W. H. AUDEN

Lectures on
Shakespeare

W. H. AUDEN: CRITICAL EDITIONS

GENERAL EDITOR
Edward Mendelson

Juvenilia: Poems, 1922–1928
Edited by Katherine Bucknell

Lectures on Shakespeare
Reconstructed and edited by
Arthur Kirsch

W. H. AUDEN

Lectures on Shakespeare

RECONSTRUCTED AND
EDITED BY

Arthur Kirsch

PRINCETON UNIVERSITY PRESS
PRINCETON, NEW JERSEY

Published by Princeton University Press, 41 William Street,
Princeton, New Jersey 08540

Library of Congress Cataloging in Publication Data

Auden, W. H. (Wystan Hugh), 1907–1973.
Lectures on Shakespeare / W.H. Auden ; reconstructed and
edited by Arthur Kirsch.
p. cm. — (W.H. Auden—critical editions)
Includes bibliographical references and index.

ISBN 0-691-05730-3 (alk. paper)
1. Shakespeare, William, 1564–1616—Criticism and
interpretation. I. Kirsch, Arthur C. II. Title. III. Series.
PR2976 .A93 2001
822.3'3—dc21   00-028479

This book has been composed in Baskerville

The paper used in this publication
meets the minimum requirements of
ANSI/NISO Z39.48-1992 (R 1997)
(*Permanence of Paper*)

www.pup.princeton.edu

Printed in the United States of America

10 9 8 7 6 5 4 3

CONTENTS

ACKNOWLEDGMENTS

The extraordinary notes Alan Ansen took when he attended Auden's lectures and discussion classes in 1946–47 are the basis of this edition. The edition would also not have been possible without the learning and generosity of Edward Mendelson, Auden's literary executor. Mendelson first let me know of the existence of Ansen's notes and helped with the edition from beginning to end, reading much of it while it was being composed as well as every word of the final manuscript, providing me with many leads, and offering constant editorial advice and encouragement.

Helen Lowenstein and Bea Bodenstein kindly provided their notes on the lectures Auden delivered in the spring term.

I am indebted to many friends and colleagues. Paul Cantor suggested that I talk to Edward Mendelson when I first became curious about Auden's lectures on Shakespeare, he read and commented on drafts of several of the lectures, and he helped me make sense of many of Auden's references. Gordon Braden, Daniel Kinney, and James Nohrnberg also were a continuous help in clarifying and tracking down references. Douglas Day, Robert Kellogg, and Anthony Spearing shared their learning in conversations about the edition, and many people helped me find particular references, including Peter Baker, Paul Barolsky, Janet Beizer, Benjamin Bennett, James Ceaser, Stephen Cushman, Robert Denommé, Hoyt Duggan, Cecil Lang, Violette Lang, Lotta Lofgren, Katharine Maus, Jacek Niecko, Stephen Railton, Richard Rorty, George Rutherglen, Walter Sokel, Herbert Tucker, and David Vander Meulen. Ronda Chollock read the entire manuscript and made many corrections and helpful suggestions.

I had extremely considerate assistance from the curators and staffs of several libraries, especially Rodney Phillips, Stephen Crook, and Philip Milito at the Henry W. and Albert A. Berg Collection of the New York Public Library, and Heather Moore at the Alderman Library of the University of Virginia. The helpfulness of Bruce Cammack, at the library of Texas Tech University, was extraordinary. At Princeton University Press, I had the help of Jane Books and Mary Murrell, as well as of Lauren Lepow, who saw the book through production with great skill and patience.

I held the Alice Griffin Chair of English Literature at the University of Virginia while working on this edition, and I am grateful to its founder as well as to the University.

I am, finally, thankful to my wife Beverly, who helped me through many problems in the book with her abiding good sense and loving support.

INTRODUCTION

THE TEXT

The New York Times reported on 27 September 1946 that "W. H. Auden, poet and critic, will conduct a course on Shakespeare at the New School for Social Research beginning Wednesday. Mr. Auden has announced that in his course, which runs through both semesters, he proposes to read all Shakespeare's plays in chronological order." The first lecture, on 2 October 1946, was an introductory one. The evening lectures on the plays began on 9 October 1946, with *Henry VI*, and continued weekly until 14 May 1947. Saturday afternoon discussion classes were offered as well to students taking the course for credit, devoted largely, in the spring term, to philological comments on particular words and phrases in *Hamlet* and *The Tempest*. Auden lectured on all the plays except *Titus Andronicus* and *The Merry Wives of Windsor*, as well as on the *Sonnets*. Rather than lecturing on *The Merry Wives of Windsor*, as he was scheduled to do, he declared that the play's only virtue was to provide "the occasion of Verdi's *Falstaff*, a very great operatic masterpiece," and he played a recording of the opera instead.

The lectures, according to the testimony of Bernadine Kielty, were "enormously popular, and the low broad auditorium" of the New School in Greenwich Village, the neighborhood in which Auden also lived, was "filled to capacity." Tickets to the lectures were sold at the door, and as many as five hundred people attended. Some people traveled a considerable distance to get to them. Robert Solotaire, then a sixteen-year-old high school student, commuted from the suburbs of New York each week with a friend, David Lougee, to hear Auden, and has written that "the thrill of the experience has stayed with me." "Auden was wonderful to listen to. I did my best to read a play a week and the pleasure of reading them has continued to this day along with the pleasure of Auden's own verse."

Auden was thirty-nine years old and had considerable experience as a teacher when he began giving the Shakespeare lectures. He had been a schoolmaster in England at Larchfield Academy (1930–32) and at the Downs School (1932–35). After arriving in the United States, he offered a course for the Writer's School of the League of American Writers in the autumn of 1939, and taught two courses at the New School in 1940: "Poetry and Culture" in the spring, and "The Language and Technique of Poetry" in the autumn. He taught for a year at the University of Michigan in 1941–42, and for three years, 1942–45, at Swarthmore College, where he offered a seminar in Shakespeare's *Sonnets* in the spring term of 1944. He spent the spring term of 1946 at Bennington College, and gave a course in the religion department of Barnard College in the spring of 1947 that overlapped with the Shakespeare lectures. He taught another course at the New School in the autumn of 1948 on "Meaning and Technique in Poetry."

None of Auden's manuscripts of the Shakespeare lectures exist. I have reconstructed the lectures primarily from notes taken by Alan Ansen, which since 1976 have been in the Henry W. and Albert A. Berg Collection of the New York Public Library. Ansen took notes on all the lectures but the opening one and those on *Twelfth Night, Hamlet,* and *All's Well That Ends Well.* He took the notes in pencil in four composition books, and also typed a copy of his notes on Auden's lecture on the *Sonnets.* Except for a few smudged and sometimes indecipherable pages on *As You Like It* and *The Tempest,* Ansen's notes on the lectures are easy to read and exceptionally detailed. They can sometimes be fragmentary and elliptical, but from time to time quotation marks indicate Auden's exact phrasing, and throughout there is a sense of attentive and intelligent fidelity to Auden's language and thought as well as to Shakespeare's. All lecturers would wish to have such a student. In the course of the lectures, Ansen became Auden's secretary and friend, and the notebooks also provide the record of Auden's conversation that has been published in *The Table Talk of W. H. Auden.* Auden dedicated *The Enchafèd Flood* to Ansen in 1950.

A second, less reliable set of notes, also in the Berg Collection, was made by Howard Griffin, who succeeded Ansen as Auden's secretary, and who later published in little magazines a series of "Conversations on Cornelia Street" that purported to be transcripts of his conversations with Auden. Griffin's notes are in typed form and were composed after the lectures, probably long after. Griffin tries to make his account of the lectures more of a continuous narrative than Ansen does, providing transitions where Ansen does not, and from time to time his notes are helpful in clarifying points that remain incomplete or obscure in Ansen. But Griffin makes almost no reference in his notes to Shakespeare's texts— Ansen always does so, specifically, accurately, and often in abundance— and his notes suggest that he was not always attentive in the lectures and that he had not always read the plays Auden was talking about. Ansen, for example, reports that in the lecture on *Coriolanus* Auden said that it is a misconception that the play represents a class war in which Corio-lanus favors the patricians, a view which *is* in Plutarch. Griffin's type-script notes on the *Coriolanus* lecture has Auden saying that the "subject" of the play is "class war" and that Shakespeare "takes the side of the aristocrats." Griffin's account of the lecture on *Richard III* scrambles the order of ideas that Ansen records, and leaves out a significant discussion drawn from a book by Hunter Guthrie that Ansen refers to and that Griffin does not mention. His notes on many other lectures are similarly incomplete. In his notes on the lecture on *Antony and Cleopatra*, Griffin records that Auden said, "In the movie they made them [Antony and Cleopatra] look too well." In Ansen's account of the lecture, Auden re-fers only to what a movie "would" do to the play. Griffin's comment seems to be an addition from a later conversation with Auden, if not his own interpolation. These mistakes, lacunae, and embellishments are typ-ical of Griffin's typescript notes on all the lectures, and I have used them very cautiously. Where I have added a reading from Griffin that is not in any way indicated in Ansen, or in conflict with him, I have recorded the fact in an endnote.

Another important source for the reconstruction of the text of the lectures is Auden's copy of George Lyman Kittredge's *The Complete Works of Shakespeare*, which is now in the library of Texas Tech University in Lubbock, Texas. Ansen describes Auden "leafing through his Kittredge" during the lecture on the *Sonnets*, and in the margins of his Kittredge text Auden marked off in pencil numerous passages that interested him in the plays. Some passages, perhaps meant for lectures he gave on other occasions, are marked in blue ink. Most of the Shakespeare quotations that Ansen indicates in his notes of the lectures, though not all, are con-firmed by Auden's markings, and I have sometimes used those markings as a warrant for the addition of a quotation that seemed specifically ger-mane to the argument Ansen indicates Auden was making. Auden also made penciled annotations, often illegible, to *Hamlet* and *The Tempest* that provided the basis for his Saturday afternoon discussions. Ansen's very sketchy notes on those Saturday afternoon classes are printed in Appendix I; the fall term final examination Auden gave the Saturday class is printed in Appendix II. A list of Auden's markings in his Kitt-redge text is printed in Appendix III. All references to Shakespeare in this edition are to Kittredge's text.

I have also referred to two other sets of notes that I received in re-sponse to a query in *The New York Times* on 11 October 1998 asking to hear from anyone who had attended the lectures. Among those who responded, Helen Lowenstein and Bea Bodenstein, both from New York, very kindly sent typed copies of the notes they had made. Both joined the course in the spring semester of 1947, which began on 5 February 1947 with the lecture on *Twelfth Night*. For the lectures which Ansen did not attend, especially those on *Twelfth Night* and *Hamlet*, their notes are indispensably helpful, and for others, they have provided details that Ansen missed. Interestingly, for example, both women note that Auden compared Cressida in *Troilus and Cressida* to Mildred in W. Somerset Maugham's *Of Human Bondage*, a comparison neither Ansen nor Griffin mentions.

The lectures were a nursery for many of the ideas developed in Auden's later prose, and on a number of occasions, always indicated in endnotes, I have incorporated sentences or brief passages from these later writings, as well as from his earlier prose, in order to clarify and enrich particular sections of the lectures—but only where and to the extent that Ansen's notes, or those of Griffin, Lowenstein, and Bodenstein, justified the additions. I have tried as much as possible to be faithful to Auden's voice in reconstructing these lectures. Auden told Ansen that he always threw away his lecture notes, which consisted of "quotations and that sort of thing," because "criticism is live conversation," and I have tried to be true to that conversational idiom, punctuating the text with commas and dashes, for example, where a more formal text might demand semicolons, in order to convey both the cadence of Auden's speech and his habit of speaking in terms of appositions and antitheses. Similarly, I have not abridged Auden's penchant for quotations, even when the quotations are long. In the effort to provide as accurate an historical record of the lectures as possible, I also have not tampered with his repetitions and plot summaries. Auden was speaking—with both his Kittredge text of Shakespeare and texts of other authors in hand and with few notes—not writing, and the lectures were not intended to be essays.

THE LECTURES

Auden's lectures on Shakespeare are at once a rich introduction to Auden's thought and an important commentary on Shakespeare's work. They vary in length and in the level of interest Auden took in different plays, but like all his work, they represent his own immensely spacious and integrated intellectual universe. As Clive James has remarked,

Auden was "a man in whom all cultural history is present," in whose "prose all the artists of the past are alive and talking among themselves." In the lectures on Shakespeare, Auden quotes most often and at length from Kierkegaard, who especially preoccupied him at the time, but the extent of his interests and of references to other writers and artists who populated his mind is prodigious, ranging from Homer to T. S. Eliot, and including an unusual number of European literatures as well as opera, contemporary newspapers and magazines, movies, and cartoons. Among the particular works that recur in the lectures, aside from Kierkegaard's, and that were loadstones for Auden's imagination, are Augustine's *City of God* and *The Confessions,* Dante's *Divine Comedy,* Pascal's *Pensées,* Mozart's *Magic Flute,* and Ibsen's *Peer Gynt.*

A central filament organizing these and a host of other artists and their works in Auden's mind was what he termed "Christian psychology." Auden says, in his concluding lecture,

> You can argue for hours as to what Shakespeare believed, but his understanding of psychology is based on Christian assumptions of the kind you'd find in every man. All men are equal not in respect of their gifts but in that everyone has a will capable of choice. Man is a tempted being, living with what he does and suffers in time, the medium in which he realizes his potential character. The indeterminacy of time means that events never happen once and for all. The good may fall, the bad may repent, and suffering can be, not a simple retribution, but a triumph.

"*Un*-Christian assumptions," he continues, include the ideas:

> first, that character is determined by birth or environment, and second, that man can become free by knowledge—that he who knows the good will will it. Knowledge only increases the danger, as Elizabethans saw. . . . The third un-Christian assumption is the understanding of God as retributive justice, where success is good and failure means wrong, and where there is no forgiveness or pity. In modern books, character is entirely the victim of circumstances, and there is the daydream of people as angels, transcendent in their power. Modern books are also devoted to the belief that success signifies the forward course of history and so is right.

Some of the results of responding to the plays with these premises are immediately evident, some are less obvious. The tragic heroes Auden

treats as essentially sinners, and most of the comedies he treats as movements toward a redeemed community, as representations of the fulfillment of Eros in Christian Agape. These ideas are as apparent as they are
fundamental in Auden's criticism, but they are neither allegorical nor
dogmatic, in part because his understanding of "Christian psychology"
was equally nourished by his eclectic knowledge of psychology, including
his reading of Freud, whose works he first encountered as a child in his
father's library. As his elegy to Freud makes clear, Auden believed that
Freud was "often . . . wrong and, at times, absurd," but he understood
both Freud's mythical power: "to us he is no more a person / now but a
whole climate of opinion / under whom we conduct our different lives";
and his artistic capacity to illuminate the infinite particularities of
human motives and behavior: "if he succeeded, why, the Generalised
Life / would become impossible." "Whoso generalises, is lost," was for
Auden "the artist's maxim," and in a review of Ernest Jones's biography
of Freud in 1953, he wrote,

> The great revolutionary step taken by [Freud], one that would make
> him a very great man still if every one of his theories should turn out
> to be false, was his decision—I am not perfectly sure that he ever
> quite realized what he had done—to treat psychological facts as be-
> longing, not to the natural order, to be investigated according to
> the methodologies of chemistry and biology, but to the historical
> order. . . . the historical world is a horrid place where, instead of
> nice clean measurable forces, there are messy things like mixed mo-
> tives, where classes keep overlapping, where what is believed to have
> happened is as real as what actually happened, a world, moreover,
> which cannot be defined by technical terms but only described by
> analogies.

At the same time that Auden insists on individual moral responsibility
in this particularized historical world, he also sees the individual's necessary dependence upon his community or society. He wrote, in an article
on *The Merchant of Venice* in *The New York Times* in 1953,

> Of all dramatists Shakespeare is, perhaps, the most "life-like." His
> plays may be in verse and, therefore, anything but "naturalistic," yet
> no one else conveys so perfectly the double truth that, while each
> man is a unique individual responsible for the choices he makes
> and not an impotent victim of circumstance, at the same time we
> are all members one of another, mutually dependent and mutually

responsible. No man is what he is or chooses what he chooses independently of the natures and choices of those with whom he is associated.

Auden views the individuals with whom Shakespeare peoples his plays—and it is a distinguishing mark of the lectures that Auden freely imagines and talks of Shakespeare's characters as "people"—through these multiple perspectives of Christian conviction and comprehensive psychological and social perception. Together they enabled him to appreciate Shakespeare's plays with an unusually inclusive combination of sympathy and judgment. T. S. Eliot, for example, a critic to whom Auden deferred, also considered Shakespeare's heroes as sinners, often very acutely, especially in his analysis of their formal Senecan derivations. But where Eliot's religious criticism of Shakespeare's tragic heroes, and of Shakespeare generally, is austere and often parched, Auden's is spacious and generous. Eliot could never forgive the lack of Dante's Thomistic precision in Shakespeare's thought and verse. Auden, who also revered Dante, and for some of the same reasons, had far greater artistic charity.

Auden's lectures on *Julius Caesar* and *Antony and Cleopatra* offer examples of the exceptional breadth of his religious sense of character and culture. Though he later modified his view of the fall of Rome, he states in the lecture on *Julius Caesar* that Roman society was "doomed not by the evil passions of selfish individuals, because such passions always exist, but by an intellectual and spiritual failure of nerve that made the society incapable of coping with its situation," by its failure "to evolve a religious pattern that was capable of grasping the world, of making sense of what was happening." Auden goes on to discuss the various characters in the play and their individual responses to this failure. He says that "Cassius is childishly envious—I swim better!" and considers him a "comic character" because "his emotional temperament is quite opposite to his Epicurean philosophy"; and he describes how the noble Brutus's attempt at Stoic detachment makes him "more at sea in the play than the unscrupulous and brutal Antony." Auden noted in his concluding lecture on Shakespeare that a historical subject simplified into a moralized history "is neither history nor moral," and he was always conscious of the extremely complex lessons of history-writing that Shakespeare learned from his apprenticeship with the chronicle plays. Nonetheless, the penetration of his analysis of *Julius Caesar* may still lie in his apprehension of the psychological and spiritual implications of the pagan undertones that Shakespeare portrays: the incapacity to create a community, the consequent power of the crowd, the failure of Stoic *ataraxia*, and the peculiar emptiness, not only the evident coldness, that shadows the play and its characters—what Kierkegaard, whom Auden quotes at length in the lecture, describes as the unconscious despair of pagan culture.

Auden's lecture on *Antony and Cleopatra*, the play he most admired, is an even richer instance of the peculiar amplitude of his understanding of "Christian psychology" and of his powers as a critic of Shakespeare. Academic criticism of *Antony and Cleopatra* in the half-century following Auden's lectures—even the best of it, like Northrop Frye's—often spends itself in disputes over whether the play depicts love or lust or both, whether its ending is transcendental, whether its numerous oxymorons and oscillating movements ever come to rest, whether its poetry is in conflict with the reality of its action. Auden cuts through these tangles by understanding the play's shimmering complexity in its presentation of "worldliness." He remarks that the "physical attraction" between Antony and Cleopatra "is real, but both are getting on, and it is less a physical need than a way of forgetting time and death." "When Romeo and Juliet express their love," he remarks, "they are saying, 'How wonderful to feel like this.' Benedick and Beatrice talk as they do about love to test each other. Antony and Cleopatra are saying, 'I want to live forever.' Their poetry, like fine cooking, is a technique to keep up the excitement of living." The flaws in the great tragic heroes, Auden continues, constitute particular and "pure states of being."

> Antony and Cleopatra's flaw, however, is general and common to all of us all of the time: *worldliness*—the love of pleasure, success, art, ourselves, and conversely, the fear of boredom, failure, being ridiculous, being on the wrong side, dying. If Antony and Cleopatra have a more tragic fate than we do, that is because they are far more successful than we are, not because they are essentially different. "Now is the time when all the lights wax dim," as Herrick writes in "To Anthea." We all reach a time when the god Hercules leaves us. Every day we can get an obsession about people we don't like but for various reasons can't leave. We all know about intrigues in offices, museums, literary life. Finally, we all grow old and die. The tragedy is not that it happens, but that we do not accept it.
>
> *Antony and Cleopatra* therefore must present a plenum of experience. An historian might complain of the irrelevance of the love story, a classical playwright of the irrelevance of the historical detail, and a theatrical producer of the multitude of tiny scenes. But Shake-

speare needs this comprehensiveness to show the temptation of the world, the real world in all its kingdoms, all its glories.

The lecture on *Antony and Cleopatra* shows Auden himself in all his plenty: the intelligence, the humor, the abiding connection with everyday life, the sympathetic response to Shakespeare that only a great writer can fully communicate. Auden's understanding of the play is incisively moral without being moralistic. He sees the worldliness in the play in traditional Christian terms, but those terms enlarge as well as crystallize the play. They are not merely homiletic, and they are certainly not dismissive. Like Shakespeare, he is entirely open to the "glories" of the world at the same time that he is uncompromising about them.

Auden's critical virtues are exceptionally compelling in the lecture on *Antony and Cleopatra* in part because the kind of adult, erotic love he saw in the play was the kind he was especially comfortable talking about. He was not comfortable talking about young, romantic love, at any rate not in the terms that have been customary for the last several centuries. He was much influenced by Denis de Rougemont's antiromantic study, *Love in the Western World*, which he had reviewed with high praise, and by Kierkegaard's commendation of the kind of love that can be proven only in the course of marriage. Both authors espoused a Christian sense of spiritual commitment in love, and both encouraged Auden in his own temperamental disposition to regard the notion of romantic sexual love as finally, if not immediately, a comic illusion. In his lecture on the *Sonnets*, he retells "a good American story" that illustrates this disposition:

A man is on a visit to Chicago. He enters a restaurant. Yes, he sees a very beautiful girl in the restaurant, exquisitely beautiful, ravishingly beautiful. Yes, she is friendly, she smiles at him, she talks to him. Yes, her conversation is very witty, she is very agreeable, she is immensely entertaining. They go to the opera. Yes, she is very intelligent, she has a fine appreciation of the beautiful things in life, is keenly aware of values. They go to a night club. Yes, she is a wonderful sport, she enters wholeheartedly into the spirit of things. Later, yes, she responds beautifully to his love-making, is very understanding, says she loves him too. In the taxi, yes, her kisses are thrilling. And after that? After that it was like it is in Cincinnati.

Auden treated romantic love skeptically throughout his work. Under the heading of "Love, Romantic" in his commonplace book, *A Certain World*, he wrote, "I must confess that I find the personal love poems of

Dante, Shakespeare, Donne, for all their verbal felicities, embarrassing. I find the romantic vocabulary only tolerable in allegorical poems where the 'Lady' is not a real human being." He added that "Simple, or elaborate, praise of physical beauty is always charming, but when it comes to writing about the emotional relation between the sexes, whether in verse or prose, I prefer the comic or the coarse note to the hot-and-bothered or the whining-pathetic."

This attitude toward romantic love makes him very sympathetic to the skepticism of comic heroes and heroines like Benedick, Beatrice and Rosalind, or to the fidelity of a married heroine like Imogen, and it enables him to speak interestingly about the plays in which they appear. His discomfort with romantic love also enables him to see discrepant moods in the plays that other critics either underestimate or miss entirely, and it is a tonic against the unexamined romanticism of much Shakespeare criticism. But it also has its obvious limitations. In his lecture on *Romeo and Juliet,* for example, he says that Romeo and Juliet "confuse romance and love" and that behind their suicides as well as their reaction to his banishment,

> is finally a lack of feeling, a fear that the relationship cannot be sustained and that, out of pride, it should be stopped now, in death. If they become a married couple, there will be no more wonderful speeches—and a good thing, too. Then the real tasks of life will begin. . . .

This comment may be true, and it is funny, but what it misses is the degree of wit and tenderness in the play that makes the catastrophe, as Northrop Frye remarks, seem almost an outrage. This note in the play Auden seems unwilling to hear, and he does not quote those "wonderful speeches," nor did he care to mark them off in his copy of Kittredge. Auden's suspicion of romantic love also prevents him, both in his lecture on *Othello* and his later essay on the play in *The Dyer's Hand,* from seeing the idealism, indeed scriptural idealism, of Desdemona, whom he dismisses simply as a "young schoolgirl who wants above all to be a grown-up," "a romantic girl going slumming," a girl who "in time . . . might well have been unfaithful."

Auden's view of Desdemona is in some sense Iago's, and this affiliation suggests a more salient feature of Auden's criticism of Shakespeare. The isolating tendencies of his dispassionate, and prodigal, intellect and his "wild, extraordinary and demonic imagination," as well as of his homosexuality, made Auden often feel like an outsider. His brother John commented on it, seeing in him an "isolation and sadness which arose from his uprooted and solitary existence," despite "his fame and wide friendships throughout America and Europe," and it affects his criticism of Shakespeare profoundly. In each of the essays or extended discussions he chose to publish on Shakespeare in *The Dyer's Hand*, his criticism is animated and made uncommonly interesting by an outsider's view, and the corresponding lectures are usually similar. The lecture on *Othello* as well as "The Joker in the Pack" examine the whole of the play from the perspective of Iago. The lecture treats him as an incarnation of the idea of the *acte gratuit*, which Augustine described in the episode of the pear tree in the *Confessions*, the doing of evil for its own sake, the doing of evil, as Auden says, "just for the hell of it." In the lecture on *The Merchant of Venice* as well as "Brothers and Others," Auden sees Shylock as both an outsider and the one serious person in "a certain kind of society, a society that is related to and can't do without someone whom it can't accept." Auden's lecture on *Henry IV* and *Henry V*, as well as "The Prince's Dog," take a markedly hostile view of Prince Hal and royal politics. In the lecture he says of Hal, "Yes, he is the Machiavellian character, master of himself and the situation—except that in the last analysis Falstaff is right when he tells him, 'Thou art essentially mad without seeming so' " (*1 Henry IV*, II.iv.540–41). "Hal is the type," Auden says, "who becomes a college president, a government head, etc., and one hates their guts." And in "The Prince's Dog," in an epiphany of his writing on Shakespeare, Auden sympathizes profoundly with Falstaff:

> The drunk is unlovely to look at, intolerable to listen to, and his self-pity is contemptible. Nevertheless, as not merely a worldly failure but also a willful failure, he is a disturbing image for the sober citizen. His refusal to accept the realities of this world, babyish as it may be, compels us to take another look at this world and reflect upon our motives for accepting it. The drunkard's suffering may be self-inflicted, but it is real suffering and reminds us of all the suffering in this world which we prefer not to think about because, from the moment we accepted the world, we acquired our share of responsibility for everything that happens in it.

In his lecture on *King Lear* Auden speaks of the Fool as "in a way the most interesting of the characters," and in *The Dyer's Hand* he devotes his discussion of *Lear* entirely to the Fool. In his lecture on *The Tempest*, Auden blames Prospero for Caliban's condition: "Prospero tried to make Caliban a conscious person, and only made him worse." In his pages on the play in *The Dyer's Hand*, he is even more antagonistic to Prospero and sympathetic to Caliban:

> As a biological organism Man is a natural creature subject to the necessities of nature; as a being with consciousness and will, he is at the same time a historical person with the freedom of the spirit. *The Tempest* seems to me a manichean work, not because it shows the relation of Nature to Spirit as one of conflict and hostility, which in fallen man it is, but because it puts the blame for this upon Nature and makes the Spirit innocent.

In his adaptation of *The Tempest* in "The Sea and the Mirror," Auden makes Caliban into a Jamesian narrator and gives him the long, almost last word.

Auden's outsider disposition is neither a reflection nor endorsement of detachment, however, which he considered the worst of illusions, "the illusion of being free of illusion." Auden quotes with approval Rosalind's judgment of Jaques in *As You Like It*: "And your experience makes you sad. I had rather have a fool to make me merry than experience to make me sad—and to travel for it too!" (IV.i.28–29). In a play with many exiles, Jaques, Auden says, "is self-exiled," and he quotes Goethe in explaining him:

> Goethe writes, "*Es bildet ein Talent sich in der Stille, / Sich ein Charakter in dem Strom der Welt,*" talent builds itself in quietness, character in the stream of the world. Jaques remains in the country. Like Shylock he won't join the dance, like Hamlet his involvement with society is unhappy, like Caliban he is unassimilable.

Finally, if some of the virtues of Auden's criticism come from the imaginative freedom and insight of his outsider's perspective, others are the result of his insider's knowledge, his experience and genius as a poet and a writer of plays and libretti. He can respond, of course, with perfect pitch to Shakespeare's verse. Auden discusses the language and verse of the plays sparingly, and he more than once simply summarizes or quotes from *Words and Poetry*, a book on Shakespeare's prose and verse by George Rylands, a critic whom, along with T. S. Eliot, C. S. Lewis, and William Empson, he may have relied on most directly in the lectures. But when he does himself consider Shakespeare's verse, his comments are arresting. In the lecture on *Cymbeline*, for example, he talks of how critics dismiss the verse in the masque with Jupiter near the end of the play as crude and un-Shakespearean, and he suggests, on the contrary, how challenging it could be to Shakespeare at that point in his career to write something deliberately unsophisticated. He points, for example, to the "remarkable" verse of the spirit who comments on Jupiter's ascension:

> The marble pavement closes; he is enter'd
> His radiant roof. Away! and, to be blest,
> Let us with care perform his great behest.
>
> (V.iv.120–22)

Auden says that these lines in *Cymbeline* as well those describing Belarius and the royal children rallying and fighting alongside the British army (V.iii.28–51) are

> not immediately noticeable, but anyone who practices verse writing returns again and again and again to such passages, more than to spectacular things. They show real technical brilliance applied to something that is not very important in subject matter, but a writer wanting to learn his trade can find out how to write verse by studying them.

Because of his interest and experience in opera, Auden is also exceptionally conscious of the songs and music and sounds in the plays. His attention to the noise of the crowd and the various martial sennets and flourishes in *Coriolanus*, for example, helps him delineate the peculiarly clinical public gaze of the play, and songs are the main focus of his trenchant analysis of *Twelfth Night*, whose "society," he says, "is beginning to smell gamey." He describes how, as opposed to the characters in *The Merchant of Venice*, those "who welcome music in Illyria are more uniformly saddened by it," and he analyzes the songs to show how the dramatic contexts in which they are presented subvert their nominal courtly or Petrarchan conventions. The audience for "O mistress mine," he points out, is "a couple of seedy old drunks," and the audience for "Come away, come away, death" is the self-absorbed Duke, who is sitting next to the disguised and suffering Viola. The clown's song, "When that I was and a little tiny boy," which ends *Twelfth Night* and is its epilogue, Auden calls "a nonsense poem. What the clown is really saying is that nothing in human life makes sense."

Auden's experience writing plays and libretti also enables him to talk often and with particular insight about Shakespeare's conceptions of genre as well as about how he conceived of character, constructed individual scenes, and put his plays together at different stages of his career. He can comment professionally on the brief scene on a Roman street between Lepidus, Maecenas, and Agrippa in *Antony and Cleopatra* (II.iv): "It swiftly shows Lepidus' feebleness, the slight contempt Maecenas and Agrippa have for him—the moment done, the scene is over." He can talk unsympathetically, but at the same time authoritatively, of what he considers the generic confusion in *The Taming of the Shrew*, a play he regards as "a complete failure." The actor in farce, he says,

> represents not a human being but a god who does not suffer, so thoroughly humble or so proud that loss of dignity means nothing to him. Custard pies thrown in his face or not being loved are equally matters of indifference to him. The farce character has no memory and no foreboding. He exists entirely in the moment. He is all body, but his body is heavy or light not in its own right but as an expression of his spirit, as if an angel should become incarnate. . . . It is fatal if a real individual is introduced. It is also fatal if the plot is connected with a serious issue.

He concludes that there is thus "too much writing in *Taming of the Shrew* for the limits of farce," and that Shakespeare was not unaware of it:

> He intended the Induction to comment on and expand the play by suggesting that the action is a daydream of Christopher Sly. But the play's a bore. Either Petruchio should have been timid and then got drunk and tamed Katherina as she wished, or, after her beautiful speech, she should have picked up a stool and hit him over the head.

Auden sees *King Lear* as crystallizing Shakespeare's turn toward opera, in particular towards an operatic conception of character:

> Lear, in the opening scene, divides up his kingdom like a birthday cake. It's not historical, but it's the way we can all feel at certain times. Shakespeare tries to do something for character development with Edgar's becoming Poor Tom, but it seems arbitrary. Shakespeare's primary treatment of character in the play is as it is in opera. The quality common to all the great operatic roles is that each of them is a passionate and willful state of being, and in recompense for the lack of psychological complexity, the composer presents the immediate and simultaneous relation of these states to each other. The crowning glory of opera is the big ensemble. The

Fool, Edgar, and the mad Lear compose such a big scene in *King Lear*. The ensemble gives a picture of human nature, though the individual is sacrificed.

In the lecture on *Pericles* and *Cymbeline*, Auden speaks of how Shakespeare continues to develop his interest in relations rather than character: "One can't talk about good and bad people, but only about good and bad relationships, and the plot creates a pattern out of these relationships." Auden then classifies the various family relations in *Pericles* and *Cymbeline*, one of many taxonomies in the lectures, in a way that reveals not only Shakespeare's central substantive interests in both plays but also their detailed dramatic composition. Auden describes the scene in which the shepherd finds the infant Perdita in *The Winter's Tale* (III.iii) as "the most beautiful scene in Shakespeare," beyond words and not needing them: "You could tell the story and describe the scene in other words and one would know at once that it is beautiful in the way that a dream can be beautiful." Auden speaks of the mythic power of *The Tempest* in similar terms, and he says that *The Tempest* is Shakespeare's farewell piece, whether he was conscious of it or not:

> I don't believe people die until they've done their work, and when they have, they die. There are surprisingly few incomplete works in art. People, as a rule, die when they wish to. It is not a shame that Mozart, Keats, Shelley died young: they'd finished their work.

Following a suggestion of Aldous Huxley, he considers all of Shakespeare's final plays as examples of the genre of the late works of major artists like Beethoven, Goya, and Ibsen, deliberately strange in their vision, unconcerned about the difficulties they may pose for an audience, and enormously interested "in particular kinds of artistic problems lovingly worked out for themselves, regardless of the interest of the whole work."

Auden's parting insider's comment on Shakespeare, delivered at the conclusion of his concluding lecture, is directly related to the increasing self-restraint of his own vast talents as a poet. He says,

> There is a continual process of simplification in Shakespeare's plays. What is he up to? He is holding the mirror up to nature. In the early minor sonnets he talks about his works outlasting time. But increasingly he suggests, as Theseus does in *A Midsummer Night's Dream*, that "The best in this kind are but shadows" (V.i.214), that art is rather a bore. He spends his life at it, but he doesn't think it's

very important. . . . I find Shakespeare particularly appealing in his attitude towards his work. There's something a little irritating in the determination of the very greatest artists, like Dante, Joyce, Milton, to create masterpieces and to think themselves important. To be able to devote one's life to art without forgetting that art is frivolous is a tremendous achievement of personal character. Shakespeare never takes himself too seriously.

Neither does Auden. His lectures on Shakespeare are as finally unassuming as their subject, as capacious, and, to alter slightly a phrase in Auden's elegy to Freud, as "life-forgiving." Together with his essays in *The Dyer's Hand*, they are among the most remarkable criticisms of Shakespeare in the twentieth century.

Lectures

Henry VI, Parts One, Two,
and Three

[9 October 1946]

Henry James, in a review of some novels, said that "Yes, circumstances of the interest are there, but where is the interest itself?" The first question to ask is what is the interest, the central kind of excitement inducing an author to write a work, as opposed to the wayside stimuli that may have amused him along the way. In the chronicle play, which is historical, not myth or fiction, the central interest is the search for cause and pattern, a depiction not merely of the event, but of the cause of it and its effect. *The Mirror for Magistrates* was the chief Elizabethan example of this kind of history and went through many editions and supplements from 1559 to 1587. It consists of imaginary, homiletic soliloquies by the ghosts of famous British statesmen, from Richard II to Henry VIII. Elizabethans believed that the chronicler's task was to determine causes. What is the pattern of retribution? To what extent is fortune conditioned by extra-human causes, the stars? How does climate influence politics, how are people affected by the stars and by humors, and by the particular balances of their temperaments? *Our* interest in history is similar in this respect, if not the same. Despite the human given, however—feelings that arise through appetite, passion, and desire—skill and free choice remain the dominant interests in historical writing.

In *The Mirror for Magistrates* the character of Salisbury, who appears early in *Henry VI*, asks himself whether Henry IV's execution of his father for trying to restore Richard II, the rightful king, to the throne, was justified. He decides that his father's purpose was

> good there is no doubt.
> What cause can be more wurthy for a knight,
> Than save his king, and helpe true heires to right?

But he concludes that the means employed were violent and therefore constituted a vice: "God hateth rigour though it furder right." Under what conditions is rebellion against the prince permissible? And what is the proper character of a prince? Elizabethans believed that the King mustn't have ordered the commission of a crime in rebelling against a usurper, and that the longer a king is on the throne, the less right there is to rebel. If the king is a tyrant—if he won the throne by violence, in other words—rebellion is proper. In the arguments between Henry VI and Edward IV, the issue of voluntary abdication is thus important.

The characters in *Henry VI* are subordinate to the action. The main interest is the nature of the body politic, what keeps it healthy, what destroys it. *Henry VI* depicts the degeneration of a society. What *is* the nature of the body politic? Today we define "society" as a voluntary association of two or more persons to pursue a common aim: to play a game of chess, for example, or to waltz. It is assumed that the individual belongs to a society through free choice, that he shares its common aim, and that he is willing to live up to its unexpressed obligations—not to lose his temper, for example, if he loses a game of chess. The Greek body politic, the *polis*, a city-state such as Athens, consisted of native, adult males and excluded women, children, slaves, foreigners. The family is a society consisting of adults and babies—the Greeks would have excluded the babies—and parents also form a nonsocial community. Babies, who have no capacity for self-government, must be ruled by force and fraud, force including rewards as well as punishments.

In the medieval body politic, the state was a nonsocial community shot through with streaks of sociality. It was split into estates and composed of people who were not citizens of their own free will, but were people who happened to be in a particular place. Some of them were sovereign, the rest subjects, and rule was by custom and then legislation. A wife was subject to the sovereignty of her husband, a person could be subject to an overlord, and the sovereign could grant liberty to his subjects. The modern view is that the Greek model of society is the desired end point. Medieval social organization is seen as a beginning that dialectically turns into the other and is always a nursery for the other, since the class barriers are upwardly permeable and there is a correspondence between the rulers and the ruled in their way of life.

The Middle Ages see the state as a natural organism, parallel to nature, and the correspondences that are drawn between the two are carried very far. Order is natural, and human society exists as part of a great chain of being extending from God to the beasts and inanimate nature. As John Fortescue argues, there is a correspondence between the high and the low, the hot and the cold, and everything occupies an inferior as well as superior position. Since the whole chain of being is regulated by God, so specifically is the human race. Fortescue maintains that man can descend in the chain and transform himself into the beast nearest his own sensuality. Greeks as well as the Middle Ages saw nature as macrocosm, man as microcosm, with a teleological relation between the two. In the Renaissance, outside of Shakespeare, and in the eighteenth century, it was understood that God made nature and man made machines. Today, nature is studied by scientists, man by historians.

Henry VI consists of three plays dealing with breakdown. The ruling class cannot rule themselves. Henry VI can rule his own self, which is immanent, but not other selves, which are transient, and the play shows a society sinking back to a nonsocial herd. Henry V was a success—we'll take up Shakespeare's personal view of him later. Henry IV was a usurper. Richard II was a bad king, but not a tyrant. The child king, Henry VI, affords an opportunity—it is not a necessity for things to go wrong.

In *Henry VI, Part One*, we are initially introduced to two generations. Gloucester and Bedford are brothers of the late king, and Gloucester is a good character. At the beginning, the bad character—he's too ambitious—is the Bishop of Winchester, later Cardinal, who is of a generation before Gloucester. The quarrel between Gloucester and Winchester is ominous. Three messengers appear—as in the Book of Job. The first reports the loss of the provinces, the second the unity of the French and the crowning of the Dauphin, and the third the capture of Talbot through the cowardice of Sir John Fastolfe. At the end of the opening scene, all the characters go off to do good except Winchester, who stays to plot how he can gain power. In the next scene, Joan of Arc is introduced. It is suggested that she has been sent to punish the English and "to be the English scourge" (Pt.1, I.ii.129). In the duels between Joan and Talbot, Joan is represented as alternately a witch and a heroic rival. She shows that she is a witch by reversing the natural order and beating Charles in a duel. The Mayor of London issues a proclamation against the violent quarrel between Gloucester and Winchester. In the three remaining scenes of Act I, Salisbury is killed by a boy's gun, Talbot is worsted in his first duel with Joan through her witchery, and Joan and the French enter Orleans in triumph. In the next act the tables are turned. Talbot makes a sally at night and drives the French out.

We are then introduced to the quarrel between the houses of the red rose of Somerset and the white rose of Richard Plantagenet, later Duke of York. Initially the dispute is not dynastic, but about the restoration of Richard's titles, despite attainder. Somerset says that Richard stands "attainted, / Corrupted, and exempt from ancient gentry" by the execution of his father, Richard Earl of Cambridge, for treason (Pt.1, II.iv.92–93).

Richard answers that his father "was attached, not attainted; / Condemn'd to die for treason, but no traitor" (96–97), and that he merits the restoration of his titles. He is right in this argument. Suffolk, when asked by Richard to judge the case, excuses himself, saying:

> Faith, I have been a truant in the law
> And never yet could frame my will to it,
> And therefore frame the law unto my will.
>
> (Pt.1, II.iv.7–9)

Warwick gives a foxy argument:

> Between two hawks, which flies the higher pitch—
> Between two dogs, which hath the deeper mouth—
> Between two blades, which bears the better temper—
> Between two horses, which doth bear him best—
> Between two girls, which hath the merriest eye—
> I have perhaps some shallow spirit of judgment;
> But in these nice sharp quillets of the law,
> Good faith, I am no wiser than a daw.
>
> (Pt.1, II.iv.11–18)

But Warwick plucks the white rose of Plantagenet. Suffolk chooses the red rose of Somerset.

The introduction of Richard's uncle, the imprisoned and dying Mortimer, in the next scene (Pt.1, II.v) recalls the atmosphere of an earlier era and an earlier injustice, the usurpation of Richard II's crown by Henry IV and the denial of Mortimer's rights. Mortimer encourages Richard, but Richard still seeks only "to be restored to my blood" (Pt.1, II.v.128). Disorder spreads between the men of Winchester and Gloucester, and Gloucester tries to patch up the quarrel. Richard is restored to his titles, but the feud with Somerset keeps things on the boil. In a battle at Rouen, first Joan triumphs, then Talbot, and subsequently Joan wins over Burgundy with an appeal to French patriotism that does not fit in with the idea of her as witch. In Paris, Talbot strips Sir John Fastolfe of the garter, the English learn that Burgundy has defected to Charles, and we see a quarrel between Vernon and Basset (Pt.1, IV.i), the whole sequence suggesting a contrast between French unity and English dissension. At Bordeaux Talbot and his son are killed because of the rivalry between Someset and York, which prevents their bringing aid to him. Talbot is betrayed now not by cowardice, or the "force of France," but by English civil dissension, "the fraud of England." (Pt.1, IV.iv.36). The wars with France had been begun by Henry IV and Henry V to distract attention from the rights of Richard II. Since these wars had not succeeded, an attempt is now made to seek peace with France through the marriage of Henry VI with the daughter of Armagnac. Joan loses power and is captured. Suffolk builds up Margaret of Anjou, his candidate to be Henry's queen, partly out of love for Margaret, partly because he wishes to increase his power by controlling her. Henry makes the mistake of accepting Margaret, thereby alienating both Gloucester and York. Henry's fault is weakness before a more passionate and clever nature than his own. No murder or treason is represented in *Henry VI, Part One*—allowing the death of Talbot is not deliberate.

Part Two is the most dramatically satisfactory of the three parts. It shows the fall of Gloucester, as well as the rise in York's fortune and the decline in his character. Henry VI, York, Gloucester: each has some of the qualities necessary for a good king. York has the best claim to the title and a more powerful character. He combines the lion and the fox. Henry is weak and disinterested, a pelican. Gloucester combines the lion and the pelican, not the fox, and displays overt signs of disloyalty. Two sides are formed: Gloucester, Salisbury, York, and Warwick on one, Winchester, Buckingham, Somerset, and Suffolk on the other. York has separate ends in mind. Both Buckingham and Somerset hope to get rid of Winchester and fight it out between themselves. The marriage of Henry and Margaret of Anjou draws the lines. Witchcraft is now English, not French. The Duchess of Gloucester resorts to witchcraft to gain power, and Suffolk and the Cardinal provide an *agent provacateur* for her. The masses begin to talk of the Duke of York as the rightful heir to the crown. An apprentice accuses his master of high treason for making that suggestion, providing an opportunity for Gloucester to decide that Somerset, not York, should be Regent of France. He thereby alienates York. The Duchess of Gloucester is caught out practicing witchcraft, and the Duke of Gloucester is forced to resign as Protector, against Henry's better judgment. The episode of Simpcox, a poor man whose claim that his sight has been restored by a miracle is easily exposed, juxtaposes the use of false magic, because of poverty, against the use of true magic by the Duchess to gain power. York gets Salisbury and Warwick to acknowledge his right to be king and lets Suffolk and the Lancastrians get rid of Gloucester, who is murdered. Warwick is shocked, and he uses the opportunity to get rid of Suffolk, who is banished. The Cardinal, who is also responsible for the murder of Gloucester, dies in terror. Suffolk is executed by pirates. He had himself behaved like a bandit.

York then eggs on Jack Cade's rebellion, which provides some of the best scenes in the trilogy. Society ends in the *Lumpenproletariat* with Cade as its leader. He attacks lawyers and proposes a communist utopia to rally his supporters:

> *Cade.* Be brave then, for your captain is brave and vows reformation. There shall be in England seven halfpenny loaves sold for a penny; the three-hoop'd pot shall have ten hoops, and I will make it felony to drink small beer. All the realm shall be in common, and in Cheapside shall my palfrey go to grass; and when I am king, as king I will be—
> *All.* God save your Majesty!
> *Cade.* I thank you, good people. There shall be no money; all shall eat and drink on my score; and I will apparel them all in one livery, that they may agree like brothers and worship me their lord.
> *Butch.* The first thing we do, let's kill all the lawyers.
> *Cade.* Nay, that I mean to do. Is not this a lamentable thing, that of the skin of an innocent lamb should be made parchment? that parchment, being scribbled o'er, should undo a man? Some say the bee stings; but I say 'tis the bee's wax; for I did but seal once to a thing, and I was never mine own man since.
>
> (Pt.2, IV.ii.69–90)

A Clerk is brought in as a prisoner:

> *Weav.* The clerk of Chatham. He can write and read and cast accompt.
> *Cade.* O monstrous!
> *Weav.* We took him setting of boys' copies.
> *Cade.* Here's a villain!
> *Weav.* Has a book in his pocket with red letters in't.
> *Cade.* Nay, then he is a conjurer.
> *Butch.* Nay, he can make obligations and write court-hand.
> *Cade.* I am sorry for't. The man is a proper man, of mine honour. Unless I find him guilty, he shall not die. Come hither, sirrah. I must examine thee. What is thy name?
> *Clerk.* Emanuel.
> *Butch.* They use to write it on the top of letters. 'Twill go hard with you.
> *Cade.* Let me alone. Dost thou use to write thy name? or hast thou a mark to thyself, like an honest plain-dealing man?

Clerk. Sir, I thank God, I have been so well brought up that I can write my name.

All. He hath confess'd! Away with him! He's a villain and a traitor!

Cade. Away with him, I say! Hang him with his pen and inkhorn about his neck.

(Pt.2, IV.ii.92–117)

Soon afterwards, a soldier is killed for calling Cade by his name:

Cade. Now is Mortimer lord of this city. And here, sitting upon London Stone, I charge and command that, of the city's cost, the pissing conduit run nothing but claret wine this first year of our reign. And now henceforward it shall be treason for any that calls me other than Lord Mortimer.

Enter a *Soldier*, running.

Sold. Jack Cade! Jack Cade!
Cade. Knock him down there.

They kill him.
(Pt.2, IV.vi.1–9)

The crowd, Cade's "rabblement," subsequently loses the power of choice, yielding successively to the speeches of Clifford and Cade. Clifford challenges the crowd to declare their allegiance to the heroic Henry V as well as the present king, and all respond, "God save the King! God save the King!" (Pt.2, IV.viii.19). Cade answers, "What, Buckingham and Clifford, are ye so brave? And you, base peasants, do ye believe them? Will you needs be hang'd with your pardons about your necks?" All then cry, "We'll follow Cade! We'll follow Cade!" (20–23, 35). Clifford again invokes Henry V as well as the crowd's fear of the French, and all cry "A Clifford! a Clifford! We'll follow the King and Clifford" (56). Cade flees and is eventually slain by Alexander Iden of Kent, a contented private citizen who provides contrast and is what Henry VI would like to be if he didn't have to be King. In the last Act of Part Two, York returns in rebellion. Warwick and Salisbury show treachery to Henry, civil war ensues, and the first battle of St. Albans is fought. Old Clifford is killed and his son vows a blood feud. At the end of Part Two, Edward and Richard, the sons of York, appear for the first time.

The third part of *Henry VI* is difficult because it portrays complete disorder and gets a little tedious. Warwick has joined York, and the third part opens with Henry's suggestion that he stay on the throne till his

death and that York succeed him. Queen Margaret says no, and prepares
to fight. At the battle of Wakefield, Margaret achieves victory, Clifford
kills the young Earl of Rutland, denying his plea to live, and he and
Margaret mock York and finally stab him. Another Lancastrian victory is
reported at the second battle of St. Albans. At the battle of Towton, first
the Lancastrians then the Yorkists prevail. Young Clifford is killed.

A deliberate parallel is drawn between the molehill upon which York
is made to stand at Wakefield before he is killed (Pt.3, I.iv.67–69) and
the molehill upon which Henry later sits at Towton as he observes the
fluctuating battle and imagines the content he would have if he were a
simple shepherd:

> Would I were dead, if God's good will were so!
> For what is in this world but grief and woe?
> O God! methinks it were a happy life
> To be no better than a homely swain;
> To sit upon a hill, as I do now,
> To carve out dials quaintly, point by point,
> Thereby to see the minutes how they run—
> How many makes the hour full complete,
> How many hours brings about the day,
> How many days will finish up the year,
> How many years a mortal man may live.
>
> (Pt.3, II.v.19–29)

Just after Henry's soliloquy, "Enter a *Son* that hath kill'd his Father, at
one door, [dragging in the body]" and then "Enter, at another door, a
Father that hath kill'd his Son, bearing of his Son['s body]" (Pt.3, II. v.54,
78). Shakespeare relies on such ritualistic techniques in the early part of
his career, leaves them in his middle period, and returns to them in the
final plays.

Henry goes to Scotland, Edward sends Warwick to woo France's
daughter, and Margaret makes her own plea to France. Henry mean-
while is captured, and Edward, who has been proclaimed King, woos and
marries Lady Grey, a widow—and here it's a demonstration of lust, not
weakness. Warwick switches sides, surprises Edward, and removes his
crown. Richard contrives Edward's escape. Clarence goes over to Warwick. Edward surprises Henry. At the battle of Barnet, Clarence having
switched sides, Warwick is defeated and killed. Queen Margaret and the
young Prince Edward are captured, and King Edward, Clarence, and
Richard stab and kill the prince in front of Margaret. Richard wishes to

kill Margaret too, but is prevented. He does, however, kill Henry. "For this (amongst the rest)," he says, "was I ordain'd." He exults as Henry bleeds: "What? Will the aspiring blood of Lancaster / Sink in the ground? I thought it would have mounted" (Pt.3, V.vi.57, 61–62). In the same soliloquy, he also says that he has "neither pity, love, nor fear," and proclaims that

> I have no brother, I am like no brother;
> And this word "love," which greybeards call divine,
> Be resident in men like one another,
> And not in me! I am myself alone.
>
> (Pt.3, V.vi.68, 80–83)

Richard also has a much longer soliloquy in the earlier scene of Edward's wooing of Lady Grey, in which he broods on his future. It is Shakespeare's first great soliloquy. After itemizing the obstacles that lie between him and the throne, Richard says,

> Well, say there is no kingdom then for Richard:
> What other pleasure can the world afford?
> I'll make my heaven in a lady's lap
> And deck my body in gay ornaments
> And witch sweet ladies with my words and looks.
> O miserable thought! And more unlikely
> Than to accomplish twenty golden crowns!
> Why, love forswore me in my mother's womb;
> And, for I should not deal in her soft laws,
> She did corrupt frail nature with some bribe
> To shrink mine arm up like a wither'd shrub;
> To make an envious mountain on my back,
> Where sits deformity to mock my body;
> To shape my legs of an unequal size;
> To disproportion me in every part,
> Like to a chaos, or an unlick'd bear-whelp,
> That carries no impression like the dam.

He concludes the soliloquy by affirming his desire for the crown:

> And I—like one lost in a thorny wood,
> That rents the thorns and is rent with thorns,
> Seeking a way and straying from the way,
> Not knowing how to find the open air
> But toiling desperately to find it out—

> Torment myself to catch the English crown;
> And from that torment I will free myself
> Or hew my way out with a bloody axe.
> Why, I can smile, and murther whiles I smile,
> And cry "Content!" to that which grieves my heart,
> And wet my cheeks with artificial tears,
> And frame my face to all occasions.
> I'll drown more sailors than the mermaid shall;
> I'll slay more gazers than the basilisk;
> I'll play the orator as well as Nestor,
> Deceive more slily than Ulysses could,
> And, like a Sinon, take another Troy.
> I can add colours to the chameleon,
> Change shapes with Proteus for advantages,
> And set the murtherous Machiavel to school.
> Can I do this, and cannot get a crown?
> Tut, were it farther off, I'll pluck it down.
>
> (Pt.3, III.ii.146–62, 174–95)

Richard is Shakespeare's first big character.

D. H. Lawrence says, in one of his poems, that he marvels when he reads Shakespeare, that "such trivial people" can speak in "such lovely language":

> Lear, the old buffer, you wonder his daughters
> didn't treat him rougher,
> the old chough, the old chuffer.
>
> And Hamlet, how boring, how boring to live with,
> so mean and self-conscious, blowing and snoring
> his wonderful speeches, full of other folk's whoring!
>
> And Macbeth and his Lady, who should have been choring,
> such suburban ambition, so messily goring
> old Duncan with daggers!
>
> How boring, how small Shakespeare's people are!
> Yet the language so lovely! like the dyes from gas-tar.

Lawrence's view of Shakespeare's characters seems to me not altogether unjust, but also not quite satisfying. After all, aren't we all SOB's? Kipling's poems show Shakespeare's characters everywhere, in Sapphic verse.

Richard III

[16 October 1946]

Henry VI is a general history. *Richard III* concentrates on an individual character: the character of a villain. There is a difference between a villain and one who simply commits a crime. The villain is an extremely conscious person and commits a crime consciously, for its own sake. Aaron in *Titus Andronicus* is an early example of the villain in Shakespeare. Barabas in *The Jew of Malta*, another crude villain, is an example in Marlowe. In appearance these characters—a Jew, a Moor, a hunchback—are all outside the norm. Barabas announces,

> As for myself, I walk abroad o' nights
> And kill sick people groaning under walls:
> Sometimes I go about and poison wells.

Aaron, after his capture, wishes he had done a "thousand more" evils:

> Even now I curse the day (and yet I think
> Few come within the compass of my curse)
> Wherein I did not some notorious ill:
> As kill a man, or else devise his death;
> Ravish a maid, or plot the way to do it;
> Accuse some innocent, and forswear myself;
> Set deadly enmity between two friends;
> Make poor men's cattle break their necks;
> Set fire on barns and haystacks in the night
> And bid the owners quench them with their tears.
>
> (V.i.125–34)

And Richard boasts, as we have seen, in his long soliloquy in the third part of *Henry VI*, that he "can smile, and murther whiles I smile," "drown more sailors than the mermaid shall," "slay more gazers than the basilisk," "and set the murtherous Machiavel to school" (III.ii.182, 186–87, 193).

Richard's opening monologue in *Richard III* is similar to the earlier soliloquy, though there is a slight difference in tone. Saying he is "rudely stamp'd" and wants "love's majesty," he announces that he is not made "to court an amorous looking glass" and has "no delight to pass away the time,"

> Unless to see my shadow in the sun
> And descant on mine own deformity.
> And therefore, since I cannot prove a lover
> To entertain these fair well-spoken days,
> I am determined to prove a villain
> And hate the idle pleasures of these days.
>
> (I.i.14–16, 25–31)

Richard III's monologue is not unlike Adolf Hitler's speech to his General Staff on 23 August 1939, in its utter lack of self-deception. The lack of self-deception is striking because most of us invent plausible reasons for doing something we know is wrong. Milton describes such rationalization in *Paradise Lost* in Eve, both before she eats the fruit of the forbidden tree and afterwards, when she justifies inducing Adam to eat:

> So dear I love him, that with him all deaths
> I could endure, without him live no life.
>
> (*PL*.IX.832–33)

Eve makes this profession of love for Adam at the moment when she is, in effect, planning to kill him.

Villains are of particular interest to artists, and there are more examples of them in art than in life. Because language is the medium of literature, people who are usable in literary works have to be conscious people. They are one of two types: (1) people who are not really conscious but who are made to be so, and (2) actually educated people, for whom artists have a natural bias. That's why most works about peasants are boring—literary works consist mostly of people's remarks. Movies do a better job with less articulate people. Drama accentuates the literary problem: characters in plays must be more verbally explicit than in novels or in life, and if they rationalize, they confuse an audience. Elizabethan drama, in addition, has the convention of characters stepping outside themselves and becoming a chorus. This puts an additional premium on highly aware characters. Richard always displays a consciousness of his ultimate goal as he is getting rid of his enemies: "My thoughts aim at a further matter. I / Stay not for the love of Edward but the crown" (*3 Henry VI*, IV.i.125–26). There is a premium on villains as interesting bad characters rather than on simple people.

Let's look now at Richard's soliloquy in *Richard III* when he awakens at Bosworth Field, after dreaming of the ghosts of people whom he has killed:

What do I fear? Myself? There's none else by.
Richard loves Richard: that is, I am I.
Is there a murtherer here? No. Yes, I am.
Then fly. What, from myself? Great reason why—
Lest I revenge myself upon myself?
Alack, I love myself. Wherefore? For any good
That I myself have done unto myself?
O no! Alas, I rather hate myself
For hateful deeds committed by myself.
I am a villain. Yet I lie, I am not.
Fool, of thyself speak well. Fool, do not flatter.
My conscience hath a thousand several tongues,
And every tongue brings in a several tale,
And every tale condemns me for a villain.
Perjury, perjury, in the high'st degree,
Murther, stern murther, in the dir'st degree,
All several sins, all us'd in each degree,
Throng to the bar, crying all "Guilty! guilty!"
I shall despair. There is no creature loves me;
And if I die, no soul shall pity me;
Nay, wherefore should they, since that I myself
Find in myself no pity to myself?

(V.iii.183–204)

This soliloquy needs to be glossed. There are two different senses to Richard's continual use of the terms "I" and "myself," and some light can be thrown on how to distinguish them by looking at Ibsen's *Peer Gynt.* When Peer is in the Troll Kingdom seeking to marry the Troll King's daughter, the King tells him that the common saying among men is, "Man, to thyself be true!" but that among the Trolls the saying is, "Troll, to thyself be—enough!" The trolls tie a tail on Peer, they serve him strange food, and they put on a show of ugly dances for him. When Peer reacts by telling the truth about what he sees despite his best intentions, the Troll King tries to persuade him to have his eye cut out in order to become like the Trolls and "cure this troublesome human nature." Peer refuses. He is only willing to do something that he can undo. Truth always creeps in.

There are two poles of the self: the essential self and the existential self. Hunter Guthrie remarks that when he talks of the essence of a thing, he means its nature. The essential self has a personal responsibility to its name and must live up to it. The essential self is always potential, a self in the process of realization. It is also a self that, since it is based on a common human nature, is central for communication and is mutually comprehensible and universal. Existence is not necessary to the essential self—characters in books have essential selves, our dead friends have essential selves. It is a characteristic of essence to want to come into being, into existence, and this characteristic is displayed in the anxiety of the weak to become strong, of the potential to become actual. The essential self wishes to be self-sufficient—internally, from compassion, externally, from other selves. Its method for dealing with external threats is to absorb, annihilate, or flee. It desires self-realization. As hunger is to food, and the desire for knowledge is to knowledge, so is the essential self to the potential it wishes to realize. It wants admiration and fears a stronger external object. The ideals of the essential self are also relative. For the Greeks, the ideals of the self were strength, beauty, and freedom from sorrow. The purpose of religious practices, for the essential self, is to prevent the hostile interest of stronger external objects.

The existential self is different: it is aware of being in the world now, it is complete, not potential, and it is contingent and unstable. Existence is not mine, a given, but depends on others. Its anxiety is different as well. The existential self is a lonely self that seeks a stronger other self to which it wishes to be attached. It seeks an infinitely strong outside appearance, it fears other objects as too weak, and it wants to be loved as it is now. Its God is not Greek, but the Absolute, and the ground of its Absolute is not logical—the Aristotelian self-sufficient, unknowable, uncaring Unmoved Mover—but an Absolute that cares infinitely. Hatred is not better than love for the existential self, but it is better than indifference. It has an admiration of quality and a love for a qualitative self. The existential self wants to be known. The essential self wants to know, and it asks for ability, not ethical importance, which is the quest of the existential self.

Look in the mirror. What does one see? One sees an object known by others, an essence. The image lacks the anxiety of the original because its existence is derived from me. What is the fascination of acting? The actor is an existing individual who expresses an essence other than his, but this essence is not anxious and does not need to become real, since the role that is played is only a possibility. Most of us make a compromise between our essential and existential selves. Parents give us affection and respect our merits, so our existential anxiety is assuaged. We seek public approval or love, and avoid public disapproval. In return for that, we abandon some objectives of the essential self so as to be loved. Most of us, most of the time, avoid the anxiety of making real choices, either by making our surroundings varied and exciting enough to keep us in a state of passion that can dictate what we do—we have our cake and eat it too—or by repressing all but one alternative so that no choice is available because all others have been repressed. Choice means willing unhappiness.

What about a person in an exceptional situation? As a hunchback, Richard III is exceptionally aware of his loneliness because his self is rejected by others and he despairs of attachment. He must either seek a real absolute to surrender to or he must make one up—make his essential self a not-self and absolutely strong so that he can worship it. His essential self is pushed into competition because it must constantly be tested to see whether it's strong enough. The existential drive of Don Giovanni is indifferent to the individuality of the girls he seduces. He keeps an impersonal list of them. The Greek gods were more selective: people they seduced had to be beautiful, and they forgot about their previous affairs. The existential drive devolves into an infinite series, not to satisfy the essential self, which wants only relief from tension, but—despite corns, tiredness—to satisfy the need for other selves, acquired either by absorption or murder.

Murder is different from other injuries: the thief may repent in a theft, the victim may forgive in a rape. Neither is possible in murder. There is a difference between anti-Negroes and anti-Semites. To anti-Semites, Jews represent a threat to existence, to anti-Negroes, Negroes are a threat to the essential self. The Southerner doesn't wish to destroy all Negroes. He is anxious that they should exist as servants. The anti-Semite wishes the Jews not to be. If the essential self despairs of the possibility of becoming strong, its recourse is the opposite of Don Giovanni's—it wishes suicidally, like Tristan, to annihilate the self and be absorbed into another.

What about Richard III? In the beginning he is a hunchback with a strong physique for whom people feel either pity or fear—fear because his physical appearance must reflect his inner nature. He is the opposite of the actor, who deliberately projects a different personality from his own. Here people draw conclusions that Richard doesn't intend. In the beginning he attempts to imitate his father, whom he admires: "Methinks 'tis prize enough to be his son" (*3 Henry VI*, II.i.20). But he overcompensates. Because he feels people will believe what they see him do, not what they hear him say—how could they believe him, looking as he does?—he first distrusts words and believes only in deeds. Thus, as he ostentatiously throws down Somerset's head, he says, "Speak thou for me, and tell them what I did" (*3 Henry VI*, I.i.16), and in the scene in which he kills Somerset, he declares, "Priests pray for enemies, but princes kill" (*2 Henry VI*, V.ii.71).

Richard discovers the power of words when his father decides not to seize the crown from Henry because of an oath he had sworn to him "that he should quietly reign." Richard playfully makes up a specious verbal justification for him to violate his oath:

> An oath is of no moment, being not took
> Before a true and lawful magistrate
> That hath authority over him that swears.
> Henry had none, but did usurp the place.
> Then, seeing 'twas he that made you to depose,
> Your oath, my lord, is vain and frivolous.
> Therefore to arms!
>
> (*3 Henry VI*, I.ii.15, 22–28)

His father immediately grasps at this speech. He watches his brother Edward have a similar initial hesitation when news is brought of their father's death. Edward, for whom the news is horrible and who does not like to think of its advantage to him, says to the messenger, "O, speak no more, for I have heard too much!" But Richard declares, "Say how he died, for I will hear it all" (*3 Henry VI*, II.i.47–48), and he soon persuades his brother to take arms as well:

> Shall we go throw away our coats of steel
> And wrap our bodies in black mourning gowns,
> Numb'ring our Ave-Maries with our beads?
>
> (*3 Henry VI*, II.i.160–62)

There is a complete difference between Richard's monologues and his conversations with others. He starts out his career with people thinking him other than he is—he's fairly decent. *Then* he makes people think him good when he's really bad. Instead of being a true mirror to his self, he is a false mirror, one that makes people look and see what they want to see, as Hastings does in *Richard III*, for example, just moments before Richard has him executed:

> I think there's never a man in Christendom
> Can lesser hide his love or hate than he,
> For by his face straight shall you know his heart.
>
> (III.iv.51–53)

As a hunchback, Richard doesn't court people to be liked. He knows you exist anyway. "I'll make my heaven," he says,

> to dream upon the crown
> And, whiles I live, t'account this world but hell
> Until my misshap'd trunk that bears this head
> Be round impaled with a glorious crown.
>
> (*3 Henry VI*, III.ii.168–71)

His brother Edward allays his anxiety by chasing one girl after another. Richard is not envious of Edward's success itself—he eventually has his own success with Anne. What he does envy is Edward's easy satisfaction with a love that has nothing to do with his nonqualitative self. Richard really wants to be loved for himself alone—not for his beauty, if he had it, or his cleverness, but for his essential self. Each person desires that. What people are in the habit of calling love is the reflection of their self-love, which is why we love or want to love people like us or like what we want to be. This is impossible for Richard, since he will not ever look like other people.

Following his realization of how his father needs a rationalization for action comes Richard's great soliloquy of the "thorny wood" (*3 Henry VI*, III.ii.124ff.), where he hasn't yet made any plans but is trying to find out what he wants. The problem is crucial for him because what he calls "this weak piping time of peace" in *Richard III* (I.i.24) is near at hand. War solves existential anxiety. The number of suicides declines in wartime. There is a Charles Addams cartoon of a little man with an umbrella—his bourgeois umbrella suggesting a magician's wand—engaged in a life-and-death struggle with a large octopus that has emerged from a man-hole in the middle of a residential street in New York. A crowd watches, saying nothing. Behind the crowd, two men with briefcases are walking along without bothering to turn their heads, and one is saying, "It doesn't take much to collect a crowd in New York." The individual exists because he is struggling for existence, the crowd exists by watching—they have both *Schadenfreude* and the feeling that "nothing ever happens to me." The two men exist negatively: whatever the crowd does, they do the opposite. In time of war Richard is needed. His postwar planning is more acute because he is more isolated and even more conscious than usual.

Richard is not ambitious in an ordinary sense. He's not interested in becoming king for the position of power, but because becoming king is so difficult. He is not so much interested in simply making people do what he wants them to do: what excites him is that they themselves don't want to do it. The wooing of Anne is a good example. The first stage of his seduction is his frank admission of his murders of members of her family, which appeals to Anne's desire for strength—her existential character. Second, he dares her to kill him and offers to kill himself at her orders, thereby treating her as infinitely strong, with his own existence deriving from hers:

> Then bid me kill myself, and I will do it.
> *[Rises, and takes up his sword.]*
>   *Anne.* I have already.
>   *Rich.*   That was in thy rage.
> Speak it again, and even with the word
> This hand, which for thy love did kill thy love,
> Shall for thy love kill a far truer love.
> To both their deaths shalt thou be accessary.
>   *Anne.* I would I knew thy heart.
>   *Rich.* 'Tis figur'd in my tongue.
>
>   (I.ii.186–93)

When Anne succumbs, Richard exults not in the prospect of possessing her, but in having won her against such odds:

> Was ever woman in this humour woo'd?
> Was ever woman in this humour won?
> I'll have her, but I will not keep her long.
> What? I that kill'd her husband and his father
> To take her in her heart's extremest hate,
> With curses in her mouth, tears in her eyes,
> The bleeding witness of my hatred by,
> Having God, her conscience, and these bars against me,
> And I no friends to back my suit withal
> But the plain devil and dissembling looks?
> And yet to win her—all the world to nothing?
> Ha! . . .
> I do mistake my person all this while!
> Upon my life, she finds (although I cannot)

Myself to be a marv'llous proper man.
I'll be at charges for a looking glass
And entertain a score or two of tailors
To study fashions to adorn my body.
Since I am crept in favour with myself,
I will maintain it with some little cost.
But first I'll turn yon fellow in his grave,
And then return lamenting to my love.
Shine out, fair sun, till I have bought a glass,
That I may see my shadow as I pass.

(I.ii.227–38, 252–63)

Richard is superstitious. He is anxious about being named Duke of Gloucester: "Let me be Duke of Clarence, George of Gloucester; / For Gloucester's dukedom is too ominous" (*3 Henry VI*, II.vi.106–7). He sees a bad omen in the gates of York being locked:

The gates made fast? Brother, I like not this!
For many men that stumble at the threshold
Are well foretold that danger lurks within.

(*3 Henry VI*, IV.vii.10–12)

And he is very troubled that the sun is not shining at Bosworth field:

Who saw the sun to-day?
Rat.   Not I, my lord.
Rich. Then he disdains to shine; for by the book
He should have brav'd the East an hour ago.
A black day will it be to somebody.

(V.iii.278–81)

Superstition treats inanimate objects and accidents as if they were intentional. The greater the success a man has in mastering the wills of others, the greater becomes the importance of the unintentional, the uncontrollable. Very strong-willed people are apt to believe in fate and signs—Carmen reading the cards, for example. In playing cards, if I lose because of my own mistakes in play, I do not mind. But if I lose because of consistently bad cards, I get mad because I am not getting the cards I think I should get. I consider it a good omen for the day if a subway train pulls in just in time for me to board it. If it pulls out of the station just as I come in, I regard it as a bad omen. But I do not think it is the driver who is responsible. I blame the train. For thinking beings are obviously controllable, but inanimate objects are not. Richard is doomed to failure in proportion to his success because ultimately if he controlled all souls, he'd be thrown back on existential anxiety: what support can he have for his own existence? So he must always make enemies, for then he can be sure he exists.

The Comedy of Errors
and *The Two Gentlemen*
of Verona

[23 October 1946]

We'll begin with the nature of the comic. It is not the same as comedy, since a comedy is not comic throughout. The comic is a contradiction in the relation of the individual or the personal to the universal or the impersonal that does not involve the spectator or hearer in suffering or pity, which in practice means that it must not involve the actor in real suffering. The second point differentiates it from tragedy. A situation in which the actor really suffers can only be found comic by children who see the contradiction and are unaware of the suffering, as when a child laughs at a hunchback. An adult does not find a hunchback comic because he realizes that a hunchback suffers from the abnormality that a child finds funny. The statements, "I'll bet my life that fountain pen's worth $3.00," and "Goliath is seven yards and three-quarters of an inch tall," are both comic because of the contrasts in scale. If a man wants to set up as an innkeeper and he does not succeed, it is not comic. If, on the contrary, a girl asks to be allowed to set up as a prostitute and she fails, which sometimes happens, it is comic—the failure of a failure. A partially drunk person is comic when he tries to appear sober. When I read *The New York Times,* I look through the obituaries first. A headline about the funeral of a baking company official strikes me as funny. A notice of the funeral of a chef is not funny. A chef is a vocation. "A baking company official" is not an adequate description of a human being. In one *New Yorker* cartoon, a Park Avenue matron tries on a hat and makes a Bronx cheer. The shop assistant says, "A simple 'yes' or 'no,' madame, will be quite sufficient." The contradiction in this instance is between individual and class.

Sydney Smith walks down a slum street in Edinburgh and sees two women arguing—fishwives from two houses. "Those two women will never agree," he says, "they argue from different premises." Communication is based on the law of language that any given verbal sound always means the same thing and only that thing. The pun comes from one word with two different meanings brought together—"premises" in the Sydney Smith story—and understood by both the speaker and the hearer. The farther apart the two meanings are, the funnier the pun.

Rhymes can have a similar comic effect if the rhymed words, on the basis of their auditory friendship, look as if they have taken charge of the situation: as if, instead of an event requiring words to describe it, words had the power to create an event. Many years ago, there appeared in *Punch* a joke that I have heard attributed to the poet A. E. Housman. The cartoon showed two middle-aged English examiners taking a country stroll in spring. And the caption ran:

> First E. E.   O cuckoo shall I call thee bird
>   Or but a wandering voice?
> Second E. E.   State the alternative preferred
>   With reasons for your choice.

A philologist doesn't enjoy puns so much.

A spoonerism depends upon a violation of a second law of language, which states that whether words make sense or nonsense depends on whether the speaker uses them correctly or incorrectly. An example of a spoonerism: a professor says to idle undergraduates, "You've hissed all the mystery lectures and tasted two worms." As opposed to the pun, where both meanings are relevant, in a spoonerism the accidental meaning is nonsensical. Also, where the pun should be immediately apparent to the hearer, it should take time before he realizes what the speaker of the spoonerism intended to say. A pun is witty and intended. A spoonerism, like a comic rhyme, should appear to be involuntary. A spoonerism in action would be a professor kissing the porter and giving his wife a quarter—an accurate general plan is not broken down into the right particulars.

Free will and necessity are different in comedy and tragedy. In comedy, if fate is to appear comic, it must be arbitrary and appear to behave like a person, and the people who are subject to fate should not be responsible for what occurs. In tragedy fate is not an arbitrary person—it is we who are responsible, and we bring our fate upon ourselves. Where fate plays too large a role, however, the effect is not tragic but pathetic. If a million people die by plague, we have pathos not tragedy. The effect of Greek tragedy can seem pathetic to us in just this way. The Greeks naively argue that the sign of guilt is misfortune and that therefore if there is misfortune, then there must be guilt. Comic fate is arbitrary and does not involve real suffering—whatever suffering is present in comedy must be temporary or imaginary.

In farce fate is all-powerful or nonexistent. You get a comic effect if you reverse the action of a movie or of a day in your life—you become passive and objects become active. What was originally the action of a person putting his hands on a tube of toothpaste to squeeze the tooth-paste out becomes the action of toothpaste drawn into the tube to push the person's hands off. Similarly, a man putting on a coat can become a coat putting on a man. There can be a comic action in which there is no fate, no essence, only existence, as when Groucho Marx feels a woman's pulse and says, "Either she's dead, or my watch has stopped." Alone in a room, you may act farce. Madmen do such things in front of everyone, which is not *then* funny.

Characters may be comic if they are so full of self-love that the object world vanishes. A saint so forgets his self that he abolishes his difference from the object world. Groucho Marx does so in reverse. Groucho offers the closest approach to a saint, aesthetically, though a real saint never draws attention to himself and therefore can't be an aesthetic subject. The tragic hero makes the mistake of thinking himself free of necessity when he ought to think himself bound to it, and he therefore moves toward doom. In tragedy, the audience and the hero move apart. In comedy, characters move from necessity—fate, passion—to freedom, and the comic characters and audience move closer together in learning to be free human beings. Only farce is *only* comic.

The comedy of *The Comedy of Errors* is set in a nominally tragic frame. The Duke of Ephesus has vowed to kill all Syracusans, but is faced with an individual Syracusan, Ægeon, whom he wishes to spare:

> Hapless Ægeon, whom the fates have mark'd
> To bear the extremity of dire mishap!
> Now trust me, were it not against our laws,
> Against my crown, my oath, my dignity,
> Which princes, would they, may not disannul,
> My soul would sue as advocate for thee.
>
> (I.i.140–45)

It is a case of the general versus the particular. There is an instance of an Icelandic saga character who vows to kill the next rider of a horse, and the next rider turns out to be his son. The story of Jepthah's daughter, in the Bible, is similar. Jepthah makes "a vow unto the Lord" that if He gives him victory over the Ammonites, he will sacrifice to Him "whoso-ever cometh forth of the doors of my house to meet me, when I return in peace from the children of Ammon":

> And Jepthah came to Mizpeh unto his house, and, behold, his daughter came out to meet him with timbrels and with dances: and she was his only child; beside her he had neither son nor daughter.

> And it came to pass, when he saw her, that he rent his clothes, and
> said, Alas, my daughter! Thou hast brought me very low, and thou
> art one of them that trouble me: for I have opened my mouth unto
> the LORD, and I cannot go back.

Hard cases make bad law, but good law will be subject to few hard cases.

The shipwreck and separation of Ægeon and his wife and children is
pathetic, not tragic, because there is no guilt. It is interesting that a shipwreck—a great Shakespearean theme—should come so early in Shakespeare's career. In his later works it becomes a great purging test—not a
punishment of guilt, but a way in which characters may learn their guilt
and repent. In those works, also, the journey in water entails deaths and
rebirths as well as the stripping off of the mask of a persona and the
discovering of the real self. But nothing much is made of the theme in
The Comedy of Errors.

The humor or farce in *The Comedy of Errors* turns on identical twins. In
The Two Gentlemen of Verona we have persons in disguise. Both turn on the
difference between existence and essence. In *The Comedy of Errors* there
are two existing people and two essences and you think it's only one
person. In the case of Dr. Jekyll and Mr. Hyde, one existence apparently
contains two essences. In disguise, you think one person is in fact two
people. There is a difference between the knowledge of self and the
knowledge of others. Look at a shadow and you see an essence separate
from existence. The effect is comic when it is not realized. It is comic, for
example, when a child and a dog see each other in mirror. If a restaurant
mirror you do not realize is there makes you step out of the way to let
yourself pass, that is comic.

For twins to be comic, one must be well known, and one must be a
complete stranger. Twins must look exactly alike, which is harder to
achieve on stage than in movies. Disguise, on the other hand, must be
obvious to the audience, which is easier in the theater. We must feel
strongly about the disguised person. The person may disclose or conceal
himself at will, but nature is more open, and his real thoughts may manifest themselves in a somatic condition. The confusion of twins is an act
of fortune, but is believed to be willed, because people lie. A disguise is
believed to be natural, but is really willed. The confusion of twins can't
be cleared up by the characters themselves but only by fate bringing
them together, and it can only be comic because no one is responsible
for it. A disguise is not usually tragic because the man fooled is not responsible. The disguiser would have to show terrific malice to make it
tragic. Universal belief throws out the comedy of mistaken twins, univer-

sal doubt throws out the comedy of disguise. To be comic, one twin must also behave strangely. A good husband acting badly is comic, for example, but not vice versa. A disguised person in comedy, finally, must not arouse serious passion.

There is considerable use of servants in comedy. It is too bad that it's getting so hard to find servants, because with their disappearance an important element in art is dying out. The servant is an instrument of his master's will, with no existence of his own, and the relationship is contractual—the master can dissolve it by firing the servant. The servant becomes a confidant to whom everything is revealed, and he may become his master's alter ego. The comedy of the relationship is that servants really have natures of their own that may contrast with or be caricatures of those of their masters. We see such contrasts between the language of Proteus and Valentine and that of Launce and Speed in *The Two Gentlemen of Verona*. Here are Valentine and Speed, for example, discussing Valentine's love for Silvia:

> *Val.* I have lov'd her since I saw her, and still I see her beautiful.
> *Speed.* If you love her, you cannot see her.
> *Val.* Why?
> *Speed.* Because love is blind. O, that you had mine eyes! or your own eyes had the lights they were wont to have when you chid at Sir Proteus for going ungarter'd!
> *Val.* What should I see then?
> *Speed.* Your own present folly and her passing deformity; for he, being in love, could not see to garter his hose; and you, being in love, cannot see to put on your hose.
> *Val.* Belike, boy, then you are in love; for last morning you could not see to wipe my shoes.
>
> (II.i.72–86)

Speed has a similar exchange with Proteus:

> *Speed.* The shepherd seeks the sheep, and not the sheep the shepherd; but I seek my master, and my master seeks not me. Therefore I am no sheep.
> *Pro.* The sheep for fodder follows the shepherd; the shepherd for food follows not the sheep. Thou for wages followest thy master; thy master for wages follows not thee. Therefore thou art a sheep.
> *Speed.* Such another proof will make me cry "baa."
>
> (I.i.88–98)

In another mocking exchange with his master Valentine, Speed says,

> *Speed.* Why muse you, sir? 'Tis dinner time.
> *Val.* I have din'd.
> *Speed.* Ay, but hearken, sir. Though the chameleon Love can feed
> on the air, I am one that am nourish'd by my victuals, and would
> fain have meat. O, be not like your mistress. Be moved, be moved.
>
> (II.i.176–82)

Both pairs, Proteus and Launce, as well as Valentine and Speed, are interested in the play on language, and in both there is a contrast between elaborate compliment versus elaborate puns. Both are a little ridiculous, but both illuminate each other. Servants in literature who have an extreme knowledge of the inner lives of their masters include Sancho Panza, the servant of Don Quixote in Cervantes' *Don Quixote,* Jeeves, the servant of Bertie Wooster in the P G. Wodehouse stories, and Crichton, the servant of Lord Loamshire in J. M. Barrie's *The Admirable Crichton.*

The comedy of the two friends in *The Two Gentlemen of Verona* is not very funny—the point of it is their final attainment of self-knowledge. In a tragedy, a character would die in a deception such as Proteus's. It's the problem of infidelity and treachery that fascinates Shakespeare in the play. What does Proteus want? The child says "me," youth says "I," and maturity says that one is "thou," addressed as "thou shalt." Because a mature person possesses the capacity and the need to disclose himself to himself, he has a thou-thou relationship with himself and possesses the capacity to enter a Thou-Thou relationship with God and his neighbors. Kierkegaard discusses the imperative "Thou shalt" in *Works of Love.* Proteus is at the stage of youth, and he wants power. In appearance he and Valentine are pledged to help each other, but in reality Proteus is competitive—he's one up on Valentine by falling in love, but the love itself is interesting to him only as long as he is not certain of returned affection. When he gains that certainty, he loses interest. Absence may make the heart grow fonder, but it also may test love. Valentine becomes equal in the contest with Proteus by falling in love himself. Proteus, however, is interested only in those whose affections are already engaged, which suggests the difference between essential and existential desire. Existential desire is only for objects of a certain class, not for a unique object. But the *self* has unique desire: "Nobody else lives like I do." If desire were really one to one, self to self, there would never be a problem of infidelity, but desire will always, without confusion, demand a particular *class.*

Caring for a unique *object* is an illusion, but the *feeling* must be unique, and though that feeling may not be natural, it is a duty. You must love your neighbor as your self, uniquely. From the personal point of view, sexual desire, because of its impersonal and unchanging character, is a comic contradiction. The relation between every pair of lovers is unique, but in bed they can only do what all mammals do. All of the relation in friendship, a relationship of spirit, can be unique. In sexual love the only uniqueness can be fidelity.

The Duke of Milan, the tyrannical father in *The Two Gentlemen of Verona*, eventually develops into King Lear. Proteus wants to *get* power; the Duke of Milan wants to *keep* power. The Duke makes his child Sylvia synonymous with the general class of daughter. By contrast, Launce loves his dog, Crab, faithfully and uniquely, endures a whipping for him, and the dog doesn't requite him. At one point Launce cannot separate his dog and his self: "I am the dog. No, the dog is himself, and I am the dog. O the dog is me, and I am myself" (II.iii.23–25), and he later goes on at length about his dog's ingratitude:

> When a man's servant shall play the cur with him, look you, it goes hard—one that I brought up of a puppy; one that I sav'd from drowning when three or four of his blind brothers and sisters went to it. I have taught him even as one would say precisely "Thus I would teach a dog." I was sent to deliver him as a present to Mistress Silvia from my master; and I came no sooner into the dining chamber but he steps me to her trencher and steals her capon's leg. O, 'tis a foul thing when a cur cannot keep himself in all companies! I would have (as one should say) one that takes upon him to be a dog indeed; to be, as it were, a dog at all things. If I had not had more wit than he, to take a fault upon me that he did, I think verily he had been hang'd for't. Sure as I live, he had suffer'd for't. You shall judge. He thrusts me himself into the company of three or four gentlemenlike dogs, under the Duke's table. He had not been there (bless the mark!) a pissing while but all the chamber smelt him. "Out with the dog!" says one. "What cur is that?" says another. "Whip him out!" says the third. "Hang him up!" says the Duke. I, having been acquainted with the smell before, knew it was Crab, and goes me to the fellow that whips the dogs. "Friend," quoth I, "you mean to whip the dog?" "Ay, marry, do I!" quoth he. "You do him the more wrong," quoth I. "'Twas I did the thing you wot of." He makes me no more ado, but whips me out of the chamber. How many masters

would do this for his servant? Nay, I'll be sworn I have sat in the
stocks for puddings he hath stol'n, otherwise he had been executed;
I have stood on the pillory for geese he hath kill'd, otherwise he had
suffer'd for't. Thou thinkst not of this now! Nay, I remember the
trick you serv'd me when I took my leave of Madam Silvia! Did not
I bid thee still mark me and do as I do? When didst thou see me
heave up my leg and make water against a gentlewoman's farthin-
gale? Didst thou ever see me do such a trick?

(IV.iv.1–42)

Proteus loves Sylvia, who, like Crab, doesn't return his affection. Launce,
however, is comic because he *knows* that his dog can't return his love in
the way he says he wishes.

Thurio is rich; he loves only his self. He is comic because he is perfectly content to be loved for his riches. He lacks passion and is not
interested in being loved for himself. You can make such a situation
tragic, when a man thinks himself loved for himself and discovers that he
isn't, as Shakespeare does with Timon.

Launce is faithful to his dog, Julia is faithful to Proteus, and Eglamour
is faithful to his dead wife. "Thyself hast lov'd," Sylvia says to Eglamour, when she turns to him for help,

> and I have heard thee say
> No grief did ever come so near thy heart
> As when thy lady and thy true-love died,
> Upon whose grave thou vow'dst pure chastity.

(IV.iii.18–21)

Kierkegaard discusses the implications of such a vow in *Works of Love*.
When death separates two friends, he writes,

the survivor—faithful in the first moment, swears that "he will never
forget the dead." Oh, how reckless! For truly, a dead man is a cunning man to talk with, except that his cunning is not like that of the
one about whom we say: "One can't always find him where one left
him"; for the cunning of the dead consists precisely in the fact that
we cannot get him away from the place where we left him. . . . When
you say to a dead man, "I shall never forget you," then it is as if he
answered, "Good! Rest assured that I shall never forget that you
have said this." And even if all your contemporaries were to assure
you that he has forgotten it, you will never hear that from the mouth
of the dead. No, he goes to his own place—but he is not *changed*. . . .

For a dead man is, although one does not notice it, a strong man: he has the strength of unchangeableness. And a dead man is a proud man. Have you not noticed that a proud man, precisely in relation to the man he despises most, takes the most pains not to betray anything, to appear entirely unchanged, to pretend to be unconscious of everything, in order to allow the despised to sink lower and lower—for the proud man only benevolently calls the attention of the one he loves to his error, in order by so doing to help him to the right!

Kierkegaard goes on to say that we should therefore fear the dead, "But if you love him, then remember him affectionately, and you will have no reason to fear." He concludes that

The work of love in remembering the dead is thus a work of the most disinterested, the freest, the most faithful love. So go out, then, and do this: remember the dead, and just by so doing learn to love the living, disinterestedly, freely, faithfully. In your relation to the dead you have a standard by which you can test yourself.

A few words about Julia's disguise. Proteus blinds himself and does not think he is in love with the person behind the disguise. He is not in love with the disguised Julia, since she is in disguise as a boy, but he does not realize that he was ever in love with the person behind the disguise. His protestations of love to Sylvia, the lover of his friend, with the disguised Julia as witness (IV.ii), reveals both his blindness and his selfishness, and his use of the disguised Julia as his servant is itself a reduplication of his selfish love of her.

The brief episode in the woods presents a contrast between the outlaws and the city and suggests St. Augustine's contrast in *The City of God* between the heavenly city and the earthly city of self-love. The outlaws' spontaneous and childlike election of Valentine as their king and general is a pastoral criticism of respectable society and evokes a sense of how things were done before we became grown up and responsible. The outlaws also eventually realize that they have committed forbidden acts and wish to be, and are ready to be, forgiven.

We come, lastly, to the problem of forgiveness. At the end of the play, Proteus is contrite and Valentine forgives him:

> *Pro.* My shame and guilt confounds me.
> Forgive me, Valentine. If hearty sorrow
> Be a sufficient ransom for offence,

> I tender't here. I do as truly suffer
> As e'er I did commit.
> *Val.*   Then I am paid;
> And once again I do receive thee honest.
> Who by repentance is not satisfied
> Is nor of heaven nor earth; for these are pleas'd;
> By penitence th' Eternal's wrath's appeas'd.
> And, that my love may appear plain and free,
> All that was mine in Sylvia I give thee.
>
> (V.iv.73–83)

Forgiveness is a relation between two people. It is nonsense to speak of forgiving a class of people, the Germans, for example. The person who forgives must regard the injury as real. If a poor man steals a nickel from a millionaire, the millionaire will consider it trivial. If a millionaire steals a widow's life savings, forgiveness arises as an issue. The offender must be considered responsible; and there must be a relationship between the one who forgives and the one who is forgiven. One must let oneself be forgiven. One must (1) confess the deed, (2) admit the deed was an injury, and (3) show repentance—and so regard oneself as personally responsible. It is harder for the guilty to admit guilt and accept forgiveness than for the innocent to forgive. Many promising reconciliations have been wrecked because both sides were ready to forgive, but neither side was ready to be forgiven.

Love's Labour's Lost

[30 October 1946]

Love's Labour's Lost is not the greatest of Shakespeare's plays, but it is one of the most perfect. Its subject, education and culture, is interesting. The forms of culture it deals with are those prevalent in Shakespeare's time and include neo-Platonic humanism, courtly manners, courtly love, and Euphuism. All humanism and learning is made fun of in the play, all social life is made fun of, all art is made fun of—it is not *specific* satire. The play begins with a scheme of four young men to found a kind of neo-Platonic academy. They already have a certain education in social manners. You might think of four men meeting in Greenwich Village in 1946. The King explains the purpose of the Academy in the play's opening lines:

> Let fame, that all hunt after in their lives,
> Live regist'red upon our brazen tombs
> And then grace us, in the disgrace of death,
> When, spite of cormorant devouring Time,
> Th' endeavour of this present breath may buy
> That honour which shall bate his scythe's keen edge
> And make us heirs of all eternity.
> Therefore, brave conquerors—for so you are
> That war against your own affections
> And the huge army of the world's desires—
> Our late edict shall strongly stand in force:
> Navarre shall be the wonder of the world;
> Our court shall be a little Academe,
> Still and contemplative in living art.

(I.i.1–14)

Any society is in danger of dismissing the virtues of another society because of its vices, and a democracy is always in danger of not paying enough attention to manners and forms. We are born grave and honest, and the first step is to learn frivolity and insincerity. The second step is to learn to be serious about other people. Each stage involves suffering, and we must progress from one to the other.

Frivolity, the first step, is bound up with convention. We are trained not to claim the attention of others. When we do, we have to deserve it.

We must learn not to monopolize conversation, and when we speak we must be funny. Without convention or manners the most aggressive will dominate. In the absence of convention, also, it is very difficult to tell what relations are developing between you and other people. Even slight departures from a convention that is shared by others enable you to get your bearings. It is a problem, if you go to a cocktail party, when people you have never met before behave as if they know you very well. We can't trust our own feelings in such a situation and so convention tides us over. We also have to remember that we are a great deal less interested in others for their own sake than for their opinions of us. Convention requires us to take an interest in people we never wish to see again, and it prevents us from boring people with our own problems. Other people's troubles are not nearly as fascinating as our own, but we must observe the conventions of social life. When people meet without them, no one knows what to do. These social conventions must be mastered by the end of the first stage.

Now, the second stage, contemplation. At the end of Plato's *Symposium*, Diotima speaks of the ladder of love that leads men from earthly to heavenly Eros. Men have a "love of generation and of birth in beauty," he says, "because to the mortal creature, generation is a sort of eternity and immortality." In a speech that lies behind the King's opening lines in *Love's Labour's Lost*, he tells Socrates how men "are stirred by the love of an immortality of fame," and describes a scale of values that informs the proper progress to the higher mysteries of love:

> For he who would proceed aright in this matter should begin in youth to visit beautiful forms; and first, if he be guided by his instructor aright, to love one such form only—out of that he should create fair thoughts; and soon he will of himself perceive that the beauty of one form is akin to the beauty of another; and then if beauty of form in general is his pursuit, how foolish would he be not to recognize that the beauty in every form is one and the same! And when he perceives this, he will abate his violent love of the one, which he will despise and deem a small thing, and will become a lover of all beautiful forms; in the next stage he will consider that the beauty of the mind is more honourable than the beauty of the outward form. So that if a virtuous soul have but a little comeliness, he will be content to love and tend him, and will search out and bring to birth thoughts which may improve the young, until he is compelled to contemplate and see the beauty of institutions and

laws, and to understand that the beauty of them all is of one family, and that personal beauty is a trifle; and after laws and institutions he will go on to the sciences, that he may see their beauty, being not like a servant in love with the beauty of one youth or man or institution, himself a slave mean and narrow-minded, but drawing towards and contemplating the vast sea of beauty, he will create many fair and noble thoughts and notions in boundless love of wisdom; until on that shore he grows and waxes strong, and at last the vision is revealed to him of the single science, which is the science of beauty everywhere.

Describing this ascent to absolute beauty further, Diotima says,

And the true order of going, or being led by another, to the things of love, is to begin from the beauties of earth and mount upwards for the sake of that other beauty, using these as steps only, and from one going on to two, and from two to all fair forms, and from fair forms to fair practices, and from fair practices to fair notions, until from fair notions he arrives at the notion of absolute beauty, and at last knows what the essence of beauty is.

The process Plato describes is a progress from the particular to the universal, from the love of one earthly being to the passion of heavenly Eros. The four men in *Love's Labour's Lost*, according to strict Platonic doctrine, want to get there all at once, and they therefore demonstrate their lack of passion for knowledge.

In the Renaissance, Platonic knowledge and the process of achieving it had been elaborated by the Italian neo-Platonists, Marsilio Ficino, Pico della Mirandola, and their followers, who developed a system of thought that attempted to harmonize Platonism and Christian mysticism. They saw the pursuit of temporal beatitude as a twofold task in which man's Reason, illuminated by his Mind, can seek to perfect human life and destiny on earth, while his Mind can seek to penetrate the realm of eternal beauty and truth. In the first case, a man practices the moral virtues comprised by *iustitia* and distinguishes himself in the active life, thereby emulating the Biblical characters of Leah and Martha and attaching himself, cosmologically, to Jupiter. In the second case he adds the theological virtues, *religio*, to the moral ones and devotes himself to the contemplative life, in which case he follows the examples of Rachel and Mary and subjects himself to Saturn. Plato was puzzled by those who did not choose the contemplative life. The source of evil was considered to be the passions of the body.

Ficino also developed a detailed cosmology. On the outside of the universe is a super-celestial and unitary God associated with Uranus. Below is the Cosmic Mind, Νοῦς, which is a purely intelligible and super-celestial realm that is like God in being incorruptible and stable, but which is unlike him in being multiple, containing ideas and intelligences and angels that are the prototypes of what exists in the lower zone. This realm is associated with Saturn, and is what the four men in *Love's Labour's Lost* want. There was another tradition that associated the planet Saturn with melancholy—which held that the wise should therefore be depressed. Beneath the Cosmic Mind is the Cosmic Soul, *anima mundana*, a realm of pure causes rather than of pure forms, and associated with Jupiter, followed by a realm of Nature, a compound of form and matter, and finally a chaotic realm of Matter alone, which is formless and lifeless. Matter and Nature—every human being, beast, plant or mineral—are influenced by one or more of the celestial bodies and are governed by fate.

Ficino and his followers found an analogous structure within the microcosm of man's soul, which they said consisted of five faculties grouped under the headings of *anima prima*, the Higher Soul, and *anima secunda*, the Lower Soul. *Anima prima* is composed of Mind and Reason. Mind is contemplative and creative. It is analogous to, and participates in, the Divine mind. It can look upwards to the super-celestial and downward to Reason. Reason, which is closer to the lower soul, coordinates sense data according to the rules of logic. In contrast with the Lower Soul, it can either permit itself to be carried away by the lower sensations and emotions or struggle to surmount them. *Anima secunda*, the Lower Soul, lives in close contact with the body and consists of the three faculties that both direct and depend on physiological functions. The first is the faculty of propagation, nourishment, and growth, the second the faculty of external perception—the five senses, and the third the faculty of interior perception, or imagination. The Lower Soul, which is not free to make choices, is governed by the conjunction of celestial bodies and fate. Reason was seen as peculiar to man alone. Its practical efforts were associated with Jupiter, its contemplative efforts with Saturn.

To the celestial and earthly Venuses discussed in Plato's *Symposium* and in Ficino's writing, Pico della Mirandola adds a third, who is an intermediary between the two. In Pico's mythology Aphrodite Urania I is the daughter of Uranus and takes a human being from the particular to the universal, from individual to divine love. Aphrodite Urania II, the figure he adds, is the daughter of Saturn and tries to make individual human love rational and compatible with the active life. Aphrodite Pandemos represents lust and is the daughter of Zeus and Dione.

The four men in *Love's Labour's Lost* think they're in the realm of Urania I, but are really in the realm of Urania II. A modern analogy of this mistake would be a missing vocation. People say, for example, "I want to write," though nothing ever gets written. Why? First, they're mistaken about writing. They aren't specific: they say they want to "be a writer," not that they want to "write such and such." The eye is on the result, not on the process, and behind that is a lack of passion and of the willingness to go through the hard stages of training and study. You must be in love with your work, not with your self. In Mozart's *The Magic Flute*, to do something involves risks, renunciations, suffering. In order to work, renouncing the pleasure principle, you must, like Tamino, fall in love before seeing. These people look at their own picture first. It's an open possibility not to follow Tamino's course—like the minor characters in *Love's Labour's Lost* and Papageno in *The Magic Flute*. The other way is the renunciation of ambition—you can't have both. When you begin writing, you find it difficult and your mind wanders. If you regard only your ego, you act as if every word has to be a masterpiece, and if not, why finish?

The four men in Shakespeare try to be serious in a frivolous way and are exposed. The ladies arrive, their resolutions are forgotten, and a courtly romance ensues, partly a parody of Christianity, and partly Platonic, with the sexes changed—the lovers are heterosexual, not homosexual as in Plato. It is a conscious game that can get too serious. Rosaline says that Cupid killed Katherine's sister, and Katherine replies that, indeed, "He made her melancholy, sad, and heavy, / And so she died" (V.ii.14–15).

The courtly manners represented in the play are also affected by the medieval and Renaissance traditions of courtly love, which began with the Troubadours in eleventh-century Provence and were codified in the early thirteenth century by Andreas Capellanus in a Latin work, *De Arte Honeste Amandi*. Andreas stipulated a number of rules of courtly love. First, the lovers must not be married. They must endure great difficulties in the achievement of their love, and must be jealous of a rival, which is undesirable in marriage, but is an essential proof of courtly love. Finally, the beloved noble lady must be treated as God. Since marriage was of *convenance*, not consent, and there was no free choice either for the man or the woman, love had to be sought outside marriage. But the beloved person must be marriageable. Rustics were not suitable, because a peasant could be coerced into intercourse. Courtly love was also not supposed to progress beyond the individual to a higher realm, unlike Platonic and neo-Platonic notions of love, and in parodic opposition to the Christian idea that you must love the persons in this world as you love yourself. The adulterous physical conclusion of courtly love was undisguised.

Andreas tells a story that clearly parodies Christian ideas of the afterworld. A knight who is searching for his horse in the woods sees three companies go by. In the first ride ladies, richly horsed and each attended by a lover on foot, who had served love wisely on earth. In the second ride ladies, surrounded by a noisy crowd of contending lovers, who had given their kindness to all who asked. In the third company ride ladies, bareback on wretched nags and entirely unattended, who had been deaf to every lover's prayer. The knight follows the three companies to a strange country. The true lovers of the first company are appointed to stay with the King and Queen of love in a place called *Amoenitas*, in the shadow of a tree bearing all kinds of fruit and beside a fountain that is as sweet as nectar and that waters the surrounding countryside. The ladies of the second company are consigned to *Humiditas*, a place of swamps in which the water from the fountain has turned icy cold. Those of the third company are confined to the outermost circle of all, the burning desert of *Siccitas*, seated on sharp thorns that tormentors keep in continual agitation beneath them.

At the end of *De Arte Honeste Amandi*, Andreas moves from Christian parody to an explicit injunction to his audience to reject earthly love and its ultimate vanity, and to embrace the love of God. We see the same turn in Chaucer, in the concluding stanzas of *Troilus and Criseyde*, and in the more harsh recantation of all his works at the end of *The Canterbury Tales*. Chaucer's disillusion is not just a means of passing the censors. No, the game must be over after a time and serious business begun. The masque of Cupid in Spenser's House of Busirane shows what happens when the game gets out of hand:

> Unquiet care and fond Unthriftyhead;
> Lewd Losse of Time, and Sorrow seeming dead,
> Inconstant Chaunge, and false Disloyalty;
> Consuming Riotise, and guilty Dread
> Of heavenly vengeaunce: faint Infirmity;
> Vile Poverty; and, lastly, Death with infamy.

Let's turn to Cupid's blindness and to the play's preoccupation with eyesight. Berowne declares himself a reluctant captive to "This wimpled, whining, purblind, wayward boy" (III.i.181) and later makes a speech in which he talks at length about the significance of eyes in love. He says to the King, Longaville, and Dumain that the richness of love is "first learned in a lady's eyes":

> From women's eyes this doctrine I derive.
> They sparkle still the right Promethean fire;
> They are the books, the arts, the academes,
> That show, contain, and nourish all the world.
>
> (IV.iii.327, 350–53)

And at the end of the play, he asks the ladies to excuse the "unbefitting strains" of their love,

> All wanton as a child, skipping and vain,
> Form'd by the eye and therefore, like the eye,
> Full of strange shapes, of habits, and of forms,
> Varying in subjects as the eye doth roll
> To every varied object in his glance;
> Which parti-coated presence of loose love
> Put on by us, if, in your heavenly eyes,
> Have misbecom'd our oaths and gravities,
> Those heavenly eyes that look into these faults
> Suggested us to make them.
>
> (V.ii.770–79)

Cupid was not represented as blind before 1215 in a German work. Sight is the most intellectual of the senses: you can *see* possibilities, your sight is under the control of your will, it is the organ of choice. Eve *saw* the apple was good to eat. The lower senses are innocent—guilt and love are conveyed by the eye. Sight is active, hearing obedient. Iconographically, the Virgin Mary in the Annunciation is represented as conceiving through the ear. At the same time, sight is also the most unreliable of the senses. It can be deceived by appearances. In the sonnets Shakespeare often contrasts the eye and the heart as the outer and the inner: "Betwixt mine eye and heart a league is took" (47), "O me, what eyes hath love put in my head" (148). Blind Cupid is used in a derogatory way in Renaissance writing, signifying the Pandemic versus the seeing, rational Cupid. The mythological figure of Anteros, who was originally understood as a god of reciprocal love, was transformed by neo-Platonic writers into a god of purification who protected man from becoming fixed on the senses and seeing alone.

We put spectacles on highbrows to caricature them. This is based on a legitimate psychosomatic observation. Myopia is appropriate to those who wish to concentrate on their own special interests and withdraw themselves from the world. For the clear-sighted, a city offers an oppressive variety of stimuli to the eye. For a myopic person, *sans* spectacles, everybody looks fresh and lovely.

The four men in *Love's Labour's Lost* must learn to love people and not the idea of love. At the end of the play, Dumain and Longaville have only to grow up and wait a year. The King, who originally conceived the idea of their academy, has to learn to be truly ascetic and to live alone. The Princess tells him to retire for twelve months "To some forlorn and naked hermitage, / Remote from all the pleasures of the world" (V.ii.804–5). Berowne has to learn to become related to people. He is a leader, but he is not satisfied with himself and is too focused upon self-improvement. His life has no necessity, only possibility, and if he does not give up his self-reflection, he will become like Hamlet. As Rosaline realizes, he requires a necessity, a need that comes from outside himself, as well as a knowledge of suffering, without which he cannot know the meaning of love. The cure that Rosaline assigns him is to spend a year in an hospital, to

> Visit the speechless sick and still converse
> With groaning wretches; and your task shall be,
> With all the fierce endeavour of your wit
> To enforce the pained impotent to smile.
>
> (V.ii.860–63)

When Berowne protests that it is impossible "To move wild laughter in the throat of death," Rosaline answers,

> Why, that's the way to choke a gibing spirit,
> Whose influence is begot of that loose grace
> Which shallow laughing hearers give to fools.
> A jest's prosperity lies in the ear
> Of him that hears it, never in the tongue
> Of him that makes it.
>
> (V.ii.864, 867–72)

"A twelvemonth?" Berowne answers, "Well, befall what will befall / I'll jest a twelvemonth in an hospital" (V.ii.879–80). Berowne is a desperate, not a frivolous man. Rosaline too is in danger from the courtly love tradition. Nobody expects her to be faithful, and if Berowne doesn't change, he will corrupt her. She has the same vices as he does, and the malice of their wit covers a desperate anxiety about themselves.

Armado is a man without a function, no money, and a certain ambition, which he is not allowed to maintain. He suffers from glossolalia, a disease of people who cannot stop talking—because of their unhappiness. It is a more innocent, if more tiresome, refuge than drink. Armado is a failure. Language is parallel to but independent of experience. It should be ahead of experience for the sake of gaining knowledge. Berowne and his cohorts, however, have too much more language than experience. Armado is the purest poet—he exhibits an extreme advance of language over experience, and Shakespeare presents the relation between the two as comic. But there is nonetheless frivolity in poetry. Shakespeare makes fun of the Euphuists in both *Love's Labour's Lost* and *Hamlet*, but he owed them a great deal and he knew it. Today Armado, to follow the fashion, would speak in Hemingway monosyllabics. There is fantastic understatement as well in modern comedy. A child must first develop language, and experience should catch up. A writer, like a child, must interest himself first in the play with words—experiments with words must come first. Affectation is a way people try out ideas of what they are and succeed in finding out about themselves. Affectation is very good at college age. If it's lacking, in five years a person will become a bore. But if it goes on into middle age, it is unpleasant.

Moth at the age of twelve or so reaches an objectivity—active intelligence, undisturbed emotion—which he can retrieve only much later in life. People at the age of twelve are more conversible than they will be later in most cases, and they make good companions. It is a good idea to represent this age on stage.

The humble in the play include Holofernes, Nathaniel, and Costard. Holofernes, a schoolmaster, is pedantic in his language, a vocational defect, but a vice on the right side—it's much better than educational theory. Nathaniel is a little mild—clergymen should not be aggressive. Costard is a stoic, a dull kind. All these people properly present the pageant of the Nine Worthies. The King ungraciously disparages their acting ability and wishes to prevent their performance, but the Princess finds pleasure in zeal and incompetence united:

> That sport best pleases that doth least know how:
> Where zeal strives to content, and the contents

Dies in the zeal of that which it presents.
Their form confounded makes most form in mirth
When great things labouring perish in their birth.

(V.ii.517–21)

To God, the right kind of human life looks well-meant but incompetent.
Zeal is more important than technique. These people are nearer the
Nine Worthies than anyone in the court party.

The introduction of the news of the death of the Princess's father also
prompts Armado to agree to marry Jacquenetta, whom he has made
pregnant, and to accept his humble position. The play closes with two
songs—the song of winter, maintained by the cuckoo, and of spring,
maintained by the owl. Spring's song is:

When daisies pied and violets blue
    And lady-smocks all silver-white
And cuckoo-buds of yellow hue
    Do paint the meadows with delight,
The cuckoo then on every tree,
Mocks married men; for thus sings he,
            "Cuckoo!
Cuckoo, cuckoo!" O word of fear,
Unpleasing to the married ear!

When shepherds pipe on oaten straws,
    And merry larks are ploughmen's clocks;
When turtles tread and rooks and daws,
    And maidens bleach their summer smocks,
The cuckoo then on every tree,
Mocks married men, for thus sings he:
            "Cuckoo!
Cuckoo, cuckoo!" O word of fear,
Unpleasing to a married ear.

Winter's song is:

When icicles hang by the wall,
    And Dick the shepherd blows his nail,
And Tom bears logs into the hall,
    And milk comes frozen home in pail,
When blood is nipp'd, and ways be foul,
Then nightly sings the staring owl:
            "Tu-who!

Tu-whit, tu-who!" a merry note,
While greasy Joan doth keel the pot.

When all aloud the wind doth blow,
   And coughing drowns the parson's saw,
And birds sit brooding in the snow,
   And Marian's nose looks red and raw;
When roasted crabs hiss in the bowl,
Then nightly sings the staring owl:
        "Tu-who!
Tu-whit, tu-who!" a merry note,
And greasy Joan doth keel the pot.

                 (V.ii.904–39)

The songs celebrate the order of nature. When the scene is nice, the emotions are nasty, when the scene is nasty, the emotions are nice. The owl and the cuckoos on every tree together suggest that though all endeavors to be worthy may, as Diotima argues, "begin from the beauties of the earth and mount upwards," they must come back again to earth.

Romeo and Juliet

[6 November 1946]

Romeo and Juliet is Shakespeare's first tragedy in the strict sense of the term. What is the nature of the aesthetically interesting in tragedy? Art is divided not between the good and the bad, but between the interesting and the boring, and what is interesting is the exceptional. The news in a work of art, tragic or comic, is the aesthetically interesting, the exception to the universal norm. Dog bites man is not interesting, man bites dog is. One can make an individual unique and interesting if he is strong, as opposed to a norm that is weak—Achilles and Hercules, for example. You can depict an ordinary man in a unique situation—the Greeks said that people in extraordinary situations were extraordinary. There can be a conflict of two universals—in *Antigone*, for example, the state versus the family. There is a story of a comic conflict during a diplomatic ball in Ankara when the dresses of the wives of the British and German naval attaches became hooked together, and they wouldn't speak to each other and couldn't move. A neutral party had to unhook them. In Inwood a man's bride died at the church door: what matters is not the girl's character, but the situation. One can compare a man's habitual life with a sudden change that makes it more interesting. It is interesting if a clergyman, rather than a burglar, steals. If a starving man steals in a country where stealing is a capital offense, it is interesting only if he is either timid or had a strict upbringing. An exceptional moment in time is interesting. Art is tied to the unique and the exceptional in character, situation, and moment.

In a tragic contradiction between the normal and the exceptional, there is suffering, in a comic contradiction, none. But tragedy can include comedy and vice versa. The Nurse's inability to understand romance in *Romeo and Juliet*, for example, is comic, though it helps lead to the tragedy. In tragedy the individual is not reconcilable with the universe, and the symbol for their opposition is death. In comedy the individual is reconcilable with the universe, and the symbol for their harmony is marriage. In ancient tragedy the universe refuses reconciliation, in modern tragedy the failure is the result of the individual's choice. Comedy includes both fate and choice.

Why do we enjoy tragedy? There are two wrong—that is to say, one-sided—ways. One is complete identification: we go to a movie and bawl.

When we do that, the actual situation portrayed is much more serious than our own. If you see a movie like your own experience, one dealing with a refugee from the Gestapo, for example, the situation is painful: one doesn't break down, one's annoyed. It's when our situation is bearable but not important enough that we identify. The other wrong way of reacting to tragedy is complete differentiation. Then we feel *Schadenfreude* arising out of envy: "He's better looking than I am, but look what happens to him! Thank God I am what I am." We must combine identification and differentiation. The wrong way of identifying with Romeo and Juliet is to sympathize with their puppy love while saying, "I'm like Romeo and Juliet, even though I won't commit suicide." But Romeo and Juliet are not right to commit suicide, and we aren't like them because we don't love enough, not because we love as much but feel a moral distaste for suicide. Romeo and Juliet confuse romance and love. The ancient tragic character is one with whom fate is passionately offended. The modern tragic character is passionately related to an untruth. It is the passion that makes the aesthetic interest, it is the untruth that makes the tragedy. I myself have insufficient passion to be a hero. In ancient tragedy the moral is, "Take care not to offend the gods." No martyr to truth, like Romeo, is possible in that drama, therefore, and no villain, who is passionately offended with truth, like Iago.

In identifying with characters and situations, the spectator also may judge, but only in terms of himself, which is what enables him to identify. Don't bother about the judgments of the audience contemporary with the author, except in cases where we can't understand why so much attention is paid to something that seems to us unimportant—the scruples of the characters in the blood feud in *Romeo and Juliet*, for example. We do better imagining ideological fights. Unless we're from Kentucky. Though Elizabethans would have condemned blood feuds, as the Prince does, they were near enough to understand and feel it as a temptation. We must correct for that: otherwise the lovers will seem more unlucky and more reasonable than they are. If you take the Nurse's view that Juliet should marry Paris and have an affair with Romeo on the side, the plot does not make any sense to us.

If the written word is reliable, the idea of romance and of falling in love has been in existence for only 800 years, and only in the West. Nobody quite knows how it started. Love is represented in classical literature as good-tempered sensuality in the story of Daphnis and Chloe, as domestic comfort and loyalty in the story of Penelope, or as tragic madness in the story of Dido and in Catullus's works. Catullus would never say it is a noble state—he treated it as a horrible distraction. Dido's love threatens Aeneas's vocation, which is to found Rome, and so he leaves her. Plato doesn't work either as a testimony to romantic love: in the *Symposium* we begin with what seems like romance, but it promptly proceeds to the love of universals—Plato does not find the individual person uniquely valuable. There is a wrenching of Ovid's *Ars Amatoria* at the start of the movement of courtly love. Ovid is mock heroic, like old gentlemen drinking brandy and talking over their good times in Paris. Ovid's loves would have been ordered out of the room at the start of serious conversation. In the Middle Ages passion was conceived as appropriate only in the relationship of the vassal and the lord, in military loyalty, and in saintliness. Roland, when he is dying, thinks of the glory he will achieve in France, not of his fiancée. The medieval Scholastics believed that the fall represented a cutting of man's rationality, and the passionate love even of one's wife was considered adultery. The purpose of marriage was to create children and provide companionship.

How did it come to pass that the phenomenon of romantic love should have become the subject of intense literary interest? Falling in love became common, but not as common as was said. Some critics connect its beginning in Provence with the presence of so many unattached knights at castles with so few marriageable ladies. The Troubadour poems in Provence were a kind of bachelor literature created in the context of the prevailing institution of the *mariage de convenance* and may well have sprung from the same neo-manichean roots as the Catharist heresy at that time, which held matter to be evil.

Now, consider the nature of falling in love. Its elements include, first, as Martin Buber explains in *I and Thou*, the discovery of a *Thou* instead of an *It*. Thou demands a relation to an *I*. *Thou* must be mysterious, numinous. From the discovery of *Thou* comes the discovery of an *I* in its fullness and unity. The *I* becomes more active, more interested, and ashamed of the condition it is in. It wants to be better. A. E. Housman refers to this convention, ironically, in *A Shropshire Lad*:

> Oh, when I was in love with you,
>   Then I was clean and brave,
> And miles around the wonder grew
>   How well did I behave.

> And now the fancy passes by,
>   And nothing will remain,
> And miles around they'll say that I
>   Am quite myself again.

The effect on Troilus of his love for Criseyde in Chaucer's *Troilus and Criseyde* is to increase his liberality, his hardiness and might, his adventurousness, his talk of love, and his interest in other lovers. Romeo tries to be friendly with Tybalt.

Second, what do you want, in falling in love? Not simply possession. It becomes important to my existence that you exist, and I want my existence to become important to you. I want to know you. Falling in love resembles other experiences that have these qualities. It is a gift, not a thing that you can make happen. There is no command, "Thou shalt *fall in* love": the scriptural command is "Thou shalt love." Falling in love does not demand the return of love. The *Thou* is not aesthetically or ethically defined, not a prettier or better person, but a *unique* person. Comparisons are futile for those who have fallen in love: lovers don't care about comparisons. The *Thou* must also seem powerful. That's why falling in love is not often reciprocated. If it is, the feeling of dependence upon one another ensues. And sex.

What are the possible experiences of *Thou*? (1) Contact with God: religious experience, and (2) the discovery of a vocation. It is characteristic of our age that no one feels that the lack of religious or vocational experience is significant, while no one doubts that the lack of love experience is. A weak self wants to be aggressive in love and to appropriate the Not-self, the lonely self wants to be related through protecting or being protected. In adolescent love, the two are brought together.

You find out who you are when you are in love. The experience is likely to appear at critical junctures—adolescence, middle age—when a stage of life is being outgrown. The courtly love people were wrong in thinking one can will falling in love, but right in thinking that falling in love is impossible in marriage. *There* either *Thou* gets weaker, or we grow to understand *Thou*, and falling in love becomes love. We see *Thou* as not a ground for our existence but as someone we can help—perhaps by separation. Parents will separate from their children, for example, in order to wean them. If we equate falling in love with love, it leads to a frenzy of cosmetics, twin beds, etc. Love is different.

In literary tradition there are always obstacles to love. For the intoxicant of romantic love to remain effective it is essential that the relationship not change into something else, dwindle into friendship or domestic, married love, for example, with its ties to the community. No, something must come between the lovers that prevents their union— one of them is already married, there is an interfamily feud, there is a barrier of race, or religion, and should no barrier be present, the lovers themselves must provide one. The purpose of the obstacle is clear: it is to intensify desire by impeding its fulfillment. Now the obstacle that the lovers ideally require must be insurmountable. That is to say, their union must be possible only through their deaths. This is the secret, the religious mystery, of Romantic Love, the mystery that is represented by the suicides of Romeo and Juliet. If people marry on the assumption that love must always overcome obstacles, they will either become unfaithful or they will make things difficult. The better you know someone, the better you can torture him: man and wife become each other's devils. Falling in love is a good thing if by means of it you become a self with whom it is possible to have a real relationship, if your *I* can develop. If a person falls in love every five minutes, people rightly suspect he has no heart. Falling in love can be bad if it leads to nothing. There are other ways of discovering oneself, but in our time falling in love seems the commonest. Because of the development of industrialization, there has been a decline in religious feeling as well as a decrease in the number of jobs that are really vocations, and in big cities there is also a shrinkage of love and of important relationships to family.

Romeo and Juliet in their suicides declare, "There's nothing to live for," which is different from the martyr who says, "There's something I have to die for." Romeo and Juliet have made each other divine. Juliet, when she learns that Romeo is banished, says,

> "Romeo is banished"—to speak that word
> Is father, mother, Tybalt, Romeo, Juliet,
> All slain, all dead.
>
> (III.ii.122–24)

Romeo says that

> banished is banish'd from the world,
> And world's exile is death. Then "banishment"
> Is death misterm'd.
>
> (III.iii.19–21)

Romeo and Juliet don't know each other, but when one dies, the other can't go on living. Behind their passionate suicides, as well as their reactions to Romeo's banishment, is finally a lack of feeling, a fear that the relationship cannot be sustained and that, out of pride, it should be stopped now, in death. If they become a married couple, there will be no more wonderful speeches—and a good thing, too. Then the real tasks of life will begin, with which art has surprisingly little to do. Romeo and Juliet are idolaters of each other, which is what leads to their suicides.

Tybalt, a Capulet, is motivated by hatred, a negative form of idolatry. The Montagues must exist for it to operate. Those who hated Hitler alone are now at loss. Foes in war, in Shakespeare's plays, use erotic metaphors. Capulet, suffering from the melancholy of old age, likes parties, likes to have light, music, and youth about him—when Tybalt recognizes Romeo at his party, Capulet is pleased, not angry—but when he is crossed, he treats Juliet not as a *Thou* but as an object:

> Wife, we scarce thought us blest
> That God had lent us but this only child;
> But now I see this one is one too much,
> And that we have a curse in having her.
> Out on her, hilding!
>
> (III.v.165–69)

Friar Lawrence and the Nurse are related in responsibility for the tragedy. The Friar thinks he knows God's will, and he arranges the marriage. He wants to play God behind the scenes. But he is a coward, afraid of anything happening to him, and he runs away from Juliet at the end out of self-conceit and fear. The Nurse sees no difference between sex and romance. Her mistake is lack of sympathy with Juliet in telling her that she should marry Paris:

> Then, since the case so stands as now it doth,
> I think it best you married with the County,
> O, he's a lovely gentleman!
> Romeo's a dishclout to him. An eagle, madam,
> Hath not so green, so quick, so fair an eye
> As Paris hath. Beshrew my very heart,
> I think you are happy in this second match,
> For it excels your first.
>
> (III.v.218–25)

She should have kept her mouth shut. As a result of this speech, Juliet no longer confides in her and doesn't tell her about the potion.

Fate and choice operate in conjunction in the play. The servant happens to hand the invitation to the Capulet party to Romeo to read for him, which is a legitimate accident, and when Romeo sees the name of his current flame Rosaline on the list of guests, it prompts him to attend the party and thereby fall in love with Juliet. Romeo's overhearing Juliet's declaration of her love for him is a similar accident. Tybalt insults Romeo and goads him to fight, but Romeo chooses not to fight and survives the temptation. Mercutio, however, is tempted to fight Romeo's battle and is killed. To his shocked surprise, he finds that a feud is more than a game and a duel more than a display of dexterity and high spirits: "A plague o' both your houses! Zounds, a dog, a rat, a mouse, a cat, to scratch a man to death! a braggart, a rogue, a villain, that fights by the book of arithmetic!" (III.i.103–6). Romeo, in turn, is tempted to avenge Mercutio and does so, thereby becoming, as he realizes, "fortune's fool" (III.i.141). Friar John's fateful failure to inform Romeo of the plan to use the potion leads to Romeo's temptation to commit suicide. The noise outside the tomb causes Friar Lawrence to run—Friar Lawrence should have stayed and told the story. But if he had, you would get a play on marriage, which is not aesthetically interesting.

In *Either/Or*, Kierkegaard distinguishes between the external history of an individual, a succession of events culminating in one intense clarifying *moment*, and internal history, in which "every little moment is of the utmost importance" and which must be understood in the context of the passage of time. The first, external history, Kierkegaard says, is the artist's or poet's natural subject because he can show it with the concentration that art requires. The second, internal history, is far more difficult to represent in art. "Imagine, then, a knight," Kierkegaard writes,

> who has slain five wild boars, four dragons, and delivered three enchanted princes, brothers of the princess whom he worships. In the romantic chain of reasoning this has complete reality. To the artist and the poet, however, it is of no importance at all whether there are five or only four monsters slain. The artist is, on the whole, more restricted than the poet, but even the latter will not be interested in relating circumstantially how the hero accomplished the destruction of each individual wild boar. He hastens on to the moment. He perhaps reduces the number, concentrates the toils and dangers with poetic intensity, and hastens on to the moment, the moment of possession. To him the whole historical succession is of comparatively little importance.

Kierkegaard continues by observing that

> since external history is the one kind of history which can without detriment be concentrated, it is natural that art and poetry choose this especially for representation, and hence, choose likewise the unopened individual and everything that has to do with him. It is said, indeed, that love opens the individual, but this is not true when

love is conceived as it is in romances. There the individual is merely brought to the point where he will open—with that it ends; or he is about to open but is interrupted. But since external history and the shut individuality will remain more especially the subjects for artistic and poetic representation, so, too, will everything which goes to compose the content of such an individuality be preferred. But substantially this is what belongs to the natural man.

Kierkegaard then offers a few examples:

Pride can very well be represented, for the essential point in pride is not succession but intensity in the moment. Humility is represented with difficulty, because here if anywhere we are dealing with succession, and whereas the beholder needs only to see pride in its culmination, in the other instance he properly requires what poetry and art cannot give, i.e., to see humility in its constant process of being, for it is essential to humility that it constantly remains, and when it is shown in its ideal moment the beholder senses the lack of something, because he feels that its true ideality does not consist in the fact that it is ideal in the moment but that it is constant. Romantic love can very well be represented in the moment, but conjugal love cannot, because an ideal husband is not one who is such once in his life but one who every day is such. If I would represent a hero who conquers kingdoms and lands, it can very well be represented in the moment, but a cross-bearer who every day takes up his cross cannot be represented either in poetry or in art, because the point is that he does it every day.

There is a warning we should heed in the love story of Paolo and Francesca in the *Inferno* of Dante's *Divine Comedy*. Dante sees the "wearied souls" of the two lovers blown about in incessant motion by the fierce winds of the second circle of hell and asks to speak to them. Francesca tells him and Virgil,

"Love, which is quickly caught in gentle heart, took him with the fair body of which I was bereft; and the manner still afflicts me.
   Love, which to no loved one permits excuse for loving, took me so strongly with delight in him, that, as thou seest, even now it leaves me not.
   Love led us to one death; Caïna waits for him who quenched our life." These words from them were offered to us.

After I had heard those wounded souls, I bowed my face, and held it low until the Poet said to me: "What art thou thinking of?"

When I answered, I began: "Ah me! what sweet thoughts, what longing led them to the woeful pass!"

Then I turned again to them; and I spoke, and began: "Francesca, thy torments make me weep with grief and pity.

But tell me: in the time of the sweet sighs, by what and how love granted you to know the dubious desires?"

And she to me: "There is no greater pain than to recall a happy time in wretchedness; and this thy teacher knows.

But if thou hast such desire to learn the first root of our love, I will do like one who weeps and tells.

One day, for pastime, we read of Lancelot, how love constrained him; we were alone, and without all suspicion.

Several times that reading urged our eyes to meet, and changed the colour of our faces; but one moment alone it was that overcame us.

When we read how the fond smile was kissed by such a lover, he, who shall never be divided from me,

kissed my mouth all trembling: the book, and he who wrote it, was a Galeotto; that day we read in it no farther."

Whilst the one spirit thus spake, the other wept so, that I fainted with pity, as if I had been dying; and fell, as a dead body falls.

A Midsummer Night's Dream

[13 November 1946]

A Midsummer Night's Dream is a very familiar work. It is the first play to show Shakespeare's unique contribution as a dramatist, presenting not only the sense of the relations of human characters to each other but also to objects, to nature. Ibsen is the only dramatist who can approach Shakespeare in this respect. Shakespeare's depiction of the relation of social classes to each other is better than that of other dramatists, but it is not unique. The subplot in Elizabethan drama generally dealt with lower class characters, and when the use of the subplot ended, English drama itself declined. Shakespeare is also better than his contemporaries at relating the subplot to the main plot.

It is very hard in drama to represent the relation of characters to the earth, though the absence of realistic sets on the Elizabethan stage facilitates it. It's easier in movies, but settings in movies are at the same time too specific and unsuggestive. We must distinguish the different senses of the term *nature*:

(1) as that which is distinctively and characteristically human—as opposed to the affected or unusual, and

(2) as that which is in contrast to man, the physical frame to which men must adapt themselves.

Classical and Chinese writers use the term *nature* in the first and traditional sense. Under the sanction of biology, the modern West uses the term *nature* in the second sense. The second sense can in turn can be divided into four subcategories:

(2a) includes all influences to which the mind is subject from without.

(2b) consists of images and things which, through our imaginative perception of (2a), we see as the world outside—our construction of the music of the wind, for example.

(2c) is an abstraction from (2b), the world of practical experience, as perceived by all men alike. The stone Dr. Johnson kicked to refute Berkeley's assertion of the nonexistence of matter is an example of this sense.

(2d) consists of the laws and theorems used by physics to describe (2a).

We confuse (2c) and (2a) and get panicky over (2b) because it includes emotion. (2d) involves elaborate abstraction and the removal of human emotion. Alfred North Whitehead, in *Modes of Thought*, criticizes the tendency of modern scientific thinking to rely exclusively on (2d), to make catalogues of forms of sense perception that are related only spatio-temporally and that are divorced from emotion. The result, he argues, is a conception of nature that is devoid of impulse and process.

Most artists treat man as totally unrelated to nature, focusing simply on the choices people make, not on how they work, how they eat, etc. As a result, people appear freer than they in fact are, and seem to be composed of pure spirit without the bodies that relate them to animals and stones. Those who make the wrong choice are thus seen as more guilty than they really are. Alternately, during the late nineteenth and twentieth centuries, a school of writers has developed that sees man as a helpless prey of nature, nature as (2d). In their view man has no will, no emotions that are relevant to action, and no responsibility for action. This view is false. It is plausible when you look at other people to say that they couldn't help doing what they did, but if that reasoning is applied to choices that we ourselves make, we get angry. Everyone is angry to hear it of themselves.

In *A Midsummer Night's Dream* Shakespeare uses a different technique to relate man and nature. He mythologically anthropomorphizes nature, making nature like man, and reducing the figurants of nature in size in comic situations. In the tragedies, however, Shakespeare does not anthropomorphize nature. Storms and shipwrecks in the tragedies are represented as the will of God, and they either reflect or contrast with human emotion.

Modern people are skeptical of mythology. They think you're being asked to believe in fairies in *A Midsummer Night's Dream*, which is not true. A minority school on the subject of myth writes serious, solemn, and insufferably boring articles that do not believe in myths but use them as a substitute for religion, Plato's "noble lie." The implication is that *we* don't need to believe in this, but for those incapable of rational thinking, it's all right. There is a difference between religious dogma and myth. Jungian myth addicts say you don't have to believe in anything. But dogma is a presupposition that has to be believed, even though it can't be proved. *Credo ut intellegam:* I believe in order that I may understand. Its confirmation is in the future, in that it changes one's life and becomes a measuring rod by which one evaluates the experience one is given. "God is love," for example, is not a statement derived from experience but a presupposition. Myth, on the other hand, is a proposition about experience, and its truth must be tested by experiment. The story of Adam and Eve in the garden, for example, is a myth, a story of general experience. It is not a question of believing the myth actually happened. The question is, does it adequately describe certain experiences that we have? St. Paul says, "For that which I do I allow not: for what I would, that do I not; but what I hate, that do I." You can say, "I don't have guilt." I say, "I think you're a liar." We may say that Freud's myth of the killing of the father is the better explanation of guilt, by an aesthetic criterion.

Freud discusses the genesis of religious belief in *Totem and Taboo*. In animism, every individual object has, like me, a will that one must either propitiate or appropriate. In polytheism, there is a finite number of universal forces, each autonomous, which must be propitiated or controlled. In monotheism, there is one God who creates the world or is imitated by it, and whose will does not change. You must either establish a relation with God that has previously been lacking, moving from ignorance to knowledge, or put a distorted relation right. Then the autonomous gods of polytheism become subsidiary and become myths. They are no longer the grounds of our own existence. In Milton's "Nativity Ode" the birth of Christ makes the gods dumb:

> The oracles are dumb,
> No voice or hideous hum
>   Runs through the arch'd roof in words deceiving.
> Apollo from his shrine
> Can no more divine,
>   With hollow shriek the steep of Delphos leaving.
> No nightly trance, or breathed spell,
> Inspires the pale-eyed priest from the prophetic cell.

Gods become accidents in substance. Dante, in the *Paradiso*, so describes the apprehension of divine love in Paradise:

> O grace abounding, wherein I presumed to fix my look on the eternal light so long that I consumed my sight thereon!
>   Within its depths I saw ingathered, bound by love in one volume, the scattered leaves of all the universe;
>   substance and accidents and their relations, as though together fused, after such fashion that what I tell of is one simple flame.

Myths present an analogous fusion of accident and substance.

The use of myths. A myth must have universal applicability, otherwise it becomes a private symbol, and the universal experience must be one to which the individual is related in a unique way—either intermittently, or happily or unhappily. There is no need for a myth on the law of gravity, since we all behave under its influence in the same way, but there is a need for a myth on the experience of falling in love, because its effects are unique. Elaborate polytheism enables one to learn certain laws of nature that you can change. But despite our knowledge, we can't control the weather, we can't control heredity or the distribution of natural gifts to people, and we can't arrange for suitable people to fall in love with each other. In our ordinary experience there is a great deal of accident. When everything falls under natural laws that are subject to control, there is no need for myth. Neither myth nor religion alter *natural* law. But if you can change the conduct of God by magic, as in polytheism, or you can alter your relation to God in yourself, as in monotheism, you have religion. Euripides' *Hippolytus* can be described without benefit of Aphrodite's anger. Its moral, in nonmythical form, is that sex is something you can't afford to make mistakes about.

In *A Midsummer Night's Dream*, mythological characters are used to describe certain universal experiences that we cannot control. You use Puck for a day when you get up and it's raining, you cut yourself shaving, you hurry over breakfast, you miss your train, your boss is sarcastic, your favorite lunch seat is taken, a bar drunk bores you with his life story, the potatoes are undercooked at dinner, and you quarrel with your wife. Or all vice versa. On a bad day, your feeling is, "Things are against me." It isn't just temperament, circumstances must also conspire. That's Puck. The role of pure mathematical chance is not as important as we suppose. We help make our luck. If we are angry with ourselves when we are shaving, we are more likely to be careless. One of my aunts, the younger one, Aunt Mildred, waited on her selfish older sister, who set up for an invalid, was pious, and distrusted pleasure. Just before they were to go on a holiday, her older sister sprained her ankle. Will is an element in such an accident. Even insurance companies take note of such things. The fairies show that these things are important, but the importance lies in how we take them. Good fortune taken too seriously leads to conceit, bad fortune taken too seriously leads to despair. There is no one-to-one relation between character and fortune: fairies are not seriously concerned with humanity. We must be grateful to good fortune and learn to accept bad fortune.

Our duties are to have (1) a right relation to God, (2) a right relation to our neighbor, and (3) a right relation to nature. You must treat your neighbor as a free agent—don't idolize or restrain him. You must help nature—don't idolize it either positively or negatively. One must accept responsibility for making nature what it should be. It is easier for me to say this, coming from Europe, an area where nature can be seen as friendly and domesticated, unlike the USA, where nature is seen as either to be exploited or to be fled to as a relief from civilization. I am continually shocked by the unhumanized nature in this country, no parks, no formal gardens. Nature never intended human beings to live in the USA—only in just a little bit of Europe and in New Zealand. Everywhere else it is either too hot or too cold. The climate in New York is savagely hot. I am happy in New York only from mid-November to March, when it's cold. One mustn't treat nature as morally responsible, or we become superstitious. But we must not regard nature as having no rights and existing solely for our convenience, because nature will revenge itself. You must not exploit nature—exploitation breeds soil erosion. But nature must be tamed.

A Midsummer Night's Dream is like a series of Chinese boxes. It was written for the occasion of someone's wedding. On the outside of the play are the bride and bridegroom and the Elizabethan audience, inside the play are the couples Theseus and Hippolyta, Titania and Oberon, the young lovers, and in the play within the play, Pyramus and Thisbe. We have festivities to mark the pauses between one form of life and another: christening, circumcision, wedding, etc. For Theseus and Hippolyta, as for any bride and bridegroom, the wedding represents the successful completion of a stage of life. Note Oberon's reference to past seductions by Theseus, and Titania's reference to the time Hippolyta was an Amazonian. The past is over, and a new life, with new failures and triumphs, begins.

The second theme of the play deals with the four lovers who have to go through what Theseus and Hippolyta have already experienced. They enter Dante's Wood of Error or Alice's world in *Through the Looking Glass*, which initiates an era of conquest of themselves or others. The quarrel between Oberon and Titania represents a disorder in nature that man is called upon to reconcile:

> The spring, the summer,
> The childing autumn, angry winter change
> Their wonted liveries; and the mazed world,
> By their increase, now knows not which is which.
> And this same progeny of evils comes
> From our debate, from our dissension;
> We are their parents and original.

(II.i.111–17)

Theseus and Hippolyta make it possible for Titania and Oberon to meet, and through human agency they are reconciled. The tragic figures, Pyramus and Thisbe, do not get out of the wood. The hunting passage (IV.i.106ff) shows that the old aggressive life has been modulated to sport, not done away with.

Theseus gives Hermia the choice of death or life in a nunnery if she doesn't obey her father, and he says of virginity,

> Thrice blest they that master so their blood
> To undergo such maiden pilgrimage;
> But earthlier happy is the rose distill'd
> Than that which, withering on the virgin thorn,
> Grows, lives, and dies in single blessedness.
>
>   (I.i.74–78)

Matters of love in *A Midsummer Night's Dream* are surrounded by imagery of the moon and moisture and Diana, all of which militate against the fire of love. The original row of Oberon and Titania is not sexual jealousy, but the punishment for it is involvement in sex. Lysander and Hermia talk like Romeo and Juliet:

> Ay, me! For aught that I could ever read,
> Could ever hear by tale or history,
> The course of true love never did run smooth.
>
>   (I.i.132–34)

The story of Pyramus and Thisbe suggests what might have happened to the people in *A Midsummer Night's Dream* as well as the frivolity of the whole business of falling in love. It says that tragic things can be due to taking the frivolous too seriously. Demetrius and Lysander, when they are not in love, are too weak to control their feelings. Hermia and Lysander at the beginning think themselves morally superior, and they are conceited over the return of their love, which is a gift of fortune only. Demetrius thinks himself stronger than Helena because he's loved while he himself is unloving—it's embarrassing but delightful. Helena's misfortune makes her spiteful, she betrays Hermia to make everyone as unhappy as she is. Lysander is equalized with Demetrius through being unfaithful and not having his love returned. Hermia is equalized with Helena because her love is not returned. Helena learns not to envy others, and she learns also that being loved isn't so grand. There is a complete reversal. Helena is punished for her spite because she doesn't believe the love offered to her is true, and Demetrius realizes what it is not to be loved. All four now, through similar experiences, have grown up, and it is now possible for them to marry.

Oberon accuses Puck, through his mistake with the potion, of confounding true and false love: "Of thy misprision must perforce ensue / Some true-love turn'd, and not a false turn'd true." Puck assumes that romantic love is accidental, however, not true, and justifies his error by an appeal to universal infidelity: "The fate o'errules, that, one man holding troth, / A million fail, confounding oath on oath" (III.ii.90–93). Puck defends himself again, shortly afterwards, by saying that he had, after all, anointed the eyes of a man wearing "Athenian garments," just as Oberon had instructed. The mix-up means that, standing on the outside, one man's like another. As Dr. Johnson remarked, "I believe marriages would in general be as happy, and often more so, if they were all made by the Lord Chancellor, upon a due consideration of characters and circumstances, without the parties having any choice in the matter."

The herb represents ambiguity. Everyone wishes to will other people to will what one wills. It can be done through (1) the exercise of power, as in rape, (2) the influence of one's essential worth: riches, etc., and (3) by sophisticated means, by making people do what you want while thinking *they* want it. Puck's use of the herb shows how dangerous the general fulfillment of such daydreams would be. In the myth of Tristan and Isolde, a love potion becomes the excuse for giving way to illicit love.

The general confusion of persons and the disharmony of nature represented in the Titania-Oberon theme can be tragic, as in *Timon of Athens*, where Timon comes to see the earth itself as a thief (IV.iii.438–45). In *A Midsummer Night's Dream* the quarrel of Oberon and Titania is comic, but it still makes the seas flood and causes a bad harvest (II.i.88–111). Oberon can be seen as Hippolyta's animus, Titania as Theseus' anima. All of their difficulties arise because of possessiveness over a trifle, a changeling boy. Titania in love with Bottom is contrasted with the confused loves of the four young Athenians, but with Titania and Bottom we have a real *mésalliance*. We like to believe that our love is due to the innate value of the object of it. We must beware: (1) for the object's sake—Bottom needs steak, not moonbeams, and (2) for the subject's sake—it is not good for Titania and no sympathy is shown for her. Bottom's relation with the fairies reveals that most unimaginative, prosaic people have aspects we wouldn't dream of. Bottom sees himself as a tough all-doer, and appears in much that way to his fellow workmen. To the audience he is seen as an ass, to Titania as a lovable, gentle, *un*tough ass. Bottom also appears as Pyramus—and maybe he is that too.

The play that Bottom and company put on raises the problem of the metaphysical distinction between existence and essence. Granted talent, etc., I could play another person so as to deceive everyone, but I can't *become* another existence. When we say it would be nice to be another person, we are imagining being ourselves with certain qualities of that other person added to our own essence. There is a difference between the theater and a bull fight. We identify ourselves with the essential suffering of actors in the theater, we can't identify with the existential suffering of the bull and gladiator. We identify with a hero taking a fall, or with a little man getting the princess and a million dollars. Or we take a play as a reversal of real life and say it is "only a play." Neither attitude is right. If we want to be heroes, we must want also to deserve disgrace, and if we don't want to be comic, we don't want to be blessed in all circumstances, but only to be rewarded as we deserve. We should be actors, not madmen who act what they are not, like the man, to take an extreme case, who believes he is Napoleon or a poached egg. Or like a pimply adolescent on the BMT looking at himself in the glass, who says, "How can I tell you how wonderful you are."

Take what you do as a game. There are two mistakes one can make in this, however: a failure to devote oneself, which is bad, and devoting oneself only when one thinks it's important, which is worse. The plays Theseus rejects include the battle of the Centaurs, because it is too personal, the riot of the Bacchanals, because he has seen it before, and the nine muses, because he feels it is too sharp for the occasion. The one he chooses is a "A tedious brief scene of young Pyramus / And his love Thisby; very tragical mirth" (V.i.56–57) and he chooses it for aesthetic reasons:

> Merry and tragical? tedious and brief?
> This is hot ice and wondrous strange snow.
> How shall we find the concord of this discord?
>
> (V.i.58–60)

The work Theseus wants must have all the elements, and it must form a pattern. It is in the nature of art that what we like is often dictated by private, not aesthetic reasons. And don't take art too seriously—the game depends on both skill and sincerity. Gifts and talents, as Theseus points out, can be overpraised:

> I will hear that play;
> For never anything can be amiss
> When simpleness and duty tender it.
>
> (V.i.81–83)

He says also,

> Our sport shall be to take what they mistake;
> And what poor duty cannot do, noble respect
> Takes it in might, not merit.
> Where I have come, great clerks have purposed
> To greet me with premeditated welcomes;
> Where I have seen them shiver and look pale,
> Make periods in the midst of sentences,
> Throttle their practis'd accent in their fears,
> And, in conclusion, dumbly have broke off,
> Not paying me a welcome. Trust me, sweet,
> Out of this silence yet I pick'd a welcome;
> And in the modesty of fearful duty
> I read as much as from the rattling tongue
> Of saucy and audacious eloquence.
> Love, therefore, and tongue-tied simplicity
> In least speak most, to my capacity.
>
> (V.i.90–105)

Theseus suggests the same imaginative generosity in his later exchange with Hippolyta:

> *Hip.* This is the silliest stuff that ever I heard.
> *The.* The best in this kind are but shadows; and the worst are no worse, if imagination amend them.
> *Hip.* It must be your imagination then, and not theirs.
> *The.* If we imagine no worse of them than they of themselves, they may pass for excellent men.
>
> (V.i.213–20)

But there are differences between good and bad art, and Theseus can be perfectly ruthless in his criticism, as he shows in his amused remarks during the performance of what he calls "this palpable, gross play" (V.i.374).

In her last novel, *Between the Acts,* Virginia Woolf describes a pageant presented outdoors by the people of a town at an English country house on the eve of World War II. Like Shakespeare, she interweaves the pageant and its actors and actresses, the reactions of the audience to them and to each other, and the fields, cows, and weather of the natural setting in which the pageant is played. And she also, writing on the eve of World War II, includes airplanes overhead. At the end of the performance, one person says, "Thank the actors, not the author. . . . Or ourselves, the audience." After the audience and players disperse and return to their individual lives, Woolf turns, in her final scene, to the husband and wife, Giles and Isa, at whose house the pageant was presented:

> The old people had gone up to bed. Giles crumpled the newspaper and turned out the light. Left alone together for the first time that day, they were silent. Alone, enmity was bared; also love. Before they slept, they must fight; after they fought, they would embrace. From that embrace another life might be born. But first they must fight, as the dog fights with the vixen, in the heart of darkness, in the fields of night.
>
> Isa let her sewing drop. The great hooded chairs had become enormous. And Giles too. And Isa too against the window. The window was all sky without colour. The house had lost its shelter. It was night before roads were made, or houses. It was night that dwellers in caves had watched from some high place among rocks.
>
> Then the curtain rose. They spoke.

The Taming of the Shrew,
King John,
and Richard II

[20 November 1946]

We shall not spend very much time on *Taming of the Shrew*. It is the only play of Shakespeare's that is a complete failure, though *Titus Andronicus* may be another. The plot of *Taming of the Shrew* belongs to farce, and Shakespeare is not a writer of farce. Ben Jonson might have made the play a success, but it is not up Shakespeare's alley.

What is the nature of farce? The characters represented must be universal—the clown, the shrew, etc.—and the actors must be individual geniuses. Farce is impromptu in nature. You cannot have a great writer of farce without the cooperation of the people who perform in it. In tragedy and comedy there is a conflict between freedom and necessity. In comedy the conflict is resolved and freedom wins. Farce is pure caprice and there is no necessity whatever. Think of Groucho, Chaplin, Grock. The characters in a farce do what an ordinary man does alone in a bathroom or dreams of doing. They do openly and sanely what only a madman would do in public.

In a world of real individuals, such behavior would inevitably cause great suffering, and it is therefore important in farce to exclude the slightest hint of individuality in the characters. The actor represents not a human being but a god who does not suffer, so thoroughly humble or so proud that loss of dignity means nothing to him. Custard pies thrown in his face or not being loved are equally matters of indifference to him. The farce character has no memory and no foreboding. He exists entirely in the moment. He is all body, but his body is heavy or light not in its own right but as an expression of his spirit, as if an angel should become incarnate. If he falls down or loses his hat, he only pretends to mind. He does not really care, because he wills what happens. It is fatal if a real individual is introduced.

It is also fatal if the plot is connected with a serious issue. Chaplin's film *The Great Dictator* fails for this reason. When you see Chaplin with a balloon, in a barbershop with Mussolini, you are prompted to think Mussolini is quite nice and could not cause suffering in any way. But it won't work. Mussolini also makes us think of Hitler, and the suffering that both caused is too near to us.

In our time the war of the sexes has become much too serious an issue to be treated in a farcical manner. This has been true in England ever since the passage of the Married Woman's Property Act in 1882. Up to that point there was no question, basically, that man was boss. I cannot tell you what a shock it was to come to this country. In England things are run for the benefit of men, and it is too bad if you are a girl. In America things are run for the benefit of women, and the men have an unfortunate time. I dropped into a bar after I had been here for a week and wondered about the unaccompanied women I saw. I still wonder. In England women are colorless. In America they are more interesting than the men. They are better educated, confident, and amusing to talk to. Perhaps, however, they suffer more in this country than they are willing to admit by holding such a dominating position, and one that is increasing. In fifty years most American men will be honorably employed as gigolos.

In the war of the sexes, a woman today should represent a masculine protest. Katherina should be physically and mentally grotesque. Petruchio should be uniquely timid and appear to be the least likely person to tame her. Shakespeare treats the problem of the war of the sexes in some depth in *Love's Labour's Lost* and *Much Ado About Nothing*, plays in which he is interested in the conflicts of the egos of men and women and in struggles between love and hate. Petruchio uses only physical means in his attempt to tame Katherina, and he remains throughout a cad. We do not see why she should grow to like or love him. She suffers as a character from her failure to protest successfully. Her final speech of submission to Petruchio (V.ii.136–79) is either unconvincing or pathetic.

There is too much writing in *Taming of the Shrew* for the limits of farce, and Shakespeare is not unaware of this. He intended the Induction to comment on and expand the play by suggesting that the action is a daydream of Christopher Sly. But the play's a bore. Either Petruchio should have been timid and then got drunk and tamed Katherina as she wished, or, after her beautiful speech, she should have picked up a stool and hit him over the head.

King John and *Richard II* form a transition from the *Henry VI* plays and *Richard III* to the great *Henry IV* plays, and to *Henry V*, where Shakespeare is getting bored. Set battle pieces remain in *King John*, as in the scenes at Angiers, but they are absent in *Richard II*. In *Henry V*, battle scenes subside into the Chorus. They are felt to be unrealistic. In *King John* and *Richard II* Shakespeare also drops the subplot, like Cade's rebellion in *Henry VI*, in favor of the depiction of a few characters. There is a consequent loss of the sense of the whole of society that we find in the earlier histories. Shakespeare brings the subplot back in *Henry IV.*

The interest in *King John* and *Richard II* centers on character and problems of language. Those mastered, Shakespeare goes on to the great studies of action of his middle period. The plays of the final period focus on feeling. There is less interest in history in *King John*. An earlier play, *The Troublesome Reign of King John*, explains historical motivation better— the falling off of the nobles, for example. Shakespeare may have written *The Troublesome Reign*, or he may just have used it. In Shakespeare, King John is not an altogether great Protestant king, as he is in *The Troublesome Reign*, nor is he altogether bad, as he shows in his repentance over Arthur. In *Richard II* there is no suspense: Richard goes downhill, Bolingbroke uphill. Bolinbroke is passive, accepts circumstances, relies on others, and has kinghood thrust upon him. York is a puzzling character: at first reluctantly disloyal to Richard, he is later anxious to execute his son for treason against Bolingbroke.

The plays are vehicles for two kinds of stars: the man of action and the lyric character. In *King John* the star is not the king, although King John has two interesting moments. The first of these moments is his suggestion to Hubert that Arthur would be better out of the way, in a speech in which the fine weather is counterpointed by his thoughts. "Give me thy hand," he says to Hubert,

> I had a thing to say,
> But I will fit it with some better time.
> By heaven, Hubert, I am almost asham'd
> To say what good respect I have of thee.
> 　*Hub.* I am much bounden to your Majesty.
> 　*K. John.* Good friend, thou hast no cause to say so yet,
> But thou shalt have; and creep time ne'er so slow,
> Yet it shall come for me to do thee good.
> I had a thing to say; but let it go.
> The sun is in the heaven, and the proud day,
> Attended with the pleasures of the world,
> Is all too wanton and too full of gauds
> To give me audience. If the midnight bell
> Did with his iron tongue and brazen mouth

Sound on into the drowsy ear of night;
If this same were a churchyard where we stand,
And thou possessed with a thousand wrongs;
Or if that surly spirit, melancholy,
Had bak'd thy blood and made it heavy, thick,
Which else runs tickling up and down the veins,
Making that idiot, laughter, keep men's eyes
And strain their cheeks to idle merriment,
A passion hateful to my purposes;
Or if that thou couldst see me without eyes,
Hear me without thine ears, and make reply
Without a tongue, using conceit alone,
Without eyes, ears, and harmful sound of words:
Then, in despite of brooded watchful day,
I would into thy bosom pour my thoughts.
But, ah, I will not! Yet I love thee well,
And, by my troth, I think thou lov'st me well.

"So well that what you bid me undertake," Hubert answers,

Though that my death were adjunct to my act,
By heaven, I would do it!
   K. John.   Do not I know thou would'st?
Good Hubert, Hubert, Hubert, throw thine eye
On yon young boy. I'll tell thee what, my friend,
He is a very serpent in my way;
And wheresoe'er this foot of mine doth tread,
He lies before me. Dost thou understand me?
Thou art his keeper.
   Hub.   And I'll keep him so
That he shall not offend your Majesty.
   K. John.   Death.
   Hub. My lord?
   K. John.   A grave.
   Hub.   He shall not live.
   K. John.   Enough.
I could be merry now.

                       (III.iii.25–67)

This speech shows an enormous advance in Shakespeare's technical skill. He gets away from conventional rhetoric, and the single word speeches—"death," "a grave," "enough"—are very skillful.

King John's other interesting moment occurs when he is dying and is semidelirious. The speech he makes has been criticized by some for the elaboration of its rhetoric, but I think the fantasticalness of the rhetoric is dramatically appropriate:

> Ay, marry, now my soul hath elbow room.
> It would not out at windows nor at doors.
> There is so hot a summer in my bosom
> That all my bowels crumble up to dust.
> I am a scribbled form drawn with a pen
> Upon a parchment, and against this fire
> Do I shrink up.
> > *Hen.*   How fares your Majesty?
> > *K. John.* Poison'd, ill fare! dead, forsook, cast off!
> And none of you will bid the winter come
> To thrust his icy fingers in my maw,
> Nor let my kingdom's rivers take their course
> Through my burn'd bosom, nor entreat the North
> To make his bleak winds kiss my parched lips
> And comfort me with cold.
>
> > (V.vii.28–41)

I don't care for the Hubert-Arthur scene (IV.i). Little kids on stage are impossible. They should be drowned. The ultimate origin of this scene is the episode of Abraham and Isaac in miracle plays—Isaac was the Shirley Temple of the day. The Chester play of "The Sacrifice of Isaac" has better rhetoric for this kind of pathos, and is tempered by the formal quality of its stanzas and its focus upon the moment of sacrifice.

The real interest in *King John* and *Richard II* lies in Shakespeare's development as a writer. Language is a means of making human feeling, and patterns of human feeling, conscious. Language and people develop side by side and, to a degree, independently. A poet is first and foremost in love with language. The love of language is either itself a poetic gift or a symptom of it. In a young writer, technical skill outruns mastery of feeling. This is the opposite of the average unliterary man or woman who grows up to develop feelings that are more mature than his or her capacity for expression. Language, like any other creature, wants to be autonomous, to go its own way. Left to itself, it wants beautiful sounds and intricate rhetorical patterns. It is also conservative. It does not want to change a pattern that works well, and it is threatened by emotions and ideas that are too strong, too disorderly, or too new for tidy expression. Language is the enemy of action. If language had its way, action would stop, and man would exist in a lyrical trance, as in the poems of Mallarmé, and in such a lyric as Peele's,

> Hot sunne, coole fire, temperd with sweet aire,
> Black shade, fair nurse, shadow my white haire,
> Shine sun, burne fire, breath aire, and ease mee,
> Black shade, fair nurse, shroud me and please me,
> Shadow (my sweet nurse) keep me from burning,
> Make not my glad cause, cause of mourning.
>> Let not my beauties fire,
>> Enflame my unstaied desire,
>> Nor pierce any bright eye,
>> That wandreth lightly.

The writer who surrenders to language—including even W. B. Yeats—is a minor poet. The relation between poet and medium is like *The Taming of Shrew*, where the writer is the husband and language the wife. In the period of courtship, the writer should fetch and carry and stand waiting in the rain. Once accepted, however, he must be the boss. If a writer doesn't love language, he isn't even a minor poet. In a young poet, look for artifice and technical skill. Everyone must begin as a minor poet. Beginning poets confine themselves to poetical feelings, either those of others or those that are their own particular discoveries. Housman is an instance of the latter. A major poet is always willing to risk failure, to look for a new rhetoric. Shakespeare, in 1595, might have startled us very much, because in 1595 he was not interested in plays, but in poems and sonnets. Highbrows then would have been much more interested in his advances in lyric poetry. It is great luck that Shakespeare had no money and was forced into drama. From observation and experience, one can say that circumstances in the theater create artistic problems that a dramatist must learn to meet. Shakespeare had to study action, which was a bore. So he had to find the rhetoric to make action interesting to him, and he thereby developed a rhetoric that enabled men of action such as Faulconbridge to transcend action and become interesting. Or, taking a particular lyric rhetoric as a given, he had to find a character to suit it, as he did with Richard II.

The really interesting character in *King John* is Faulconbridge, who dominates the play out of proportion to his historical importance. A bastard can be represented in two ways. First, as an example of nature versus society, an honest and graceful child as opposed to the hypocritical and weak offspring of a loveless marriage. The other way is to represent him as a criminal outlaw, as opposed to a legitimate child—Edmund versus Edgar in *King Lear*, for example. Faulconbridge is dubious about all human nature—including his own—but he remains loyal.

Shakespeare's real interest is in the bastard's diction. Consider his long speech on "commodity":

> that same purpose-changer, that sly devil,
> That broker that still breaks the pate of faith,
> That daily break-vow, he that wins of all,
> Of kings, of beggars, old men, young men, maids,
> Who, having no external thing to lose
> But the word "maid," cheats the poor maid of that—
> That smooth-fac'd gentleman, tickling Commodity,
> Commodity, the bias of the world—
> The world, who of itself is peised well,
> Made to run even upon even ground
> Till this advantage, this vile drawing bias,
> This sway of motion, this Commodity,
> Makes it take head from all indifferency,
> From all direction, purpose, course, intent—
> And this same bias, this Commodity,
> This bawd, this broker, this all-changing word,
> Clapp'd on the outward eye of fickle France,
> Hath drawn him from his own determin'd aid,
> From a resolv'd and honourable war,
> To a most base and vile-concluded peace.
> And why rail I on this Commodity?
> But for because he hath not woo'd me yet:
> Not that I have the power to clutch my hand
> When his fair angels would salute my palm,
> But for my hand, as unattempted yet,
> Like a poor beggar, raileth on the rich.
> Well, whiles I am a beggar, I will rail
> And say there is no sin but to be rich;
> And being rich, my virtue then shall be
> To say there is no vice but beggary.

(II.i.567–96)

For a moment this looks like a traditional villain's speech, but Faulconbridge in fact acts as a loyal man. This type of speech is serviceable for a cynic turning villain, like Iago, for example, or for an honest man in despair, like Timon. It looks back also to Berowne's speech on marriage in *Love's Labour's Lost*:

> What, I? I love? I sue? I seek a wife?
> A woman, that is like a German clock,
> Still a-repairing, ever out of frame,
> And never going aright, being a watch,
> But being watch'd that it may still go right.
>
> (III.i.191–95)

And it looks forward to Hotspur's speech on Glendower in *Henry IV*:

> O, he is as tedious
> As a tired horse, a railing wife;
> Worse than a smoky house. I had rather live
> With cheese and garlic in a windmill far
> Than feed on cates and have him talk to me
> In any summer house in Christendom.
>
> (*1 Henry IV*, III.i.159–64)

All these speeches use unliterary language as an offset to the conventional language affected by most men of action. Faulconbridge uses such language in his fleering of Lewis when Lewis invades—"a beardless boy, / A cock'red silken wanton" (V.i.69–70). And he expresses himself with the same kind of diction when he accuses Hubert of killing Arthur:

> If thou didst but consent
> To this most cruel act, do but despair;
> And if thou want'st a cord, the smallest thread
> That ever spider twisted from her womb
> Will serve to strangle thee; a rush will be a beam
> To hang thee on. Or wouldst thou drown thyself,
> Put but a little water in a spoon,
> And it shall be as all the ocean,
> Enough to stifle such a villain up.
>
> (IV.iii.125–33)

Faulconbridge is apparently unconscious of literary style, but he actually displays an enormous literary gift. Shakespeare is interested in how men of action *should* talk, *not* in conventional braggadocio. Out of this interest was to come the great development of his verse in the future.

Constance in *King John* and Richard II in *Richard II* represent a combination of dramatic and lyrical writing. Shakespeare was learning to find a character suitable to a lyric style. Mark Van Doren notes that Constance is the last of Shakespeare's wailing women. She is not used as chorus, but is presented instead as a grieving individual who plays incessantly on words and has a good deal of acting in her nature. She derisively mocks Elinor by playing fleeringly on the word, "grandam":

> *Eli.*   Come to thy grandam, child.
> *Const.* Do, child! go to it grandam, child!
> Give grandam kingdom, and it grandam will
> Give it a plum, a cherry, and a fig.
> There's a good grandam!
>
> (II.i.159–63)

And she plays on the word "day," when France declares that people shall never see the day of the marriage of Lewis and Blanch but as "a holiday": "A wicked day, and not a holy day!" (III.i.83). The style of Constance's speeches is like that of Sonnet 135—"Whoever hath her wish, thou hast thy Will"—which was written at about the same time. When Cardinal Pandulf tells Constance, "you utter madness and not sorrow," she goes off into a dialectic of grief to prove that she cannot be mad:

> Thou art not holy to belie me so.
> I am not mad. This hair I tear is mine;
> My name is Constance; I was Geffrey's wife;
> Young Arthur is my son, and he is lost.
> I am not mad. I would to heaven I were!
> For then 'tis like I should forget myself.
> O, if I could, what grief should I forget!
> Preach some philosophy to make me mad,
> And thou shalt be canoniz'd, Cardinal;
> For, being not mad, but sensible of grief,
> My reasonable part produces reason
> How I may be deliver'd of these woes
> And teaches me to kill or hang myself.
> If I were mad, I should forget my son,
> Or madly think a babe of clouts were he.
> I am not mad. Too well, too well I feel
> The different plague of each calamity.
>
> (III.iv.43–60)

Constance is a minor character. In *Richard II* the lyric type of character takes center stage, and Richard's language overflows onto other characters as well. When Bushy asks the Queen to lay aside her heaviness and "entertain a cheerful disposition," she answers:

> To please the King, I did; to please myself,
> I cannot do it. . . .
> I cannot but be sad—so heavy sad
> As, though in thinking on no thought I think,
> Makes me with heavy nothing faint and shrink.
>> *Bushy.* 'Tis nothing but conceit, my gracious lady.
>> *Queen.* 'Tis nothing less. Conceit is still deriv'd
> From some forefather grief. Mine is not so,
> For nothing hath begot my something grief,
> Or something hath the nothing that I grieve.
> 'Tis in reversion that I do possess;
> But what it is that is not yet known what,
> I cannot name. 'Tis nameless woe, I wot.
>
> (II.ii.4–6, 30–40)

Even John of Gaunt can go in for this kind of speech, as when he says goodbye to his exiled son, Bolingbroke, and recommends that he adopt the behavior of Richard, that of an actor (I.iii. 279–93).

Richard is an early version of Hamlet. He can also be compared to other unsuitable kings, to Henry VI, a pious man who would be a monk and is forced to be king in time of stress, and to Richard III, a man of action who insists upon becoming king and, in spite of justice, plans ahead to get rid of people who stand in his way—which is what Bolingbroke does *not* do. Richard II is interested in the idea of kingship rather than in ruling. Like a writer of minor poetry—he is good at that—he is interested more in the idea than in the act. He is good at presiding over a tournament, not at taking an action that means something, and his passion for ritual even embraces self-humiliation. He says, for example, when he looks in the looking glass in the scene in which he gives up the crown,

> O flattering glass,
> Like to my followers in prosperity,
> Thou dost beguile me! Was this face the face
> That every day under his household roof
> Did keep ten thousand men? Was this the face

That like the sun did make beholders wink?
Was this the face that fac'd so many follies
And was at last outfac'd by Bolingbroke?
A brittle glory shineth in this face.
As brittle as the glory is the face,

                              [*Dashes the glass to the floor*]
For there it is, crack'd in a hundred shivers.
Mark, silent king, the moral of this sport—
How soon my sorrow hath destroy'd my face.

                                        (IV.i. 279–91)

Richard has few feelings, but he enjoys those situations that should produce feelings. When Bolingbroke says, after Richard has broken the mirror, "The shadow of your sorrow hath destroy'd / The shadow of your face," Richard seizes upon the remark in order to elaborate upon it as a literary conceit:

                          Say that again.
The shadow of my sorrow? Ha! let's see!
'Tis very true: my grief lies all within;
And these external manners of laments
Are merely shadows to the unseen grief
That swells with silence in the tortured soul.

                                        (IV.i.293–98)

In his farewell to the Queen, Richard doesn't think of his wife or even of himself, but of how his story will sound in literature:

Think I am dead, and that even here thou takest,
As from my deathbed, thy last living leave.
In winter's tedious nights sit by the fire
With good old folks, and let them tell thee tales
Of woful ages long ago betid;
And ere thou bid good-night, to quite their griefs
Tell thou the lamentable tale of me,
And send the hearers weeping to their beds.
For why, the senseless brands will sympathize
The heavy accent of thy moving tongue
And in compassion weep the fire out;
And some will mourn in ashes, some coal-black,
For the deposing of a rightful king.

                                        (V.i.38–50)

In his last soliloquy, Richard is really happy. He compares the prison he is in to the world and finds the comparison interesting:

> I have been studying how I may compare
> This prison where I live unto the world;
> And, for because the world is populous,
> And here is not a creature but myself,
> I cannot do it. Yet I'll hammer it out.

(V.v.1–5)

Richard has only literary gifts, and he is stupid. Hamlet has intellectual ones, and can see that what happens to him is universal. Richard sees only himself. Both characters are egotistic, though Hamlet does more harm. Behind both is the real grief of the reflective melancholic person over the problem of whether to be or not to be. For Hamlet, it is an open possibility to choose one or the other. The only escape for Richard is into language. Shakespeare is able to work the lyrical style out of his system through the depiction of Richard II and proceed to the men of action in the plays of his middle period. In his last period he develops lyrical plays that avoid men of action.

The Merchant of Venice

[27 November 1946]

With memories of the horrors of the last ten years and forebodings about anti-Semitism, it is difficult to look objectively at a play in which the villain is a Jew. But we must, in order to understand it. In England in Shakespeare's day, English writers didn't know Jews, who had been expelled by Edward I in 1290 and not readmitted until the time of Cromwell. A few years before the play was written, there had been a law case in which Dr. Roderigo Lopez, a Portuguese Jew who was physician to the Queen, was tried and executed for treason—it was a frame-up. Whatever prejudice against the Jews existed among Elizabethans, it was not racial. Lorenzo marries Shylock's daughter—there is no thought of racial discrimination. The only racial remark in the play is made by Shylock, and the Christians refute it. Religious differences in the play are treated frivolously: the question is not one of belief, but of conformity. The important thing about Shylock is not that he is a Jew or a heretic, but that he is an outsider.

The Merchant of Venice is about a certain kind of society, a society that is related to and can't do without someone whom it can't accept. The Gentile Venetian society is a newborn bourgeois capitalist society, no longer feudal, not yet industrial. Feudal society is based on status by birth. In such a society, marriage must be arranged between the right people. But in *The Merchant of Venice* the issue is breeding, not inheritance. Jessica makes clear that though she is "a daughter" to Shylock's "blood, / I am not to his manners." (II.iii.18–19), and Lorenzo shows his lack of prejudice in perceiving this and marrying her. Portia, too, has no racial prejudice. She explains to the Moor that were she not bound by the test of the caskets,

> Yourself, renowned Prince, then stood as fair
> As any comer I have look'd on yet
> For my affection.

(II.i.19–21)

There is also no sense of a stratified class structure in the play: Gratiano, who marries Nerissa, Portia's maid, is treated as an equal by Bassanio and Antonio, and Nerissa is treated in the same way by Portia. There is a free choice in personal relationships. Even the choice of caskets is not an arrangement to provide a particular person for Portia, but a device to insure her marrying a person with a particular kind of character, someone capable of making her happy. The first four suitors announce that even if they win Portia by choosing the right casket, they won't insist that she marry them unless she is willing. This is not feudal. Feudal society has fixed obligations. In this play personal obligations are unlimited, as Antonio's conduct to Bassanio shows. Antonio tells Bassanio, when he is asked for help,

> You know me well, and herein spend but time
> To wind about my love with circumstance;
> And out of doubt you do me now more wrong
> In making question of my uttermost
> Than if you had made waste of all I have.
> Then do but say to me what I should do
> That in your knowledge may by me be done,
> And I am prest unto it.

(I.i.153–60)

Bassanio displays the same limitless generosity when he rushes to Antonio without first lying with Portia, whom he has just won and married. Today there are no personal obligations in a laissez-faire society. In *The Merchant of Venice* you are free to form the personal relationships you choose, but your obligations are then enormous. There are few plays of Shakespeare in which the word "love" is used more frequently, and the understanding of love is not unlike E. M. Forster's in his essay "I Believe," in which he says, "if I had to choose between betraying my country and betraying my friend, I hope I should have the guts to betray my country."

There is an aesthetic awareness in all the characters in this play. Lorenzo shows it when he describes the moonlight to Jessica:

> How sweet the moonlight sleeps upon this bank!
> Here will we sit and let the sounds of music
> Creep in our ears. Soft stillness and the night
> Become the touches of sweet harmony.
> Sit, Jessica. Look how the floor of heaven
> Is thick inlaid with patens of bright gold.

(V.i.54–59)

Lorenzo also says that

> The man that hath no music in himself,
> Nor is not mov'd with concord of sweet sounds,

Is fit for treason, stratagems, and spoils;
The motions of his spirit are dull as night,
And his affections dark as Erebus.
Let no such man be trusted.

(V.i.83–88)

Lorenzo shows the same sensibility in all his other speeches, and an aesthetic consciousness is evident as well in Bassanio's descriptions of Portia and her wealth:

Nor is the wide world ignorant of her worth;
For the four winds blow in from every coast
Renowned suitors, and her sunny locks
Hang on her temples like a golden fleece,
Which makes her seat of Belmont Colchos' strond,
And many Jasons come in quest of her.

(I.i.167–72)

Portia's wish that music accompany Bassanio's choice of the casket shows and creates a similar aesthetic attentiveness:

Let music sound while he doth make his choice;
Then, if he lose, he makes a swanlike end,
Fading in music. That the comparison
May stand more proper, my eye shall be the stream
And wat'ry deathbed for him. He may win;
And what is music then? Then music is
Even as the flourish when true subjects bow
To a new-crowned monarch. Such it is
As are those dulcet sounds in break of day
That creep into the dreaming bridegroom's ear
And summon him to marriage.

(III.ii.43–53)

Portia shows the same disposition in criticizing the various suitors she has not liked: the Neapolitan who boasts of his horse—gents don't boast—and the Count Palatine, who is gloomy, full of "unmannerly sadness" (I.ii.54)—one must be gay. Though gaiety must have a limit. At a lunch party in the south of France, during the Spanish Civil War, a voice pipes up, "Spain must be madly ungay this summer." The story goes that in the last war a Guards officer who was home on leave was asked what war was like, and answered, "So annoying—the noise, and the *people.*" Again, in the last war, a friend of mine who went over the top and didn't shoot, took a rug and a book, was wounded, and lay comfortably and read until they came for him. Portia criticizes Monsieur Le Bon because "He is every man in no man" (I.ii.64–65)—one must be an individual and have a center, whether it is shown or not. She finds fault with Falconbridge because, though he tries, he's not chic, speaks no languages, and is "oddly . . . suited" (I.ii.79)—one mustn't be provincial. The Scottish lord, who "borrowed a box in the ear of the Englishman, and swore he would pay him again when he was able" (I.ii.84–86), is rejected for lacking esprit, being too dull. The Duke of Saxony's nephew, a drunken boor, is rejected because one must have good manners.

One must also be quite carefree and unpossessive. When Jessica joins this society, the first thing that upsets Shylock is that she spends four score ducats in one evening and buys a monkey for a ring. Be free with money, be imprudent, always gamble, and as in Gratiano's marriage, act on impulse. Bet on the first boy, always wagering money on chance. The Venetians are fashionably frivolous, and it is true that, like all frivolous people, they're also a little sad. In the opening lines of the play, Antonio says,

> In sooth, I know not why I am so sad.
> It wearies me; you say it wearies you;
>
> (I.i.1–2)

and he tells Gratiano,

> I hold the world but as the world, Gratiano—
> A stage, where every man must play a part,
> And mine a sad one.
>
> (I.i.77–79)

Portia echoes him at the start of the second scene when she says, "By my troth, Nerissa, my little body is aweary of this great world" (I.ii.1–2). She treats the feeling more lightly than it in fact is in order not to bore people. Gratiano, a frivolous chatterbox, a Gentile opposite of Shylock, is a type of his society, and he's the only one who doesn't wish to pardon Shylock. Speaking at one point of Lorenzo's lateness, Gratiano says that chasing is more fun than catching: "All things that are / Are with more spirit chased than enjoy'd" (II.vi.12–13).

Unlike a feudal society, which is based on land, the basis of this society is money coming from speculative trade, not from production, as in an industrial society. It is possible to become suddenly rich or suddenly poor, and money has commodity as well as exchange value. As a money-lender, Shylock is guilty of usury. Antonio, when he asks for the loan from Shylock, says:

> If thou wilt lend this money, lend it not
> As to thy friends—for when did friendship take
> A breed for barren metal of his friend?
> But lend it rather to thine enemy,
> Who if he break, thou mayst with better face
> Exact the penalty.
>
> (I.iii.133–38)

The condemnation of the breeding of money by money goes back to Aristotle, and in Canto XI of the *Inferno*, Virgil castigates the money-lenders and associates them with sodomists:

> Violence may be done against the Deity, in the heart denying and blaspheming Him; and disdaining Nature and her bounty:
> and hence the smallest round seals with its mark both Sodom and Cahors, and all who speak with disparagement of God in their hearts.

Cahors was a center of non-Jewish usury and of misbelievers. Virgil also instructs Dante that Genesis "behoves man to gain his bread and prosper" and that "because the usurer takes another way, he contemns Nature in herself and in her follower, placing elsewhere his hope."

At the time *The Merchant of Venice* was written, however, these traditional attitudes against usury were breaking down. In an economy for direct consumption or barter borrowing, the borrowing of money is an exception, and money is not a commodity that one sells for a profit—which is how we would feel if we were asked for interest on the loan of a dollar from a friend. In a society where money becomes generally needed, a conflict arises between the abhorrence of usury and the necessity for it. The hypocrisy is that though moneylending will be condemned and the lender despised, men will still go to the moneylender. Shylock's argues that Laban's method of producing parti-colored sheep, though not "directly int'rest," "was a way to thrive, and he was blest; / And thrift is blessing, if men steal it not" (I.iii.78, 90–91). Antonio objects, saying,

> This was a venture, sir, that Jacob serv'd for;
> A thing not in his power to bring to pass,

> But sway'd and fashion'd by the hand of heaven.
> Was this inserted to make interest good?
> Or is your gold and silver ewes and rams?
>
> (I.iii.92–96)

Nonetheless, Shylock's commentary on Laban's sheep was actually used by theologians trying to give interest canonical legality. Moneylending serves the need for ready cash. Because it is regarded as immoral, however, it is handed over to outsiders. The madame runs the brothel, but the senator still visits it. It's a bad situation for outsiders, who will go to a job from which they are not excluded, to the most lucrative job, but one that is socially condemned: moneylending.

Wealth in Venetian society depends upon speculation and exploitation. Shylock points this out when he justifies his possession of the pound of flesh by arguing from the Gentiles' unwillingness to free their slaves:

> What judgment shall I dread, doing no wrong?
> You have among you many a purchas'd slave,
> Which, like your asses and your dogs and mules,
> You use in abject and in slavish parts,
> Because you bought them. Shall I say to you,
> "Let them be free, marry them to your heirs!
> Why sweat they under burthens? Let their beds
> Be made as soft as yours, and let their palates
> Be season'd with such viands"? You will answer,
> "The slaves are ours." So do I answer you.
> The pound of flesh which I demand of him
> Is dearly bought, 'tis mine, and I will have it.
>
> (IV.i.89–100)

Within the charmed social circle of Venice and Belmont, all is love, affection, grace, wit, beauty, riches. The improper suitors are seen as outsiders. Shylock sums them up as an outsider par excellence. He is an outsider partly by religion, which is not too important, more a formal, social matter, and partly by profession, which partially reflects the extravagance of society itself. But he is an outsider chiefly by character, for which society is partly responsible, though social conditions are never quite enough to determine character. In contrast to the others, he's gloomy, priggish, and hates music. He enjoins Jessica not to listen to the masques:

What, are there masques? Hear you me, Jessica.
Lock up my doors; and when you hear the drum
And the vile squeaking of the wry-neck'd fife,
Clamber not you up to the casements then,
Nor thrust your head into the public street
To gaze on Christian fools with varnish'd faces;
But stop my house's ears—I mean my casements.
Let not the sound of shallow fopp'ry enter
My sober house.

(II.v.28–36)

Shylock is too serious. He's not really more acquisitive than the other Venetians—they, too, clearly seek profit—but he is more possessive, he keeps his possessions to himself, and he does not value personal relationships. He is more concerned about his ducats and diamonds than his daughter, and he cannot imagine making a sacrifice to personal relations.

Why, there, there, there, there! A diamond gone cost me two thousands ducats in Frankford! The curse never fell upon our nation till now; I never felt it till now. Two thousand ducats in that, and other precious, precious jewels. I would my daughter were dead at my foot, and the jewels in her ear! Would she were hears'd at my foot, and the ducats in her coffin! No news of them? Why, so—and I know not what's spent in the search. Why, thou loss upon loss! the thief gone with so much, and so much to find the thief; and no satisfaction, no revenge! nor no ill luck stirring but what lights o' my shoulders; no sighs but o' my breathing; no tears but o' my shedding.

(III.i.87–101)

Why does Shylock finally alienate our sympathy, even though we can understand his wanting revenge? Part of the reason is that his revenge is in excess of the injury—a characteristic of revenge plays. But he mainly alienates our sympathy because he tries to play it safe and use the law, which is universal, to exact a particular, personal revenge. A private quest for revenge may have started a feud, but would be forgivable. What is not forgivable is that he tried to get revenge safely. Shylock's unlimited hatred is the negative image of the infinite love of Venetian and Belmont society, which proposes that one should behave with a love that is infinitely imprudent. "Who chooseth me must give and hazard all he hath," the motto of the lead casket, is also the motto of the play.

Legality is a problem in the play, as in *Measure for Measure*. A law is either a law *of* or a law *for*. The law of gravitation is a law *of*, a description of a pattern of regular behavior observed by disinterested observers. There must be no exception and no caprice. Conformity is necessary for the law to exist, for if an exception is found, the law has to be rewritten in such a way that the exception becomes part of the pattern, for it is a presupposition of science that events in nature conform to law—in other words, a physical event is always related to some law, even if it be one of which scientists are at present ignorant. Laws *for*, like human legislation, are patterns of behavior imposed on behavior that was previously lacking in pattern. In order for the laws to come into existence, there must be at least some people who don't conform to them—there is no American law, for example, dealing with cannibalism. Unlike laws *of*, which must completely explain how events occur, laws *for* are only concerned with commanding or prohibiting the class of actions to which they refer, and a man is only related to the law when it is a question of doing or not doing one act of such a class. When his actions are not covered by law, when alone in a room reading a book, for example, he is related to no law at all. *The Merchant of Venice* shows that morals are not to be thought of as laws *of*, that laws *for* can't account for all actions, and that ethics can't be based on right, but must be based on duty.

How do we judge the means and ends of action? Utilitarian theory doesn't consider the choice of means, but argues that utility and right are identical. But why is a key "right" in opening a door and a bent wire "wrong"? Kant and Fichte ask, what is your ethical duty if you know where A is, and B, who intends to murder A, asks you where A is? If your assumption is that you must tell the truth, then what? Kant argues that you must tell. Or, if your assumption is that human life is sacred, then you don't tell. Duty is not what is conformable to right, but to what I owe. There is no refuge in generality, the choice is specific. There are no alternatives, the choice must be *mine*. And ought implies can. Antonio's sense of infinite obligation links utility and duty, as utility and right cannot be linked. Right states that a man should help friends, but doesn't explain why. Shylock thinks of duty upside down, and sees a one-to-one relation between action and intention. He tries to get Antonio. His mistake is that he tries to invoke the law and gets caught out. Laws are not adapted to particular ends, but deal with generalities. It's amazing that the Doge and others didn't realize that the bond involved bloodshed, but we have to accept that.

The question the play raises is, how shall I behave? I might assume that if I follow the rules, I'm okay, but Portia points out that obediences differ:

> Therefore, Jew,
> Though justice be thy plea, consider this—
> That, in the course of justice, none of us
> Should see salvation. We do pray for mercy,
> And that same prayer doth teach us all to render
> The deeds of mercy. I have spoke thus much
> To mitigate the justice of thy plea.
>
> (IV.i.197–203)

Portia, on the other hand, does trust to a legal generalization to free a man from an evil character:

> But in the cutting it if thou dost shed
> One drop of Christian blood, thy lands and goods
> Are, by the laws of Venice, confiscate
> Unto the state of Venice.
>
> (IV.i.309–12)

A shyster lawyer uses the same kind of argument. A "Profile" of the nineteenth-century New York criminal law firm, Howe and Hummel, in the *New Yorker*, describes how William F. Howe got one his clients off on a charge of arson. Howe arranged for a plea bargain on the charge of attempted arson, and when his client, Owen Reilly,

came up for sentence, Howe arose and pointed out that the law provided no penalty for attempted arson. The court begged enlightenment. The sentence for attempted arson, Howe explained, like the sentence for any crime attempted but not actually committed, was half the maximum imposed by law for the actual commission of the crime. The penalty for arson was life imprisonment. Hence, if the court were to determine a sentence for Reilly, it would have to determine what half a life came to. "Scripture tells us that we knoweth not the day nor the hour of our departure," Howe said. "Can this court sentence this prisoner at the bar to half of his natural life? Will it then sentence him to half a minute or to half the days of Methuselah?" The court agreed that the problem was beyond its earthbound wisdom.

By a similar kind of argument, Howe argued in 1888 that a convicted cop-killer, Handsome Harry Carlton, could not be executed. The Electrical Death Penalty law of that year had suspended hanging as of 4 June 1888 and installed electrocution as of 1 January 1889. Howe was able to argue that between June 4th and January 1st, murder was legal, since through the careless syntax of the bill, the law appeared to read that during that period there was no legal penalty for murder. And without a penalty, Howe said, there could be no crime. A higher court disposed of the problem, and Handsome Harry didn't get off, but for a while in New York murder seemed technically legal. Ergo, law is fundamentally frivolous, whereas a moral sense is serious. Hard cases make bad law. "Sell all thou hast and give to the poor" is a particular command, not a law.

Shylock is the outsider because he is the only serious person in the play. He may be serious about the wrong things, the acquisition of property, since property is itself a frivolous *thing*. In contrast, however, we have a society that is frivolous because certain gifts are necessary to belong to it—beauty, grace, wit, riches. Nothing that doesn't apply to everyone can be serious, and a frivolous society makes life a game. But life is not a game because one cannot say: "I will live if I turn out to be good at living." No, gifted or not, I must live. Those who cannot play a game can always be spectators, but no one can be a spectator of life; he must either live himself or hang himself. The Greeks, being aesthetes, regarded life as a game, i.e., as a test of inborn *areté*. The compensation for the chorus who could not play was to enjoy seeing the star players come one by one to a sticky end.

An aesthetically conceived society depends on the exploitation of the ungifted. A society constructed to be like a beautiful poem—as was imagined by some aesthetically-minded Greek political theorists—would be a nightmare of horror, for given the historical reality of actual men, such a society could only come into being through selective breeding, extermination of the physically and mentally unfit, absolute obedience to its Director, and a large slave class kept out of sight in cellars. The people in *The Merchant of Venice* are saved by their excess of love, which destroys the pattern of exclusiveness generated by self-love.

Whenever a society is exclusive, it needs something excluded and unaesthetic to define it, like Shylock. The only serious possession of men is not their gifts but what they all possess equally, independent of fortune, namely their will, in other words, their love, and the only serious matter is what they love—themselves, or God and their neighbor. The people in *The Merchant of Venice* are generous, and they behave well out of a sense of social superiority. Outside of them is Shylock, but inside is melancholy and a lack of serious responsibilities—which they'd have as farmers or producers, but not as speculators. They are haunted by an anxiety that it is not good sense for them to show.

The caskets are the key to the play. All the suitors are in the right social "set." Two of them do what the "set" does. The first chooses the gold casket, "to gain what many men desire," and inside is a death's head. Death is what the aesthete is most afraid of. The second suitor, seeking to "get as much as he deserves," chooses the silver casket, and inside is a portrait of a grinning idiot, the specter behind natural gifts. The third casket, which Bassanio must choose, is made of lead—common, universal, and unaesthetic—and it must be chosen with complete passion, for Bassanio must give and hazard all he has.

I am glad that Shakespeare made Shylock a Jew. What is the source of anti-Semitism? The Jew represents seriousness to the Gentile, which is resented, because we wish to be frivolous and do not want to be reminded that something serious exists. By their existence—and this is as it should be—Jews remind us of this seriousness, which is why we desire their annihilation.

Sonnets

[4 December 1946]

Shakespeare's *Sonnets* were published in 1609, but the bulk of them were written between 1593 and 1596, so that's why we're reading them now. How far are they personal? How far are they technical exercises? There has been more nonsense written about Shakespeare's *Sonnets* than about any other piece of literature extant. Wordsworth said, "With this key / Shakspeare unlocked his heart," and Browning said, "'*With this same key / Shakespeare unlocked his heart,*' once more! / Did Shakespeare? If so, the less Shakespeare he!" In one sense the artist is always unlocking his heart, in another he is always dramatic. But actually there must be a difference between Shakespeare's dramatic works and poems about experiences that were happening to him. The question we must ask about lyric verse is: how far is it personal, how far is it dramatic? Most of these sonnets were addressed to a man. That can lead to a variety of nonsensical attitudes from exercises in special pleading to discreet whitewashing. It is also nonsensical, no matter how accurate your results may be, to waste time trying to identify characters. It is an idiot's job, pointless and uninteresting. It is just gossip, and gossip, though it can be exceedingly interesting when the parties are alive, is not at all interesting when they're dead.

Why should so much poetry be written about sexual love and so little about eating—which is just as pleasurable and never lets you down—or about family affection, or about the love of mathematics? Sexual love has, in very acute form, the double impress of nature and spirit and is therefore ideally representative of our human condition. The weak self that desires to be strong is hungry. The lonely self desires to be attached. The spirit desires to be free and unattached, and not at the mercy of natural appetite. It also desires to be important, and that conflicts with its desire for freedom. The weak self wants other things to exist so it may encroach on them, the lonely self wants other existences to hold on to, in extreme cases to be absorbed in. But the spirit wants to be only "I," wants its attachment to other things to be its free choice. Consciousness plays the least part in the pleasure of eating, but it plays some—that's why we recognize gluttony as a sin. But the element of consciousness is so small that gluttony is a staple only of comedy—for example, the story of the man who gives up a beautiful girl to marry an ugly woman who happens to be a good cook. His choice can't involve difficulty, for eating is a comparatively innocent occupation. It also has a generalized object of desire: it doesn't make very much difference what the food is. It is comic to see an individual overcome by something general. Take the man who is conversing very elaborately, very beautifully, on matters of the highest spiritual nature. Suddenly, when no one is looking, he snatches a cake. As in all natural humor, though, the amusement to be derived from this sort of situation, where the individual comes in contact with the universal, is limited. For example, there's a party. Everyone is waiting expectantly for the great writer to put in an appearance. He enters. Instead of producing illuminating conversation, the first thing he does is ask where the bathroom is. At the other extreme, the passion for mathematics, though it can be in selected persons quite as intense as any love affair, is too spiritual. But because mathematicians are still obstinately people, you can still get a mild comic effect from the contrast between their interest and their human situation: for instance, the absent-minded professor who forgets the day of his wedding.

Sexual love has both nature and spirit and the desire for personal choice. The desire begins with the individual object but ends in bed where things are generalized. I think that there's a good American story to illustrate this point. A man is on a visit to Chicago. He enters a restaurant. Yes, he sees a very beautiful girl in the restaurant, exquisitely beautiful, ravishingly beautiful. Yes, she is friendly, she smiles at him, she talks to him. Yes, her conversation is very witty, she is very agreeable, she is immensely entertaining. They go to the opera. Yes, she is very intelligent, she has a fine appreciation of the beautiful things in life, is keenly aware of values. They go to a night club. Yes, she is a wonderful sport, she enters wholeheartedly into the spirit of things. Later, yes, she responds beautifully to his love-making, is very understanding, says she loves him too. In the taxi, yes, her kisses are thrilling. And after that? After that it was like it is in Cincinnati. You see, any description of the sex act must be pornographic. To an outsider, to a child watching, it looks like eating. There is no realization that individuals are concerned. But they are, even at the last, though the fact may be not be evident. The nature of the act is that we must not remain self-conscious, it is destroyed if we do. Of course, to the child the act is comic, but it is not to the adult because he knows that spirit is involved. Literature makes people fornicating self-conscious and so violates the nature of the experience.

Why is love so peculiarly the subject of lyric poetry? War and work are dealt with dramatically, not lyrically. You often get people writing poetry when they fall in love who are not moved by their other equally important experiences to do any writing about them. It isn't at all because love poetry has any practical value. No one was ever seduced by a beautiful poem, though a bad one may be effective on occasion. Work and war are less subjective, they can be imposed on one for pragmatic reasons. Of course, subjective reasons, the combative instinct, loving your work, may enter in, but you always advance pragmatic, causal reasons—I have to defend my country, I have to earn my living. Now, these reasons are never advanced in love. The sex drive is enough, and reasons are always inadequate. It is an entirely personal affair, it is *my* love. It is a matter of necessity, I can't help myself. Duty does not enter into falling in love, though it may later enter into love itself.

Falling in love is the discovery of what "I exist" means. Now here we see the difference between essence and existence. I can readily imagine other people's feelings by analogy with my own, but I cannot readily imagine other people's existence by analogy with my own. My feelings, desires, etc., can be objects of my knowledge and hence I can imagine what other people feel. My existence cannot become an object of knowledge, and hence while, if I have the necessary histrionic imagination and talent I can act the part of another in such a way that I deceive his best friends, I can never imagine what it would be like to *be* that other person but must always remain pretending to be him. Falling in love is an intense interest in the existence of another person. That existence is not alone an object of knowledge, nor is it exclusively a goal of desire. That is why people write under these circumstances as they do not at other times. They are confronted with the question, "What is existence?" and with a tension between nature and spirit. To illustrate this tension one common rhetoric, used by Shakespeare, is to contrast the essential eye and the existential heart. Sonnet 46:

> Mine eye and heart are at a mortal war
> How to divide the conquest of thy sight;
> Mine eye my heart thy picture's sight would bar,
> My heart mine eye the freedom of that right.
> My heart doth plead that thou in him dost lie
> (A closet never pierc'd with crystal eyes);
> But the defendant doth that plea deny
> And says in him thy fair appearance lies.

To 'cide this title is impanneled
A quest of thoughts, all tenants to the heart,
And by their verdict is determined
The clear eye's moiety and the dear heart's part:
    As thus—mine eye's due is thy outward part,
    And my heart's right thy inward love of heart.

Also, Sonnet 24:

Mine eye hath play'd the painter and hath stell'd
Thy beauty's form in table of my heart;
My body is the frame wherein 'tis held,
And perspective it is best painter's art.
For through the painter must you see his skill
To find where your true image pictur'd lies,
Which in my bosom's shop is hanging still,
That hath his windows glazed with thine eyes.
Now see what good turns eyes for eyes have done:
Mine eyes have drawn thy shape, and thine for me
Are windows to my breast, wherethrough the sun
Delights to peep, to gaze therein on thee.
    Yet eyes this cunning want to grace their art—
    They draw but what they see, know not the heart.

I can talk about "my" feelings but not about "my" existence, as if I owned and lived outside it. Because you exist, my existence becomes important—Sonnet 62:

Sin of self-love possesseth all mine eye
And all my soul and all my every part;
And for this sin there is no remedy,
It is so grounded inward in my heart.
Methinks no face so gracious is as mine,
No shape so true, no truth of such account,
And for myself mine own worth do define
As I all other in all worths surmount.
But when my glass shows me myself indeed,
Beated and chopt with tann'd antiquity,
Mine own self-love quite contrary I read;
Self so self-loving were iniquity.
    'Tis thee (myself) that for myself I praise,
    Painting my age with beauty of thy days.

Or, one may react, "My feelings give your existence importance"—
Sonnet 141:

> In faith, I do not love thee with mine eyes,
> For they in thee a thousand errors note;
> But 'tis my heart that loves what they despise,
> Who in despite of view is pleas'd to dote.
> Nor are mine ears with thy tongue's tune delighted;
> Nor tender feeling to base touches prone,
> Nor taste, nor smell, desire to be invited
> To any sensual feast with thee alone;
> But my five wits nor my five senses can
> Dissuade one foolish heart from serving thee,
> Who leaves unsway'd the likeness of a man,
> Thy proud heart's slave and vassal wretch to be.
> > Only my plague thus far I count my gain,
> > That she that makes me sin awards me pain.

The testimony of the five wits and the five senses are not of primary importance.

Dr. Johnson refuted determinism by kicking a stone, and that was a very sound thing, for freedom is the first order of consciousness, and you can't argue about it. Translated into the rhetoric of love, that means the lover can say, "You transform the world for me," in two ways. First, you transform my condition vis-à-vis the world, as in Sonnet 29:

> When, in disgrace with Fortune and men's eyes,
> I all alone beweep my outcast state,
> And trouble deaf heaven with my bootless cries,
> And look upon myself and curse my fate,
> Wishing me like to one more rich in hope,
> Featur'd like him, like him with friends possess'd,
> Desiring this man's art, and that man's scope,
> With what I most enjoy contented least;
> Yet in these thoughts myself almost despising,
> Haply I think on thee, and then my state,
> Like to a lark at break of day arising
> From sullen earth, sings hymns at heaven's gate;
> > For thy sweet love rememb'red such wealth brings
> > That then I scorn to change my state with kings.

Or, you may transform other objects, as in Sonnet 99:

> The forward violet thus did I chide:
> Sweet thief, whence didst thou steal thy sweet that smells,
> If not from my love's breath? The purple pride
> Which on thy soft cheek for complexion dwells
> In my love's veins thou hast too grossly dy'd.
> The lily I condemned for thy hand;
> And buds of marjoram had stol'n thy hair.
> And roses fearfully on thorns did stand,
> One blushing shame, another white despair;
> A third, nor red nor white, had stol'n of both,
> And to his robb'ry had annex'd thy breath;
> But, for his theft, in pride of all his growth
> A vengeful canker eat him up to death.
>   More flowers I noted, yet I none could see
>   But sweet and colour it had stol'n from thee.

Another characteristic extremely important in the *Sonnets* is the experience of Time as a perpetual presence by which the past and future are judged, as set against the experience of a changing outside world in time. So, fading beauty is immortalized in art. Now what would be a good poem to illustrate that? Sonnet 65 will do:

> Since brass, nor stone, nor earth, nor boundless sea,
> But sad mortality o'ersways their power,
> How with this rage shall beauty hold a plea,
> Whose action is no stronger than a flower?
> O, how shall summer's honey breath hold out
> Against the wrackful siege of batt'ring days,
> When rocks impregnable are not so stout,
> Nor gates of steel so strong, but Time decays?
> O fearful meditation! Where, alack,
> Shall Time's best jewel from Time's chest lie hid?
> Or what strong hand can hold his swift foot back?
> Or who his spoil of beauty can forbid?
>   O, none! unless this miracle have might,
>   That in black ink my love shall still shine bright.

Notice how frequently the concluding couplets of the sonnets are poor. Unlike many of even the greatest artists, Shakespeare is not interested in completely flawless wholes. He says what he wants to say and lets the sonnet end anyhow. But that is the fault of a major artist, for a minor one always completes the work carefully. For instance, when we read Dostoevsky, we feel, yes, this is wonderful, this is marvelous, now go home and write it all over again. And yet if he did, the effect might well be lost. Most of us, however, can't get away with that attitude toward our writing.

There are two kinds of past in Shakespeare. The first is the personal past, as in Sonnet 31:

> Thy bosom is endeared with all hearts,
> Which I by lacking have supposed dead;
> And there reigns love, and all love's loving parts,
> And all those friends which I thought buried.
> How many a holy and obsequious tear
> Hath dear religious love stol'n from mine eye,
> As interest of the dead, which now appear
> But things remov'd that hidden in thee lie!
> Thou art the grave where buried love doth live,
> Hung with the trophies of my lovers gone,
> Who all their parts of me to thee did give:
> That due of many now is thine alone.
>   Their images I lov'd I view in thee,
>   And thou (all they) hast all the all of me.

The second kind of past is the historical past, as in Sonnet 53:

> What is your substance, whereof are you made,
> That millions of strange shadows on you tend?
> Since every one hath, every one, one shade,
> And you, but one, can every shadow lend.
> Describe Adonis, and the counterfeit
> Is poorly imitated after you.
> On Helen's cheek all art of beauty set,
> And you in Grecian tires are painted new.
> Speak of the spring, and foison of the year:
> The one doth shadow of your beauty show,
> The other as your bounty doth appear,
> And you in every blessed shape we know.
>   In all external grace you have some part,
>   But you like none, none you, for constant heart.

Parallel to this is the theme of the young man as inspiration about whom Shakespeare can always write.

Anxiety, pride, despair, faith—these cannot be called emotions like fear, anger, envy, or lust. They can't be observed directly, but only by symptoms. Anxiety, pride, and so forth refer to existence—we can't stand outside them so as to judge whether or not they are actually present. We can tell when a person is greedy or amorous, but we can never tell if he's proud: all symptoms can be deceitful. Conceit, on the other hand, is perfectly visible.

In the *Sonnets* we seem to be confronted with the anxiety into which the behavior of another person can throw you. For instance, Sonnet 57, "Being your slave, what should I do but tend," or better, Sonnet 75:

> So are you to my thoughts as food to life
> Or as sweet-season'd showers are to the ground;
> And for the peace of you I hold such strife
> As 'twixt a miser and his wealth is found:
> Now proud as an enjoyer, and anon
> Doubting the filching age will steal his treasure;
> Now counting best to be with you alone,
> Then better'd that the world may see my pleasure;
> Sometime all full with feasting on your sight,
> And by-and-by clean starved for a look;
> Possessing or pursuing no delight
> Save what is had or must from you be took.
>   Thus do I pine and surfeit day by day,
>   Or gluttoning on all, or all away.

The desire of spirit comes into conflict with the demand of nature, lust into conflict with envy. There is always the inevitably unsuccessful attempt to separate them. One can desire an ugly person and love someone whom one distrusts. Sonnet 129, "Th' expense of spirit in a waste of shame," deals with that, but it's too well known. Let's look at Sonnets 151 and 137. Sonnet 151:

> Love is too young to know what conscience is;
> Yet who knows not conscience is born of love?
> Then, gentle cheater, urge not my amiss,
> Lest guilty of my faults thy sweet self prove.
> For, thou betraying me, I do betray
> My nobler part to my gross body's treason;

My soul doth tell my body that he may
Triumph in love; flesh stays no farther reason,
But, rising at thy name, doth point out thee
As his triumphant prize. Proud of this pride,
He is contented thy poor drudge to be,
To stand in thy affairs, fall by thy side.
    No want of conscience hold it that I call
    Her "love" for whose dear love I rise and fall.

Sonnet 137:

Thou blind fool, Love, what dost thou to mine eyes
That they behold, and see not what they see?
They know what beauty is, see where it lies,
Yet what the best is take the worst to be.
If eyes, corrupt by over-partial looks,
Be anchor'd in the bay where all men ride,
Why of eyes' falsehood hast thou forged hooks,
Whereto the judgment of my heart is tied?
Why should my heart think that a several plot
Which my heart knows the wide world's common place?
Or mine eyes seeing this, say this is not,
To put fair truth upon so foul a face?
    In things right true my heart and eyes have erred,
    And to this false plague are they now transferred.

Let's consider the text of the *Sonnets* for a moment. It's obvious they were printed in an entirely higgledy-piggledy way. The marriage series is interrupted by Sonnet 15, "When I consider every thing that grows." Sonnet 70, "That thou art blam'd shall not be thy defect," should accompany Sonnets 94, "They that have pow'r to hurt and will do none," and 95, "How sweet and lovely dost thou make the shame." Sonnets 40 through 43 should go with the other sonnets about the dark lady. Sonnets 153 and 154—the last two—are formal exercises about taking the waters at Bath. Sonnet 145, "Those lips that Love's own hand did make," is an unconnected minor exercise in octosyllabics. Sonnet 146, "Poor soul, the centre of my sinful earth," is completely unconnected with the rest of the sequence.

It seems likely that there was more than one young man. The marriage sonnets were probably addressed to a patron. But other sonnets were not. The social distinction between Shakespeare's class and that of any likely patron would make personal passion and the criticism in which he sometimes indulges impossible. "When, in disgrace with Fortune and men's eyes" is a sonnet that could not have been addressed to a patron: the contrast between fortune and love would not have been applicable, since once a poet had found a complaisant patron, he no longer had to worry about fortune. Sonnet 41, "Those pretty wrongs that liberty commits," and Sonnet 38, "How can my Muse want subject to invent," and the sonnets on the immortality of writing may be addressed to a patron, or they may be addressed to a person whose social status is lower than Shakespeare's, though Shakespeare treats him ironically as a patron. In the sonnet about the rival poet, there are two alternatives. Either it is addressed to a patron, in which case Chapman or someone of that class is involved; or it may be intended as irony, and the rival may be a very bad poet whom the young man had the bad taste to like. That explanation is very possible, and a situation that can arouse a good deal of bitterness. What, after all, would you *say* if you had a bad poet for a rival.

Though there may be several young men throughout the series, there is predominantly one particular young man whom by Sonnet 104 Shakespeare has known for three years. There is a period of reciprocated love, a separation, at least one journey, the young man seems to have given Shakespeare his picture, both exchanged memorandum books, and Shakespeare gave his away and apologized. The young man behaved badly to Shakespeare, and Shakespeare behaved badly to him, as we can see from Sonnets 119, "What potions have I drunk of Siren tears," and 120, "That you were once unkind befriends me now." All this suggests sexual infidelity, which wouldn't make sense if there hadn't been a prior sex relationship between Shakespeare and the young man. The young man gets into bad company, Shakespeare has an affair with the dark lady, where love but not liking is involved, so does the young man, and neither is happy. The young man is beautiful, charming, and calculating. He isn't a nice person, but he's a powerful one. The lady is neither beautiful nor nice—she's therefore sexually attractive as an infernal genius. The young man is no nicer, but Shakespeare's thoughts about him are different.

You know, there aren't any pure accidents in love. When you are unhappy in love, it may be because your love is not returned, you may be in love with a bad character, or you may be treated badly. But always the question arises, how far is one responsible for one's unhappiness? If you tend to be fond of strong, domineering people, you may be completely uninterested when your affection is returned, since that may be a proof of weakness on the part of the person you'd admired. An artist, again, is interested in seeing just how much he can stand. But don't worry. The artist is tough, tough as leather. He is never in any danger of being destroyed, though he may destroy others. That is why there is so much higher a proportion of difficult and complex affairs among artists.

Most men are confronted with the difficulty that they tend to separate sexual passion from liking. That's not true of women, but men think that sex is something you have with those you don't respect and that love is something different—but sex enters where it's least expected. Women tend to fuse the two. Unless they're very strange indeed, they don't want to sleep with a man they don't like. Yeats writes in his poem, "A Last Confession":

> What lively lad most pleasured me
> Of all that with me lay?
> I answer that I gave my soul
> And loved in misery,
> But had great pleasure with a lad
> That I loved bodily.
>
> Flinging from his arms I laughed
> To think his passion such
> He fancied that I gave a soul
> Did but our bodies touch,
> And laughed upon his breast to think
> Beast gave beast as much.
>
> I gave what other women gave
> That stepped out of their clothes,
> But when this soul, its body off,
> Naked to naked goes,
> He it has found shall find therein
> What none other knows.
>
> And give his own and take his own
> And rule in his own right;
> And though it loved in misery
> Close and cling so tight,
> There's not a bird of day that dare
> Extinguish that delight.

Women think liking makes a good marriage, but that's not always so.

What does the particular idea of a handsome young man mean? This particular beauty is very evanescent and so comes to stand for the importance of the irrevocable moment. It must be rescued from time and made eternal. It is an aesthetic beauty entirely unrelated to function. You know, from a sexual point of view, the looks of a man is a biological luxury and so can stand as a symbol of the beauty of art because both are unrelated to anything, they are gratuitous. The beauty of women is functional, but it's recently been discovered that the beautiful plumage of male birds is not at all, as was thought, a result of sexual selection. Now this may be just jealousy on my part, but when one looks at the faces of men who have had great success with women, one certainly finds it extraordinarily easy to credit those experiments.

Youth is an internal possibility, but a visible completeness. It is a double symbol of art: it takes a potential and completes it, it emphasizes—and this is applicable to beauty in women as well—the division between beauty and goodness. Where you have, as in America, a culture putting a premium, in its fashions and elsewhere, on youth in women, you have a culture with dominant homosexual traits.

Art, as a general rule, is practiced by people with a highly developed consciousness and highly developed tensions, with a nostalgia for the innocence of unconsciousness. Artists are drawn to simple people, to beautiful young men of action. Let me read you Hölderlin's "Sokrates und Alkibiades":

> "Warum huldigest du, heiliger Sokrates,
>   Diesem Jünglinge stets? kennest du Grössers nicht,
>   Warum siehet mit Liebe,
>   Wie auf Götter, dein Aug' auf ihn?"

And Socrates answers:

> Wer das Tiefste gedacht, liebt das Lebendigste
> Hohe Tugend versteht, wer in die Welt geblickt,
>   Und es neigen die Weisen
>   Oft am Ende zu Schönem sich.

Now let me read the poem again, in English:

> Why should you continually praise this youth,
>   Saintly Socrates? Do you know nothing greater? Why
>   Does your eye look on him
>   Lovingly, as on the gods?

> Who most deeply has considered, loves what is most alive. He
>   Only understands the best, who has beheld the world,
>   And the wise in the end shall
>   Often incline to the beautiful.

You know there is a myth that Orpheus was a homosexual and that that is why he was killed by the ladies. How did that myth arise? On one side the artist starts with an acute ego problem. Art is completely unnecessary. Like love, it is not a matter of duty, it can't serve a practical end. It involves a mastery of emotion by consciousness, and through it one can play god and make the world in one's own image. From one point of view, art is simply the most prudent of occupations because all suffering short of acute physical violence becomes an object of interest. But art may spill over from creating a world of language into the dangerous and forbidden task of trying to create a human being. But for that one has to have someone of the same sex. You can *act* as somebody else—that's all right, you're just pretending. But this is *creating* someone else, you've involved yourself with a person, not a dream. He is actual, but you try to know him existentially as you know yourself—therefore, he must be of the same sex. This may look like Narcissus, but it really isn't because the other person must exist. He must have free will, and yet his free will must be a phase of one's own. Now that sort of relationship always involves great anxiety and a perpetual need of testing to see if the magic is working. No wonder both parties sooner or later behave very badly to each other. Shakespeare must have introduced the man and girl to each other—one more experiment that, as one might have predicted, didn't work. Now when we come to read *Henry IV* and *Henry V*, we shall see certain analogies between Prince Hal and the young man and between Falstaff and the artist.

The speech of Palamon before the temple of Venus in the fifth act of *The Two Noble Kinsmen* is one of the last speeches Shakespeare ever wrote on love. Here in treating love Shakespeare maintains a balance by which he avoids both over-romanticism and cynicism. One example he gives of the power of Venus, the marriage of an old man and a young girl who has a child very quickly, is extremely ugly, but it is set in a context of prayerful respect for the goddess:

> Hail, sovereign queen of secrets, who hast power
> To call the fiercest tyrant from his rage,
> And weep unto a girl; that hast the might,
> Even with an eye-glance, to choke Mars's drum

And turn th' alarm to whispers; that canst make
A cripple flourish with his crutch, and cure him
Before Apollo; that mayst force the king
To be his subject's vassal, and induce
Stale gravity to dance; the polled bachelor—
Whose youth, like wanton boys through bonfires,
Have skipp'd thy flame—at seventy thou canst catch,
And make him, to the scorn of his hoarse throat,
Abuse young lays of love. What godlike power
Hast thou not power upon? To Phoebus thou
Add'st flames, hotter than his; the heavenly fires
Did scorch his mortal son, thine him. The huntress
All moist and cold, some say, began to throw
Her bow away, and sigh. Take to thy grace
Me thy vow'd soldier, who do bear thy yoke
As 'twere a wreath of roses, yet is heavier
Than lead itself, stings more than nettles. I
Have never been foul-mouth'd against thy law;
Nev'r reveal'd secret, for I knew none—would not,
Had I kenn'd all that were. I never practis'd
Upon man's wife, nor would the libels read
Of liberal wits. I never at great feasts
Sought to betray a beauty, but have blush'd
At simp'ring sirs that did. I have been harsh
To large confessors, and have hotly ask'd them
If they had mothers. I had one, a woman,
And women 'twere they wrong'd. I knew a man
Of eighty winters—this I told them—who
A lass of fourteen brided. 'Twas thy power
To put life into dust. The aged cramp
Had screw'd his square foot round,
The gout had knit his fingers into knots,
Torturing convulsions from his globy eyes
Had almost drawn their spheres, that what was life
In him seem'd torture. This anatomy
Had by his young fair feere a boy, and I
Believ'd it was his, for she swore it was,
And who would not believe her? Brief, I am
To those that prate and have done, no companion;
To those that boast and have not, a defier;

To those that would and cannot, a rejoicer.
Yea, him I do not love that tells close offices
The foulest way, nor names concealments in
The boldest language. Such a one I am,
And vow that lover never yet made sigh
Truer than I. O, then, most soft-sweet goddess,
Give me the victory of this question, which
Is true love's merit, and bless me with a sign
Of thy great pleasure.

> *Here music is heard and doves are seen to flutter. They*
> *fall again upon their faces, then on their knees.*

O thou that from eleven to ninety reign'st
In mortal bosoms, whose chase is this world,
And we in herds thy game, I give thee thanks
For this fair token; which being laid unto
Mine innocent true heart, arms in assurance
My body to this business.—Let us rise
And bow before the goddess.

(V.i.77–136)

Henry IV, Parts One and Two,
and Henry V

[11 December 1946]

It is difficult to imagine that a historical play as good as *Henry IV* will ever again be written.

In the second part of the play, Henry IV makes a speech on the subject of time:

> O God, that one might read the book of fate
> And see the revolution of the times
> Make mountains level, and the continent,
> Weary of solid firmness, melt itself
> Into the sea! and other times to see
> The beachy girdle of the ocean
> Too wide for Neptune's hips; how chances mock,
> And changes fill the cup of alteration
> With divers liquors! O, if this were seen,
> The happiest youth, viewing his progress through,
> What perils past, what crosses to ensue,
> Would shut the book and sit him down and die.
>
> (*2 Henry IV*, III.i.45–56)

There are two or three different kinds of time. There is natural time and historical time. The effects of the passage of natural time in space are reversible: hydrogen and oxygen can combine to make water, water can decompose into hydrogen and oxygen. The individual process of natural time is irreversible, with constant new replacements, each competitive with the other. An irreversible succession of events constitutes history. Those most afraid of death and most afraid of failing powers think of time as the immediate moment looking after them, and they demand that *this* moment decide their lives. Those who fear not certainty but uncertainty want to control time, and look at the moment as something to be conquered and as having no rights of its own. The latter type either make great careers or are destroyed. It is good for them if they understand the moment, but if they do not, they are destroyed by those who understand it better than they. The first type are cynical about change and history—*plus ça change, plus c'est la même chose.* The other sort are cynical in believing that whatever succeeds is right. There are two corresponding attitudes towards politics: the first holds that "they are all crooks," the other that the successful ones are historically progressive: "All weather is fair to the winner." Falstaff, the first type, is unpolitical. He makes the moment his mother and his nurse. Hal, the second type, makes the moment his slave. At the end Falstaff is physically destroyed, but Hal is morally destroyed—he has no self left. Hotspur is a failure: he wants to be Hal, but he doesn't understand the political situation and is destroyed. Bardolph, Nym, and Pistol try to be Falstaff, but they lack trust in the immediate moment.

The plays present many antitheses. One, reflecting an interest in circular time, is youth versus age. On the one hand, there is youth in Hotspur, Hal, John, Falstaff's page, on the other hand, there is age in the King, Northumberland, Mistress Quickly, and Doll Tearsheet. Prince Hal is young physically, but not in mind. Falstaff is old physically, but he is like a child in refusing to live historically. Falstaff dominates, however, and our sense of the meaning of history is enhanced by having a hero who denies it meaning and acts as a mirror to it. Another antithesis is the sophisticated versus the naive. Hal and Falstaff are sophisticated in respect to each other and naive also. Falstaff understands things that Hal doesn't, Hal understands things about history that Falstaff doesn't. Henry IV is sophisticated, so is Worcester. Hotspur, Blunt, Chief Justice, Coleville, Shallow, Silence—they are all naive. Pistol is naive, though he thinks himself sophisticated. Yet another antithesis is the old order versus the new order. The old order believes in the decentralized, liberal, feudal state. It is composed of the North and West, including the Percies and Glendower, who are even further outside the mainstream, coming from an even older culture that is still allied to magic. Opposed to them is the more efficient, less liberal, more cynical centralized monarchy of the new order, consisting of Henry IV and his sons, the South and East, and London.

There are a number of individuals in the play who are on the wrong side, given their characters. Falstaff and his group are closer to the old order. They come from Gloucestershire, almost a geographical accident. York and an old fox like Worcester are by temperament on the other side. Hotspur, by accident, is also on the wrong side. There is a real old order and a real new order. An imaginary new order of the state withering away is imagined by Falstaff for Hal's succession. There is also a contrast between private character and public character in the play, often involving a double pretense. Falstaff counterfeiting a man of action is exposed. Hal counterfeiting an anarchist bohemian is revealed not to be one.

Shakespeare makes constant use of images of disease in the plays. In one of the first of many parallels, the short-winded peace is mirrored in Falstaff's short-windedness. The King declares to Warwick,

> you perceive the body of our kingdom,
> How foul it is; what rank diseases grow,
> And with what danger, near the heart of it
>
> (*2 Henry IV*, III.1.38–40),

and the sickness of dissension in the body politic is counterpointed with various specific diseases: Falstaff's great stomach, Doll's syphilis, Northumberland's sickness. We hear of the testing of Falstaff's water (*2 Henry IV*, I.ii.1–5). The Archbishop of York describes public opinion in the kingdom as a disease:

> Let us on
> And publish the occasion of our arms.
> The commonwealth is sick of their own choice;
> Their over-greedy love hath surfeited.
> An habitation giddy and unsure
> Hath he that buildeth on the vulgar heart.
> O thou fond Many! with what loud applause
> Didst thou beat heaven with blessing Bolinbroke
> Before he was what thou wouldst have him be!
> And being now trimm'd in thine own desires,
> Thou (beastly feeder) art so full of him
> That thou provok'st thyself to cast him up.
> So, so (thou common dog) didst thou disgorge
> Thy glutton bosom of the royal Richard;
> And now thou wouldst eat thy dead vomit up,
> And howl'st to find it.
>
> (*2 Henry IV*, I.iii.85–100)

The imagery of surfeit in this speech is clearly paralleled in Falstaff's characterization. Later, York says again,

> we are all diseas'd
> And with our surfeiting and wanton hours

Have brought ourselves into a burning fever,
And we must bleed for it; of which disease
Our late King, Richard, being infected, died.

(*2 Henry IV*, IV.i.54–58)

Mowbray, after a toast, just before Prince John's betrayal, suspects what is to come and says, "You wish me health in very happy season, / For I am on the sudden something ill" (*2 Henry IV*, IV.ii.79–80). In a similar psychosomatic demonstration, after hearing of the defeat of the rebels, the King feels he can die, having done his work:

And wherefore should these good news make me sick?
Will Fortune never come with both hands full,
But write her fair words still in foulest letters?
She either gives a stomach, and no food
(Such are the poor, in health), or else a feast,
And takes away the stomach—such are the rich
That have abundance and enjoy it not.
I should rejoice now at this happy news;
And now my sight fails and my brain is giddy.
O me! come near me. Now I am much ill.

(*2 Henry IV*, IV.iv.102–111)

And at the end, just before he sees Hal for the last time, Falstaff says, "I know the young king is sick for me" (*2 Henry IV*, V.iii.139–40).

Why do people get fat?—we'll take up that question later. Another interest in the play is the relation between honesty and acting. Most dishonest are those who are unaware that they are acting, or who come to believe in their own act. Honesty with one's self requires that you know you are an actor and not take yourself too seriously. You can be dishonest with others and still be honest with yourself. Hotspur can be honest with others, but is dishonest with himself. Falstaff counterfeits dishonesty. Henry V is dishonest both ways—his formal will and a powerful ego are the only things he has left.

Pretending is harped on in the play. Hal pretends to be one of the boys, a "sworn brother to a leash of drawers" on one occasion (*1 Henry IV*, II.iv.7), Hal and Poins pretend to be pickpurses, and, on a totally different level, Falstaff pretends to have been wounded on Gadshill. Falstaff and Hal act out father and son and the reverse, the latter, with the child acting the father, suggesting *King Lear*. Poins pretends to be a customer in order to bid for Francis in the tavern. Vernon and Worcester disguise Henry IV's generosity. Blunt "counterfeit'st the person of a king" (*1 Henry IV*, V.iv.28). Falstaff pretends that he is deaf to the Lord Chief Justice, that his pistol case is a bottle of sack, that his ring is of value, that he is dead, that he killed Hotspur. Pistol, who pretends to choler, Shallow, to being a gay dog, and Silence: they are all not what they seem. John pretends to honesty with the rebels. Hal tries on the King's crown. Some of these pretenses are serious, some are trivial. A few characters, like Coleville, don't pretend at all. Fluellen and Gower have developed a vocational theater of their own. Hal and Falstaff really dominate all in pretending.

In *Richard II*, Henry Bolingbroke is a younger man, self-confident, hopeful, and in a sense a naive character. Later, he says he acted on impulse in gaining the throne:

> Though then, God knows, I had no such intent,
> But that necessity so bow'd the state
> That I and greatness were compell'd to kiss.
>
> (*2 Henry IV*, III.i.72–74)

In *Henry IV, Parts One and Two*, however, Henry has grown older. The physical effect of age and the experience of politics have made him rather melancholic and a little *rusé*. He fails to see that Hal is even more *rusé*, and that his son is older than he is in his understanding of policy. Henry thinks Hotspur is the son he'd wish to have, noble and respectable, but Hotspur has no political sense. As a father, Henry doesn't appreciate the real political genius of Hal, and doesn't, as Hal does, see the politics of the future, the politically new.

Tel père tel fils, however—they are essentially similar in their calculation of effects. Hal reveals the premeditated policy behind his association with Falstaff at the very start:

> I know you all, and will awhile uphold
> The unyok'd humour of your idleness.
> Yet herein will I imitate the sun,
> Who doth permit the base contagious clouds
> To smother up his beauty from the world,
> That, when he please again to be himself,
> Being wanted, he may be more wond'red at
> By breaking though the foul and ugly mists
> Of vapours that did seem to strangle him.
> If all the year were playing holidays,

> To sport would be as tedious as to work;
> But when they seldom come, they wish'd-for come,
> And nothing pleaseth but rare accidents.
> So, when this loose behaviour I throw off
> And pay the debt I never promised,
> By how much better than my word I am,
> By so much shall I falsify men's hopes;
> And, like bright metal on a sullen ground,
> My reformation, glitt'ring o'er my fault,
> Shall show more goodly and attract more eyes
> Than that which hath no foil to set it off.
> I'll so offend to make offence a skill,
> Redeeming time when men think least I will.
>
> (*I Henry IV*, I.ii.219–41)

Compare the advice that Henry later gives Hal when he rebukes him for his association with Falstaff:

> Had I so lavish of my presence been,
> So common-hackney'd in the eyes of men,
> So stale and cheap to vulgar company,
> Opinion, that did help me to the crown,
> Had still kept loyal to possession
> And left me in reputeless banishment,
> A fellow of no mark nor likelihood.
> By being seldom seen, I could not stir
> But, like a comet, I was wond'red at;
> That men would tell their children, "This is he!"
> Others would say, "Where? Which is Bolingbroke?"
> And then I stole all courtesy from heaven,
> And dress'd myself in such humility
> That I did pluck allegiance from men's hearts,
> Loud shouts and salutations from their mouths
> Even in the presence of the crowned King.
>
> (*1 Henry IV*, III.ii.39–54)

Keep exclusive and get people excited—Richard skipped up and down the kingdom too much. But both Henry IV and Hal have a sense of what is the politically wise thing to do. Bolingbroke's behavior is dictated by the need to contrast himself to Richard, Hal's by the need to contrast himself to his father. In politics you have to surprise. As he is dying, Henry gives Hal Machiavellian advice:

> Be it thy course to busy giddy minds
> With foreign quarrels, that action, hence borne out,
> May waste the memory of the former days.
>
> (*2 Henry IV*, IV.v.214–16)

Henry IV had planned a crusade to the Holy Land, which is more idealistic than Henry V's invasion of France on flimsy grounds.

Both father and son talk of the uneasiness of being a king, Henry IV in a speech on sleep that ends, "Uneasy lies the head that wears a crown" (*2 Henry IV*, III.i.31), and Henry V, in a speech on sleep that is one of the few passages in *Henry V* that can be said to make up a poem:

> 'Tis not the balm, the sceptre, and the ball,
> The sword, the mace, the crown imperial,
> The intertissued robe of gold and pearl,
> The farced title running fore the king,
> The throne he sits on, nor the tide of pomp
> That beats upon the high shore of this world—
> No, not all these, thrice-gorgeous ceremony,
> Not all these, laid in bed majestical,
> Can sleep so soundly as the wretched slave,
> Who, with a body fill'd, and vacant mind,
> Gets him to rest, cramm'd with distressful bread;
> Never sees horrid night, the child of hell;
> But like a lackey, from the rise to set,
> Sweats in the eye of Phoebus, and all night
> Sleeps in Elysium; next day after dawn,
> Doth rise and help Hyperion to his horse;
> And follows so the ever-running year
> With profitable labour to his grave;
> And but for ceremony, such a wretch,
> Winding up days with toil and nights with sleep,
> Had the forehand and vantage of a king.
>
> (*Henry V*, IV.i.277–97)

This is terribly bad poetry, which is just as it should be. Henry IV is conscious of the corruptions of power because he has had to struggle for power, Henry V is less conscious of it because he is always successful, and Henry VI pays the price. Northumberland is sick, old, and finally unsure of himself, like Henry IV: these two get old, have had their political day, and become a little like what Falstaff always is—cynical about politics.

Hotspur, like Falstaff, is a terrific talker—especially when facing opposition. Like Thomas Carlyle, who extolled the virtues of silence for twenty volumes. Hotspur is a young man with enormous energy, who finds himself in a situation without opportunity, and who suffers from a lack of meaning in life. His defense is to force circumstances to give him opportunity. Falstaff surrenders to the moment, Hal uses the moment. Hotspur is halfway between the two and therefore fails. He tries to work up the quarrels that he lacks. As Worcester says, Hotspur actively "apprehends a world of figures here," but he cannot remain passive enough to perceive "the form of what he should attend" (*1 Henry IV*, I.iii.209–10). Falstaff purges himself of melancholia by language, but Hotspur only succeeds in stirring himself up. Pistol counterfeits Hotspur and pretends to energy, but he doesn't have to pretend resentment, as Hotspur does. Pistol is the nasty drunk—you can meet him at cocktail parties. Hotspur has a rhetoric based on everyday words. Pistol has elaborate, poetical diction, a parody of Marlowe that remains fustian.

Prince Hal. Yes, he is the Machiavellian character, master of himself and the situation—except that in the last analysis Falstaff is right when he tells him, "Thou art essentially mad without seeming so" (*1 Henry IV*, II.iv.540–41). Hal has no self. In talking with Poins, he despises himself for wanting small beer: "Doth it not show vilely in me to desire small beer?" (*2 Henry IV*, II.ii.7–8). He can be a continuous success because he can understand any situation, he can control himself, and he has physical and mental charm. But he is cold as a fish. Hal says to Poins, "What wouldst thou think of me if I should weep" for my father, and Poins answers, "I would think thee a most princely hypocrite." The Prince says,

> It would be every man's thought, and thou art a blessed fellow to think as every man thinks. Never a man's thought in the world keeps the roadway better than thine. Every man would think me an hypocrite indeed. And what accites your most worshipful thought to think so?
>
> *Poins.* Why, because you have been so lewd and so much engraffed to Falstaff.
>
> *Prince.* And to thee.
>
> (*2 Henry IV*, II.ii.56–68)

"And to thee": Poins is right about the fact that Hal would be suspected of hypocrisy, but wrong about the reason why. Hal plays with Falstaff's love, as he plays with the conspirators Cambridge, Scroop, and Grey. He is capable of gratuitous cruelty, as he shows in his joke on Francis, a boy who is an idiot. He knows how to talk to anyone. He can speak to the troops en masse, "Once more unto the breach, dear friends, once more" (*Henry V*, III.i.1), and differently in disguise with William, an individual soldier. He can talk to a depressed noble, he can threaten a town with sacking, and he can express bogus piety.

There is a questionable religious atmosphere in Shakespeare's history plays. Only scoundrels like Richard III and Henry V talk of religion. The clerics in *Henry V* are depicted in a bad light, they don't want to lose their lands, and they speciously justify Henry's claim to France. Henry gives himself away. He doesn't know God in a personal way, but thinks he can manage Him. His offer of two chantries in penance for the killing of Richard is a bribe:

> I have built
> Two chantries, where the sad and solemn priests
> Sing still for Richard's soul. More will I do!
> Though all that I can do is nothing worth,
> Since that my penitence comes after all,
> Imploring pardon.
>
> (*Henry V*, IV.i.317–22)

The most brutal scene in Shakespeare is Henry's wooing of Katherine. It is cold and calculated, and most shocking is Henry's certainty of success. Richard's wooing of Anne is a tour de force. Henry's wooing of Katherine is too easy:

Marry, if you would put me to verses or to dance for your sake, Kate, why, you undid me. For the one I have neither words nor measure; and for the other I have no strength in measure, yet a reasonable measure in strength. If I could win a lady at leapfrog, or by vaulting into my saddle with my armour on my back, under the correction of bragging be it spoken, I should quickly leap into a wife. Or if I might buffet for my love, or bound my horse for her favours, I could lay on like a butcher and sit like a jackanapes, never off. But, before God, Kate, I cannot look greenly nor gasp out my eloquence, nor I have no cunning in protestation; only downright oaths, which I never use till urg'd, nor never break for urging. If thou canst love a fellow of this temper, Kate, whose face is not worth sunburning, that never looks in his glass for love of anything he sees there, let thine eye be thy cook. I speak to thee plain soldier. If thou canst love me for this, take me; if not, to say to thee that I shall die, is true—but for thy love, by the Lord, no; yet I love thee too. And while thou liv'st, dear Kate, take a fellow of plain and uncoined constancy; for he perforce must do thee right, because he hath not the gift to woo in other places. For these fellows of infinite tongue that can rhyme themselves into ladies' favours, they do always reason themselves out again. What! A speaker is but a prater; a rhyme is but a ballad. A good leg will fall, a straight back will stoop, a black beard will turn white, a curl'd pate will grow bald, a fair face will wither, a full eye will wax hollow; but a good heart, Kate, is the sun and the moon; or rather, the sun, and not the moon, for it shines bright and never changes, but keeps his course truly. If thou would have such a one, take me; and take me, take a soldier; take a soldier, take a king. And what say'st thou then to my love? Speak my fair—and fairly, I pray thee.

(*Henry V,* V.ii.137–77)

Henry pretends to be a bluff wooer, but he *could* dance and make verses for Katherine's sake if he would. As he himself tells her dryly, he will die—but certainly not for her.

Why, essentially, does Hal associate with Falstaff and his companions? Not just for the surprise of his "reformation," but because he must possess a knowledge of human weakness. Court manners hide too much. Let people take liberties and they'll give themselves away. Then he can rule them. "I am so good a proficient in one quarter of an hour," he tells Poins, "that I can drink with any tinker in his own language during my life" (*1 Henry IV,* II.iv.20–22). Hal and Falstaff are eternal antitypes, sworn foes. Hal is the type who becomes a college president, a government head, etc., and one hates their guts. On the other side, we can't govern ourselves. If Falstaff were running the world, it would be like the Balkans, of former and better days. Neither Hal nor Falstaff can do without the other. Falstaff, unhistorical and unpolitical, gives Hal an education in the nature of politics. After Falstaff is gone, Hal becomes a formal public figure, and his style becomes fat, like Falstaff's stomach. Falstaff's style is short-winded and good. Hal's style is all fat, no muscle—the man is swallowed up in the office, and we have no interest in him. Falstaff is perpetually interesting.

Falstaff has a number of things to say about his stomach:

'Sblood, I am as melancholy as a gib-cat or a lugg'd bear.

(*1 Henry IV,* I.ii.82–83)

A plague of sighing and grief! It blows a man up like a bladder.

(1 Henry IV, II.iv.365–66)

I am not only witty in myself, but the cause that wit is in other men. I do here walk before thee like a sow that hath overwhelm'd all her litter but one.

(2 Henry IV, I.ii.11–14)

The young prince hath misled me. I am the fellow with the great belly, and he my dog.

(2 Henry IV, I.ii.164–66)

I have a whole school of tongues in this belly of mine, and not a tongue of them all speaks any other word but my name. An I had but a belly of any indifferency, I were simply the most active fellow in Europe. My womb, my womb, my womb undoes me!

(2 Henry IV, IV.iii.20–25)

Why do people get fat?—because they eat humble pie as their food and swallow their pride as their drink. What does drink do? It destroys the sense of time and makes one childlike and able to return to the innocence one enjoyed before one had sex. Why do people get fat? "Getting the wind up": men imitate pregnancy in fatness, which is a symbol for the frustrated creative deed. A fat man looks like a cross between a very young child and a pregnant mother. The Greeks thought of Narcissus as a slender youth, but I think they were wrong. I see him as a middle-aged man with a corporation, for, however ashamed he may be of displaying it in public, in private a man with a belly loves it dearly—it may be an unprepossessing child to look at, but he's borne it all by himself.

Falstaff hides the realization that Hal does not love him and that he is a failure. He is also a displaced person, a country boy who leaves his playmates and comes to the city. Most people in Greenwich Village don't know how to live in the city. They try to live in the city as if they were in the country, where nature provides the rhythm of life—or did before industrialization—and where the less you do the truer you can be to it. But in the city, you have to be like Hal. Time will tell you nothing—you must decide your life. The sense of time is disoriented in the city. When Falstaff asks Hal, in his first words in the play, "Now, Hal, what time of day is it, lad?" Hal answers,

Thou art so fat-witted with drinking of old sack, and unbuttoning thee after supper, and sleeping upon benches after noon, that thou

hast forgotten to demand that truly which thou wouldest truly know.
What a devil hast thou to do with the time of the day?

(*1 Henry IV*, I.ii.1–7)

You can't extemporize in the city. Set against Shallow and Silence,
Falstaff is enormously more aware. He is inactive, however, he has no
land and beeves, and as he says, "I can get no remedy against this consumption of the purse. Borrowing only lingers and lingers it out, but the
disease is incurable." But he also says, "A good wit will make use of anything. I will turn diseases to commodity (*2 Henry IV*, I.ii.264–66, 277–79).
The Justices are looked after by time.

Falstaff loves Hal for his youth and power because he knows he can't
manage his own life. He wants by charm to attach himself to Hal both as
a child and as a mother. Falstaff, like Hamlet, is an actor living in a world
of words. Falstaff is attached positively to life through Hal, and when he
is rejected, he dies. Hamlet is attached negatively to life by the crime of
his mother and uncle, and he sees politics as personal relations. That's
why so many of us can't dislike Tammany Hall. Under the circumstances
of today, we must have a decently dishonest bureaucracy. If a policeman
won't take a $10 bribe, you're sunk. Falstaff is never on time, he borrows
money he doesn't pay back, he always extemporizes. He is the artist—but
not really. He will talk, but he can't sit down to convert possibility into
reality. The artist has to mix Falstaff and Hal, Falstaff's childlikeness and
Hal's Machiavellianism and prudence.

Falstaff's death changes things. Hal becomes a public figure, and the
not so innocent children, Bardolph, Pistol, and Nym—who goes to the
gallows—are drawn into history, and suffer.

Much Ado About Nothing

[18 December 1946]

The first thing to notice about *Much Ado About Nothing* is that the subplot overwhelms and overshadows the main plot. The main plot consists of the story of Hero and Claudio and the conspiracy of Don John. Its sources are Bandello, Ariosto, and a Greek romance. Shakespeare treats the story perfunctorily, and except for Don John, it's boring. And Shakespeare shows some carelessness in putting it together: for example, Margaret—didn't she know what she was doing? And Borachio's plans to be called Claudio from the window don't come off—anyhow, Claudio is listening. The whole story is a foil to the duel of wits between Beatrice and Benedick.

How have we seen Shakespeare use the subplot? First, as a parallel. In *Love's Labour's Lost* Armado parallels the gentry—his affected language is a comment on Berowne's poetic affectations, and he has to accept Jacqueline, an inferior wife, as Berowne has to "jest a twelvemonth in an hospital" (V.ii.880). In *A Midsummer Night's Dream* Bottom suffers from the same kinds of illusion as the lovers, and, like the lovers, he is eventually delivered from them. Shakespeare also uses the subplot as a contrast: Shylock is juxtaposed against Venetian life in *The Merchant of Venice,* and Falstaff is elaborately developed as a contrast to the heroic life of Hal and the nobles in *Henry IV.* There is also a very sketchy contrasting subplot in the *Comedy of Errors*—the tragic background of the father doomed to death unless he can raise the money to pay a large fine.

Much Ado provides another case of contrast, with the comic, light duel of wits in the foreground and the dark malice of Don John in the background. How does Shakespeare keep the tragic plot from getting too serious? He treats it perfunctorily as a background. This draws attention to an artistic point—the importance of boredom. In any first-class work of art, you can find passages that in themselves are extremely boring, but try to cut them out, as they are in an abridged edition, and you lose the life of the work. Don't think that art that is alive can remain on the same level of interest throughout—and the same is true of life.

The relation of pretense and reality is a major concern of the play, and the keys to understanding it can be found in two passages. One is Balthazar's song, "Sigh no more, ladies, sigh no more" (II.iii.64–76). Where and how songs are placed in Shakespeare is revealing. Let's look first at two or three other examples. In *The Two Gentlemen of Verona*, we have the song, "Who is Silvia? What is she, / That all our swains commend her?" (IV.ii.39–53). The song, which is sung to Silvia, has standard Petrarchan rhetoric—cruel fair, faithful lover—but the music is being used with conscious evil intent. Proteus, who has been false to his friend, has forsworn his vows to Julia, and is cheating Thurio, serenades Silvia while his forsaken Julia, disguised as a boy, listens:

> *Host.* How now? Are you sadder than you were before? How do you, man? The music likes you not.
> *Jul.* You mistake, the musician likes me not.
> *Host.* Why, my pretty youth?
> *Jul.* He plays false, father.
> *Host.* How? Out of tune on the strings?
> *Jul.* Not so; but yet so false that he grieves my very heartstrings.
> *Host.* You have a quick ear.
> *Jul.* Ay, I would I were deaf! It makes me have a slow heart.
> *Host.* I perceive you delight not in music.
> *Jul.* Not a whit, when it jars so.
> *Host.* Hark, what fine change is in the music!
> *Jul.* Ay, that change is the spite.
> *Host.* You would have them always play but one thing?
> *Jul.* I would always have one play but one thing.
>
> (IV.ii.54–72)

"O mistress mine, where are you roaming?" in *Twelfth Night* (II.iii.40–53), which is sung to Sir Toby Belch and Sir Andrew Aguecheek, is in the "Gather ye rosebuds" tradition, but taken seriously the lines suggest the voice of elderly lust, not youth, and Shakespeare makes us conscious of this by making the audience for the song a pair of aging drunks. In *Measure for Measure*, the betrayed Mariana is serenaded by a boy in a song that does not help her forget her unhappiness but indulges it. Being the deserted lady has become a role. The words of the song "Take, O, take those lips away" (IV.i.1–6) mirrors her situation exactly, and her apology to the Duke when he surprises her gives her away:

> I cry you mercy, sir, and well could wish
> You had not found me here so musical.
> Let me excuse me, and believe me so,
> My mirth it much displeas'd, but pleas'd my woe.
>
> (IV.i.10–13)

In each of these three cases, the setting criticizes the song's convention. The same is true in *Much Ado About Nothing*. The serenade convention is turned upside down in Balthazar's song, and its effect is to suggest that we shouldn't take sad lovers too seriously. The song is sung to Claudio and Don Pedro for the benefit of Benedick, who is overhearing it, as they plot to make him receptive to loving Beatrice. In the background, also, is the plot of Borachio and Don John against Claudio.

> Sigh no more, ladies, sigh no more!
>   Men were deceivers ever,
> One foot in sea, and one on shore;
>   To one thing constant never.
>   Then sigh not so,
>   But let them go,
>   And be you blithe and bonny,
> Converting all your sounds of woe
>   Into Hey nonny, nonny.
>
> Sing no more ditties, sing no moe,
>   Of dumps so dull and heavy!
> The fraud of men was ever so,
>   Since summer first was leavy.
>   Then sigh not so, &c.
>
> (II.iii.64–76)

Claudio, in his dreamy love-sick state, is shortly to prove such a lover as the song describes, and Benedick, who thinks himself immune to love, is shortly to acknowledge his love for Beatrice. If one imagines the sentiments of the song being an expression of character, the only character they suit is Beatrice, and I do not think it is too far-fetched to imagine that the song arouses in Benedick's mind an image of Beatrice, the tenderness of which alarms him. The violence of his comment when the song is over is suspicious: "An he had been a dog that should have howl'd thus, they would have hang'd him; and I pray God, his bad voice bode no mischief. I had as live have heard the night raven, come what plague could have come after it" (II.iii.81–85).

Historically and individually there are new discoveries, like courtly love, which create novelty and give new honesty to new feelings. As time goes on, the discovery succeeds because of its truth. Then the convention petrifies and is employed by people whose feelings are quite different. Petrarchan rhetoric had its origin in a search for personal fidelity versus arranged marriage, and was then used to make love to a girl for an evening. To dissolve the over-petrified sentiments and unreality of a convention, one must apply intelligence. "Sigh no more, ladies, sigh no more" is Petrarchan convention seen comically through the lens of a critical intelligence.

Man must be an actor, and one always has to play with ideas before one can make them real. But one must not forget one is playing and mix up play with reality. When Antonio tries to comfort his brother Leonato about Hero, Leonato resists his counsel:

> My griefs cry louder than advertisement.
> *Ant.* Therein do men from children nothing differ.
> *Leon.* I pray thee peace. I will be flesh and blood;
> For there was never yet philosopher
> That could endure the toothache patiently,
> However they have writ the style of gods
> And made a push at chance and sufferance.

(V.i.32–38)

This is the other key to the issue of pretense and reality in *Much Ado:* just as feeling can petrify, there can be a false rhetoric of reason that genuine grief can detect. Too much concern for play widens the gap between convention and reality, resulting in either a brutal return to reality or a flight to a rival convention. Leonato's grief is not real—it is an expression of social embarrassment. Antonio, though he tries to console Leonato, is the one who really grieves, as his curses against Claudio and Don Pedro for their lack of faith show:

> God knows I lov'd my niece,
> And she is dead, slander'd to death by villains,
> That dare as well answer a man indeed
> As I dare take a serpent by the tongue.
> Boys, apes, braggarts, Jacks, milksops! . . . .
> Scambling, outfacing, fashion-monging boys,
> That lie and cog and flout, deprave and slander.

(V.i.87–91, 94–95)

So it is Antonio who really feels, Leonato who puts on an act.

Beatrice and Benedick are essentially people of good will—their good will and honesty are what create their mockery and duels of wit. Don John is honest and cynical, but behind that is ill will. All three characters are intelligent, able, and honest. *Much Ado About Nothing* is not one of Shakespeare's best plays, but Benedick and Beatrice are the most lovable, amusing, and good people—the best of combinations—he ever created. They are the characters of Shakespeare we'd most like to sit next to at dinner. The great verbal dexterity of Beatrice and Benedick is paralleled by the great verbal ineptitude of Dogberry, an ineptitude which itself becomes art. All three love words and have good will—they are divided in verbal skill and intelligence. The honest, original people in the play use prose, the conventional people use verse. A general criticism of an Elizabethan sonneteer is that he is too "poetic." Every poet has to struggle against "poetry"—in quotes. The real question for the poet is what poetic language will show the true sensibility of the time.

Much Ado About Nothing is full of deception and pretense. Benedick and Beatrice fool themselves into believing they don't love each other— they mistake their reactions against the conventions of love for lovelessness. Claudio, Hero, and Don Pedro pretend to Benedick and Beatrice that the two love each other, and—with good will—they use Benedick and Beatrice to bolster their own conventions of love. Don John, Borachio, and Margaret's pretense, on the other hand, is animated by pure malice and ill will. Their deception succeeds because those who are deceived are conventionally-minded. They are stupid and don't recognize malice, unlike Benedick, who at once suspects Don John (IV.i.189–90), and Beatrice, who at once believes that Hero is innocent (IV.i.147).

Claudio turns away from Hero, Hero faints instead of standing up for herself, and Leonato is taken in by Don John's pretense because he doesn't want to believe that princes lie—he's a snob. When Beatrice says that she was not Hero's bedfellow on the night in question, though she has been so for a twelvemonth, Leonato declares:

> Confirm'd, confirm'd! O, that is stronger made
> Which was before barr'd up with ribs of iron!
> Would the two princes lie? And Claudio lie,
> Who lov'd her so that, speaking of her foulness,
> Wash'd it with tears? Hence from her! Let her die.
>
> (IV.i.151–55)

Leonato and Hero subsequently follow the Friar's advice to pretend that Hero is dead and to disguise her as a cousin—yet more pretense. And, finally, Dogberry pretends to know language and to be wiser than he is.

The individual versus the universal. Among animals there is no universal like marriage or justice—only man can be false by following his nature. A human being is composed of a combination of nature and spirit and individual will. Laws are established to help defend his will against nature and to get the individual meaningfully related to the universal. When the individual has only an abstract relation with the universal, there is a hollow rhetoric and falsity on both sides. There are three possibilities in relating to law. First is the defiant rebel, who is a destructive misfit. Second is the conformist, whose relation to law remains abstract. And third is the creative, original person, where the individual relation to law is vivifying and good on both sides. Don John the bastard is in the first, temperamentally melancholic, group. Don John uses that temperament to take a negative position outside the group, like Shylock, as opposed to a character like Faulconbridge, who is an outsider with a positive attitude. "I thank you," Don John says sullenly to Leonato at the start of the play, "I am not of many words, but I thank you." (I.i.158–59). To Conrade, who advises him to behave more ingratiatingly to his brother Don Pedro, he says,

> I had rather be a canker in a hedge than a rose in his grace, and it better fits my blood to be disdain'd of all than to fashion a carriage to rob love from any. In this, though I cannot be said to be a flattering honest man, it must not be denied that I am a plain-dealing villain. I am trusted with a muzzle and enfranchis'd with a clog; therefore I have decreed not to sing in my cage. If I had my mouth, I would bite; if I had my liberty, I would do my liking. In the meantime let me be that I am, and seek not to alter me.
>
> *Con.* Can you make no use of your discontent?
> *John.* I make all use of it, for I use it only.
>   Enter *Borachio*
> Who comes here? What news, Borachio?
> *Bora.* I came yonder from a great supper. The Prince your brother is royally entertain'd by Leonato, and I can give you intelligence of an intended marriage.
> *John.* Will it serve for any model to build mischief on? What is he for a fool that betroths himself to unquietness?
>
>   (I.iii.28–50)

Don John's discontent is infinite. His view of marriage is superficially like Benedick and Beatrice's, but his motive is the hatred of happiness. Like the Devil, he wants to be unique. He has little feeling, great intelligence, and great will.

Claudio is chief among the conventional characters—characters who are either functions of the universal or are destroyed by it. Claudio has some intelligence, some feeling, and very little will. Don Pedro has to coax him to declare his love for Hero. When Claudio asks whether Leonato has a son, he's indirectly saying he wants to marry for money, an attitude that Benedick's honesty has already detected: "Would you buy her, that you enquire after her?" (I.i.181–82). There's some conventional stuff about his having been at war and having had no time for love. He really wants to get married—no matter to whom, and he turns to entirely conventional forms of love-making. Benedick says of him,

> I have known when there was no music with him but the drum and fife; and now had he rather hear the tabor and the pipe. I have known when he would have walk'd ten mile afoot to see a good armour; and now will he lie ten nights awake carving the fashion of a new doublet. He was wont to speak plain and to the purpose, like an honest man and a soldier; and now is he turn'd orthography; his words are a very fantastical banquet—just so many strange dishes.
>
> (II.iii.13–23)

Claudio is a conventional tough soldier, a conventional Petrarchan lover—and his jealousy is conventional, expressed in conventional puns: "fare thee well, most foul, most fair! Farewell, / Thou pure impiety and impious purity!" (IV.i.104–5). The remedy for the conventional is the exceptional: Hero's supposed death makes him a killer, and he is punished by being forced to marry her "cousin," which proves that he's not an individual. The song Claudio sings for Hero in the churchyard, "Pardon, goddess of the night" (V.iii.12–21) is a suitably bad song that keeps the tragedy cursory. Don Pedro and Claudio skip off to the final reconciliation nonchalantly.

Now to the people who are both critical and creative. The conventions of love-making are criticized in the courtship of Berowne and Rosaline in *Love's Labour's Lost*, in which Rosaline is superior, and in the courtship and marriage of Petruchio and Katherina in *The Taming of the Shrew*, in which Petruchio is superior. Benedick and Beatrice mark the first time that both sides are equally matched. Both are critics of Petrarchan convention, and both hate sentimentality because they value feeling. When they really love, they speak directly:

> *Bene.* I do love nothing in the world so well as you. Is not that strange?

Beat. As strange as the thing I know not. It were as possible for me to say I loved nothing so well as you. But believe me not; and yet I lie not. I confess nothing, nor I deny nothing. I am sorry for my cousin.

Bene. By my sword, Beatrice, thou lovest me.

Beat. Do not swear, and eat it.

Bene. I will swear by it that you love me, and I will make him eat it that says I love not you.

Beat. Will you not eat your word?

Bene. With no sauce that can be devised to it. I protest I love thee.

Beat. Why then, God forgive me!

Bene. What offence, sweet Beatrice?

Beat. You have stayed me in a happy hour. I was about to protest I loved you.

Bene. And do it with all thy heart.

Beat. I love you with so much of my heart that none is left to protest.

Bene. Come, bid me do anything for thee.

Beat. Kill Claudio.

(IV.i.269–91)

Beatrice wants action here, though Benedick is right in thinking Claudio is not entirely responsible.

Beatrice and Benedick have a high ideal of marriage. Before the dance, Beatrice kids Hero:

For, hear me Hero: wooing, wedding, and repenting is as a Scotch jig, a measure, and a cinque-pace: the first suit is hot and hasty like a Scotch jig—and full as fantastical; the wedding, mannerly modest, as a measure, full of state and ancientry; and then comes Repentance and with his bad legs falls into the cinque-pace faster and faster, till he sink into his grave.

Leon. Cousin, you apprehend passing shrewdly.

Beat. I have a good eye, uncle; I can see a church by daylight.

(II.i.75–86)

Beatrice and Benedick demand a combination of reason and will, a combination Benedick displays in the soliloquy in which he resolves to love Beatrice after hearing how she loves him:

This can be no trick. The conference was sadly borne; they have the truth of this from Hero; they seem to pity the lady. It seems her affections have their full bent. Love me? Why, it must be requited. I hear how I am censur'd. They say I will bear myself proudly if I perceive the love come from her. They say too that she will rather die than give any sign of affection. I did never think to marry. I must not seem proud. Happy are they that hear their detractions and can put them to mending. They say the lady is fair—'tis a truth, I can bear them witness; and virtuous—'tis so, I cannot reprove it; and wise, but for loving me—by my troth, it is no addition to her wit, nor no great argument of her folly, for I will be horribly in love with her. I may chance have some odd quirks and remnants of wit broken on me because I have railed so long against marriage. But doth not the appetite alter? A man loves the meat in his youth that he cannot endure in his age. Shall quips and sentences and these paper bullets of the brain awe a man from the career of his humour? No, the world must be peopled. When I said I would die a bachelor, I did not think I should live till I were married.

(II.iii.228–53)

Benedick's reasons are not those of feelings. Conventional people protest in a rhetoric of feeling.

There is a gay conclusion for Benedick and Beatrice. At the end one feels absolutely confident of the success of their marriage, more than of other marriages in Shakespeare. They have creative intelligence, good will, a lack of sentimentality, and an ability to be open and direct with each other in a society in which such directness is uncommon. For us, the modern convention of "honesty" is now the danger. People must learn to hide things from each other a little more. We need a post-Freudian-analytic rhetoric.

The play presents law in a comic setting. Dogberry is an imperfect human representation of the law, and he's conceited. He and the Watch don't understand what's happening, and they succeed more by luck than ability. Dogberry's "line" is like Falstaff's, but he's not against law. He says to the Watch and Verges,

If you meet a thief, you may suspect him, by virtue of your office, to be no true man; and for such kind of men, the less you meddle or make with them, why, the more is for your honesty.

2. Watch. If we know him to be a thief, shall we not lay hands on him?

Dog. Truly, by your office you may; but I think they that touch pitch will be defil'd. The most peaceable way for you, if you do take a thief, is to let him show himself what he is, and steal out of your company.

Verg. You have been always called a merciful man, partner.

(III.iii.52–65)

Dogberry and his company do indeed raise the problem of mercy versus justice. They are successful against probability, and that they are suggests (1) that police are dangerous because they become like crooks in dealing with crooks, and (2) that good nature pays off better than efficiency. Efficiency at the expense of kindness must be checked, which is more a British than an American attitude.

A contrast between light and dark is always present in Shakespeare. It is made explicit in *Much Ado About Nothing* in the contrast Don Pedro draws, after visiting Hero's tomb, between kindness and the possibilities of malice and tragedy, between the gentle day and the wolves of prey:

> Good morrow, masters. Put your torches out.
>   The wolves have prey'd, and look, the gentle day,
> Before the wheels of Phoebus, round about
>   Dapples the drowsy east with spots of grey.
> Thanks to you all, and leave us. Fare you well.

(V.iii.24–27)

With this passage in mind, let me conclude by reading from Rimbaud's "Génie":

> He is affection and the present since he has made the house open to foamy winter and to the murmur of summer—he who has purified food and drink—he who is the charm of fleeing places and the super-human delight of stations.—He is affection and the future, love and force whom we, standing among our rages and our boredoms, see passing in the stormy sky and banners of ecstasy.
>
> . . . .
>
> And we remember him and he has gone on a journey . . . And if Adoration goes, rings, his promise rings: "Away! superstitions, away! those ancient bodies, those couples, and those ages. It is this present epoch that has foundered!"
>
> He will not go away, he will not come down again from any heaven, he will not accomplish the redemption of the angers of women and the gaieties of men and all this Sin: for it is done, he being and being loved.
>
> . . . .

He has known us all and all of us has loved; take heed this winter night, from cape to cape, from the tumultuous pole to the castle, from the crowd to the shore, from look to look, force and feelings weary, to hail him, to see him and to send him away, and under the tides and high in the deserts of snow, to follow his views,—his breaths,—his body,—his day.

The Merry Wives of Windsor

[8 January 1947]

The Merry Wives of Windsor is a very dull play indeed. We can be grateful for its having been written, because it provided the occasion of Verdi's *Falstaff*, a very great operatic masterpiece. Mr. Page, Shallow, Slender, and the Host disappear. I have nothing to say about Shakespeare's play, so let's hear Verdi.

Julius Caesar

[15 January 1947]

Tonight I hope to reassure the less musical, because I'm going to talk and talk and talk. *Julius Caesar* is one of the best known and most performed of Shakespeare's plays. Like *Hamlet*, the play is a puzzle. It doesn't conform to the idea of Aristotelian tragedy in presenting a noble man with a conspicuous flaw, nor to Elizabethan melodrama in presenting a conspicuous villain. Some critics think Shakespeare combined two plays in *Julius Caesar*. Certainly he combined two plots. Shakespeare's two significant tragedies preceding *Julius Caesar*—we can forget *Titus Andronicus*—are *Richard III* and *Romeo and Juliet*.

It was natural in the thirties of this century for theatrical directors to make Caesar a Fascist dictator and the conspirators noble liberals. That's a misreading, I think, but there are things to be said for it. It draws attention to *Julius Caesar* as a historical play, and it helps us bear in mind Shakespeare's continuing interest in the genre. The last play he wrote was a historical play, *Henry VIII*, an excellent collaboration with Fletcher. In the later Roman plays, history is superficial in the sense that it could be changed without changing the characters. But time and history are essential in *Julius Caesar*. What is Shakespeare's interest in writing the play? He sets himself the problem, in depicting Roman society, of whether he can understand Roman history and society as he has English history. At that time, people in Europe grew up more with Roman history, but it is still difficult for Shakespeare. There is a poetic problem alongside the technical one: what kind of rhetoric must the characters use? How must they speak? In the English chronicle plays, characters speak romantically out of the Herod character of the miracle plays and the *miles gloriosus* of Marlowe. *Julius Caesar* is unique for a plain, direct, bleak, public style of rhetoric. The language of the characters often consists of monosyllables. Brutus, for example, at the end of his first meeting with Cassius, says,

> For this time I will leave you.
> To-morrow, if you please to speak to me,
> I will come home to you; or if you will,
> Come home to me, and I will wait for you.

(I.ii.307–10)

Brutus says to his servant Lucius, "I should not urge thy duty past thy might. / I know young bloods look for a time of rest" (IV.iii.261–62). Calphurnia says, in warning Caesar not to leave his house,

> The noise of battle hurtled in the air,
> Horses did neigh, and dying men did groan,
> And ghosts did shriek and squeal about the streets.
>
> (II.ii.22–24)

Contrast this speech with its imitation in *Hamlet*, when Horatio says,

> In the most high and palmy state of Rome,
> A little ere the mightiest Julius fell,
> The graves stood tenantless, and the sheeted dead
> Did squeak and gibber in the Roman streets.
>
> (I.i.113–16)

Julius Caesar has great relevance to our time, though it is gloomier, because it is about a society that is doomed. Our society is not doomed, but in such immense danger that the relevance is great. Octavius only succeeded in giving Roman society a 400-year reprieve. It was a society doomed not by the evil passions of selfish individuals, because such passions always exist, but by an intellectual and spiritual failure of nerve that made the society incapable of coping with its situation, which is why the noble Brutus is even more at sea in the play than the unscrupulous and brutal Antony. The Roman-Hellenic world failed to evolve a religious pattern that was capable of grasping the world, of making sense of what was happening. The Platonic-Aristotelian politics of the good life proved ineffective for the public world, and Stoic-Epicurean thought proved incapable of saving the individual. The play presents three political responses to this failure. The crowd-master, the man of destiny, Caesar. The man who temporarily rides the storm, Antony. And Caesar's real successor, the man who is to establish Roman order for a time, Octavius. Brutus, who keeps himself independent, is the detached and philosophic individual.

Julius Caesar begins with a crowd scene. First things in Shakespeare are always important. There are three types of groups of people: societies, communities, and crowds. A society is something I can belong to, a community is something I can join, a crowd is something I add to. A society is defined by its function. A string quartet, for example, is a society with a specific function, to play works of music composed for a string quartet. It has a specific size, and you cannot change its size without changing the society. An individual is irreplaceable in his function to his society.

A community is an association of people with a common love. If you get a collection of people all of whom, say, love music, they form a community of music lovers. A cello player in a string quartet, for example, who hates music but plays because he must eat and playing a cello is all he knows, is a member of a society. He is not a member of the community of music lovers. A community has no definite size. If what they love is good—for example, God—the optimum size of a community is infinite. If what they love is bad—for example, marijuana—the optimum size is zero. In a community, also, "I" precedes "we."

The third form of a plurality of people is a crowd. Its members neither belong to nor join it, but merely add to it. The members of a crowd have nothing in common except togetherness. The individual is a contradiction in a crowd. The "we" precedes the "I." In itself the crowd has no function. When does a crowd or a mass or public develop? (1) When there are an insufficient number of societies and the individual can't find a meaningful function, so that he feels like a cog in a machine, or if he cannot belong to a society—he's unemployed, for example. (2) If communities disappear, individuals cease to love anything in particular and become incapable of making a choice between loves. Why can't they choose? In order to choose, there must be a number of values in terms of which a choice becomes meaningful. Lose those values, and one becomes incapable of a choice between loves. Combine that condition with an absence of society, and individuals become members of the crowd or the public. It has nothing whatever to do with education. Knowing a lot does not make one believe in anything. Knowledge can't make people believe in a society or give them a function in it. The educated and the rich can become members of the crowd and the public.

Describing the characteristics of the public, Kierkegaard writes in *The Present Age*:

> The real moment in time and the real situation being simultaneous with real people, each of whom is something: that is what helps to sustain the individual. But the existence of a public produces neither a situation nor simultaneity. . . . The man who has no opinion of an event at the actual moment accepts the opinion of the majority, or if he is quarrelsome, of the minority. But it must be remembered that both majority and minority are real people, and that is why the individual is assisted by adhering to them. A public, on the contrary, is an abstraction. . . . A people, an assembly or a man can change to such an extent that one may say: they are no longer the same; a public on the other hand can become the very opposite and

still be the same—a public. . . . A public is neither a nation, nor a
generation, nor a community, nor a society, nor these particular
men, for all these are only what they are through the concrete; no
single person who belongs to the public makes a real commitment;
for some hours of the day, perhaps, he belongs to the public—at
moments when he is nothing else, since when he really is what he is
he does not form part of the public. Made up of such individuals, of
individuals at the moments when they are nothing, a public is a kind
of gigantic something, an abstract and deserted void which is everything and nothing. But on this basis any one can arrogate to himself
a public, and just as the Roman Church chimerically extended its
frontiers by appointing bishops *in partibus infidelium,* so a public is
something which every one can claim, and even a drunken sailor
exhibiting a "peep-show" has dialectically absolutely the same right
to a public as the greatest man.

Kierkegaard says that if he tried "to imagine the public as a particular
person,"

I should perhaps think of one of the Roman emperors, a large well-
fed figure, suffering from boredom, looking only for the sensual
intoxication of laughter, since the divine gift of wit is not earthly
enough. And so for a change he wanders about, indolent rather
than bad, but with a negative desire to dominate. Every one who has
read the classical authors knows how many things a Caesar could try
out in order to kill time.

Kierkegaard then turns to the relationship of the public and the press,
the public's "dog": "In the same way the public keeps a dog to amuse
it. That dog is literary scum. If there is some one superior to the rest,
perhaps even a great man, the dog is set on him and the fun begins."
Eventually the public tires and says the press may stop, but "the public is unrepentant, for it is not they who own the dog—they only
subscribe."

With the proper gift, a man can turn the crowd into a mob—in other
words, a passionate crowd. The mob is a pseudosociety that sets out to do
something, but what it wishes to do is often both negative and general. The Cinna the Poet incident in *Julius Caesar* provides a very good
illustration.

3. *Pleb.* Your name, sir, truly.
Cin. Truly, my name is Cinna.
1. *Pleb.* Tear him to pieces! He's a conspirator.

Cin. I am Cinna the poet ! I am Cinna the poet!

4. Pleb. Tear him for his bad verses! Tear him for his bad verses!

Cin. I am not Cinna the conspirator.

4. Pleb. It is no matter; his name's Cinna! Pluck but his name out of his heart, and turn him going.

3. Pleb. Tear him, tear him! Come, brands, ho! firebrands! To Brutus', to Cassius'! Burn all!

(III.iii.28–42)

The function of the mob, to destroy, is general. It is incapable of making differentiations upon which a society depends.

The negative impulse is easier for an orator to instill in a crowd. A crowd is passive, and therefore notoriously fickle. In *Henry VI, Part Two,* during Jack Cade's rebellion, both Clifford and Jack Cade speak (IV.viii), and the crowd changes its mind with each speech. In *Julius Caesar,* Brutus speaks—the crowd approves. Antony speaks—"We'll hear him, we'll follow him, we'll die with him!" (III.ii.214). A comparison of the scenes from the two plays shows Shakespeare's dramatic development. In *Henry VI,* Clifford and Cade both speak in the same way. In *Julius Caesar,* the speeches of Brutus and Antony are differentiated, so we can see not only that the crowd is fickle, but also that Brutus doesn't understand how to move them, because he tries to allay their feelings, while Antony does understand how to move them, because he tries to excite their feelings—a successful technique. Directors should make the citizens supporting Brutus different from those supporting Antony.

In a community, defective lovers require political leaders. Shakespeare's successful leaders are Henry IV, Henry V, Richard III, Caesar, Antony. His unsuccessful leaders are Richard II, Henry VI, Brutus. A successful leader needs the theatrical gift of arousing emotions, of moving and persuading others, without appearing self-interested and moved himself. Just before the assassination, when Artemidorus tries to press his suit because it's one that "touches Caesar nearer" than the others, Caesar replies, "What touches us ourself shall be last serv'd" (III.i.7–8). Richard III first refuses a crown. Caesar, Casca tells us, twice puts back the crown Antony offers him—reluctantly though, he wants it a bit. Henry V and Antony assume a bluntness of manner. Antony tells the crowd,

> I come not, friends, to steal away your hearts.
> I am no orator, as Brutus is,
> But (as you know me all) a plain blunt man
> That love my friend.

(III.ii.221–24)

President Roosevelt used his smile and cigarette holder to show his disinterest, Churchill both uses gestures and keeps his hands in his pockets. Obviously one shouldn't sneer at such devices. A good leader understands that emotion precedes effective action. A study of anthropology, for example, is not a good beginning for eradicating race prejudice—one must arouse a passion for treating one's neighbor as one's self. A teacher must be a clown and arouse in his pupils a love of knowledge—the more love there is in the pupil, the less work for the teacher—he mustn't annoy or discourage the pupil. "Disingenuous compliances," Dr. Johnson called it. The love of power in a good politician—one whom one respects—is subservient to his zeal for a just society. Power is uppermost for a bad politician, a demagogue. He is like a writer who writes because he wants to be famous, rather than because he wants to write well. A good politician and a good teacher labor to abolish their own vocations.

The Peloponnesian War created a vacuum by the end of Greek society. The Third Punic War enlarged Roman society and created classes, the *Lumpenproletariat*. As Hegel wrote, "Minerva's owl takes flight in the evening," philosophy always arrives too late to give advice. The Greek's ethical cosmology formulated by Plato and Aristotle held that God, the unmoved Mover, and Nature are co-eternal and unrelated. In Aristotle, matter, in an effort to escape from the innate disorder of its temporal flux, falls in love with the Mover. In Plato an intermediary party, the Demiurge, loves the Ideas and then imposes them on matter. Matter is the limiting cause of evil, and the first task of man is to contemplate Ideas and will the good. It was assumed that sin is ignorance and that to know the good is to will it. But what can be done about the ignorant who are sinful, or those who are sinful because, even with knowledge of the good, they do not will it? Impose order on them. But if the way of wisdom is to withdraw from the temporal flux, how can the wise impose such order and control society? The best thing is to have the philosopher get hold of the king and advise him. Plato tried that, however, and it didn't work.

Ancient political philosophy is either archaistic or futuristic. Either the philosopher has to discover a timeless order, or a Hercules-savior must step in to save society from change. Aristotle's practical observation of a small middle class as the best rulers doesn't tell how society can be kept from growing and therefore changing. The successful man of action tended to be given a demiurgic, semidivine status. With the decline of the city-state and the development of agrarian Rome, the ideal of a wise man became detachment. The ideal took two slightly different forms, the philosophy of Epicurus, which Cassius professes, and the philosophy of the Stoics, such as Zeno, with which Brutus associates himself.

The man of action in the play is Caesar, the savior on horseback who appears to have arrived. Having become a legend, Caesar has to live up to the role. "Beware the ides of March," the Soothsayer tells him. Caesar's answer, "He is a dreamer. Let us leave him. Pass." (I.ii.24–25), illustrates the necessity for confident speech in a ruler. Such speech may not necessarily be a manifestation of pride, though it may become so. A general or an assertive leader in a time of sudden financial depression, for example, must give people the impression that he has no fear, or they'll lose heart, too. Like Caesar with the Soothsayer, he must exaggerate his confidence. Great men in politics like flatterers to give them confidence, which they can then radiate back. Sometimes they lose their sense of intuition and fail, a point that Caesar has perhaps reached. It is unfortunate for a ruler to be fatalistic, to make a religion of necessity, as Caesar begins to do when he rejects all warnings, "Seeing," as he says, "that death, a necessary end, / Will come when it will come" (II.ii.36–37). The most successful know the role fortune plays, they believe in the stars.

Antony has a sanguine character and he's also politically quite skillful, though not as skillful as he thinks he is. In a crisis he's in his element. He's in politics for fun, he craves excitement. He's not good at slow, patient plotting. After he has successfully turned the plebians into a mob, he says, almost indifferently,

> Now let it work. Mischief, thou art afoot,
> Take thou what course thou wilt.
>
> (III.ii.265–66)

Octavius or Caesar would never make such a playboy remark. Antony's bored. Later we'll see the tragedy of a bored man and bored woman. Antony impolitically gives himself away to Octavius in revealing his feelings about Lepidus:

> Octavius, I have seen more days than you;
> And though we lay these honours on this man
> To ease ourselves of divers sland'rous loads
> He shall but bear them as the ass bears gold.
>
> (IV.i.18–21)

Octavius would never talk that way. He is far too guarded and calculating, as he demonstrates in his sudden decision to take the right wing just before the battle of Philippi:

> *Ant.* Octavius, lead your battle softly on
> Upon the left hand of the even field.
>   *Oct.* Upon the right hand I. Keep thou the left.
>   *Ant.* Why do you cross me in this exigent?
>   *Oct.* I do not cross you; but I will do so.
>
>   (V.i.16–20)

Octavius is a very cold fish.

Cassius is a choleric man—a General Patton. He is passionate, short-tempered, sentimental. He is also politically shrewd. Before the assassination, he sees that Antony will be dangerous to the conspiracy and argues that he should be killed. Later he tries to conciliate Antony—"Your voice shall be as strong as any man's / In the disposing of new dignities." (III.i.177–78)—at the same time that he warns Brutus of the danger of letting Antony speak at Caesar's funeral. He also doesn't want to fight at Phillipi, "to set / Upon one battle all our liberties" (V.i.74–75), as Brutus does, and he probably has the better military knowledge. He is a follower of Epicurus, as he says explicitly at the end of the play (V.i.76–77). Epicurean thought was largely determinist and materialist, it sought to achieve the condition of imperturbability, *ataraxia*, it was moderate, and it rejected, as Lucretius especially did, the irrational and the superstitious as a destroyer of life. Its aim was to show that life was rational and that there was nothing to fear. Cassius is thus a comic character, because his emotional temperament is quite opposite to his Epicurean philosophy. Early on in the play he says that "the fault, dear Brutus, is not in our stars, / But in ourselves" (I.ii.140–41), and when Casca becomes superstitious about a thunderstorm, Cassius calmly and learnedly interprets the storm as an encouragement to the conspirators to act against Caesar (I.iii.57–99). Before the battle of Philippi, however, Cassius becomes superstitious:

> You know that I held Epicurus strong
> And his opinion. Now I change my mind
> And partly credit things that do presage.
>
>   (V.i.76–78)

And his desperate suicide is based on a misinterpretation.

There are no lymphatic characters in the play, "men that are fat," as Caesar says, "Sleek-headed men, and such as sleep a-nights" (I.ii.192–

93). It's too rough a time. Brutus is a melancholic. "I am not gamesome," he tells Cassius, "I do lack some part / Of that quick spirit that is in Antony" (I.ii.28–29), and he tells his wife Portia that she is as dear to him "as are the ruddy drops / That visit my sad heart" (II.i.289–90). Brutus at the same time strives for the Stoic virtue of *ataraxia*, of freedom from disturbance and perturbation. He says to the conspirators, to encourage and calm them,

> Good gentlemen, look fresh and merrily.
> Let not our looks put on our purposes,
> But bear it as our Roman actors do,
> With untir'd spirits and formal constancy.
>
> (II.i.224–27)

His detachment is most evident during the quarrel with Cassius, when he doesn't reveal that Portia has just died until he and Cassius have reconciled:

> *Cass.* I did not think you could have been so angry.
> *Bru.* O Cassius, I am sick of many griefs.
> *Cass.* Of your philosophy you make no use
> If you give place to accidental evils.
> *Bru.* No man bears sorrow better. Portia is dead.
>
> (IV.iii.143–47)

When Messala enters with hints of news about his wife, he pretends not to know about her death in order to serve as an example to his troops.

> *Mes.* Then like a Roman bear the truth I tell;
> For certain she is dead, and by strange manner.
> *Bru.* Why, farewell, Portia. We must die, Messala.
> With meditating that she must die once,
> I have the patience to endure it now.
> *Mes.* Even so great men great losses should endure.
> *Cass.* I have as much of this in art as you,
> But yet my nature could not bear it so.
>
> (IV.iii.187–95)

Brutus maintains the same calm in the presence of Caesar's ghost:

> *Bru.* Well; then I shall see thee again?
> *Ghost.* Ay, at Philippi.
> *Bru.* Why, I will see thee at Philippi then.
>
> [*Exit Ghost.*]

> Now I have taken heart thou vanishest,
> Ill spirit, I would hold more talk with thee.
>
> (IV.iii.284–88)

The one thing that can throw the detached man into perturbation, as Brutus shows, is the prospect of action:

> Since Cassius first did whet me against Caesar,
> I have not slept.
> Between the acting of a dreadful thing
> And the first motion, all the interim is
> Like a phantasma or a hideous dream.
>
> (II.i.61–65)

There is really a will in Brutus to commit suicide, and when he finally does so, he has to run on someone else's sword to establish contact with others.

Cassius is childishly envious—I swim better! The conspirators don't really have a good motive. Brutus, as a man of thought and feeling, wants to play the man of action. He is haunted by two ghosts. The invisible ghost that haunts him is his ancestor Brutus, who drove Tarquin "from the streets of Rome" (II.i.53–54)—he thinks of him just before he speaks of the "phantasma" that precedes the taking of action. The visible ghost that haunts Brutus is Caesar's. Brutus really has nothing against Caesar, "no personal cause to spurn at him" (II.i.11), and nothing has happened that he condemns. He kills a man he is fond of, a man of action whom he can never replace. Brutus and Cassius are Shakespeare's criticism of the ideal of detachment, an ideal that ends up in an absorption with the idea of death, and an ideal that is ultimately suicidal. Toynbee writes in *A Study of History* that the "logical goal" of Epicurean and Stoic *ataraxia* was "self-annihilation."

We can see in A. E. Housman's poetry a good contemporary example of the morbid outcome of the ideal of detachment. In one of the poems in *A Shropshire Lad*, he writes,

> From far, from eve and morning
>   And yon twelve-winded sky,
> The stuff of life to knit me
>   Blew hither: here am I.
>
> Now—for a breath I tarry
>   Nor yet disperse apart—

> Take my hand quick and tell me,
> What have you in your heart.
>
> Speak now, and I will answer;
> How shall I help you, say;
> Ere to the wind's twelve quarters
> I take my endless way.

In another poem, which refers to Rome, Housman writes,

> On Wenlock Edge the wood's in trouble,
> His forest fleece the Wrekin heaves;
> The gale, it plies the saplings double,
> And thick on Severn snow the leaves.
>
> 'Twould blow like this through holt and hanger
> When Uricon the city stood:
> 'Tis the old wind in the old anger,
> But then it threshed another wood.
>
> Then, 'twas before my time, the Roman
> At yonder heaving hill would stare:
> The blood that warms an English yeoman,
> The thoughts that hurt him, they were there.
>
> There, like the wind through woods in riot,
> Through him the gale of life blew high;
> The tree of man was never quiet:
> Then 'twas the Roman, now 'tis I.
>
> The gale, it plies the saplings double,
> It blows so hard, 'twill soon be gone:
> To-day the Roman and his trouble
> Are ashes under Uricon.

Time is up, and what's more you're not likely to enjoy yourself if you overstay your welcome!

Epictetus argued that the peace Caesar can bring is limited in nature, but that philosophers can give peace in all:

> Behold now, Caesar seems to provide us with profound peace, there are no wars any longer, nor battles, no brigandage on a large scale, nor piracy, but at any hour we may travel by land, or sail from the rising of the sun to its setting. Can he, then, at all provide us with

peace from fever too, and from shipwreck too, and from fire, or earthquake, or lightning? Come, can he give us peace from love? He cannot. From sorrow? From envy? He cannot—from absolutely none of these things. But the doctrine of the philosophers promises to give us peace from these troubles too. And what does it say? "Men, if you heed me, wherever you may be, whatever you may be doing, you will feel no pain, no anger, no compulsion, no hindrance, but you will pass your lives in tranquillity and in freedom from every disturbance." When a man has this kind of peace proclaimed to him, not by Caesar—why, how could *he* possibly proclaim it?—but proclaimed by God through the reason, is he not satisfied, when he is alone?

The detachment of Stoic philosophy cannot really admit love or pity, you must never sacrifice eternal calm, though you must do your best to help your fellow man. What are the modern forms of detachment? Professionalism—keep at the job. And go to psychoanalysts for a perfect personality.

Brutus is related to Hamlet. Hamlet knows he's in despair, but Brutus and other characters in *Julius Caesar* don't know. In *The Sickness Unto Death*, Kierkegaard emphasizes that unconscious despair is the most extreme form of despair, and he sees it as a condition of paganism. He praises the great "aesthetic" achievements of pagan societies, but rejects the pagan's aesthetic definition of spirit:

> No, it is not the aesthetic definition of spiritlessness which furnishes the scale for judging what is despair and what is not; the definition which must be used is the ethico-religious: either spirit / or the negative lack of spirit, spiritlessness. Every human existence which is not conscious of itself as spirit, or conscious of itself before God as spirit, every human existence which is not thus grounded transparently in God but obscurely reposes or terminates in some abstract universality (state, nation, etc.), or in obscurity about itself takes its faculties merely as active powers, without in a deeper sense being conscious whence it has them, which regards itself as an inexplicable something which is to be understood from without—every such existence, whatever it accomplishes, though it be the most amazing exploit, whatever it explains, though it were the whole of existence, however intensely it enjoys life aesthetically—every such existence is after all despair. It was this the old theologians meant when they talked about the virtues of the pagans being splendid vices. They

meant that the most inward experience of the pagan was despair, that the pagan was not conscious of himself before God as spirit.

"Hence it came about," Kierkegaard continues,

> . . . that the pagans judged self-slaughter so lightly, yea, even praised it, notwithstanding that for the spirit it is the most decisive sin, that to break out of existence in this way is rebellion against God. The pagan lacked the spirit's definition of the self, therefore he expressed such a judgment of *self*-slaughter—and this the same pagan did who condemned with moral severity theft, unchastity, etc. . . . The point in self-slaughter, that it is a crime against God, entirely escapes the pagan. One cannot say, therefore, that the self-slaughter was despair, which would be a thoughtless hysteron proteron; one must say that the fact that the pagan judged self-slaughter as he did was despair.

T. S. Eliot writes, in "Coriolan,"

> Cry what shall I cry?
> All flesh is grass:
>
> .   .   .   .
> Mother mother
> Here is a row of family portraits, dingy busts, all looking
>   remarkably Roman,
> Remarkably like each other, lit up successively by the flare
> Of a sweaty torchbearer, yawning.
> O hidden under the . . . Hidden under the . . . Where the
>   dove's foot rested and locked for a moment,
> A still moment, a repose of noon, under the upper
>   branches of noon's widest tree
> Under the breast feather stirred by the small wind after noon
> There the cyclamen spreads its wings, there the clematis
>   droops over the lintel
> O mother (not among these busts, all correctly inscribed)
> I a tired head among these heads
> Necks strong to bear them
> Noses to break the wind. . . .

As You Like It

[22 January 1947]

I don't know how it is in America, but in England students had to read
As You Like It a good deal in schools and act it too, and at that time I
found it dull. The trouble is that it's not a play for kids. It's very sophisticated, and only adults can understand what it's about. You have to be
acquainted with what it means to be a civilized person, and a child or
adolescent won't have such knowledge. Those who have read William
Empson's *Some Versions of Pastoral* will have to excuse me for taking over
some of his ideas on pastoral convention—they're very good. Those who
haven't read the book should read it.

Any idea of pastoral involves a conception of the primitive. Erwin Panofsky discusses three categories of primitivism: (1) "soft" primitivism,
(2) "hard" primitivism, and (3) the Hebraic idea of the Garden of Eden
and the Fall. Soft or positivistic primitivism depicted the primitive form
of existence as a Golden Age, in comparison with which the subsequent
phases of existence were nothing but successive stages of one prolonged
fall from grace. The first classical description of the Golden Age is found
in Hesiod's *Works and Days*. Hesiod discriminates five ages of man: the
age of gold, the age of silver, the age of bronze, the age of the heroic
demigods, and the age of iron. Compare Jaques's speech on the seven
ages of man (II.vii.139–66). Hesiod says of the "golden race of mortal
men" who lived in the first age:

> And they lived like gods without sorrow of heart, remote and free
> from toil and grief: miserable age rested not on them; but with legs
> and arms never failing they made merry with feasting beyond the
> reach of all evils. When they died, it was as though they were over-
> come with sleep, and they had all good things; for the fruitful earth
> unforced bare them fruit abundantly and without stint. They dwelt
> in ease and peace upon their lands with many good things, rich in
> flocks and loved by the blessed gods.

Of the fifth and last age, the Iron Age, Hesiod writes,

> Thereafter, would that I were not among the men of the fifth gener-
> ation, but either had died before or been born afterwards. For now
> truly is a race of iron, and men never rest from labour and sorrow by

day, and from perishing by night; and the gods shall lay sore trouble upon them. But, notwithstanding, even these shall have some good mingled with their evils. And Zeus will destroy this race of mortal men also when they come to have grey hair on the temples at their birth. The father will not agree with his children, nor the children with their father, nor guest with his host, nor comrade with comrade; nor will brother be dear to brother as aforetime. Men will dishonour their parents as they grow quickly old, and will carp at them, chiding them with bitter words, hard-hearted they, not knowing the fear of the gods. They will not repay their aged parents the cost of their nurture, for might shall be their right: and one man shall sack another's city. There will be no favour for the man who keeps his oath or for the just or for the good; but rather men will praise the evil-doer and his violent dealing. Strength will be right and reverence will cease to be; and the wicked will hurt the worthy man, speaking false words against him, and will swear an oath upon them. Envy, foul-mouthed, delighting in evil, with scowling face, will go along with wretched men one and all. And then Aidôs and Nemesis, with their sweet forms wrapped in white robes, will go from the wide-pathed earth and forsake mankind to join the company of the deathless gods: and bitter sorrows will be left for mortal men, and there will be no help against evil.

In Hesiod, civilization represents a continuous decline.

A modern sophisticated version of this idea is represented in Jean-Jacques Rousseau's conception of the noble savage, who is born good and free, but is corrupted by human institutions. Another version is D. H. Lawrence's opposition of the reflective and destructive mental consciousness to the dark gods of the blood of the instinctive man, who acts naturally. We can see the expression of these feelings in our selves. In an industrial civilization, in the big city, we live a certain type of life. We take summer vacations in the country among comparatively unselfconscious and simple people. We feel that they are happier than we are and think they behave better. We can understand Flaubert's saying of them that "*Ils sont dans le vrai,*" that they are right.

"Hard," or negativistic, primitivism, on the other hand, described by such writers as Lucretius, Virgil, and Pliny, as well as Hobbes, imagines the primitive form of existence as a truly bestial state, in which the condition of man in the world was brutal, disorderly, and savage. Through technical and intellectual progress, civilization brings the transformation of the brutal into an orderly, knowing, and civil world. In myth this conception is associated with Vulcan and the coming of fire, and with Hercules, Prometheus, and Demeter.

Would I like to have lived in an earlier period, when there was less knowledge, less power over disease, less plumbing and less police? No, I would not like to have lived then. If one thinks in terms of happiness, or in terms of human love, behavior is worse now. If one thinks in terms of knowledge and power and the potential for good, one can say there has been an advance. The Golden Age view is dangerous. It appeals not to conservatism but to anarchism and nihilism, a feeling that we are all sunk and had better withdraw. The withdrawal can take the form of an attempt to lead a simple life, to live in a simple way, or it can take the form of drink, whose object is to reduce self-consciousness. There can be a retreat from trying to do anything. A Marxist would point out that the Golden Age view is natural to people like myself who belong to a dying class. The hard view appeals to people, either reactionary or forward-looking, Fascists or Communists, who seek and really enjoy power. They are like Prince Hal. The Falstaffs of the world counter the hard view with a millennial appeal to the recovery of a Golden Age in the future. The soft Hesiodic view and the hard Lucretian view are both historical, though for Hesiod things get worse without reason.

The Hebraic view of the Garden of Eden is Hesiodic, but it is prehistoric and has to be told in mythical as well as historical terms, because the Fall is what conditions history. In Genesis there is not a race of people, there is first a man and a woman. And the first thing they do is eat of the tree of good and evil and get turned out of Eden. Their first act, the act that loses them their innocence, begins history. Like Lucretius, the Hebraic view asserts that all human beings are born bad and have to redeem themselves. But there is a different attitude toward history and civilization in the Hebraic view of primitivism. To the soft Hesiodic view, things are gloomy because every advance is really a decline—the cycle always has to begin with the primitive. This is Spengler's premise. The hard view, that every advance of law and knowledge brings progress, deifies historical process. The Hebraic and Christian view is that civilization is neutral. The knowledge of good and evil increases, but the knowledge in itself is ambiguous. It is a temptation. A man can behave better through understanding, or worse. Neither knowledge nor ignorance has anything to do with the perversion of the will through the love of self, and neither can make you choose good or reject evil. Correspondingly, you cannot have advances in science, including the cure of diseases, without having both good and bad results. One attempt to resolve this problem is to declare, like Hesiod, that it's better not to change anything. The other view, one held by Victorians, is more sure that things will get better and better—but today's history has shown us that such a view is imaginary. But we can't turn to Hesiod completely, because the radius of evil has simply grown too great.

In the Old Irish myth depicted in "The Sea-God's Address to Bran," translated by Kuno Meyer, paradise does not degenerate through historical succession nor is it reclaimed through hard primitivism's promise of the final subjugation of nature. It is, rather, redeemed from the loss imposed by man's sinful quest for independence. Manannan, the sea-god, sings to Bran, who is at sea in his coracle:

> Sea-horses glisten in summer
> As far as Bran can stretch his glance:
> Rivers pour forth a stream of honey
> In the land of Manannan, son of Ler.

> The sheen of the main on which thou art,
> The dazzling white of the sea on which thou rowest about—
> Yellow and azure are spread out,
> It is a light and airy land.

> Speckled salmon leap from the womb
> Out of the white sea on which thou lookest:
> They are calves, they are lambs of fair hue,
> With truce, without mutual slaughter.

> Though thou seest but one chariot-rider
> In the Pleasant Plain of many flowers,
> There are many steeds on its surface,
> Though thou dost not see them.

> Large is the plain, numerous is the host,
> Colours shine with pure glory:
> A white stream of silver, stairs of gold
> Afford a welcome with all abundance.

> An enchanting game, most delicious,
> They play over the luscious wine:
> Men and gentle women under a bush
> Without sin, without transgression.

> Along the top of a wood
> Thy coracle has swum across ridges:

There is a wood laden with beautiful fruit
Under the prow of thy little skiff.

A wood with blossom and with fruit
On which is the vine's veritable fragrance,
A wood without decay, without defect,
On which is foliage of golden hue.

From the beginning of creation we are
Without old age, without consummation of clay:
Hence we expect not there should be frailty—
The sin has not come to us.

An evil day when the serpent came
To the father into his citadel!
He has perverted the ages in this world,
So that there came decay which was not original.

By greed and lust he has slain us,
Whereby he has ruined the noble race:
The withered body has gone to the fold of torment,
An everlasting abode of torture.

It is a law of pride in this world
To believe in the creatures, to forget God:
Overthrow by diseases, and old age,
Destruction of the beguiled soul.

A noble salvation will come
From the King who has created us:
A white law will come over seas—
Besides being God, He will be man.

The everlasting garden is the primitive site of the pastoral tradition, but though at the end of Dante's *Purgatorio*, Dante arrives at the Garden of Eden, beyond that is the *Civitas Dei*, the City of God, which is the opposite of the pastoral convention.

The pastoral is an aristocratic form. It begins roughly with Theocritus, and, in a "hard" version, Virgil's *Georgics*. The landscapes of the medieval works of the *Roman de la Rose* and *Pearl* are presented quite differently. The classical form of the pastoral returns in the Renaissance. The greatest Renaissance works in the genre are Góngora's *Soledades* and, in English, Sidney's *Arcadia* and Milton's *Lycidas*. In these works, shepherds speak in extremely formal, sophisticated, and aristocratic language, presenting civilized language in a bucolic setting. These people, as peasants, *sont dans le vrai* in their life. Lao-tse would read them as corrupting their innocence through their speech, since in their simpleness they have the power to be free and are better than their social betters. But in order to be better in the pastoral form, they must speak very well.

On the other side, related to hard primitivism, the shepherds are like the nobles whose words they use. There is the same relation between the governors and the governed, between the shepherd and nature—man is the ruler of nature, the sheep are the ruled. The good shepherd protects the sheep from the wolves, the bad shepherd neglects them.

Other forms of pastoral that Empson deals with include the animal in contrast with man. An animal is undisturbed by self-consciousness, and really acts instinctively—what he wills and what he does are the same. Walt Whitman writes in *Leaves of Grass*:

> I think I could turn and live with animals, they are so placid
>   and self-contain'd,
> I stand and look at them long and long.
>
> They do not sweat and whine about their condition,
> They do not lie awake in the dark and weep for their sins,
> They do not make me sick discussing their duty to God,
> Not one is dissatisfied, not one is demented with the mania of
>   owning things.
> Not one kneels to another, nor to his kind that lived thousands
>   of years ago,
> Not one is respectable or unhappy over the whole earth.

For instance, "If men were as much men as lizards are lizards, / They'd be worth looking at"—the idea of lizards is better.

Children compose another kind of pastoral in their freedom from self-consciousness and sex, and in their detachment. They are incapable of hiding things. If you want to decide whether the Garden of Eden is true, just watch children and you see it work. Both Alice in Wonderland and Jaques can't conceal anything. The fool, the Fool in *King Lear* for example, provides another form of pastoral. The fool is fearless and untroubled by convention—like a child, he isn't even aware of convention. He's not all there, but he is prophetic, because through his craziness he either sees more or dares to say more.

Another pastoral figure is the outlaw, who provides a kind of inverted pastoral, a view from the other side of the tracks: Falstaff, Shylock, and John Gay's *The Beggar's Opera* are examples. So are gangster films and detective stories, though not Mickey Spillane's Mike Hammer series or Chandler's studies of a criminal milieu. The primary interest in the detective story is the identification of the murderer. If all the characters are potential criminals, that interest disappears. The best setting for a detective story is the vicarage or college, both of which correspond to the Edenic pastoral garden. You begin with a discovery of a corpse, and the story then involves guilt, the entry of the law, detection, the apprehension of the murderer, the exit of the law, and the renewal of pastoral peace. False innocence is replaced by true innocence, and the city or court is contrasted with the field or village, a humanized nature that is comparable to that depicted in ordinary pastoral.

Another version of pastoral lumps the village and city together over against nature in the raw. The modern feeling for wild nature is a product of industrialization, in which civilized life is felt to annihilate the individual in the mass. The *idiotes*, the private citizen, is opposed by the *banausos*, the tiny specialist with a nondirected, aimless ambition. Wild nature becomes a place of adventure, in which I can't be a *banausos*, a specialist—wild nature fights me and forces me to become a whole individual, gives me a *raison d'être*. Earlier society saw rough nature as an unpleasant necessity. Wordsworth's description of the city of London in *The Prelude*, presents the modern view of the city as the enemy of the individual:

> Oh, blank confusion! And a type not false
> Of what the mighty City is itself
> To all except a Straggler here and there,
> To the whole Swarm of its inhabitants;
> An undistinguishable world to men,
> The slaves unrespited of low pursuits,
> Living amid the same perpetual flow
> Of trivial objects, melted and reduced
> To one identity, by differences
> That have no law, no meaning, and no end.

To this we may contrast Sydney Smith's comment: "O it's terrible in the country, one feels that the whole creation is going to expire at tea-time."

Of all of Shakespeare's plays, *As You Like It* is the greatest paean to civilization and to the nature of a civilized man and woman. It is dominated by Rosalind, a triumph of civilization, who, like the play itself, fully embodies man's capacity, in Pascal's words, "to deny, to believe, and to doubt well"—*nier, croire, et douter bien*. The play presents a balance of dialectical opposites: the country versus the court, detachment versus love, honesty versus poetry, nature versus fortune, nature and fortune versus art. We begin in an orchard, a cultivated garden, and the first name we hear is Adam. The resonances are hardly unconscious on Shakespeare's part, since Adam and Orlando are going to be driven out of the garden. At the same time that the garden is parallel to Eden, however, it is different. The biblical Adam shuts himself out of Eden through guilt. Here Orlando is driven out in innocence by an older brother who is jealous of his nicer brother. Orlando complains that Oliver is training him in pastoral rusticity:

> You shall hear me. My father charg'd you in his will to give me good education. You have train'd me like a peasant, obscuring and hiding from me all gentlemanlike qualities. The spirit of my father grows strong in me, and I will no longer endure it. Therefore allow me such exercises as may become a gentleman, or give me the poor allottery my father left me by testament.
>
> (I.i.69–78)

This is an appeal to hard primitivism, to the kind of military exercises recommended for Jesuits by St. Ignatius Loyola.

The other exile is of Duke Senior by Duke Frederick, who possesses what doesn't belong to him and represents the brutal element in civilization. Duke Senior is forced to retire to the pastoral life of the Forest of Arden, which Charles initially describes in terms of soft primitivism:

> They say he is already in the Forest of Arden, and a many merry men with him; and there they live like the old Robin Hood of England. They say many young gentlemen flock to him every day, and fleet the time carelessly as they did in the golden world.
>
> (I.i.120–25)

Rosalind and Celia appear, just emerging from the innocence of childhood, another pastoral form. They talk of nature and fortune a little, a bit uncertain as to which is which (I.ii.34–53). Both the Duke and Orlando are in the forest through acts of fortune. But the nature of the people involved is also a concern. Oliver is by nature envious, and there is something in the nice Orlando to arouse his envy. The same is true of Duke Frederick's relation to Duke Senior. Compare Antonio's relation to Prospero in *The Tempest*. Nature gives the characters the wit to flout fortune. There is no distinction, rightly none, between nature and art in human beings, because we are inherently artifice-making creatures and have a psychosomatic constitution in which mind affects matter. The use of nature in *As You Like It* depends first on the characters themselves and then on fortune.

In bidding farewell to Orlando, M. le Beau says, "Hereafter, in a better world than this, / I shall desire more love and knowledge of you" (I.ii.295–96). The court is pictured as an evil from which the good withdraw, either compulsorily, as in the case of Orlando and Rosalind, or voluntarily through love for the exiles, as in the case of Adam and Celia, though to leave even a court represented as evil is exile. Orlando, in the language of soft primitivism, says to Adam,

> O good old man, how well in thee appears
> The constant service of the antique world,
> When service sweat for duty, not for meed!
> Thou art not for the fashion of these times,
> Where none will sweat but for promotion,
> And having that, do choke their service up
> Even with the having. It is not so with thee.

(II.iii.56–62)

In the language of hard primitivism, he asks Adam earlier, when Adam tells him he must leave,

> What, wouldst thou have me go and beg my food,
> Or with a base and boist'rous sword enforce
> A thievish living on the common road?

(II.iii.31–33)

"O, how full of briers is this working-day world!" Rosalind says to Celia, and Celia responds, "They are but burrs, cousin, thrown upon thee in holiday foolery. If we walk not in the trodden paths, our very petticoats will catch them" (I.iii.12–15). There is a danger in the departure from regular society.

Duke Senior, in the Forest of Arden, first adopts a conventional pastoral posture:

> Now, my co-mates and brothers in exile,
> Hath not old custom made this life more sweet
> Than that of painted pomp? Are not these woods
> More free from peril than the envious court?
> Here feel we but the penalty of Adam,
> The seasons' difference; as, the icy fang

And churlish chiding of the winter's wind,
Which, when it bites and blows upon my body
Even till I shrink with cold, I smile, and say
"This is no flattery; these are counsellors
That feelingly persuade me what I am."
Sweet are the uses of adversity,
Which, like the toad, ugly and venemous,
Wears yet a precious jewel in his head;
And this our life, exempt from public haunt,
Find tongues in trees, books in the running brooks,
Sermons in stones, and good in everything:
I would not change it.

The First Lord immediately puts the Duke's speech in perspective:

Happy is your Grace
That can translate the stubbornness of fortune
Into so quiet and so sweet a style.

(II.i.1–20)

So the speech of Duke Senior is not priggish—he hasn't chosen his condition.

The first Lord's subsequent description of Jaques's homily on a hunted and wounded deer puts the hardness of life in the wood and in the court together—even other deer abandon the one wounded by hunters, as men abandon someone who is bankrupt:

"Poor deer," quoth he, "thou mak'st a testament
As worldlings do, giving thy sum of more
To that which had too much." Then, being alone,
Left and abandoned of his velvet friends:
"'Tis right!" quoth he, "thus misery doth part
The flux of company." Anon a careless herd,
Full of the pasture, jumps along by him
And never stays to greet him: "Ay," quoth Jaques,
"Sweep on, you fat and greasy citizens!
'Tis just the fashion! Wherefore do you look
Upon that poor and broken bankrupt there?"
Thus most invectively he pierceth through
The body of the country, city, court;
Yea, and of this our life, swearing that we

> Are mere usurpers, tyrants, and what's worse,
> To fright the animals and to kill them up
> In their assign'd and native dwelling place.
>
> (II.i.47–63)

Shakespeare treats Petrarchan literary conventions with a sophisticated sensibility in his new pastoral. The love of Silvius and Phoebe, the conventional shepherd and shepherdess, foreshadows that of Orlando and Rosalind, but Rosalind's view of Silvius and Phoebe is, "I must get you out of this madness." On the one hand, she chides Silvius for being too much of a doormat and Phoebe for being vain:

> You are a thousand times a properer man
> Than she a woman. 'Tis such fools as you
> That makes the world full of ill-favour'd children.
> 'Tis not her glass, but you, that flatters her,
> And out of you she sees herself more proper
> Than any of her lineaments can show her.
> But, mistress, know yourself. Down on your knees,
> And thank heaven, fasting, for a good man's love;
> For I must tell you friendly in your ear,
> Sell when you can! you are not for all markets.
>
> (III.v.51–60)

On the other hand, Rosalind is aware that, as Amiens sings in his song, "Most friendship is feigning, most loving mere folly" (II.vii.181). Rosalind tells Orlando, "Love is merely a madness, and, I tell you, deserves as well a dark house and a whip as madmen do; and the reason why they are not so punish'd and cured is that the lunacy is so ordinary that the whippers are in love too" (III.ii.420–24). "Yet I profess curing it by counsel," Rosalind says, and she describes how she once cured a lover of such lunacy:

He was to imagine me his love, his mistress; and I set him every day to woo me. At which time would I, being but a moonish youth, grieve, be effeminate, changeable, longing, and liking, proud, fantastical, apish, shallow, inconstant, full of tears, full of smiles; for every passion something and for no passion truly anything, as boys and women are for the most part cattle of this colour; would now like him, now loathe him; then entertain him, then forswear him; now weep for him, then spit at him; that I drave my suitor from his mad humour of love to a living humour of madness, which was, to forswear the full stream of the world and to live in a nook merely monastic. And thus I cur'd him.

(III.ii.425–42)

A mistaken attachment can lead to a complete withdrawal.

Touchstone says to Audrey, quite correctly, that "the truest poetry is the most feigning, and lovers are given to poetry; and what they swear in poetry may be said, as lovers, they do feign" (III.iii.19–22). In a pastoral reversed, Touchstone stands up both for love, however unfaithful, and for the city: "as a wall'd town is more worthier than a village, so is the forehead of a married man more honourable than the bare brow of a bachelor; and by how much defence is better than no skill, by so much is a horn more precious than to want" (III.iii.59–64).

Jaques is a detached man, as Rosalind sees clearly in the following dialogue:

> *Jaq.* I have neither the scholar's melancholy, which is emulation; nor the musician's, which is fantastical; nor the courtier's, which is proud; nor the soldier's, which is ambitious; nor the lawyer's, which is politic; nor the lady's, which is nice; nor the lover's, which is all these: but it is a melancholy of mine own, compounded of many simples, extracted from many objects, and indeed the sundry contemplation of my travels, in which rumination wraps me in a most humourous sadness.
>
> *Ros.* A traveller! By my faith, you have great reason to be sad, I fear you have sold your own lands to see other men's. Then to have seen much and to have nothing is to have rich eyes and poor hands.
>
> *Jaq.* Yes, I have gain'd my experience.

Rosalind answers, "And your experience makes you sad. I had rather have a fool to make me merry than experience to make me sad—and to travel for it too!" (IV.i.10–29). Jaques is self-exiled.

Rosalind keeps a dialectical balance. When Orlando says that he will die if his love is not requited, Rosalind says,

> No, faith, die by attorney. The poor world is almost six thousand years old, and in all this time there was not any man died in his own person, videlicet, in a love cause. Troilus had his brains dash'd out with a Grecian club; yet he did what he could to die before, and he is one of the patterns of love. Leander, he would have liv'd many a fair year though Hero had turn'd nun, if it had not been for a hot midsummer night; for (good youth) he went but forth to wash him

in the Hellespont, and being taken with the cramp, was drown'd; and the foolish chroniclers of that age found it was "Hero of Sestos." But these are all lies. Men have died from time to time, and worms have eaten them, but not for love.

(IV.i.94–108)

At the same time, Rosalind confesses to Celia how much she loves Orlando: "O coz, coz, coz, my pretty little coz, that thou didst know how many fathom deep I am in love! But it cannot be sounded. My affection hath an unknown bottom, like the Bay of Portugal" (IV.i.209–13).

Touchstone stands up for the similarity of the court and the rustic in his argument with Corin:

> *Cor.* Sir, I am a true labourer; I earn that I eat, get that I wear; owe no man hate, envy no man's happiness; glad of other men's good, content with my harm; and the greatest of my pride is to see my ewes graze and my lambs suck.
>
> *Touch.* That is another simple sin in you: to bring the ewes and the rams together and to offer to get your living by the copulation of cattle; to be bawd to a bell-wether, and to betray a she-lamb of a twelvemonth to a crooked-pated old cuckoldly ram, out of all reasonable match. If thou beest not damn'd for this, the devil himself will have no shepherds; I cannot see else how thou shouldst scape.
>
> (III.ii.77–90)

The representation of wild nature in the lioness contributes to the apparent absurdity of the resolution. Through grace, Oliver overcomes his temptation to let the lioness eat Orlando, and thus converted, he marries Celia. Duke Frederick meets a hermit in the desert—which is important—and is converted by him both from his intention of taking vengeance upon his brother in the forest and "from the world" (V.iv.168). He leaves his crown to Duke Senior. Nature has become a place of repentance, from which the exiles can return. Oliver and Duke Frederick retire to the country not because of its pastoral superiority, but because it is necessary for them to repent—just as, perhaps, the exiles have learned through the suffering of exile. Nature is not a place to retire as *idiotes*, but as a preparation for a return to the world. For others, like Duke Frederick, the retirement to the country is a penance.

Goethe writes, "*Es bildet ein Talent sich in der Stille, / Sich ein Charakter in dem Strom der Welt*," talent builds itself in quietness, character in the stream of the world. Jaques remains in the country. Like Shylock he won't join the dance, like Hamlet his involvement with society is un-happy, like Caliban he is unassimilable. He is too self-conscious, he must go and see things, there is much to be learned—he has an obstinate intellect, as opposed to Caliban's passion. Civilization is a dance between the ocean of barbarism, which is a unity, and the desert of triviality, which is diverse. One must keep a dialectical balance, and keep both faith—through will, and humor—through intellect. Jaques has the lat-ter, Rosalind has both, so she is able to get the returning exiles to join in the rite of dance.

Alice dances so with Tweedledum and Tweedledee:

> ... she took hold of both hands at once: the next moment they were dancing round in a ring. This seemed quite natural (she remem-bered afterwards), and she was not even surprised to hear music playing: it seemed to come from the tree under which they were dancing, and it was done (as well as she could make it out) by the branches rubbing one across the other, like fiddles and fiddle-sticks. . . . "I don't know when I began it, but somehow I felt as if I had been singing it a long long time!"

Twelfth Night

[5 February 1947]

Twelfth Night is one of Shakespeare's unpleasant plays. It is not a comedy for schoolchildren, as is commonly felt. Most of the characters are not individual enough to provide comic depth, and at the time Shakespeare wrote the play, he seems to have been averse to pleasantness. The comic convention in which the play is set prevents him from giving direct expression to this mood, but the mood keeps disturbing, even spoiling, the comic feeling. One has a sense, and nowhere more strongly than in the songs, of there being inverted commas around the "fun." The plays that followed *Twelfth Night* are the tragedies, as well as *Measure for Measure* and *All's Well That Ends Well*, which are considered his dark comedies.

Shakespeare wrote four different kinds of comedy, the first two of classical derivation:

(1) Plautine comedy in *The Comedy of Errors* and *The Two Gentlemen of Verona*, in which plot is supreme and characterization unimportant.

(2) Comedy of humours, like Ben Jonson's, in *The Taming of the Shrew*. Katherina, the shrew, is a humour character. Shakespeare later uses humours for tragedy as well—humour becomes the dominant passion of the tragic heroes. *Hamlet* and *Timon of Athens* are tragedies of humour.

(3) Comedy of character. These comedies represent individuals in relation to their social milieu, offering intricate contrasts and interrelations between the characters and their social surroundings. Shakespeare is always conscious of the individual *apart* from his social status and milieu at the same time that he understands the individual as a representative of his class. Examples of comedy of character include *Love's Labour's Lost*, *The Merchant of Venice*, which particularly examines the "outsider" Shylock, *Much Ado About Nothing*, in which the outsider is John the Bastard, *Henry IV*, in which the Prince in the tavern presents a contrast between the individual and his social surroundings, and *As You Like It*, in which the social milieux of the country and court are contrasted, and in which Rosalind's disguise flows from her character—it is not merely a convenient device.

(4) Comedy of emotion, the lyrical drama of the last plays, which one hesitates to call comedies: *Pericles, Cymbeline, The Winter's Tale,* and *The Tempest.* These plays are all related to the masque and opera. They present plots that are subordinate not to character but to patterns of passionate emotions, and they are comedies of conversion. Characters are transformed, though they are often too scorched or old to be very interesting. The plays are dramatizations of the human psyche rather than of people as people you would know or have a drink with.

Twelfth Night cannot be classified under any of these four types. What is the reason? Probably that Shakespeare intended it for a more intimate audience than at the Globe Theater, one which was more select and not so large, and for whom a pleasant comedy would have been inappropriate.

Shakespeare returns to the use of twins in the play, as in *The Comedy of Errors.* Viola's motivation for disguising herself is capricious—it is necessary only to set the plot in motion—and the shipwreck has merely a technical use, to get the characters in place. In the last plays, storms and shipwrecks are elaborately developed as symbols of death, rebirth, and purgation by suffering.

The characters in *Twelfth Night* are rich and idle, and their society is pervasively melancholic, which contrasts with the social characteristics and mood of the characters in *The Merchant of Venice.* Both plays have characters who dislike music, Shylock in *The Merchant of Venice* and Malvolio in *Twelfth Night,* but the characters who welcome music in Illyria are more uniformly saddened by it. Orsino sounds this note in the play's opening speech:

> If music be the food of love, play on,
> Give me excess of it, that, surfeiting,
> The appetite may sicken, and so die.
> That strain again! It had a dying fall;
> O, it came o'er my ear like the sweet sound
> That breathes upon a bank of violets,
> Stealing and giving odour! Enough, no more!
> 'Tis not so sweet now as it was before.
>
> (I.i.1–8)

Compare to this Lorenzo's lyrical speech to Jessica about "the sounds of music" in Belmont:

> There's not the smallest orb which thou behold'st
> But in his motion like an angel sings,
> Still quiring to the young-ey'd cherubins;
> Such harmony is in immortal souls;
> But whilst this muddy vesture of decay
> Doth grossly close it in, we cannot hear it.
>
> (V.i.60–65)

Illyria, in *Twelfth Night*, is generally more self-conscious, weary, and less productive than the society in *The Merchant of Venice*, which is busy making money, trading, and doing business. The attitude toward money is also different in the two plays. The characters in *The Merchant of Venice* are careless about it, throwing it about freely and generously. In contrast, there is cynicism about money in *Twelfth Night*, an awareness that services must be paid for, that people can be bought, and that money can get you what you want. There are many examples of this attitude. Sir Toby says Sir Andrew Aguecheek is "as tall a man as any's in Illyria" because "he has three thousand ducats a year" (I.iii.20–23). Viola assures the Sea Captain she will pay him "bounteously" (I.ii.52) for his help in presenting her in disguise as Cesario to Duke Orsino. And Olivia, when she falls in love with Cesario, thinks of what she can "bestow of him" to win him, "For youth is bought more oft than begg'd or borrow'd" (III.iv.2–3).

Women have become dominant in *Twelfth Night* and take the initiative. Malvolio lacks self-confidence and self-control and is weak, and with the exception of Antonio, the other men are passive. The women are the only people left who have any will, which is the sign of a decadent society. Maria, in love with Sir Toby, tricks him into marrying her. Olivia starts wooing Cesario from the first moment she sees him, and Viola is a real man-chaser. All the ladies in this play get what they want.

The society in *Twelfth Night* is beginning to smell gamey. The characters in the play are out for gain, they are generally seedy, and they are often malicious. Unlike Falstaff, who also drinks and is idle, and who might at first seem comparable, especially to Sir Toby, they are neither wise and intelligent, nor full of self-knowledge, nor capable of real love. The turnabouts in the marriages at the end are emblematic. The Duke, who up till the moment of recognition had thought himself in love with Olivia, drops her like a hot potato and falls in love with Viola on the spot, and Sebastian accepts Olivia's proposal of marriage within two minutes of meeting her for the first time. Both appear contemptible, and it is impossible to imagine that either will make a good husband. Unlike

Falstaff, these people emerge victorious and have their nasty little triumph over life. Falstaff is defeated by life.

The three famous songs in *Twelfth Night* are in many ways keys to its tone. "O mistress mine, where are you roaming?" is in the "gather ye rosebuds," carpe diem tradition of Andrew Marvell's "To His Coy Mistress":

> O mistress mine, where are you roaming?
> O, stay and hear! Your true-love's coming,
> > That can sing both high and low.
> Trip no further, pretty sweeting;
> Journeys end in lovers meeting,
> > Every wise man's son doth know.
>
> What is love? 'Tis not hereafter;
> Present mirth hath present laughter;
> > What's to come is still unsure:
> In delay there lies no plenty;
> Then come kiss me, sweet and twenty!
> > Youth's a stuff will not endure.

(II.iii.40–53)

These lines are charming enough, if taken playfully, but suppose one asks, "For what kind of person would these lines be an expression of their true feelings?" True love certainly does not plead its cause by telling the beloved that love is transitory; and no young man, trying to seduce a girl, would mention her age. He takes her youth and his own for granted. Taken seriously, as I mentioned in the lecture on *Much Ado About Nothing*, these lines are the voice of aged lust, with a greed for possession that reflects the fear of its own death. Shakespeare forces this awareness on our consciousness by making the audience to the song Sir Toby and Sir Andrew, a couple of seedy old drunks.

The conventions of "O mistress mine" developed from parts of the courtly love tradition. We can still find residues of it in A. E. Housman's poem:

> If truth in hearts that perish
> > Could move the powers on high,
> I think the love I bear you
> > Should make you not to die.
>
> Sure, sure, if stedfast meaning,
> > If single thought could save,

The world might end to-morrow,
   You should not see the grave.

This long and sure-set liking,
   This boundless will to please,
—Oh, you should live for ever
   If there were help in these.

But now, since all is idle,
   To this lost heart be kind,
Ere to a town you journey
   Where friends are ill to find.

The most metrically elaborate of all of Shakespeare's songs is "Come away, come away, death," which also plays upon a courtly love convention, the idea of the "fair cruel maid":

Come away, come away, death,
   And in sad cypress let me be laid.
Fly away, fly away, breath;
   I am slain by a fair cruel maid.
My shroud of white, stuck all with yew,
     O, prepare it!
My part of death, no one so true
     Did share it.

Not a flower, not a flower sweet,
   On my black coffin let there be strown;
Not a friend, not a friend greet
   My poor corpse, where my bones shall be thrown.
A thousand thousand sighs to save,
     Lay me, O, where
Sad true lover never find my grave,
     To weep there!

(II.iv.52–67)

This is not the folk song that the Duke's request for "that old and antique song we heard last night" (II.iv.3) would lead us to expect, but a sophisticated treatment of a folk theme. What began as a theme of courtly love for higher classes and progressed to folk ballads has now returned to a sophisticated form. This process often occurs with conventional material: ballads provide matter for epics, courtly love themes move through folk songs to pastorals, and in America hymns are transformed into spirituals.

"Come away, come away, death" also casts light on the Duke. Shake-speare has so placed the song as to make it seem an expression of the Duke's real character. Beside him sits the disguised Viola, for whom the Duke is not a playful fancy but a serious passion. It would be painful enough for her if the man she loved loved another, but it is much worse to be made to see that he loves only himself, and it is this insight that at this point Viola has to endure. In the dialogue about the difference be-tween man's love and woman's that follows the song, Viola is, I think, being anything but playful when she says,

> We men say more, swear more; but indeed
> Our shows are more than will; for still we prove
> Much in our vows but little in our love.
>
> (II.iv.119–21)

The Duke is interested in being either a faithful Tristan or a dashing Don Juan. He ends up marrying the first woman who asks him.

The third of the famous songs in *Twelfth Night* is sung by the clown at the end of the play, when the stage is cleared:

> When that I was and a little tiny boy,
>   With hey, ho, the wind and the rain,
> A foolish thing was but a toy,
>   For the rain it raineth every day.
>
> But when I came to man's estate,
>   With hey, ho, the wind and the rain,
> 'Gainst knaves and thieves men shut their gate,
>   For the rain it raineth every day.
>
> But when I came, alas! to wive,
>   With hey, ho, the wind and the rain,
> By swaggering could I never thrive,
>   For the rain it raineth every day.
>
> But when I came unto my beds,
>   With hey, ho, the wind and the rain,
> With tosspots still had drunken heads,
>   For the rain it raineth every day.
>
> A great while ago the world begun,
>   With hey, ho, the wind and the rain;
> But that's all one, our play is done,
>   And we'll strive to please you every day.
>
> (V.i.398–417)

These are the last words of the play, its epilogue, and it is a nonsense poem. What the clown is really saying is that nothing in human life makes sense.

There is a disparity between a writer's life and what he puts into his work. The greater the writer's sense of genre and the more he understands his characters, the greater this disparity becomes. The plays that follow *Twelfth Night* are dark. The characters bring destruction upon themselves, in contrast to classical tragedy in which their fall is caused by forces external to them, and they do not atone through their suffering. The darkness is pulled down over their heads. The plays are gloomy. In Shakespeare's last plays, the characters survive and are changed for the better by their suffering.

Hamlet

[12 February 1947]

If a work is quite perfect, it arouses less controversy and there is less to say about it. Curiously, everyone tries to identify with Hamlet, even actresses—and in fact Sarah Bernhardt did play Hamlet, and I am glad to say she broke her leg in doing it. One says that one is like a character, but one does not say, "This is me." One says, "I am more like Claudius, perhaps, than I am like Laertes," or "I would rather be Benedick than Orsino." But when a reader or spectator is inclined to say, "This is me," it becomes slightly suspicious. It is suspicious when all sorts of actors say, "This is a part I would like to do," not "This is a part I have a talent to do." I would question whether anyone has succeeded in playing Hamlet without appearing ridiculous. *Hamlet* is a tragedy where there is a part left open, as a part is left open for an improvisational actor in farce. But here the part is left open for a tragedian.

Shakespeare took a great deal of time over this play. With a writer of Shakespeare's certainty of execution, a delay of this kind is a sign of some dissatisfaction. He has not got the thing he wants. T. S. Eliot has called the play an "artistic failure." Hamlet, the one inactive character, is not well integrated into the play and not adequately motivated, though the active characters are excellent. Polonius is a pseudo-practical dispenser of advice, who is a kind of voyeur where the sex life of his children is concerned. Laertes likes to be a dashing man-of-the-world who visits all houses—but don't you touch my sister! And he is jealous of Hamlet's intellect. Rosencrantz and Guildenstern are yes men. Gertrude is portrayed as a woman who likes to be loved, who likes to have romance in her life. And Horatio is not too bright, though he has read a lot and can repeat it.

The plays of the period in which Shakespeare wrote *Hamlet* have great richness, but one is not sure that at this point he even wants to be a dramatist. *Hamlet* offers strong evidence of this indecision, because it indicates what Shakespeare might have done if he had had an absolutely free hand: he might well have confined himself to dramatic monologues. The soliloquies in *Hamlet* as well as other plays of this period are *detachable* both from the character and the plays. In earlier as well as later works they are more integrated. The "To be or not to be" soliloquy in *Hamlet* (III.i.56–90) is a clear example of a speech that can be separated from both the character and the play, as are the speeches of Ulysses on time in *Troilus and Cressida* (III.iii.145–80), the King on honor in *All's Well That Ends Well* (II.iii.124–48), and the Duke on death in *Measure for Measure* (III.i.5–41).

Shakespeare, at this time, is interested in various technical problems. The first is the relation between prose and verse in the plays. In the early plays, the low or comic characters—Shylock as well as Launcelot Gobbo in *The Merchant of Venice*, for example—speak prose. An intellectual character like Falstaff speaks prose, in contrast to a passionate character like Hotspur, who speaks verse. In *As You Like It*, contrary to tradition, both the hero and heroine speak prose. In *Twelfth Night*, Viola speaks verse at court and prose to herself, and the characters in the play who are false or have no sense of humor speak verse. Those who are wiser and have some self-knowledge speak prose. In the tragedies Shakespeare develops an extremely fertile prose style for the tragic characters. Hamlet speaks both verse and prose. He speaks verse to himself, in his soliloquies, and in speeches of violent passion to others, as in the scene with his mother. He otherwise usually speaks prose to other people. There is a highly developed relation of prose and poetry in all the plays of this period. In the last plays Shakespeare exploits verse more exclusively, and tends to use prose when he is bored, or when he needs to fill in the gaps. In *Antony and Cleopatra*, the boring characters use prose, the rounded characters, verse.

Shakespeare is also developing a more flexible verse. He started off with the end-stopped Marlovian and lyric lines that were suitable to high passion. In *Hamlet* he experiments with the *caesura*, the stop in the middle of the line, to develop a middle voice, a voice neither passionate nor prosaic. *Hamlet* also shows a development in Shakespeare's use of the double adjective. From such a phrase as "sweet and honey'd sentences" in *Henry V* (I.i.50), which is tautological, he moves to pairs of adjectives in *Hamlet* that combine the abstract and the concrete: Laertes' "And keep you in the rear of your affection / Out of the shot and danger of desire" (I.iii.34–35), for example, Horatio's "These are but wild and whirling words, my lord" (I.v.133), and Hamlet's "Led by a delicate and tender prince" (IV.iv.48). George Rylands's book, *Words and Poetry*, is very good on Shakespeare's language and style.

In this period, also, Shakespeare appears to be tired of writing comedy, which he could do almost too well—he was probably bored because of his facility in the genre. Comedy is limited in the violence of language and emotion it can present, although Shakespeare can include a remarkable amount of both in his comedies. But though he wants to get away from comedy, he doesn't want to go back to the crude rhetoric of *King John* and *Richard III* or to the lyric and romantic rhetoric of *Romeo and Juliet* and *Richard II*. He doesn't want a childish character, who doesn't know what is going on, like Romeo and Richard II, nor a crude character like Brutus, who is a puppet in a plot of historical significance, where the incidents are more important than the characters. Finally, he doesn't want a character of fat humour that the situation must be constructed to reveal. And having done Falstaff, he doesn't want to go back to the crude character.

Shakespeare's very success as a dramatic poet may have led him to a kind of dissatisfaction with his life that is reflected in *Hamlet*. A dramatic poet is the kind of person who can imagine what anyone can feel, and he begins to wonder, "What am I?" "What do *I* feel?" "*Can* I feel?" Artists are inclined to suffer not from too much emotion but rather from too little. This business of being a mirror—you begin to question the reality of the mirror itself.

Shakespeare develops Hamlet from a number of earlier characters who are in differing ways proto-Hamlets. Richard II is a child, full of self-pity, who acts theatrically but who is not, like Hamlet, conscious of acting. Falstaff is like Hamlet, an intellectual character and the work of an artist who is becoming aware of his full powers, but he is not conscious of himself in the way Hamlet is. When Falstaff does becomes conscious of himself, he dies, almost suicidally. Brutus anticipates Hamlet by being, in a sense, his opposite. Hamlet is destroyed by his imagination. Brutus is destroyed by repressing his imagination, like the Stoic he is. He tries to exclude possibility. The nearest to Hamlet is Jaques, who remains unexplained and can take no part in the action.

It is perhaps more important to consider the sources of this play than any other of Shakespeare's plays. The story of Hamlet originally appears in Saxo Grammaticus's *Historia Danica*, but Shakespeare went to Belleforest's *Histoires Tragiques* for an expanded and moralized version of the story. Belleforest's tale was translated into English in 1608. Another influence was Thomas Kyd's play *The Spanish Tragedy*, a prototype of the revenge play, which was printed in 1594 and was exceptionally popular on the Elizabethan stage.

The first major exploration of the idea of revenge occurs in *The Oresteia*, the legend of Orestes, Agamemnon and Clytemnestra. Saxo's version of the Hamlet story had comparatively little to do with emotions—revenge is treated as an absolute duty. In Elizabethan plays, though a wrong is done a person, the wronged one carries his grievances too far and Nemesis turns back on him—Shylock is an instance. What was a duty now becomes a question of passion and hatred. Hamlet's disgust and revulsion towards his mother, for example, seem out of all proportion to her actual behavior.

Hamlet has many faults—it is full of holes both in action and motivation. The sketchy portrayal of Fortinbras is one. We hear early about his plans, when Claudius sends word for him to stop. Fortinbras agrees, but wants permission to pass through Denmark on his way to Poland. We see him pass across the stage on the way to Poland, and he returns when everyone is dead. This subplot is needed, but it is not properly incorporated into the play. The action involving Laertes also poses problems. When Laertes returns from France the second time, why hasn't someone told him Hamlet killed his father, and when he storms the palace, why is all the excitement over in a few moments? Polonius is secretly buried. Why? Polonius' death is necessary to get Laertes back to England, but again the subplot is not really knit into the action. And why does Claudius delay in killing Hamlet and make elaborate plans which could miscarry? Ophelia is a silly, repressed girl and is obscene and embarrassing when she loses her mind over her father's death. But though her madness is very shocking and horrible, it is not well motivated. She was not so wild about her meddling Papa, nor was she tremendously *interested* in Papa.

Hamlet's age is a great mystery. His conversation with the Clown suggests he is about thirty years old (V.i.154–77), but if he is, why is he still a university student? And, if he is young enough to be a student, his speeches—which sound mature and middle-aged—are inappropriate to him. And how old, then, is Gertrude?

Was Hamlet ever seriously in love with Ophelia? He says so in the end:

> I lov'd Ophelia. Forty thousand brothers
> Could not (with all their quantity of love)
> Make up my sum.

> (V.i.292–94)

But we may wonder. Hamlet's earlier disgust with Ophelia and his repudiations of her are, in any case, out of proportion to what we see of their relation, and poorly motivated. He suspects her of being a spy, which probably came from an earlier version of *Hamlet* in which she was a spy on him.

Finally, why doesn't Claudius react to the dumb-show, why wait till the play within the play? This suggests that there was an earlier version with a dumb-show and a later one with a play within a play, and that Shakespeare incorporated both without bothering about the rest of the speeches.

The Elizabethans had a number of conventions about ghosts. A ghost would appear to the guilty party, or to call for vengeance. He could haunt a place where he was not properly buried, his appearance could be a portent, and if he had buried money in his lifetime and not told his heirs where to find it, his duty was to let them know. Horatio asks all the proper questions of a ghost.

Hamlet's melancholy, finally, is hard to relate to the body of the play, and his last speech has the same kind of vanity as a suicide note:

> Had I but time (as this fell sergeant, Death,
> Is strict in his arrest) O, I could tell you—
> But let it be. Horatio, I am dead;
> Thou liv'st; report me and my cause aright
> To the unsatisfied. . . .
> O good Horatio, what a wounded name
> (Things standing thus unknown) shall live behind me!
> If thou didst ever hold me in thy heart,
> Absent thee from felicity awhile,
> And in this harsh world draw thy breath in pain,
> To tell my story.
>
> (V.ii.347–51, 355–60)

Hamlet's procrastination. Hamlet *can* act when outward circumstances threaten him in any way, and when he does, as in his killing of Polonius, he shows a considerable lack of feeling. The play within the play he engineers and directs is presented not as a comic but a tragic contradiction, where the innocence of the players is contrasted with the guilt of the people who speak well, and what is meant to entertain in a harmless way causes real suffering.

Hamlet is intensely self-absorbed and that self-interest continues to the very last moment. He delays. The task is to choose oneself, to accept the *now*. Not to say, "The time is out of joint. O cursed spite / That ever I was born to set it right" (I.v.189–90)—"I would be all right if things were different." I must not want to be somebody else. I must realize that I mustn't hide part of myself from myself and make the situation easier than it is, in the way Brutus does. I have to choose myself. How can I transcend this self I have accepted, and then forget all about it? I must not leave this choice to fate or circumstances, as a person who plunges into dissipation or uncoordinated action does. I mustn't say I can't deal with life because my mother didn't love me or my mother loved me too much, or whatever it is. Hamlet could either avenge his father promptly or he could say it isn't my business to judge other people, it is God's business. He does neither. Instead, he finds the situation interesting, and takes notes on how "one may smile, and smile, and be a villain" (I.v.108).

Aversion keeps one related but detached. Either hatred or love means an alteration in situation. Why doesn't he act? He has to find an answer to the question, "Who am I?" He lacks a basic sense of a reason for existence at all. Hamlet lacks faith in God and in himself. Consequently he must define his existence in terms of others, e.g., I am the man whose mother married his uncle who murdered his father. He would like to become what the Greek tragic hero is, a creature of situation. Hence, his inability to act, for he can only "act," i.e., play at possibilities. He is fundamentally *bored*, and for that reason he acts theatrically. The play is written entirely out of spite against actors, and by its nature the role of Hamlet cannot be done by an actor. An actor can act everything except an actor. Hamlet should be played by an actor brought in off the street, and the rest of the characters should be professional actors. The point about Hamlet is that he is an actor and you can't act yourself. You can only *be* yourself.

It is no longer possible for people to believe in something because a lot of other people do. To believe in something is not now a naive act. The normal reaction is to try not to go forward, but rather to retreat from desire and will back to passion, where one can act. The cost, however, is the sacrifice of one's reason, and you have to invent a terrific kind of technique to arouse such a passion in reflective people. The opposite of a passionate leap into fate is a gratuitous leap into activity, like Iago's.

Kierkegaard writes in *Either/Or* that "Boredom is the root of all evil":

> Starting from a principle is affirmed by people of experience to be a very reasonable procedure; I am willing to humor them, and so begin with the principle that all men are bores. Surely no one will prove himself so great a bore as to contradict me in this. This principle possesses the quality of being in the highest degree repellent, an essential requirement in the case of negative principles, which are

in the last analysis the principles of all motion. It is not merely repellent, but infinitely forbidding; and whoever has this principle back of him cannot but receive an infinite impetus forward, to help him make new discoveries. For if my principle is true, one need only consider how ruinous boredom is for humanity, and by properly adjusting the intensity of one's concentration upon this fundamental truth, attain any desired degree of momentum. Should one wish to attain the maximum momentum, even to the point of almost endangering the driving power, one need only say to oneself: Boredom is the root of all evil. Strange that boredom, in itself so staid and stolid, should have such power to set in motion. The influence it exerts is altogether magical, except that it is not the influence of attraction, but of repulsion.

"Boredom," Kierkegaard says, "is the demoniac side of pantheism."

Pantheism is, in general, characterized by fullness; in the case of boredom we find the precise opposite, since it is characterized by emptiness; but it is just this which makes boredom a pantheistic conception. Boredom depends on the nothingness which pervades reality; it causes a dizziness like that produced by looking down into a yawning chasm, and this dizziness is infinite.

Troilus and Cressida

[19 February 1947]

In considering *Troilus and Cressida, All's Well That Ends Well,* and *Measure for Measure,* not wholly successful plays, the first thing that comes to mind is the difference between a major and a minor writer—which is not necessarily the difference between better and worse. We can forget the bad writers. The minor artist, who can be idiosyncratic, keeps to one thing, does it well, and keeps on doing it—Thomas Campion, for example, A. E. Housman, and in music, Claude Debussy. There are minor writers who can mean more to us than any major writer, because their worlds are closest to ours. Great works of art can be hard to read—in a sense, boring to read. Whom do I read with the utmost pleasure? Not Dante, to my mind the greatest of poets, but Ronald Firbank. The minor writer never risks failure. When he discovers his particular style and vision, his artistic history is over.

The major writer, on the other hand, is of two kinds. One is the kind who spends most of his life preparing to produce a masterpiece, like Dante or Proust. Such writers have a long history in developing their writing, and they risk dying before it bears fruit. The other kind of major artist is engaged in perpetual endeavors. The moment such an artist learns to do something, he stops and tries to do something else, something new—like Shakespeare, or Wagner, or Picasso. How do the two different types of major writers create their work, and what is important to them? The first type is interested in finding out what the masterpiece will be, the second is more interested in discovering how to tackle a new problem and is not concerned about whether the work will succeed. Shakespeare is always prepared to risk failure. *Troilus and Cressida, Measure for Measure* and *All's Well That Ends Well* don't quite come off, whereas almost every poem of Housman does. But if we don't understand these plays, we won't understand the great tragedies.

What are Shakespeare's problems in *Troilus and Cressida?* First, the technical ones: he must perfect a style to deal with matter he has not previously dealt with. Second, he must decide what, in his material, is interesting and important. Initially, as we saw in *Hamlet,* there is the problem of vocabulary, particularly the use of a Latinized vocabulary—in *Troilus and Cresida,* words such as "vindicative" (IV.v.107), "tortive," "errant" (I.iii.9), and "prenominate" (IV.v.250). There are also many double nouns and adjectives in *Henry V, Hamlet,* and *Troilus and Cressida*—"in the fan and wind of your fair sword" (V.iii.41) or "ridiculous and awkward action" (I.iii.149), for example, in *Troilus and Cressida*—that result in a very elaborate and involved style of speech. Metaphors are developed elaborately to illustrate thought, in contrast with *Julius Caesar,* for example, where they are decorative.

Shakespeare inherited two kinds of style. The first was the passionate choleric style, inherited from Marlowe, that is found in Talbot's speeches in *Henry VI.* Ajax's speech to the trumpeter is an example in *Troilus and Cressida*:

> Now crack thy lungs and split thy brazen pipe.
> Blow, villain, till thy sphered bias cheek
> Outswell the colic of puff'd Aquilon.
> Come, stretch thy chest and let thy eyes spout blood.
>
> (IV.v.7–10)

The other style Shakespeare inherited was the affective, antithetically balanced style of lyric and reflective character that we find in *The Rape of Lucrece*:

> "Time's glory is to calm contending kings,
> To unmask falsehood and bring truth to light,
> To stamp the seal of time in aged things,
> To wake the morn and sentinel the night,
> To wrong the wronger till he render right,
>   To ruinate proud buildings with thy hours,
>   And smear with dust their glitt'ring golden tow'rs;
>
> "To fill with wormholes stately monuments,
> To feed oblivion with decay of things,
> To blot old books and alter their contents,
> To pluck the quills from ancient ravens' wings,
> To dry the old oak's sap and cherish springs,
>   To spoil antiquities of hammer'd steel
>   And turn the giddy round of Fortune's wheel;
>
> "To show the beldame daughters of her daughter,
> To make the child a man, the man a child,
> To slay the tiger that doth live by slaughter,
> To tame the unicorn and lion wild,

To mock the subtle in themselves beguil'd,
        To cheer the ploughman with increaseful crops
        And waste huge stones with little water-drops.

                                                            (939–59)

In *Troilus and Cressida*, by contrast, Shakespeare is developing the kind of reflective and intellectual style we see in Ulysses' speech to Achilles on Time:

Time hath, my lord, a wallet at his back,
Wherein he puts alms for oblivion,
A great-siz'd monster of ingratitudes.
Those scraps are good deeds past, which are devour'd
As fast as they are made, forgot as soon
As done. Perseverance, dear my lord,
Keeps honour bright. To have done is to hang
Quite out of fashion, like a rusty mail
In monumental mock'ry. Take the instant way;
For honour travels in a strait so narrow
Where one but goes abreast. Keep then the path,
For emulation hath a thousand sons
That one by one pursue. If you give way,
Or hedge aside from the direct forthright,
Like to an ent'red tide they all rush by
And leave you hindmost;
Or, like a gallant horse fall'n in first rank,
Lie there for pavement to the abject rear,
O'errun and trampled on. Then what they do in present,
Though less than yours in past, must o'ertop yours;
For Time is like a fashionable host,
That slightly shakes his parting guest by th' hand,
And with his arms outstretch'd as he would fly
Grasps in the comer. The welcome ever smiles,
And farewell goes out sighing. Let not virtue seek
Remuneration for the thing it was!

                                                            (III.iii.145–70)

This is a style of reflection in a specific situation, calculated for a particular effect: Ulysses is trying, with intellectual argument, to get Achilles to act. Shakespeare had previously represented this kind of argument in prose.

Parallel to this verse, Shakespeare is developing something new in prose, a kind of violent prose that reaches its full flower in the speeches of the Fool in *King Lear.* We see it in Thersites' diatribe against Agamemnon and Menelaus:

> With too much blood and too little brain these two may run mad; but if with too much brain and too little blood they do, I'll be a curer of madmen. Here's Agamemnon, an honest fellow enough and one that loves quails, but he has not so much brain as earwax; and the goodly transformation of Jupiter there, his brother, the bull, the primitive statue and oblique memorial of cuckolds, a thrifty shoeing horn in a chain, hanging at his brother's leg—to what form but that he is should wit larded with malice, and malice forced with wit, turn him to? To an ass were nothing: he is both ass and ox: to an ox were nothing; he is both ox and ass. To be a dog, a mule, a cat, a fitchook, a toad, a lizard, an owl, a puttock, or a herring without a roe, I would not care; but to be Menelaus, I would conspire against destiny. Ask me not what I would be if I were not Thersites; for I care not to be the louse of a lazar, so I were not Menelaus—Hoy-day! sprites and fires!
>
> (V.i.53–73)

Hamlet uses verse for great emotions in *Hamlet,* and prose for ordinary relations. In the opening scene of *Troilus and Cressida,* Troilus speaks in verse and Pandarus in prose, and in the next scene Pandarus and Cressida speak in prose to each other, and Cressida speaks in verse when she is alone. The third scene, the Greek council scene, is entirely in verse. In the first scene of Act II, Ajax and Thersites speak to each other in prose, in the next, the Trojan council scene, there is only poetry, and in the third scene, in the Greek camp, the men talk in prose to Thersites and largely in verse to each other. The beginning and the end of the orchard scene (III.ii) are in verse, otherwise Troilus and Cressida's wooing is in prose, except at its emotional height. Pandarus, Thersites, and other detached characters always talk in prose. Troilus, Cressida, and others, when they know what their relation is—warrior, lover—use poetry, and when they are uncertain or indifferent, as in the scene of Pandarus, Helen, and Paris together (III.i), they use prose.

The matter of the play is: (a) the Homeric story of the Trojan War, the archetype of male heroism, with its accompanying issues of courage, honor, comradeship in arms, and (b) the love story of Troilus and Cressida, the great medieval archetype of courtly love. The conventions of

both stories, one of tragic heroism, the other of pathetic love, are transformed in the play. In what does the tragedy of Homer consist? What
happens is really ordained by the gods, and human emotion is juxtaposed against the indifference of everlasting nature. In the foreground
are men locked in battle, killing and being killed, farther off their wives,
children, and servants waiting anxiously for the outcome, overhead,
watching the spectacle with interest and at times interfering, the gods
who know neither sorrow nor death, and around them all indifferent
and unchanging, the natural world of sky and sea and earth. Though
Castor and Pollux are dead, the life-giving earth is our mother still. The
same sense of how things are, how they always have been, and always
will be, is conveyed in *Beowulf* in the final dirge for Beowulf, and in Achilles' dialogue with old Priam at the end of the *Iliad*: "Neither may I tend
[my father] as he groweth old, since very far from my country I am dwell-
ing in Troy-land, to vex thee and thy children." Life makes no sense, but
the moment of heroism, the moment of loyalty, does. "*Hige sceal þe
heardra, / heorte þe cenre, / mod sceal þe mare / þe ure mægen lytlað,*" Byrhtwold
says to his expiring warriors in *The Battle of Maldon*. "Mind must be the
resoluter, / heart the bolder, / courage must be the greater, / as our
strength dwindles."

In *Troilus and Cressida* the characters are not driven by a fate from
which they cannot escape. They know what they are doing and don't
believe in it. Troilus says of the war, at the very beginning of the play,

> Peace, you ungracious clamours! peace, rude sounds!
> Fools on both sides, Helen must needs be fair
> When with your blood you daily paint her thus!
> I cannot fight upon this argument;
> It is too starv'd a subject for my sword.

> (I.i.92–96)

Hector and Troilus are the only two characters in the play with the faint-
est pretense of nobility. In the Trojan council scene, Hector argues that
reason demands Helen should be given up and Troilus that honor demands she should be kept:

> *Hect.* Brother, she is not worth what she doth cost
> The holding.
> *Tro.*   What is aught but as 'tis valu'd?
> *Hect.* But value dwells not in particular will:
> It holds his estimate and dignity
> As well wherein 'tis precious of itself

As in the prizer. 'Tis mad idolatry
To make the service greater than the god;
And the will dotes that is attributive
To what infectiously itself affects
Without some image of th' affected merit. . . .
                    Or, is your blood
So madly hot that no discourse of reason,
Nor fear of bad success in a bad cause,
Can qualify the same?

                              (II.ii.51–60, 115–18)

Hector continues to chide the Trojans for perpetuating wrong by doing more wrong, but then suddenly and lamely agrees with Troilus' appeal to honor:

                         Thus to persist
In doing wrong extenuates not wrong,
But makes it much more heavy. Hector's opinion
Is this in way of truth. Yet ne'ertheless,
My sprightly brethren, I propend to you
In resolution to keep Helen still;
For 'tis a cause that hath no mean dependence
Upon our joint and several dignities.

                                    (II.ii.186–93)

The Homeric hero finds himself in a tragic situation from which there is no escape. Shakespeare's people, for the sake of glory, refuse to escape when escape is possible. Diomedes tells Paris quite plainly that Helen is worthless and that both he and Menelaus are fools for fighting over her:

                         Both alike.
He merits well to have her that doth seek her,
Not making any scruple of her soilure,
With such a hell of pain and world of charge;
And you as well to keep her, that defend her,
Not palating the taste of her dishonour,
With such a costly loss of wealth and friends.
He like a puling cuckold would drink up
The lees and dregs of a flat tamed piece;
You, like a lecher, out of whorish loins
Are pleas'd to breed out your inheritors.
Both merits pois'd, each weighs nor less nor more;
But he as he, the heavier for a whore.

> *Par.* You are too bitter to your countrywoman.
> *Dio.* She's bitter to her country. Hear me, Paris:
> For every false drop in her bawdy veins
> A Grecian's life hath sunk; for every scruple
> Of her contaminated carrion weight
> A Troyan hath been slain. Since she could speak
> She hath not given so many good words breath
> As for her Greeks and Troyans suff'red death.

Paris answers, cynically,

> Fair Diomed, you do as chapmen do,
> Dispraise the thing that you desire to buy;
> But we in silence hold this virtue well,
> We'll not commend what we intend to sell.

(IV.i.54–78)

In many other ways as well, the play doesn't conform to heroic convention. Achilles gets a letter from Hecuba with a token from her daughter, his "fair love" (V.i.45), and he refuses to fight. He forgets his cause, so there is no tragic conflict, as in heroic tragedy. When he remembers it after Patroclus is killed, he takes the extremely unheroic line of butchering the unarmed Hector:

> *Achil.* Look, Hector, how the sun begins to set;
> How ugly night comes breathing at his heels.
> Even with the vail and dark'ning of the sun,
> To close the day up, Hector's life is done.
> 　*Hect.* I am unarm'd; forgo this vantage, Greek.
> 　*Achil.* Strike, fellows, strike! This is the man I seek.

[*Hector falls.*]
(V.viii.5–10)

Ajax and Achilles have no loyalty, they are interested only in themselves. The other comradeship in arms, the relationship of Achilles and Patroclus—compare the biblical story of David and Jonathan—is reduced to sexual love. Patroclus admits he has little stomach for the wars. His biggest thing is his ability to amuse Achilles with imitations. The characters are like the grubby little boys from Steig cartoons, except that they know what they're doing and people get killed.

Æneas and Diomedes, when they greet each other in Troy, are courteous, but also defiant and savage:

Æne.　　Health to you, valiant sir,
During all question of the gentle truce;
But when I meet you arm'd, as black defiance
As heart can think or courage execute!
　　Dio. The one and other Diomed embraces.
Our bloods are now in calm, and so long, health!
But when contention and occasion meet,
By Jove, I'll play the hunter for thy life
With all my force, pursuit, and policy.
　　Æne. And thou shalt hunt a lion that will fly
With his face backward. In humane gentleness
Welcome to Troy! now by Anchises' life,
Welcome indeed! By Venus' hand I swear,
No man alive can love in such a sort
The thing he means to kill more excellently.
　　Dio. We sympathize. Jove let Æneas live,
If to my sword his fate be not the glory,
A thousand complete courses of the sun!
But in mine emulous honour let him die,
With every joint a wound, and that to-morrow!

(IV.i.10–29)

Directions to the stage director of *Troilus and Cressida*: everything should be made grotesque, the characters presented as caricatures in the Dickens tradition. Agamemnon, Menelaus, Achilles, Ajax, must be enormous. Nestor must be a tiny, incredibly drivelling old man, Patroclus a 52nd Street queen, Helen an expensive whore, like the Second Mrs. Tanqueray, and Cressida like Mildred in *Of Human Bondage*. Pandarus must be fat and plainly syphilitic.

The story of Troilus and Cressida draws upon a tradition including Dares, Boccaccio, Chaucer, and Henryson. In Chaucer, Criseyde doesn't yield to Troilus until midway in the third book, the fourth book treats their love, and the fifth is about her betrayal. In Shakespeare there is no wooing. First, Cressida likes Troilus, second, they go to bed, and third, she betrays him very soon after. C. S. Lewis sees Chaucer's Criseyde as "a woman who in a chaste society would certainly have lived a chaste widow." But if, Lewis says, in the society and circumstances in which she does live,

she yields, she commits no sin against the social code of her age and country: she commits no unpardonable sin against any code I know of—unless, perhaps, against that of the Hindus. By Christian standards, forgivable: by the rules of courtly love, needing no forgiveness: this is all that need be said of Cryseide's act in granting the Rose to Troilus. But her betrayal of him is not so easily dismissed.

Here there is, of course, no question of acquittal. "False Cryseide" she has been ever since the story was first told, and will be till the end. And her offence is rank. By the code of courtly love it is unpardonable; in Christian ethics it is as far below her original unchastity as Brutus and Iscariot, in Dante's hell, lie lower than Paolo and Francesca. But we must not misunderstand her sin; we must not so interpret it as to cast any doubt upon the sincerity of her first love.

Lewis goes on to say that if we ask how this sincerity "is compatible with her subsequent treachery," the answer is a further consideration of her character:

Chaucer has so emphasized the ruling passion of his heroine, that we cannot mistake it. It is Fear—fear of loneliness, of old age, of death, of love, and of hostility; of everything, indeed, that can be feared. And from this Fear springs the only positive passion which can be permanent in such a nature; the pitiable longing, more childlike than womanly, for protection. . . . What cruelty it is, to subject such a woman to the test of absence—and of absence with no assured future of reunion, absence compelled by the terrible outerworld of law and politics and force (which she cannot face), absence amid alien scenes and voices.

> With wommen fewe, among the Grekes stronge.

Every one can foresee the result.

Once she is in Greek hands, Lewis writes,

Diomede becomes, no longer the alternative to Troilus, but the alternative to flight. The picture of herself in Diomede's arms gains the all but irresistible attraction that it blots out the unbearable picture of herself stealing out past the sentries in the darkness. And so, weeping and half-unwilling, and self-excusing, and repentant by anticipation before her guilt is consummated, the unhappy creature becomes the mistress of her Greek lover, grasping at the last chance of self-respect with the words

> To Diomede algate I wol be trewe.

Shakespeare's Cressida, on the other hand, wants power and can play hard to get:

> Yet hold I off. Women are angels, wooing:
> Things won are done; joy's soul lies in the doing.
> That she belov'd knows naught that knows not this:
> Men prize the thing ungain'd more than it is.
> That she was never yet that ever knew
> Love got so sweet as when desire did sue.
> Therefore this maxim out of love I teach:
> Achievement is command; ungain'd, beseech.
> Then, though my heart's content firm love doth bear,
> Nothing of that shall from mine eyes appear.
>
> (I.ii.312–21)

The first conversation between Troilus and Cressida is coarse and sexual.

Tro. O, let my lady apprehend no fear! In all Cupid's pageant there is presented no monster.

Cres. Nor nothing monstrous neither?

Tro. Nothing but our undertakings when we vow to weep seas, live in fire, eat rocks, tame tigers—thinking it harder for our mistress to devise imposition enough than for us to undergo any difficulty imposed. This is the monstruosity in love, lady, that the will is infinite and the execution confin'd, that the desire is boundless and the act a slave to limit.

Cres. They say all lovers swear more performance than they are able, and yet reserve an ability that they never perform, vowing more than the perfection of ten, and discharging less than the tenth part of one. They that have the voice of lions and the acts of hares, are they not monsters?

(III.ii.79–96)

Ulysses ticks Cressida off at once:

> Fie, fie upon her!
> There's language in her eye, her cheek, her lip;
> Nay, her foot speaks. Her wanton spirits look out
> At every joint and motive of her body.
> O, these encounterers so glib of tongue,
> That give accosting welcome ere it comes
> And wide unclasp the tables of their thoughts

> To every ticklish reader—set them down
> For sluttish spoils of opportunity
> And daughters of the game!
>
> (IV.v.54–63)

She's sunk when she attempts to deal with Diomedes. His interest is entirely physical, and he has a better trick than she has. He does what she did with Troilus: he threatens to leave her. At the end she gives him Troilus' sleeve, saying that it belonged to one "that lov'd me better than you will" (V.ii.89–90).

Pandarus is reduced from the interesting, complicated servant of *Amour* we find in Chaucer to an old syphilitic man depending upon second-hand pleasures. The only pleasure that his own impotence allows him is the voyeuristic encouragement of others, like the Earl of Rochester's maimed debauchee:

> Thus, Statesman-like I'll saucily impose,
>   And, safe from danger, valiantly advise;
> Shelter'd in Impotence urge you to Blows,
>   And, being good for nothing else, be wise.

Pandarus is loyal both to Troilus and courtly love in Chaucer, he is loyal just to pandering in Shakespeare.

Troilus is supposed to be fairly nice by comparison to Pandarus and Cressida, but not if we look closely. Compare the speech in which Juliet looks forward to her night with Romeo with the speech in which Troilus anticipates sleeping with Cressida. Juliet's speech, "Come, civil night," in which she anticipates the loss of her maidenhead and the consummation of her marriage, is frankly sexual—"O, I have bought the mansion of a love, / But not possess'd it" (III.ii.26–27), but it is the speech of someone thinking of a particular person:

> Come, night; come, Romeo; come thou day in night;
> For thou wilt lie upon the wings of night
> Whiter than new snow upon a raven's back.
> Come, gentle night; come, loving, black-brow'd night;
> Give me my Romeo.
>
> (III.ii.17–21)

Troilus says, in expectation of Cressida's coming,

> I am giddy; expectation whirls me round.
> Th' imaginary relish is so sweet

That it enchants my sense. What will it be
When that the wat'ry palates taste indeed
Love's thrice-repured nectar? Death, I fear me;
Sounding destruction; or some joy too fine,
Too subtile-potent, tun'd too sharp in sweetness
For the capacity of my ruder powers.
I fear it much; and I do fear besides
That I shall lose distinction in my joys,
As doth a battle when they charge on heaps
The enemy flying.

(III.ii.19–30)

Troilus's reverie is a marvellous analysis of a particular experience, but it is quite independent of the person with whom he is going to sleep. Chaucer's Troilus is kind and chivalrous—"the smale bestes leet he gon biside." Shakespeare's Troilus is not. He is "more dangerous" than Hector, Ulysses says,

For Hector in his blaze of wrath subscribes
To tender objects, but he in heat of action
Is more vindicative than jealous love.

(IV.v.105–7)

Troilus makes his nature clear in telling Hector,

Brother, you have a vice of mercy in you
Which better fits a lion than a man. . . .
            For th' love of all the gods,
Let's leave the hermit Pity with our mother;
And when we have our armours buckled on,
The venomed vengeance ride upon our swords,
Spur them to ruthful work, rein them from ruth!
    Hect. Fie, savage, fie!

(V.iii.37–38, 44–49)

Troilus and Cressida is not a satire merely. There are two kinds of satire. There is a satire of sacred abuse, whose purpose is to produce a catharsis of resentment, a holiday from conventions designed to keep the conventions solid. The second kind exposes abuses, and even attacks the so-called norm in order to establish a new norm. But the very idea of a norm is attacked in Shakespeare's *Troilus and Cressida.* There is no universal in the play. In *Hamlet,* where the ego and the self are separate, the self becomes questionable, and this separation means an awareness of, and a responsibility for, the self. The process is not reversible. Once it's experienced, it is very hard to think back to your prior state. One can imagine people different from oneself, but it is difficult to imagine a person with less degree of consciousness than oneself. We write about others as if they were aware of what we see to be their rationalizations. What makes *Troilus and Cressida* unsatisfactory and at the same time so malign is that the characters behave with awareness in a way that aware characters would not behave. Hamlet tries to free his self by freeing it of all relations, all the ties to society that determined his nature, but he is also afraid of losing himself. The next stage is the detached, observing ego—which differs from Brutus's *ataraxia* because Brutus is unaware of his nature. An aware person recognizes the lack of freedom of feeling, but his awareness gives him the freedom of analysis and an aversion to emotional display in which only honest emotion is admissible. Hamlet's detachment works backwards into emotion.

The characters in *Troilus and Cressida* have an extraordinary verbosity. Words are vehicles of detachment, a means to *ataraxia*, as Robert Graves points out:

> Children are dumb to say how hot the day is,
> How hot the scent is of the summer rose,
> How dreadful the black wastes of evening sky,
> How dreadful the tall soldiers drumming by.
>
> But we have speech, that cools the hottest sun,
> And speech that dulls the hottest rose's scent.
> We spell away the overhanging night,
> We spell away the soldiers and the fright.
>
> There's a cool web of language winds us in,
> Retreat from too much gladness, too much fear:
> We grow sea-green at last and coldly die
> In brininess and volubility.
>
> But if we let our tongues lose self-possession,
> Throwing off language and its wateriness
> Before our death, instead of when death comes,
> Facing the brightness of the children's day,
> Facing the rose, the dark sky and the drums,
> We shall go mad no doubt and die that way.

Thersites says, when he refuses to fight Margarelon the Bastard,

I am a bastard too; I love bastards. I am bastard begot, bastard instructed, bastard in mind, bastard in valour, in everything illegiti-
mate. One bear will not bite another, and wherefore should one
bastard? Take heed, the quarrel's most ominous to us. If the son of
a whore fight for a whore, he tempts judgment. Farewell, bastard.

(V.vii.16–23)

If we compare this speech to Falstaff's soliloquy on honor, we see that
Falstaff is arguing for straight self-preservation, Thersites for ego preser-
vation. It is a triumph of the ego to be honest about the self. Shakespeare
works through this process in the plays of this period in a way that reveals, in the tragedies, how pride differs from hybris. In classical tragedy,
man thinks his self to be more secure than it is. In Shakespearean tragedy, pride begins with the desire to be a god, a desire to escape from
one's finiteness. One tries to hide this finiteness by power over others,
like Macbeth, or by the idolatry of the individual in the romantic tradition, or by the idolatry of convention in law, of the infinite We in which
the individual is annihilated. In the great tragedies the knowledge of
what they are doing is hidden from the heroes, and a really mad world is
created by the hero with a dynamic mania. In *Troilus and Cressida*, where
the characters are and remain maniacs and are aware of it, we get the
feeling that this is the world, not *a* world. Only by reading plays like this
can we see how terrifying *Othello* and *Macbeth* really are.

Once there is a revelation of what's going on, there is either destruction or a new relationship. A man who hasn't questioned the value of his
own existence or of any social effort is still a child. As Martin Buber
explains, it is only at that point that man achieves individual history.
Beasts of prey can have a biography and even state annals, but only man
can have history, by having responsibility. In order to reach that point of
responsibility, to be related to truth, one must see truth as over against
the self. That is why all progress depends upon the experience in which
life and one's nature are called into question. As G. K. Chesterton writes
in "The Sword of Surprise,"

> Sunder me from my bones, O sword of God,
> Till they stand stark and strange as do the trees;
> That I whose heart goes up with the soaring woods
> May marvel as much at these.

Sunder me from my blood that in the dark
I hear that red ancestral river run,
Like branching buried floods that find the sea
But never see the sun.

Give me miraculous eyes to see my eyes,
Those rolling mirrors made alive in me,
Terrible crystal more incredible
Than all the things they see.

Sunder me from my soul, that I may see
The sins like streaming wounds, the life's brave beat;
Till I shall save myself, as I would save
A stranger in the street.

All's Well That Ends Well

[26 February 1947]

All's Well That Ends Well and *Measure for Measure* are plays that are not concerned with individual character but with concepts—in *All's Well That Ends Well*, the code of honor, in *Measure for Measure*, the principle of law and justice. Both plays are the most suited to modern dress and staging of all of Shakespeare's plays.

In the worldly city, society is built up either on the idea of a code of honor or on the principle of law and justice. *All's Well That Ends Well* is concerned with honor. If one starts with individual will, the first thing one can say about honor is that it is a way of conduct that I choose for myself to obey and that I would not expect of others. Usually it occurs—in origin always—when the "I" is identified with a particular group, an aristocratic group that chooses to obey the principles of conduct that it does not expect of an inferior group. It differs from law in that the whole point of a code is that it not be written, that it be transmitted by individual to individual. The imperative of the code is never: "This is legal, or this is forbidden." No, it is: "This is not done." It is not done by me or my group. The penalty for breaking the code is chiefly self-contempt, which is derived from the consciousness of being expelled from the group by friends. The reason for keeping to the code is ego-respect. It means that I or my group desire a world that is interesting, a world in which there are admirable individuals. All codes of honor attach a moral value to things that lie outside the realm of justice—good looks, for example, wit, skill.

Honor has nothing to do with justice. A person is expected to pay his gambling debts before he pays his tailor's bill. This is unjust—the tailor needs the money more. If someone insults me, I must challenge him to a duel. In that case he has a choice of weapon. If the choice is pistols, and the other person is a better shot than I am, I cannot claim that this is unjust. That's not the point of a duel. There is a valid idea in the concept of honor. It is valid to the extent to which there are aesthetic inequalities among people, inequalities that cannot be changed. Some people are better than others in many ways, and more is expected of them in a society governed by honor, and should be.

Honor breaks down in various ways. Its limitation is that honor presupposes that everyone who has an unusual gift may *belong*. The moment people *who are capable* of obeying the code are excluded, the thing becomes ridiculous. The limitation exists because we find inequalities that are not aesthetic inequalities, that is, they are removable. The fact that one is born with more intelligence than another and that more will be expected of the intelligent one and should be: that is OK. But it is another thing to say that only certain people are to get a chance of an education. This does not follow. The code becomes corrupt in the degree to which the passion of pride and self-respect is lost and only the sense of superiority remains. The moment people hold to superiority and do not obey the code when it demands sacrifices of them—then it falls to pieces. Those who live by a sense of honor are spared the temptation of those who live by law, in that they do not divide others into good and bad. Their division is the nice people on one side, and on the other side, the bleak and dim people, the ugly and the poor.

Law implies obedience to something outside ourselves, ideally according to a reason that everyone can agree to, because everyone should have to obey the law. The penalty for breaking it is not the loss of respect, but—in the ideal case—self-contradiction. It may be somebody I've never seen before, my social inferior, who arrives and puts handcuffs on me. There is a necessary contradiction between the individual and society as a universal. The motive for honor is the desire for an interesting world. A law has to ignore that the individual is unique, and it cannot know the degree of an individual's virtue in keeping or transgressing a particular ordinance. The more clear it becomes that everyone's relation to the law is unique, the more impossible it becomes to think of the law as an expression of right. The motive of law is the desire for a reasonable world. It has nothing directly to do with honor. If I recognize a law as something that I don't choose to obey, but something I am compelled to obey either by my reason or my fear, my obedience is a humiliation to my ego and a loss of honor. Justice and law are valid where men are really equal. They break down or are unworkable where there are real differences, as there are today.

According to the code of honor in the society in *All's Well That Ends Well* in which Bertram is born, you are expected to be physically brave, you are expected to tell the truth when you are questioned by your equals. You must be polite. In regard to women, you must not marry a person you will be socially ashamed of. With women who are your social equals you may kiss, but in that case you must never tell. With women who are not of your class, you may have affairs, but you mustn't marry them or get involved.

It is more difficult for a child to succeed in a house where the parents are intelligent. The son feels: "I cannot ever be equal to my parents." The sons of great men usually turn out badly. The son feels the great weight of intelligence on him. Bertram is in this kind of position. His widely admired and dead father is repeatedly held up to him as an exemplar of virtue, and Bertram's choice is either to equal papa by doing something quite different from him or to equate with papa by being like him. The great love of parents, like that of the Countess for Bertram, is also a burden for a child, first because the child knows that it isn't deserved, and second because he tries to deserve it, which is of course impossible.

In *All's Well That Ends Well*, the Countess, Lafeu and the Clown are all rather old, and Bertram has been brought up rather too strictly, with a strong sense of honor and family heritage. With his birthright, virtue and goodness are expected of him. But he is even more unhappy at court, where he is considered too young to be sent to war, than he is at home. He gets satisfaction out of displeasing the King by refusing Helena and asserting himself, and it is understandable why he refuses. But the King's displeasure is also understandable. People are not nice when they are ill, as the King is, and in addition, according to the King's code, you don't feel sorry when you are ill, you feel ashamed.

There are two kinds of ego satisfaction for a man. First, there is the public one, which might be success in business, or in Elizabethan times, bravery in war. But primarily you must show yourself by the conquest of women who are hard to get. Bertram declares that "War is no strife / To the dark house and the detested wife" (II.iii.308–9), and goes off to the fighting in Florence, where he does prove his bravery. But he also seduces Diana and lies about it. Parolles tells the King, "He did love her, sir, as a gentleman loves a woman. . . . He lov'd her, sir, and lov'd her not" (V.iii.245–48). But Bertram violates a gentleman's code in his affair with Diana, both by the dishonorable vow he makes to her when he thinks he is seducing her and by lying about it afterwards. When he finally admits his dishonor, he can go on from there—he can accept the fact that he may need and love Helena. Helena understands Bertram well and is willing to sacrifice herself so that he can return home.

Parolles is the only man Bertram can talk to who is his own age. Parolles treats Bertram as a grown-up warrior, which flatters him, and the Countess believes that Bertram "corrupts a well-derived nature / With his inducement" (III.ii.90–91). But Parolles doesn't deceive himself about himself, he only tries to deceive others. When he is finally and fully exposed as both a coward and a liar, he says,

> Yet am I thankful. If my heart were great,
> 'Twould burst at this. Captain I'll be no more;
> But I will eat, and drink, and sleep as soft
> As captain shall. Simply the thing I am
> Shall make me live. Who knows himself a braggart,
> Let him fear this; for it will come to pass
> That every braggart shall be found an ass.
> Rust, sword! Cool, blushes! and, Parolles, live
> Safest in shame! Being fool'd, by fool'ry thrive!
> There's place and means for every man alive.
>
>   (IV.iii.366–75)

The gift of the artist is being shameless, too—and the artist doesn't go in for action either.

Measure for Measure

[5 March 1947]

Measure for Measure is about three things: the nature of justice, the nature of authority, and the nature of forgiveness. Cicero, in *De Re Publica*, defines society as a group of people associated by a common sense of advantage and of right, *jus*. St. Augustine, in *The City of God*, defines a society as a group of rational beings associated in respect to things they love. One of the points of the play is to assert that Augustine's definition is correct, and that if people are united by a common sense of advantage, they cannot also be united by a common sense of right.

The play presents the problem of the earthly city and the vanity of the secular hope for creative politics, the hope that justice precedes love and that law can make people good—the hope, in other words, that you can start with the law and make people love it because it is right. Insofar as what people love is themselves, law is necessary. If you loved God and loved your neighbor as your self, there would be no need for law. Law can only function negatively. Politics expressed in law can never make someone who loves himself into someone who loves his neighbor. Laws can only make self-love social, by making people see that if men are to survive in communities—and men must exist in communities—they must have a contract. If I don't scratch their back, they won't scratch mine. Don't talk about right, but about social equity.

Real justice is the effect, not the cause, of love. Justice is a human abstraction, it cannot be loved. The moment we proceed from barbarism to anything we can call civilization, we conceive of law as universally right and no longer the whim of an individual with superior power. Since the time of the Roman Empire, no one has ever dared to proclaim a law without claiming that it was a universal law. That child labor had to be justified by arguments, that Hitler had to think up reasons for killing the Jews, and that Southerners have to justify their treatment of Negroes marks an advance, whether or not it is hypocrisy, as Marx claims, or a moral advance. It is no longer possible simply to say, "This is what I want, and I will have it because I am stronger." Law assumes that people recognize the rule of law and feel they ought to obey it, and laws range from moral imperatives like "Honor thy father and mother" to laws of general utility, like traffic laws. Law also assumes that people have sufficient power of will to obey, that they are able to do it.

Laws either command or forbid certain actions to a given class of people. If we claim a law is unjust, there are four heads under which the claim can be made:

(1) The action commanded is felt to be wrong or unjust. This tends to be more true of customs, as, for example, when Hamlet criticizes the King's wassail: "a custom / More honour'd in the breach than the observance" (I.iv.15–16).

(2) The acts forbidden seem either just or harmless, like smoking.

(3) The law treats as one class of action something that belongs to another: manslaughter and murder, for example, unintentional and intentional killing, belong to different classes. *Measure for Measure* is concerned with this category of injustice.

(4) The law treats people separately who belong together—a law, for example, that permits a combination of capital and forbids a combination of employees in a union. A law that establishes a color bar for voting is unjust, since a restriction on voting according to race is not a real distinction. A law is similarly unjust if it treats together people who belong apart. Prohibition could be considered unjust, for example, because it failed to distinguish between the alcoholic and the social drinker. These distinctions are quite obvious.

What must law ignore in order to be law at all? Law deals with classes, with types of action. It has to ignore what the individual does when he is not in relation to law, when he is not obeying it or disobeying it, and it has to ignore the individual's uniqueness. It cannot know the degree of the individual's virtue either in keeping to the law or in transgressing it. The more it is realized that everybody's relation to law is unique, the more it is realized that law is not about right but about equity. The law can't judge guilt or innocence, but only the act. It should say only: "I don't want X done to me." Stealing, for instance—no sane person will say that he wishes someone to steal from him. Then, if people break the law, we can treat them not as good or bad, but rather as social nuisances. The criminal becomes the man who claims to be an exception, who claims a license to do what he denies to others. The idea of retributive punishment for a criminal is silly. The criminal must be restrained and educated. Membership in human society is involuntary—society is not like Isabella's nunnery, which you can leave—and the criminal has nowhere to leave to.

The problem of punishment. There are three different ideas of punishment. First, there is atonement or restitution, to which the lawbreaker freely consents. If I break a taboo and don't make restitution, either the gods or society will punish me. I must placate the gods, or I must placate the human injured party who demands satisfaction, who demands that I "pay up." What is the punishment?—what the gods or the injured party will accept and what the law-breaker willingly consents to. Second is strict retribution in which a penalty is imposed on the lawbreaker against his will. If a law is conceived as right, and therefore a universal, it becomes apparent that God doesn't automatically punish the law-breaker, and human beings must take the place of God. In cases where nothing the law-breaker can do will placate and satisfy the injured party, we resort to the punishment of "an eye for an eye, a tooth for a tooth." An eye for an eye is a simple punishment, until a man puts out 50 eyes—how much penalty can atone for that? Eventually, in retributive punishment, the penalties approach infinity: first death, then torture.

The third idea of punishment sees it as a deterrent to those people who know an act is wrong and still want to commit it. The goal of this conception of punishment is to prevent a man from repeating the act as well as to make him an example to warn others. The problem for justice is that the punishment may be enough to deter A but not B, and if you increase the punishment you may be unjust to A without deterring B. The idea of deterrence can ultimately lead to the death penalty. In *Measure for Measure*, a character like Lucio, who represents the average man, will be deterred by his fear of consequences, but a character like Barnardine will break the law, however severe the penalty. You can't tell what penalty is right, even though justice *should* be universal. What should be the penalty for smoking in the subway? Is $5.50 better than $5.00? We make rough and ready compromises, with some element slipping through. In most countries inheriting a Christian attitude, there is a lurking suspicion that social equity and right are not synonymous. Where social equity and right are identified, all breaking of the law becomes assimilated into the serious crime of treason and the penalties are stepped up severely.

However tolerant we are, we all agree that certain sex acts are moral violations. But from the point of view of equity, no one's rights are violated if both parties consent. Let us exclude rape, which is a direct violation of rights, and offenses against people arbitrarily assumed to be minors, who can't consent. In *Measure for Measure* we have mutual consent, but it is here, in this sphere of action, that for the ordinary man the moral difficulties begin and remain. Lucio, Mistress Overdone, and Pompey demonstrate a real moral offense, and Lucio is the reason why laws are enacted. He is a man of the immediate moment, a selfish man who won't be a hermit, who wants to live in society and demands that others behave toward him in a way in which he is not prepared to behave toward them. He exhibits a low form of good fellowship—he wants to be liked. He will go to Isabella for Claudio, but when he is asked to take a real risk, he drops out—he refuses to go bail for Pompey, on whom he has depended for getting his girls. He's meanly vindictive when he's afraid. Mistress Overdone tells how Lucio informed against her because he'd gotten a girl with child. He wants to use the girl, but not to give anything back.

Lucio frequents brothels, which raises the question of prostitution. The society of the brothel in the play is an interesting reversal of a family and its community of love, which is what society is usually built on. It shows that even selfishness can create a society. Food and greed are the two great human drives. For the girls, sex is not love, but a form of work and a source of money. For the customers it is not love, but food. The transaction is based on mutual consent and is equitable, because one want is exchanged for another. In the last analysis, law can't deal with them. Pompey and Mistress Overdone, Abhorson the hangman and his helpers, or a pirate gang make up a society within society. They show the truth of Augustine's definition of society. Lucio speaks of

> the sanctimonious pirate, that went to sea with the Ten Commandments, but scrap'd one out of the table.
> *2. Gent.* "Thou shalt not steal"?
> *Lucio.* Ay, that he raz'd.
> *1. Gent.* Why, 'twas a commandment to command the captain and all the rest from their functions: they put forth to steal.
>
> (I.ii.7–14)

The brothel depends, similarly, on the desire for fornication. And on other conditions: as Mistress Overdone says, "Thus, what with the war, what with the sweat, what with the gallows, and what with poverty, I am custom-shrunk" (I.ii.83–85). When she hears that the bawdy-houses are to be torn down in the suburbs, she complains, "Why here's a change indeed in the commonwealth. What shall become of me?" Pompey assures her humorously that her trade will continue and that she will be taken care of:

Come, fear not you! Good counsellors lack no clients. Though you change your place, you need not change your trade. I'll be your tapster still. Courage, there will be pity taken on you. You that have worn your eyes almost out in the service, you will be considered.

(I.ii.107–14)

There is humor also in Abhorson's snobbery about taking Pompey as an assistant: "A bawd, sir? Fie upon him! he will discredit our mystery. . . . For I do find your hangman is a more penitent trade than your bawd; he doth oftener ask forgiveness" (IV.ii.29–30, 52–54). Abhorson's trade has more serious consequences than Pompey's—Abhorson kills people— but he's on the right side of the tracks.

In the squalid world of these people, law is felt to be necessary to correct evils. But Barnardine proves a type who is insensible to law. He is, the Provost tells the Duke,

A man that apprehends death no more dreadfully but as a drunken sleep; careless, reckless, and fearless of what's past, present, or to come; insensible of mortality and desperately mortal. . . . Drunk many times a day, if not many days entirely drunk. We have very oft awak'd him, as if to carry him to execution, and show'd him a seeming warrant for it. It hath not moved him at all.

(IV.ii.149–53, 157–61)

Barnardine acts out the Provost's description shortly afterwards:

Abhor. Sirrah, bring Barnardine hither.

Pom. Master Barnardine, you must rise and be hang'd! Master Barnardine!

Abhor. What ho, Barnardine!

Bar. (*within*) A pox o' your throats! Who makes that noise there? What are you?

Pom. Your friends, sir; the hangman. You must be so good, sir, to rise and be put to death.

Bar. (*within*) Away, you rogue, away! I am sleepy.

Abhor. Tell him he must awake, and that quickly too.

Pom. Pray, Master Barnardine, awake till you are executed, and sleep afterwards.

Abhor. Go in to him and fetch him out.

Pom. He is coming, sir, he is coming. I hear his straw rustle.

Enter *Barnardine.*

Abhor. Is the axe upon the block, sirrah?

Pom. Very ready, sir.

Bar. How now, Abhorson? What's the news with you?

Abhor. Truly, sir, I would desire you to clap into your prayers; for, look you, the warrant's come.

Bar. You rogue, I have been drinking all night. I am not fitted for't.

Pom. O, the better, sir! for he that drinks all night, and is hanged betimes in the morning, may sleep the sounder all the next day.

                    Enter *Duke*, [disguised as before]

Abhor. Look you, sir, here comes your ghostly father. Do we jest now, think you?

Duke. Sir, induced by my charity, and hearing how hastily you are to depart, I am come to advise you, comfort you, and pray with you.

Bar. Friar, not I! I have been drinking hard all night, and I will have more time to prepare me, or they will beat out my brain with billets. I will not consent to die this day, that's certain.

Duke. O, sir, you must! and therefore I beseech you
Look forward on the journey you shall go.

Bar. I swear I will not die to-day for any man's persuasion.

Duke. But hear you—

Bar. Not a word! If you have anything to say to me, come to my ward; for thence will not I to-day.

                                                    (IV.iii.22–67)

It is because of Barnardine's very insensibility that we see the Duke eventually pardoning him at the end of the play. Why is he treated more leniently than Lucio? Because he's brave, he doesn't demand mercy or to be treated any differently, and he tells the truth. From the point of view of justice, to execute him is as meaningless as to kill a wild dog. The other alternative: let him go. There is the suggestion that the surprise of mercy may shock him into membership in society. Certainly he can't be frightened into law.

Hard cases make bad law. Claudio is an example of the hard case. He has a common-law marriage with Juliet for prudential reasons, to get a dowry. Compare Angelo's behavior to Mariana—Angelo abandons Mariana when she loses her dowry. In a strict moral sense, if Claudio had loved Juliet more, he would have waited, or renounced the dowry. There are three classes of violation of the commandment "Thou shalt not commit fornication" in the play. (1) Claudio loves and wants to marry, but goes to bed first. (2) Lucio goes to brothels. (3) Angelo compels or tries to compel others to go to bed. Since every case is unique, the law over-laps—hard cases make bad law, but there is no law without at least some hard cases. In the play, in every case, marriage is substituted for the death penalty. For Claudio and Juliet marriage is desirable and wel-comed. Lucio, who is a bawd, doesn't want it and thinks it worse than death, though he may learn. The marriages either work out secular equity or offer the promise of something different that may be achieved through suffering. Angelo's atonement isn't what he thinks—death—but marriage to Mariana.

The Duke seems like an awful snooper. Why does he let it go on? Because he is not just a character, but Vienna, and a mirror in which the other characters learn to know themselves. He creates an educational process that allows the characters to undergo and emerge from their sufferings.

It's hard for us not to see Isabella as a prude for refusing to sacrifice her virginity for Claudio's life. But let's go back to the Elizabethans. The vow of chastity involves a duty to God, and the duty to God is more im-portant to fulfill than what your neighbor thinks he wants. It is hard for us nowadays to see this idea clearly. Isabella was trying to take what was for her an absolute vow. Change the situation for a moment. Suppose Angelo were an enemy agent who told Isabella that she had to give up the plans of a secret airplane base or he would kill her brother. People then would understand and say that she is quite right in her vow.

Shakespeare gives a number of warning notes about Isabella's charac-ter. The first is the vanity, and perhaps fear, she displays in wanting the nuns of St. Clare, an extremely strict order, to have even fewer privileges than they do:

> I speak not as desiring more,
> But rather wishing a more strict restraint
> Upon the sisterhood, the votarists of Saint Clare.
>
> (I.iv.3–5)

The second warning is her rage in refusing her brother. She doesn't just say, "No, I won't." She says,

> O you beast!
> O faithless coward! O dishonest wretch!
> Wilt thou be made a man out of my vice?
> Is't not a kind of incest to take life
> From thine own sister's shame? . . .
> Die, perish! Might but my bending down

> Reprieve thee from thy fate, it should proceed.
> I'll pray a thousand prayers for thy death,
> No word to save thee.

(III.i.136–40, 144–47)

Isabella is really tempted by Angelo as a man, and an actress playing the role should bring this out. She starts out thinking she has a vocation for a celibate life, she ends up knowing she hasn't. Her very excess of feeling about that vocation means that she is not qualified for it. The Duke, who has been her confessor, is therefore able to propose to her.

Angelo starts off thinking that the law against fornication is a good law, both for him and for others, and others think he can fulfill the law easily, that he is passionless. They are both wrong. He has a unique relation to law. He wants to be celibate, but there is a difference between his and Isabella's wish to be so. Isabella wants to give her self to celibacy for the sake of God and her neighbor, Angelo wants to be celibate as a matter of pride because he doesn't want to be weak like Lucio. A terrible revenge is taken on him. He values chastity aesthetically, he envies Isabella as a stronger character, and he wishes to go to bed with her to appropriate her chastity as something he can absorb. The difference between the superego and conscience is demonstrated in Angelo. He has the former, not the latter. He wishes to show his superior power by judging others, and he becomes involved in a situation with Isabella in which he demonstrates a very conscious, deliberate malice that wouldn't be true of a less powerful character. When you want to be good for the sake of strength, you can get much worse.

Angelo broke off the match with Mariana when she lost her dowry. Mariana loves him all the more: she's in love with the idea of unhappy love—it's clever of Shakespeare to make her fond of melancholy music. Angelo must learn to love a person, not an abstract idea, to love Mariana and to accept ordinary human weaknesses. Mariana must learn to love Angelo as a husband and not as a romantic, cruel figure at a distance. Both must be brought down to earth, from the abstract to the concrete and to the love of real people.

So much for justice, now for authority. There are three forms of authority: aesthetic authority, ethical authority, and religious authority. Aesthetic authority is based on the understanding that there are necessary inequalities between people that are either permanent, like intelligence, good looks, and health, or temporary, like riches and social power. We see the Duke and Escalus exercising aesthetic power in exerting society's control over outlaws like Claudio and Barnardine, and we see Isabella's superiority to Angelo. Aesthetic authority demands greater responsibility for self-judgment, and for mercy towards those who are not in power. The Provost and Escalus fulfill these responsibilities, Angelo does not. The temptation of the aesthetic authority of those who are superior is to treat it as ethical authority. On the other side, inferiors must admire superiors, but they are tempted either to envy them, as Lucio envies and resents the Duke, or they are tempted to appropriate their superiority, as Angelo is with Isabella.

Ethical authority depends on accidental superiority. Parents, for example, know more than children and should teach them, just as the children may eventually learn more and teach the parent. The ethically superior person's temptation is to treat his superiority aesthetically, to keep it to himself and refuse to share it. The ethically inferior person is tempted to be indolent, to deny responsibility and depend on others for everything—he also treats himself aesthetically.

Religious authority is shown through forgiveness. X is wronged by Y. Y is guilty. X must not be so superior aesthetically that the offense is not aesthetically real, as, for example, a beggar stealing a nickel from a millionaire. The Duke remits his penalty against Lucio because his slander is too trivial. Y must not be so inferior, ethically, that he can't understand the offense, a kleptomaniac, for example, or poor whites who insult Negroes. They cannot be regarded as free agents. The guilty person must admit that the act was wrong, that he committed it freely, and he must demand punishment. Angelo at the end quite correctly concentrates on his offense and demands punishment:

> No longer session hold upon my shame,
> But let my trial be mine own confession.
> Immediate sentence then, and sequent death,
> Is all the grace I beg.
>
> (V.i.376–79)

The wronged person must also find all extenuating circumstances without denying the offender's central guilt. Thus, Mariana says, looking to the future,

> They say best men are moulded out of faults,
> And, for the most, become much more the better
> For being a little bad. So may my husband.
>
> (V.i.444–46)

And Isabella offers extenuation in her plea to the Duke by referring to
Angelo's goodness in the past:

> I partly think
> A due sincerity governed his deeds,
> Till he did look on me. Since it is so,
> Let him not die.

(V.i.450–53)

Both are extenuations, neither denies Angelo's guilt, and Angelo does
repent. Being forgiven is harder than being punished. Many promising
reconciliations break down because people come prepared to forgive,
not to be forgiven.

   Lucio won't do right except for reasons of self-preservation, which is
as far as the secular city of self-love can get. There are many evils where
law in the secular city should not, as well as cannot, intervene. It seeks an
equitable society, but that doesn't mean it makes a good city. As long as
men live in the earthly city, the city of self-love, as Claudio recognizes,

> every scope by immoderate use
> Turns to restraint. Our natures do pursue,
> Like rats that ravin down their proper bane,
> A thirsty evil, and when we drink we die.

(I.ii.131–34)

Othello

[12 March 1947]

Between the ages of 40 and 44, Shakespeare wrote his great tragedies. There are various peaks in his career. In the first period, he solves the problem of the historical chronicle play in *Henry IV*, and of a certain kind of comedy in *As You Like It*. Then, after a slight uncertainty, he solves the problem of tragedy and produces the five tragic masterpieces: *Othello*, *Macbeth*, *King Lear*, *Antony and Cleopatra*, and *Coriolanus*.

The particular kind of tragedy Shakespeare writes differs from Greek tragedy. Both assume that the tragic figure is a great or good man suffering from a flaw that brings him to destruction. If one asks, what is the matter with the Greek character, the answer is *hybris*, which is not translatable by our word *pride*. Hybris is the belief that one is omnipotent, a god. This doesn't cause a radical difference in the way you behave, but the tragedy is the gods' punishment for a man's feeling like this. The envy of the gods is aroused when someone powerful—a power derived from them—should claim to be their equal. The gods show the heroes that they aren't. The tragic heroes in Greek drama must therefore be great men, in a worldly sense. Members of the chorus in Greek tragedy can't be heroes. The whole point in a Greek tragedy is that the hero and his tragic fate are exceptional.

Shakespeare's tragic characters, on the other hand, suffer from the Christian sin of pride: knowing you aren't God, but trying to become Him—a sin of which any of us is capable. Hybris is the manifestation of overweening self-confidence, of over-security. Pride is the manifestation of a lack of security, of the anxiety that is due to lack of faith, and of a defiance of one's finite limitations as a human being. It is a form of despair. There are two types of despair: one is the despair of willing not to be oneself, the other is the despair of willing to be oneself. The official heroes of Shakespeare's tragedies are men of passion who will not to be themselves—their passions, not unlike the humours of Jonson's characters, are the attempt to hide from themselves what they are. The other type of tragic figure is Iago, a tragic hero without passion, who refuses to yield to what he knows, who wills to be himself, who knows what he is and refuses to change, who refuses to relate himself in love to others and insists on standing outside the community. Iago relates to others only negatively.

All great Shakespearean tragedies are about first, anxiety and security, and second, freedom and necessity. In Greek tragedy the pity lies in the inevitability of the hero's fate, in Shakespearean tragedy what is pitiable is that the hero chose as he did, because he could have chosen otherwise. *Romeo and Juliet* is a play that is untypically pathetic because Romeo and Juliet are too young to be entirely responsible for their choices—they are before the age of consent. For theatrical reasons it is convenient to pick people who play prominent roles in society, but pride can exist in anyone. In Greek tragedy, a member of the audience is part of the chorus, a spectator, but in Shakespearean tragedy, whatever his position, a member of the audience must say, "This is me." He is a participant as well as a spectator.

The only thing that's pure fate in Othello is the storm. Even the dropping of the handkerchief does not occur by absolutely pure chance. The storm (1) allows Desdemona and Cassio to meet before Othello gets to Cyprus, and (2) disposes of the Turkish fleet and gives the Venetians leisure. All the rest of the tragedy is character, either personal or sociopolitical. Because Othello himself, as a general, is indispensible to Venice in the political struggle with the Turks, the Venetians permit his miscegenation. But fate is also a function of other people's characters. As we see in *Othello*, there are two wrong attitudes that people can take toward events: they can pretend what happens isn't so, or they can succumb to what happens. Brabantio could have taken Desdemona in, Cassio needn't have gotten drunk, Emilia needn't have given the handkerchief to Iago, Desdemona needn't have lied about its being lost, Roderigo needn't have attacked Cassio, etc.

The play suffers from a certain contradiction of interest. Shakespeare began writing a tragedy about a man suffering from jealousy. Iago was just a necessary agent in that case. In the original story Iago was a plain villain who was in love with Desdemona, thinking she was in love with Cassio. As Shakespeare went on, however, he became interested in why people like evil, not for their own advantage but for its own sake. The effect of this shift in interest is that Othello becomes a secondary character and Iago dominates the whole play, which finally raises difficult problems for Shakespeare.

Aaron, Shylock, Richard III, and Don John the Bastard are all patently villainous characters. Nobody trusts them. The moment they come on stage, we say, "This is the bad man." Claudius, Proteus, Oliver, and Angelo are the same. They all have direct and visible motives: Claudius is possessed by ambition, Proteus by rivalry, Oliver by envy, and Angelo by jealousy of purity. But the point about Iago is that everyone must trust him. He resembles Boyet, Friar Lawrence, Puck and Oberon, Prince Hal-Henry V, Hamlet, Pandarus, and the Duke of Vienna—all Machiavellian characters who manage people, though Iago is more like the characters in the comedies, Boyet and Puck, in that he does what he does for fun. Hal wants to rule, Hamlet to trap, Pandarus to revivify love, the Duke to make people conscious of what they are. Most Iagos on stage are impossible because they act sinister, like regular villains, so that no one will trust them. Iago must be plain and inconspicuous, absolutely ordinary, someone who could be chosen as a Secret Service man today, "honest" because he is what he looks like. Yet he must dominate the play by his will. Iago also says nothing poetically or intellectually interesting. His monologues don't square with this because, though Shakespeare may have begun the characterization of Iago as an ordinary malcontent, a then new idea, he soon realized that without soliloquies the audience would be at sea. But unlike Hamlet's soliloquies, which are most important, Iago's soliloquies reveal nothing—Iago can't explain his self to himself. To perform these soliloquies you must play them like Ariel or Puck, slightly mad and with terrific gaiety.

Iago is an example of the idea of the *acte gratuit,* a concept that is foreign to Greek thought. It first comes up in St. Augustine's *Confessions,* in the episode of the pear tree. Augustine writes that when he was young,

I lusted to thieve, and did it, compelled by no hunger, nor poverty, but through a cloyedness of welldoing, and a pamperedness of iniquity. For I stole that, of which I had enough, and much better. Nor cared I to enjoy what I stole, but joyed in the theft and sin itself. A pear tree there was near our vineyard, laden with fruit, tempting neither for colour nor taste. To shake and rob this, some lewd young fellows of us went, late one night, (having according to our pestilent custom prolonged our sports in the streets till then,) and took huge loads, not for our eating, but to fling to the very hogs, having only tasted them. And this, but to do, what we liked only, because it was misliked. Behold my heart, O God, behold my heart, which Thou hadst pity upon in the bottom of the bottomless pit. Now, behold let my heart tell Thee, what it sought there, that I should be gratuitously evil, having no temptation to ill, but the ill itself. It was foul, and I loved it; I loved to perish, I loved mine own fault, not that for which I was faulty, but my fault itself.

The idea of such an action, a pure assertion of self-autonomy, seemed to Augustine to be the central problem of ethics. One acts not on a motive of pleasure or pain, or of the rational and the irrational, but just for the hell of it. St. Augustine was the first real psychologist for he was the first to see the basic fact about human nature, namely that the natural man hates nature, and that the only act that can really satisfy him is the *acte gratuit.* His ego resents every desire of his natural self for food, sex, pleasure, logical coherence, because desires are given not chosen, and his ego seeks constantly to assert its autonomy by doing something of which the requiredness is not given, something which is completely arbitrary, a pure act of choice. The *acte gratuit* may be considered as a special case under the heading of pleasure and pain or of rational and irrational, or it may be considered primary, with the other categories secondary—it depends upon your view of psychology. One can't prove it one way or the other. If you think the *acte gratuit* is primary, you believe that a man's deepest desire is to be free of necessity through an act of pure choice.

At the same time man wants to feel important, and it is from the immediately given feelings with which he identifies himself that the natural man derives his sense of self-importance. This places him in a dilemma, for the more he emancipates himself from given necessity, the more he loses his sense of importance and becomes prey to anxiety. Necessity—hunger, for example—conditions importance. Games of all kinds, including art, are *actes gratuits* in which the players obey the necessity of rules freely chosen by themselves. Other *actes gratuits* are criminal: a man asserts his freedom by disobeying a law and retains a sense of self-importance because the law he has disobeyed is an important one, one established either by God or his society. Much crime is magic, an attempt to make free with necessities. All *actes gratuits* involve the Fall of Man.

Charles Williams gives the best account of the Fall. "The nature of the Fall," he writes,

> —both while possible and when actual—is clearly defined. The "fruit of the tree" is to bring an increase of knowledge. That increase, however, is, and is desired as being, of a particular kind. It is not merely to know more, but to know in another method. It is primarily the advance (if it can be so called) from knowing good to knowing good and evil; it is (secondarily) the knowing "as gods." A certain knowledge was, by its nature, confined to divine beings. Its communication to man would be, by its nature, disastrous to man. . . .

God, Williams continues, may know evil through intelligence, but

> It was not so possible for man, and the myth is the tale of that impos-
> sibility. However solemn and intellectual the exposition of the
> act sounds, the act itself is simple enough. It is easy for us now, after
> the terrible and prolonged habit of mankind; it was not, perhaps,
> very difficult then—as easy as picking a fruit from a tree. It was
> merely to wish to know an antagonism in the good, to find out what
> the good would be like if a contradiction were introduced into it.
> Man desired to know schism in the universe. It was a knowledge
> reserved to God; man had been warned that he could not bear it—
> "in the day that thou eatest thereof thou shalt surely die." A serpen-
> tine subtlety overwhelmed that statement with a grander promise—
> "Ye shall be as gods, knowing good and evil." Unfortunately to be as
> gods meant, for the Adam, to die, for to know evil, for them, was to
> know it not by pure intelligence but by experience. It was, precisely,
> to experience the opposite of good, that is, the deprivation of the
> good, the slow destruction of the good, and of themselves with the
> good.

Adam and Eve, Williams concludes, "knew good," but

> they wished to know good and evil. Since there was not—since there
> never has been and never will be—anything else than the good to
> know, they knew good as antagonism. All difference consists in the
> mode of knowledge. They had what they wanted. That they did not
> like it when they got it does not alter the fact that they certainly
> got it.

Iago tells Roderigo that he doesn't like the way Cassio, not he, got the
Lieutenancy, and Roderigo asks why Iago then doesn't leave Othello.
Iago professes an intention to take revenge—"I follow him to serve my
turn upon him" (I.i.42)—and plays the worldly-wise cynic for Roderigo's
benefit. But no one else seems to think that Iago has lost out for the job.
Neither Othello, nor Cassio, nor Emilia thinks Iago should be jealous of
Cassio's promotion. Iago also puts up the idea that Othello has cuck-
olded him, without taking it seriously, and again speaks faintly of taking
revenge by seducing Desdemona:

> Now I do love her too;
> Not out of absolute lust (though peradventure
> I stand accountant for as great a sin)

But partly led to diet my revenge,
For that I do suspect the lusty Moor
Hath leap'd into my seat. . . .

(II.i.299–305)

If Iago had wanted revenge, he would have tried to have Desdemona
seduced by someone. But he doesn't care about that—he just wants to
make Othello jealous:

And nothing can or shall content my soul
Till I am even'd with him, wife for wife;
Or failing so, yet that I put the Moor
At least into a jealousy so strong
That judgment cannot cure.

(II.i.307–11)

Othello asks at the end, very reasonably, why Iago has done what he has
done. Iago refuses to answer. He can't, any more than Leopold and Loeb
could for their killing of the young boy. The whole point of revenge is to
confront people: "Now I'll pay you for what you did." But Iago wants to
destroy everyone. Out of Desdemona's goodness, he says, he will "make
the net / That shall enmesh them all" (II.iii.367–68). Iago must confine
himself to temptation. He must make people destroy themselves by making them instruments of his will. Once he has to take a hand, once he has
to commit murder himself, he's lost. And I think Iago never lies about a
point of fact. He may hold out false hopes to people who would never
believe these hopes were they not blinded by their own desires, and he
may select aspects of truth, but he doesn't lie about facts.

We are able to see what other characters are like by the way Iago acts
towards them, and they emerge through their interactions with his
greater consciousness. You'd expect Emilia to know Iago best—yet she
gives him the handkerchief. She is stupid. She thinks men are all crazy
anyway, that you must put up with them or they'll make a fuss. Anything
for a quiet life. She calls Iago "wayward" when she steals the handkerchief to please him:

My wayward husband hath a hundred times
Woo'd me to steal it; but she so loves the token
(For he conjur'd her she should ever keep it)
That she reserves it evermore about her
To kiss and talk to. I'll have the work ta'en out
And give't Iago.

What he will do with it heaven knows, not I;
I nothing but to please his fantasy.

(III.iii.292–99)

Emilia doesn't think too clearly about what life is about. She has a drive
not to think about what she is like or what anyone else is like. She con-
dones adultery, and then rails on Bianca. Stupid Emilia, by stealing the
handkerchief, kills Desdemona.

Roderigo is the stupidest of the men whom Iago deals with, but he is
the one who destroys Iago. Roderigo is neither handsome nor bright,
and he is envious of those who are, but he does have one asset—money.
He is the type who buys what he wants with money, including sleeping
with a lot of girls. He won't love anyone, however, because he is unattrac-
tive and afraid he won't be loved back. He may, though, care for Desdemona a little. He wants to be like Cassio and Iago. Iago manages him by
treating him as worldly-wise. Iago tries to get Roderigo to get Desdemona's marriage to Othello annulled, and Brabantio says that he wishes
Roderigo had her. But when the marriage is confirmed, Roderigo is
ready to give up because of the element of affection for Desdemona.
Iago then talks of the great power of his money—"Put money in thy
purse. . . . Fill thy purse with money. . . . Make all the money thou canst"
(I.iii.346, 354, 362)—which is what Roderigo would like to believe. In the
next Act, Iago suggests to Roderigo that Desdemona is in love with Cassio because of Cassio's beauty as well as Othello's physical unattractive-
ness, again reasons that appeal to Roderigo and that Iago uses to con-
vince him that he must get rid of Cassio:

Iago. First, I must tell thee this: Desdemona is directly in love with
him.

Rod. With him? Why, 'tis not possible.

Iago. Lay thy finger thus, and let thy soul be instructed. Mark me
with what violence she first lov'd the Moor, but for bragging and
telling her fantastical lies; and will she love him still for prating? Let
not thy discreet heart think it. Her eye must be fed; and what delight
shall she have to look on the devil? When the blood is made dull
with the act of sport, there should be, again to inflame it and give
satiety a fresh appetite, loveliness in favour, sympathy in years, manners, and beauties; all which the Moor is defective in. Now for want
of these requir'd conveniences, her delicate tenderness will find itself abus'd, begin to heave the gorge, disrelish and abhor the Moor.
Very nature will instruct her in it and compel her to some second

choice. Now, sir, this granted (as it is a most pregnant and unforc'd position), who stands so eminent in the degree of this fortune as Cassio does?

(II.i.220–42)

In Act IV, in their last set-to, Roderigo becomes suspicious, and Iago puts forth the idea that Roderigo kill Cassio. Roderigo is not suited to this employment—he's cowardly and he's shocked, and Iago has to incite him very strongly. But because of his fear and guilt, he fails to bring the murder off, and this causes Iago's downfall. Iago thought Roderigo was easier to handle than he proves.

Brabantio is an old widower, with an only child, who puts his trust in birth and breeding. His real satisfaction in life is a daughter who adores him, and he resents her having any suitor. Brabantio wants his daughter to remain a child. Iago knows just how to treat him, repeatedly stressing the image of his beautiful, nobly-born daughter in bed with a black man:

Even now, now, very now, an old black ram / Is tupping your white ewe. . . . you'll have your daughter cover'd with a Barbary horse. . . . I am one, sir, that come to tell you your daughter and the Moor are now making the beast with two backs.

(I.i.88–89, 111–12, 116–18)

The business about magic (I.i.172–74) is truer than Brabantio or others realize. Mysteriously, we're told at the end of the play that he died of grief over the marriage.

Cassio is a quite familiar type—he gets on with women much better than with men. He's a ladies' man, not a seducer, but he's better at holding wool in the drawing room than being in a barroom where he's ill at ease—women shouldn't be there, anyway. He wants to be authoritative and one of the boys, but when in trouble, he runs to the ladies. How right that he should be the one to be quarrelsome when he gets tight, a characteristic of a person who has hidden resentments. He wants to get friendly with Iago, the "simple soldier," and he fights Montano, the governor of Cyprus, whom he would like to be. Innocent bystanders at drunken parties often become the target of hidden resentments. Iago gets Cassio to drink by playing on his wish to be one of the boys, and afterwards he finds it easy to get him to go to Desdemona.

The nasty side of Cassio shows up in his relation to Bianca. She loves him and he doesn't love her, and she is of a lower class, both of which give him an unaccustomed feeling of power, but he abuses his power over her out of a sense of his own inferiority. He's cruel in giving the handkerchief to Bianca to copy, knowing she will think it's from another woman and become jealous—that is sadism. Cassio doesn't treat Bianca badly in private, but he talks unpleasantly about her in public, which eventually helps undo him and precipitate the climax of the play, since Othello overhears him and thinks he is talking of Desdemona. He refuses to stay with Othello during his fit. He might have given or been given an explanation, but Cassio is frightened by Iago's description of Othello's bad temper.

Desdemona is a young schoolgirl who wants above all to be a grown-up. Othello wins her by the tale of what he has done, by the romantic idea of adventure—ironically, this really is a kind of magic, though not Brabantio's notion of magic. He does not win her by sexual attraction. She is afraid of sex. Othello is an older man and a father image to her. At the same time she behaves as if she knows she's conferring a favor on him, because her color puts her in a superior position. She's a romantic girl going slumming. And she wants to get away from home. She pushes Cassio's case tactlessly, because she's excited by the idea of a woman's power over a soldier. She's never done anything, she wants to do something, and she overdoes it. She drops the handkerchief when she is shocked by Othello's being short with her for the first time. When she has to confess the loss of the handkerchief, Othello's rage makes her see him as a person for the first time, and she doesn't understand him at all and is frightened. When she hears him call her a strumpet and a whore, "that cunning whore of Venice / That married with Othello" (IV.ii.89–90), she doesn't ask for an explanation, she cries. In her last conversation with Emilia, Desdemona begins to talk like a woman for the first time, and begins to realize the meaning of adultery as a circumstance of life, not just of books. She may see her love for Othello as romantic, but in calling Ludovico a "proper man," she may also be thinking that he is the sort of man she should have married. In time she might well have been unfaithful.

Othello is the black outsider who wants to become a member of the community that only tolerates him because it cannot do without his military competence. He sees Desdemona as a way of uniting himself to the community and being loved and accepted as a person. The marriage is a way of making the grade, but it also masks his own inner insecurity. He initially thinks people love him very much for fear that they don't love him at all. His paranoiac suspicion is an expression of fear that people are ignoring him. He therefore makes himself the center of the universe in a negative way, preferring a negative interest in him to no interest at all.

There are two kinds of sexual jealousy. Ordinary sexual jealousy involves the infidelity of a person who has given himself to you when you discover that you can't retain that gift. The bigger type is the jealousy of a person seen as a goddess or god-idol. In this type, (a) the idol must act in accord with your will, and (b) must act so of his own free will. Here, the moment you doubt, you're sunk, because once the idol is seen as human, like oneself, all assurances, all acts, can have a double interpretation. Either you must give up the idol or you must realize that you're dependent on another human being. Iago has only to suggest suspicion to Othello. All he has to do is cite a fact, like Desdemona's deception of Brabantio, and Othello's whole world quickly collapses:

> I had been happy if the general camp,
> Pioners and all, had tasted her sweet body,
> So I had nothing known. O, now for ever
> Farewell the tranquil mind! farewell content!
> Farewell the plumed troop, and the big wars
> That make ambition virtue! O, farewell!
> Farewell the neighing steed and the shrill trump,
> The spirit-stirring drum, th' ear-piercing fife,
> The royal banner, and all quality,
> Pride, pomp, and circumstance of glorious war!
> And O ye mortal engines whose rude throats
> Th' immortal Jove's dread clamours counterfeit,
> Farewell! Othello's occupation's gone.
>
> (III.iii.345–57)

But Othello knows nothing. What does he know? Doubt and jealousy. Iago's report of Cassio's dream (III.iii.413–26) may be read as simply a lie. But it can also be thought of as perfectly true—I'm more in accord with this interpretation. It leaves Othello to answer his own questions. In the last scene Desdemona finally asks for evidence, but too late.

The big figures in Shakespeare's tragedies do not learn anything—that is the ultimate tragedy of Shakespearean tragedy. Othello says in his last speech,

> Soft you! A word or two before you go.
> I have done the state some service, and they know't—

No more of that. I pray you, in your letters,
When you shall these unlucky deeds relate,
Speak of me as I am. Nothing extenuate,
Nor set down aught in malice. Then must you speak
Of one that lov'd not wisely, but too well;
Of one not easily jealous, but, being wrought,
Perplex'd in the extreme; of one whose hand
(Like the base Indian) threw a pearl away
Richer than all his tribe; of one whose subdu'd eyes,
Albeit unused to the melting mood,
Drop tears as fast as the Arabian trees
Their med'cinable gum. Set you down this;
And say besides that in Aleppo once,
Where a malignant and a turban'd Turk
Beat a Venetian and traduc'd the state,
I took by the throat the circumcised dog
And smote him—thus.   *He stabs himself.*
                                       (V.ii.338–56)

Othello learns nothing, remains in defiance, and is damned. He cannot think why he did what he did, or realize what was wrong. His thoughts are not on Desdemona at all. He just recalls he did some service to the state, and he ends by identifying himself with another outsider, the Moslem Turk. He has no realization of why he was jealous. It's easy for us to see that Othello and Desdemona should not have married, but he never does.

Given Iago's knowledge, he should be a saint. There must be some significance in the fact that Iago is the only person in the play who exhibits a knowledge of Holy Writ: "I am not what I am" (I.i.65), he says, and he can lecture and catechize on virtue like a theologian. His lines, in fact, have frequent theological overtones and allusions. In Iago we have, I think, a very remarkable portrait by Shakespeare of the villain as an inverted saint, a saint manqué. On the surface, nothing might seem less probable. Yet Shakespeare was surely right in suggesting this, because the saint and the villain have very similar psychologies. In both, ethics and aesthetics become almost the same thing. There is a similar detachment and similar freedom in both with respect to human relations, an absence of the usual scruples and motivations that govern or trouble most living.

Iago has the knowledge of living described by the hero in Dostoevsky's
Notes from Underground:

I believe that the best definition of man is the ungrateful biped. But
that is not all, that is not his worst defect; his worst defect is his
perpetual moral obliquity, perpetual—from the days of the Flood to
the Schleswig-Holstein period. . . . The only thing one can't say
[about the history of the world] is that it's rational. The very word
sticks in one's throat. And, indeed, this is the odd thing that is continually happening: there are continually turning up in life moral
and rational persons, sages and lovers of humanity, who make it
their object to live all their lives as morally and rationally as possible,
to be, so to speak, a light to their neighbours simply in order to show
them that it is possible to live morally and rationally in this world.
And yet we all know that those very people sooner or later have been
false to themselves, playing some queer trick, often a most unseemly
one. Now I ask you: what can be expected of man since he is a being
endowed with such strange qualities? Shower upon him every
earthly blessing, drown him in a sea of happiness, so that nothing
but bubbles of bliss can be seen on the surface; give him economic
prosperity, such that he should have nothing else to do but sleep,
eat cakes and busy himself with the continuation of his species, and
even then out of sheer ingratitude, sheer spite, man would play you
some nasty trick. He would even risk his cakes and would deliberately desire the most fatal rubbish, the most uneconomical absurdity, simply to introduce into all this positive good sense his fatal fantastic element. It is just his fantastic dreams, his vulgar folly, that he
will desire to retain, simply in order to prove to himself—as though
that were so necessary—that men still are men and not the keys of
a piano, which the laws of nature threaten to control so completely
that soon one will be able to desire nothing but by the calendar.
And that is not all: even if man really were nothing but a piano-key,
even if this were proved to him by natural science and mathematics,
even then he would not become reasonable, but would purposely
do something perverse out of simple ingratitude, simply to gain his
point. . . . the whole work of man really seems to consist in nothing
but proving to himself every minute that he is a man and not a
piano-key! . . .

You will scream at me (that is, if you condescend to do so) that no
one is touching my free will, that all they are concerned with is that

my will should of itself, of its own free will, coincide with my own normal interests, with the laws of nature and arithmetic.

Good heavens, gentlemen, what sort of free will is left when we come to tabulation and arithmetic, when it will all be a case of twice two makes four? Twice two makes four without my will. As if free will meant that!

Macbeth

[19 March 1947]

Macbeth is the best known of Shakespeare's plays. It is difficult to say anything particularly new or revealing about it. I can only raise some fairly obvious points in talking about three themes: murder, the nature of time and fate, and the three communities in the play—the community of light, the community of darkness and malice, and the world of the human being, which is in middle earth and is pulled simultaneously towards both of the others.

I don't know how many of you are, like myself, detective story addicts. Why must you have a murder rather than a lesser crime in a detective story? Because unless it's a murder, you don't want to find out who did it. In *Macbeth* there are various kinds of death and bloodshed. In the beginning of the play there is a description of how Macbeth killed Macdonwald and we learn of the execution of the treacherous Thane of Cawdor. Neither is a murder. A war killing is not murder in that the killer and the killed are not in a personal relationship: each sees in the other a representative of the enemy force. And an executioner sees not a person but an example of a certain crime, while the executed one sees the executioner as a representative of justice. Murder is defined by the intent to kill in a situation in which the relation between the killer and the killed is personal.

There are three classes of crime: (A) offenses against God and one's neighbor or neighbors, (B) offenses against God and society, and (C) offenses against God. All crimes, of course, are offenses against oneself, not only direct ones like suicide or drink or drugs. Murder is a member and the only member of Class B, offenses against God and society. The characteristic common to all crimes in Class A, offenses against God and one's neighbor, is that it is possible, at least theoretically, either that restitution can be made to the injured party—for example, stolen goods can be returned—or that the injured party can forgive the criminal—for example, in the case of rape. Consequently society as a whole is only indirectly involved. Its representatives—the police, etc.—act in the interests of the injured party. Murder is unique in that it abolishes the party it injures. No one is there to accept restitution or to grant forgiveness, and the murderer ceases to be related to the injured party. Murderers are often said to see ghosts, because a ghost is an expression of the murderer's desire not to be left alone with the consciousness of his crime, of his need to keep up the relationship with the person he has killed. We want to discover the murderer in a detective story because in other offenses the law acts on behalf of the injured person, but in murder, law and society must be substitutes for the injured party and must act on his behalf.

As to the murderer's end, of the three alternatives—execution, suicide, and madness—the first is preferable. If the murderer commits suicide, he refuses to repent, and if he goes mad, he cannot repent, but if he does not repent, society cannot forgive. Execution, on the other hand, is the act of atonement by which the murderer is forgiven by society. In real life I disapprove of capital punishment, but in a detective story we demand capital punishment as the only proper end. The object of capital punishment is justice, the fulfillment of the assumption that blood will have blood, that there be a life for a life. The murderer must desire to confess and must die willingly, and society must forgive him— the executioner asks forgiveness of the man he hangs. If you want life imprisonment, you are saying that the murderer refuses to acknowledge or realize his guilt and that all that can be done is to exclude him from society. There can be no question of expiation—death alone is an expiation. If the murderer admits guilt, either you must execute him or take it upon yourself to know the will of the victim and let him go.

In *Macbeth*, the parallel to murder is treachery. The Thane of Cawdor is treacherous, admits his guilt, and willingly pays his debt. Malcolm reports that he has spoken

> With one that saw him die; who did report
> That very frankly he confess'd his treasons,
> Implor'd your Highness' pardon, and set forth
> A deep repentance. Nothing in his life
> Became him like the leaving it.

> (I.iv.4–8)

Macbeth, and secondarily Lady Macbeth, show how the murderer is isolated from the society that represents the injured party and can see to restitution. Macbeth can't sleep.

> Methought I heard a voice cry "Sleep no more!
> Macbeth does murther sleep."—the innocent sleep,
> Sleep that knits up the ravell'd sleave of care,
> The death of each day's life, sore labour's bath,

> Balm of hurt minds, great nature's second course,
> Chief nourisher in life's feast.
>
> (II.ii.35–40)

Neither can he forget, because there is no one else to remember. He is unable to enter the world of wish and dream because the wish has become a fact, and the past cannot remain the past because it is related to him and to no other:

> Better be with the dead,
> Whom we, to gain our peace, have sent to peace,
> Than on the torture of the mind to lie
> In restless ecstasy.
>
> (III.ii.19–22)

Macbeth makes three revealing remarks to the ghost of Banquo that are based on his horror of the fact that the ghost isn't conscious and cannot say, "You did it":

> Thou canst not say I did it. Never shake
> Thy gory locks at me.
>
> (III.iv.50–51)

> Blood hath been shed ere now, i' th' olden time,
> Ere humane statute purg'd the gentle weal;
> Ay, and since too, murthers have been perform'd
> Too terrible for the ear. The time has been
> That, when the brains were out, the man would die,
> And there an end! But now they rise again,
> With twenty mortal murthers on their crowns,
> And push us from our stools. This is more strange
> Than such a murther is.
>
> (III.iv.75–83)

> Avaunt, and quit my sight! Let the earth hide thee!
> Thy bones are marrowless, thy blood is cold;
> Thou hast no speculation in those eyes
> Which thou dost glare with!
>
> (III.iv.93–96)

In the final battle scene Macbeth refuses to commit suicide and says, "Why should I play the Roman fool and die / On mine own sword?" (V.viii.1–2). He says this because he wants justice, he wants relation with other human beings. If he is killed in battle, relation is restored.

Lady Macbeth is in a different position. She does commit suicide. She does not herself murder, but she is guilty in intention, and really more guilty than Macbeth because she stirs him up:

> The raven himself is hoarse
> That croaks the fatal entrance of Duncan
> Under my battlements. Come, you spirits
> That tend on mortal thoughts, unsex me here,
> And fill me, from the crown to the toe, top-full
> Of direst cruelty! Make thick my blood;
> Stop up th' access and passage to remorse,
> That no compunctious visitings of nature
> Shake my fell purpose nor keep peace between
> Th' effect and it!
>
> (I.v.39–48)

> Was the hope drunk
> Wherein you dress'd yourself? Hath it slept since?
> And wakes it now to look so green and pale
> At what it did so freely? From this time
> Such I account thy love. Art thou afeard
> To be the same in thine own act and valour
> As thou art in desire?
>
> (I.vii.35–41)

> I have given suck, and know
> How tender 'tis to love the babe that milks me.
> I would, while it was smiling in my face,
> Have pluck'd my nipples from his boneless gums
> And dash'd the brains out, had I sworn as you
> Have done to this.
>   *Macb.*   If we should fail?
>   *Lady.*   We fail?
> But screw your courage to the sticking place,
> And we'll not fail.
>
> (I.vii.54–61)

Consciously, Lady Macbeth gets what she asks for, though not entirely. She commits suicide because she's more lonely than Macbeth, and she is more lonely because she's related to the victim only through Macbeth. She cannot see ghosts and apparitions, only images of what has happened. She has only memories. There is no way in which she can be directly reconciled.

Usually in tragedy a good person is made to suffer through a flaw in his goodness. In *Macbeth* this pattern is reversed: it is the streak of goodness that causes pathos and suffering. Macbeth and Lady Macbeth attempt to be murderers without malice. The Witches, who, like Iago, represent the world of malice, may suffer in much worse ways, but their suffering can't be seen—they enjoy what they do. What Macbeth does can only be done without suffering if it is entirely malicious. Richard III finally breaks down, but in most murders there is no remorse, because the murderer is full of malice. Macbeth and Lady Macbeth never show direct malice. They would act as devils without becoming so, and that destroys them. Macbeth tells Lady Macbeth that during the murder of Duncan, Duncan's grooms cried "God bless us" and "Amen" in their sleep and that

>   I could not say "Amen!"
> When they did say "God bless us!"
> *Lady.*   Consider it not so deeply.
> *Macb.* But wherefore could not I pronounce "Amen"?
> I had most need of blessing, and "Amen"
> Stuck in my throat.
> *Lady.*   These deeds must not be thought
> After these ways. So, it will make us mad.
>
>   (II.ii.29–35)

What Lady Macbeth warns Macbeth of applies to her as well, though she doesn't yet know it because she is less imaginative than Macbeth.

Time, free will, and necessity make up the second theme of the play. The Witches foretell future events, and Macbeth is thereby tempted to his destruction. There is a difference between classical and Christian attitudes toward consulting oracles about the future. In classical times you should consult oracles—it was prohibited by the Caesars only for reasons of their own political security. Since everything is willed by Zeus, there is no distinction between what will happen and what ought to happen. You consult Zeus to see if a particular design will fail, and if it will, it ought not to be done. The Christian view is that man has free will, in other words, that what will happen is not the same as what ought to happen. God permits what he forbids, and God, being outside time, can see what man will do without making him do it. Spirits are believed to have similar, though lesser, powers of prevision. Consulting oracles is forbidden. As a finite historical creature, man has a past to repent of, a present to choose in, and a future to hope for. God can foresee the future as experience, but man can never believe in the future except as a possibility depending on his own choice, which is the reverse of his knowledge of evil, which he can know only through experience. As Henry IV's speech on reading "the book of fate" suggests (*2 Henry IV*, III.i.45–56), one either takes the future as despair or as a function of choice.

The Witches do not appear except to people who in a sense call on them. They tell Macbeth that he is to be King. He could accept it as a fated fact—"If chance will have me King, why chance may crown me, / Without my stir" (I.iii.143–44)—but he doesn't do so, nor does he ask what he should do. Instead, he says,

> why do I yield to that suggestion
> Whose horrid image doth unfix my hair
> And make my seated heart knock at my ribs
> Against the use of nature? Present fears
> Are less than horrible imaginings.
> My thought, whose murther yet is but fantastical,
> Shakes so my single state of man that function
> Is smother'd in surmise and nothing is
> But what is not.
>
> (I.iii.134–42)

Macbeth thinks he knows the particular way the Witches' prophecy will come to pass. It is a belief in a particular fulfillment in time, but not a complete acceptance of fate, because he cannot think about the future with the certainty that exists about the past. There is a slight suggestion that Banquo is tempted by the Witches too, but he doesn't yield to the temptation:

> Merciful powers,
> Restrain in me the cursed thoughts that nature
> Gives way to in repose!
>
> (II.i.7–9)

After seeing Banquo's ghost, Macbeth consults the Witches again. He has no moral obligation to go to them, he has a compulsion to go:

> More shall they speak; for now I am bent to know
> By the worst means the worst. For mine own good
> All causes shall give way. I am in blood
> Stepp'd in so far that, should I wade no more,
> Returning were as tedious as go o'er.
>
> (III.iv.134–38)

If the future is determined, all causes shall not give way, but Macbeth doesn't believe fully in a determined future.

The Witches present Macbeth with four apparitions. The first, "*an Armed Head*," whom the First Witch says "knows thy thought" (IV.i.69), tells him to beware Macduff. The second, "*a Bloody Child*," tells him that "none of woman born / Shall harm Macbeth" (IV.i.80–81), but this doesn't change his mind about killing Macduff:

> But yet I'll make assurance double sure
> And take a bond of fate. Thou shalt not live!
> That I may tell pale-hearted fear it lies
> And sleep in spite of thunder.
>
> (IV.i.83–86)

The third apparition, "*a Child Crowned, with a tree in his hand*," warns Macbeth of the movement of Birnam Wood to Dunsinane, which doesn't perturb him, but he still worries about Macduff's issue. The final apparition is the show of kings in Banquo's line. When he is informed, a few moments afterwards, that Macduff has fled to England, Macbeth decides to murder Macduff's wife and children.

> Time, thou anticipat'st my dread exploits.
> The flighty purpose never is o'ertook
> Unless the deed go with it. From this moment
> The very firstlings of my heart shall be
> The firstlings of my hand. And even now,
> To crown my thoughts with acts, be it thought and done!
>
> (IV.i.144–49)

Macbeth tries to control the future. He never asks the Witches, "Should I do this or that?" and he never asks them about the means he should employ.

The consequence of the wish to control the future, for both Macbeth and Lady Macbeth, is to destroy the significance of time completely. At the end of the play, when he is told that Lady Macbeth is dead, Macbeth says,

> She should have died hereafter;
> There would have been a time for such a word.
> To-morrow, and to-morrow, and to-morrow
> Creeps in this petty pace from day to day
> To the last syllable of recorded time;

And all our yesterdays have lighted fools
The way to dusty death.

(V.v.17–23)

The whole sequence of past, present, and future is broken for them, and so, too, is the circular revolution of natural time, of sleeping and waking.

The third theme of *Macbeth* is the depiction of three kinds of societies. The first, the world of light, is the coinherence of all flesh in love. The second, the coinherence of a certain group, a community of friends, in truth, justice, and love is possible, but it is not complete. The third is the pseudocoinherence of the world of malice, the world of the Witches and witchcraft, in which "Fair is foul, and foul is fair" (I.i.10). Macbeth's first line in the play—"So foul and fair a day I have not seen" (I.iii.38)—suggests that inversion, though he can't quite say it. The world of the Witches, too, is not complete in itself. The Witches try to get hold of people to use for their purposes. Their likely victims include unmarried women who have fallen out with their lovers, unimportant people who are ambitious, and morally ugly or greedy people. The duties of the Witch include both personal malice—as, for example, the Witch who proposes to pursue the sailor's wife to Aleppo for refusing to give her chestnuts (I.iii.4–9)—and general malice, to raise storms, for example, to "untie the winds and let them fight / Against the churches" (IV.i.52–53). Spirits can enter human bodies, but the bodies cannot become theirs.

In a perfect society all human beings would be neighbors. In the society of the middle earth, this is not so. Certain groups can compose an internal neighborhood, though each group is not necessarily a neighbor to the other. In *Macbeth* there are two hostile groups—Norway, led by Macdonwald, and Scotland, led by Duncan. Killing between the two is not regarded as murder. Malice can affect the world of middle earth and create abnormalities, including treachery and murder within the group. Deaths caused by struggle between the groups are compensable. Who belongs to your group? Blood relations, relations through the feudal loyalty of oaths freely given, and a guest. Even a stranger who has come to the group as a guest in disguise and is your deadliest enemy is included: his physical proximity makes him your neighbor.

There are two doctors in *Macbeth*, the Scottish doctor who tells Macbeth he cannot help the sick Lady Macbeth, and the English doctor who tells Malcolm and Macduff how the good King of England is able to heal people with his touch. Macbeth turns in despair to the Scottish doctor for help in healing Scotland as well as his wife:

> If thou couldst, doctor, cast
> The water of my land, find her disease,
> And purge it to a sound and pristine health,
> I would applaud thee to the very echo,
> That should applaud again.—Pull't off, I say.—
> What rhubarb, senna, or what purgative drug,
> Will scour these English hence?
>
> (V.iii.50–56)

But Macbeth, not the English, is the disease of his kingdom.

In his dialogue with Macduff on the good king, Malcolm accuses himself of various crimes. He says he is lustful, and Macduff answers that lust does more harm to the king than to his kingdom. He says he is avaricious, and Macduff says that's worse, but not fatal. Malcolm says, finally,

> The king-becoming graces,
> As justice, verity, temp'rance, stableness,
> Bounty, perseverance, mercy, lowliness,
> Devotion, patience, courage, fortitude,
> I have no relish of them, but abound
> In the division of each several crime,
> Acting it many ways. Nay, had I pow'r, I should
> Pour the sweet milk of human concord into hell,
> Uproar the universal peace, confound
> All unity on earth.
>
> (IV.iii.91–100)

To this declaration of total malice, Macduff responds, "Fit to govern? / No, not to live" (IV.iii.102–3). Civilization can endure a good many ills, but unless people will fulfill their word, there can be no civilization.

The idea of love or obligation versus malice is played out in terms of light and darkness as well as in imagery of blood in *Macbeth*. The play takes place largely in the physical darkness of nature at night, which for the good is a time of rest and danger, and for the guilty a time of hiding and dread—and bad dreams. There is also the internal darkness of the malicious, the conscience-stricken, the frightened, the injured. The opening scene of the play, the first Witches' scene, presents the darkness of malice as well as thunder and lightning. The following scene in the camp takes place in light (I.ii), with the shadow of treachery invisible, and it presents honest bloodshed. The next scene shows the Witches again (I.iii.), and the scene after that reveals the light in Duncan's palace, but also Macbeth's inner darkness:

> The Prince of Cumberland! That is a step
> On which I must fall down, or else o'erleap,
> For in my way it lies. Stars, hide your fires!
> Let not light see my black and deep desires.
>
> (I.iv.48–51)

As he approaches Macbeth's castle, Duncan, a man of light, says, "This castle hath a pleasant seat," and Banquo says it is approved by "This guest of summer / The temple-haunting martlet" (I.vi.1, 3–4). In the scene before, within the castle and also in daylight, Lady Macbeth has called upon the dark raven as well as the night:

> Come, thick night,
> And pall thee in the dunnest smoke of hell,
> That my keen knife see not the wound it makes,
> Nor heaven peep through the blanket of the dark
> To cry "Hold, hold!"
>
> (I.v.51–55)

It should be dark in the murder scene, with the lights of people wrongfully moving about, and with the visible wrong of blood on Macbeth's and Lady Macbeth's hands. The Porter is a character of light and heralds the coming of morning, but the blood on the grooms again shows the opposite. Macbeth consults with the two murderers at the palace in the afternoon light (III.i), and, still at the palace, he calls upon night:

> Come, seeling night,
> Scarf up the tender eye of pitiful day,
> And with thy bloody and invisible hand
> Cancel and tear to pieces that great bond
> Which keeps me pale! Light thickens, and the crow
> Makes wing to th' rooky wood.
>
> (III.ii.46–51)

The light struck out during the murder of Banquo (III.iii) allows Fleance to escape. The feast in the palace is lighted, there is blood on the murderer's face, the Ghost of Banquo appears to Macbeth, and Macbeth says, "It will have blood, they say; blood will have blood" (III.iv.122). Act III ends with Lennox and a Lord, two men of light with the shadow of fear upon them. The scene in which Macbeth sees the apparitions (IV.i) presents again the dark of the Witches. In the succeeding scene with Macduff's wife and child (IV.ii), there is physical light and an innocent child, but the shadow of fear turns into reality. In the next scene in England the two fugitives, Malcolm and Macduff, speak to each other in a "desolate shade" (IV.iii.1), but after Malcolm tests Macduff and overcomes his suspicion of him, light breaks for a moment. Then Macduff hears the news of Macbeth's slaughter of his family. The opening scene of Act V introduces the doctor who talks of the darkness of guilt, and it contrasts Macbeth's darkness with the light of a battle in which blood is rightfully shed and restitution is made.

Lady Macduff's line, "All is the fear, and nothing is the love" (IV.ii.12), might be the motto of *Macbeth*, and at the end of the play, it is shown to be no longer true. But the play is incomplete. The Hecate scene is put in by another author. And the motivation of Macduff's flight is not clear. When Ross tells Lady Macduff that she cannot know whether Macduff left her and their children because of "his wisdom or his fear," she answers:

> Wisdom? To leave his wife, to leave his babes
> His mansion, and his titles, in a place
> From whence himself does fly? He loves us not,
> He wants the natural touch. For the poor wren,
> (The most diminutive of birds) will fight,
> Her young ones in her nest, against the owl.
> All is the fear, and nothing is the love,
> As little is the wisdom, where the flight
> So runs against all reason.
>
> (IV.ii.6–14)

And Malcolm too voices suspicions:

> Why in that rawness left you wife and child,
> Those precious motives, those strong knots of love,
> Without leave-taking?
>
> (IV.iii.26–28)

Some material must have dropped out of the text involving Macduff's uncertainty as to which side he would be on. Considering Macbeth's character, why does he act in this completely crazy way?

King Lear

[26 March 1947]

It is embarrassing to talk for an hour or an hour and a half about great masterpieces. It's fun to talk about minor and neglected works because one can point out new stuff. Even Dante has difficulties that need to be explained. But *Othello, King Lear, Antony and Cleopatra* are works that are perfectly easy to understand. Is *Lear* better read or acted? —a great controversy. If I finally come down on the side of those who think it is *not* actable . . . but let's postpone that.

First, the construction of *King Lear*. The play divides into only two parts, possibly three. The first scene of Act I introduces Gloucester, Kent, and Edmund, in a minor key, and then Lear and his three daughters. It is followed by Edmund's plot against his father, Gloucester (I.ii). There is then an interval of time, the only one, during which, as in Act I, scene iii, we are shown Lear's quarrels with Goneril and Regan. Act III is the crisis: the storm on the heath, the madness of Lear, the blinding of Gloucester, the arrival of the French army to the rescue. There is an interval in Act IV, which is composed of Goneril's and Regan's intrigues for Edmund, the meeting of the mad Lear and the blind Gloucester—a critical scene—and the reconciliation scene between Cordelia and the no longer passionately mad, but childish, Lear. The weather is now fine, the storm is over. Act V presents the battle and the climax of the play: the self-destruction of one daughter, the murder of the other, the killing of Cordelia, the death of Lear.

King Lear is unique among the tragedies in having a fully developed subplot, the first in the plays since *Henry IV*. In *Henry IV* Falstaff is the antithesis of Hal. Gloucester and Lear are similarly opposed in *King Lear*. In the main plot Lear is mistaken about his daughters and banishes the good daughter, in the subplot Gloucester is mistaken about his sons and banishes the good son. Lear is directly responsible, Gloucester less so, because he believes someone else. One father goes mad, the other father is blinded. One father meets his good daughter and recognizes her, the other father meets and fails to recognize his good son. Two daughters destroy each other, the good son kills the bad son. Lear discovers his dead daughter and dies of grief, Gloucester discovers his good son, who has tended him, and also dies. In the main plot, unreasoning passion, good and bad, causes catastrophe. In the subplot, reason, good and bad, causes the smash. The violence in the subplot is thus designed to make up for its comparative prose. Lear is more tragic because he wills his feelings, Gloucester more pathetic because he tries to avoid suffering.

The direction in which Shakespeare's interests are moving is from individuals towards states, the kind of states of being in which individuals exist that Blake wished to represent in his prophetic books. Beatrice and Benedick in *Much Ado About Nothing* and Rosalind in *As You Like It* are among Shakespeare's most perfectly realized characters. Look at Beatrice or Benedick: you say, yes, here is a person I might meet and have dinner with and talk to. In the later plays, with people like Iago and Lear, you say, no, I don't think this is a person I might meet, but this is a state which in the life of man everybody at one time or another experiences. Nobody's Iago all of the time. The representation of states resembles the effect we get from opera. A certain universality is gained. We get a picture of a human heart and of every human heart together. Certain things are sacrificed, especially probability. Lear, in the opening scene, divides up his kingdom like a birthday cake. It's not historical, but it's the way we can all feel at certain times. Shakespeare tries to do something for character development with Edgar's becoming Poor Tom, but it seems arbitrary. Shakespeare's primary treatment of character in the play is as it is in opera. The quality common to all the great operatic roles is that each of them is a passionate and willful state of being, and in recompense for the lack of psychological complexity, the composer presents the immediate and simultaneous relation of these states to each other. The crowning glory of opera is the big ensemble. The Fool, Edgar, and the mad Lear compose such a big scene in *King Lear.* The ensemble gives a picture of human nature, though the individual is sacrificed. The meeting between Lear and Gloucester in the storm doesn't further the action. In fact, it's a mystery how Lear got loose. Shakespeare wants to put two ruined characters together, one a victim of pride, the other a victim of credulity. The motivation for the French army is left vague, except that they must arrive for Lear and Cordelia to reunite—that's all-important. It is improbable that Kent should keep up his disguise before Cordelia or that Edgar should keep his disguise with Gloucester. It has to be done to keep the scene of Lear and Cordelia's reunion strong. Lear's recognition of Kent would weaken the impact of the reunion. Gloucester's recognition of Edgar on stage would do so also. When Kent is revealed, the word "Kent" doesn't mean anything to Lear any more. What interests Shakespeare now is states of being. Crucial actions that in the chronicle plays would have been elaborated—Goneril and Regan's competition for the love of Edmund, the battle between the English and French—are treated perfunctorily. They are significant only for enabling the representation of states of being. But clearly sacrifices are made. Both Gloucester's blinding and his suicide run the risk of seeming funny. The states of passion, as we shall see, are contrasted with a passionless storm.

The play revolves about various meanings of the word "nature." Lear says:

> Which of you shall we say doth love us most?
> That we our largest bounty may extend
> Where nature doth with merit challenge.
>
> (I.i.52–54)

Lear exiles Kent for coming "between our sentence and our power,—/ Which nor our nature nor our place can bear" (I.i.173–74). Lear speaks to France of Cordelia's being "a wretch whom nature is asham'd / Almost t' acknowledge hers" (I.i.215), and France answers that her offense "Must be of such unnatural degree / That monsters it" (I.i.222–23). Kent meets Oswald before Gloucester's castle and says, "You cowardly rascal, nature disclaims in thee; a tailor made thee" (II.ii.59–60). Cornwall says that Kent affects "A saucy roughness, and constrains the garb / Quite from his nature" (II.ii.103–4). Lear at first tries to excuse Cornwall's behavior by saying that

> We are not ourselves
> When nature, being oppress'd, commands the mind
> To suffer with the body.
>
> (II.iv.108–10)

Regan tells Lear that he is old: "Nature in you stands on the very verge / Of her confine" (II.iv.149–50). Lear, in pleading with Regan for her care, says that she knows "The offices of nature, bond of childhood" better than Goneril (II.iv.181). Lear cries out to Regan:

> O, reason not the need! Our basest beggars
> Are in the poorest thing superfluous,
> Allow not nature more than nature needs,
> Man's life is cheap as beast's.
>
> (II.iv.267–70)

Lear, contending with the storm, calls upon it to "Crack Nature's moulds, all germains spill at once, / That make ingrateful man!" (III.ii.8–9), and Kent says, in urging Lear to take shelter, "The tyranny of the open night's too rough / For nature to endure" (III.iv.2–3). When Edmund betrays his father, he tells Cornwall, "I may be censured, that nature thus gives way to loyalty" (III.v.3–4). Lear asks, "Is there any cause in nature that makes these hard hearts?" (III.vi.81–82). Albany says:

> O Goneril,
> You are not worth the dust which the rude wind
> Blows in your face! I fear your disposition.
> That nature which contemns its origin
> Cannot be bordered certain in itself.
>
> (IV.ii.29–33)

The Doctor says that "Our foster nurse of nature is repose" (IV.iv.12). The blinded Gloucester exclaims, when he meets Lear, "O ruined piece of nature!" (IV.vi.137), and Lear says, "I am even / The natural fool of fortune" (IV.vi.194–95). The Gentleman proclaims that Lear has "one daughter / Who redeems nature from the general curse / Which twain have brought her to" (IV.vi.209–11), and Cordelia asks the gods to "Cure this great breach" in Lear's "abused nature!" (IV.vii.15). Finally, in the last reference to nature in the play, Edmund says, after he has a change of heart, "Some good I mean to do, / Despite of mine own nature" (V.iii.243–44).

Edmund, in the first of two great addresses to nature in the play, announces:

> Thou, Nature, art my goddess; to thy law
> My services are bound. Wherefore should I
> Stand in the plague of custom, and permit
> The curiosity of nations to deprive me,
> For that I am some twelve or fourteen moonshines
> Lag of a brother? Why bastard? Wherefore base?
> When my dimensions are as well compact,
> My mind as generous, and my shape as true,
> As honest madam's issue? Why brand they us
> With base? with baseness? bastardy? base, base?
> Who, in the lusty stealth of nature, take
> More composition and fierce quality
> Than doth, within a dull, stale, tired bed,
> Go to th' creating a whole tribe of fops
> Got 'tween asleep and wake?
>
> (I.ii.1–15)

A few moments later, after Edmund has made Gloucester suspect his legitimate son Edgar, Gloucester says:

These late eclipses in the sun and moon portend no good to us. Though the wisdom of nature can reason it thus and thus, yet nature finds itself scourg'd by the sequent effects. Love cools, friendship falls off, brothers divide. In cities, mutinies; in countries, discord; in palaces treason; and the bond crack'd 'twixt son and father. This villain of mine comes under the prediction; there's son against father: the King falls from bias of nature; there's father against child. We have seen the best of our time.

(I.ii.112–23)

But Edmund rejects laying sins off on the stars:

This is the excellent foppery of the world, that, when we are sick in fortune, often the surfeit of our own behaviour, we make guilty of our disasters the sun, the moon, and the stars; as if we were villains on necessity; fools by heavenly compulsion; knaves, thieves, and treachers by spherical predominance; drunkards, liars, and adulterers by an enforc'd obedience of planetary influence; and all that we are evil in, by a divine thrusting on. An admirable evasion of whoremaster man, to lay his goatish disposition to the charge of a star!

(I.ii.128–39)

The other major address to nature in the play is Lear's curse against Goneril:

> Hear, Nature, hear! dear goddess, hear!
> Suspend thy purpose, if thou didst intend
> To make this creature fruitful.
> Into her womb convey sterility;
> Dry up in her the organs of increase;
> And from her derogate body never spring
> A babe to honour her! If she must teem,
> Create her child of spleen, that it may live
> And be a thwart disnatur'd torment to her.
> Let it stamp wrinkles in her brow of youth,
> With cadent tears fret channels in her cheeks,
> Turn all her mother's pains and benefits
> To laughter and contempt, that she may feel
> How sharper than a serpent's tooth it is
> To have a thankless child!

(I.iv.297–311)

We must start to classify these occurrences of the word. What various meanings are there? First, nature as an individual human being's inborn disposition, and second, that which is truly and typically human. You can have these two meanings contrasted in the same person, as when a monster Lear calls his daughters "unnatural hags" (II.iv.281). The third meaning of nature is instinct as opposed to social law: Edmund as a natural son, for example, or instinct and will as opposed to convention. The fourth sense is of a "natural," a feeble-minded fool, also conceived as opposed to convention. In Edmund, however, both will and reason are opposed to law. The Fool, who is without the gift of reason, is not conscious of social law and may, therefore, often tell the truth. The Fool and Edgar in different ways represent that sense of nature. The fifth sense is a personified force of that which endows matter with form, as in Lear's curse against Goneril. The sixth sense of nature is physical existence contrasted with people's wishes: this is the sense conveyed when Regan brutally tells her father that he is old and dying, that "Nature . . . stands on the very verge / Of her confine" in him (II.iv.149–50).

Nature in the sense of inorganic matter is *not* used in *King Lear* to contrast with human consciousness. Such nature is present in the storm, but it is referred to as the heavens, the elements. What is the *cause* of thunder, asks Lear—thunder is regarded as not nature. What is the cosmology of *King Lear*? Lear refers to the gods creating the storm, "this dreadful pudder o'er our heads" (III.ii.50), and Gloucester says, "As flies to wanton boys are we to th' gods. / They kill us for their sport" (IV.i.36–37). Edmund talks of Nature, superstitious Gloucester talks of the stars and, to an extent, Kent too speaks of the stars.

The real counterpointing in the play is the world of passion, of *man's* nature, versus the elements, the physical world of the universe. The storm is infinitely strong compared to man, and is of the moment only. It is pitiless, but innocent. It has no malice, it doesn't want to be anything else but a storm. The poor, bare, forked animal, man, on the other hand, has an infinite wish to be infinitely great, to become what he is not. In his *Pensées*, Pascal asks, "For in fact what is man in nature? A Nothing in comparison with the Infinite, an All in comparison with the Nothing, a mean between nothing and everything. . . . he is equally incapable of seeing the Nothing from which he was made, and the Infinite in which he is swallowed up." "The whole visible world," Pascal says,

> is only an imperceptible atom in the ample bosom of nature. No idea approaches it. We may enlarge our conceptions beyond all imaginable space; we only produce atoms in comparison with the

reality of things. It is an infinite sphere, the centre of which is every-where, the circumference nowhere. . . . let man consider what he is in comparison with all existence; let him regard himself as lost in this remote corner of nature; and from the little cell in which he finds himself lodged, I mean the universe, let him estimate at their true value the earth, kingdoms, cities, and himself. What is a man in the Infinite?

"*Un roseau qui pense,*" Pascal answers:

Man is but a reed, the most feeble thing in nature; but he is a think-ing reed. The entire universe need not arm itself to crush him. A vapour, a drop of water suffices to kill him. But, if the universe were to crush him, man would still be more noble than that which killed him, because he knows that he dies and the advantage which the universe has over him; the universe knows nothing of this.

All our dignity consists, then, in thought. By it we must elevate ourselves, and not by space and time which we cannot fill.

Let's consider *King Lear* and Pascal's conception of how a human being is greater than the universe in understanding and will. What do the characters in the play desire? What is the contrast between their na-tures and their offices or social functions? Lear desires absolute power over others, and absolute love from others—to an infinite extent. He's a father, a king, and he has authority. He has authority by his nature and his office. He gives his office away. He still is a king in his natural author-ity, but becomes a subject by office. Provoked, he becomes a passion, and the idea of kingship is placed in the sharpest contrast to the body of an old, weak man in a storm. His kingship dissolves. His nature is that of a child, and socially he becomes a father-son to Cordelia. The two bad daughters may not initially have an infinite wish, just a desire for free-dom from parental authority, but having that, they develop an infinite, maniac passion for getting their own way that makes them kill, and fi-nally makes them perish—Regan is poisoned and Goneril kills herself in the last act. Inwardly they both are wolves.

Cordelia wants to love freely, without compulsion, and paradoxically she describes love as a duty. When Lear awakens from his madness, he says to her,

> I know you do not love me; for your sisters
> Have, as I do remember, done me wrong.
> You have some cause, they have not.

Cordelia's answer is, "No cause, no cause" (IV.vii.73–75). Compare Leonora's "*Nichts, nichts, mein Florestan*" in Beethoven's *Fidelio*. Cordelia
doesn't want authority, she wishes to love freely.

Edmund begins by simply wanting to be Edgar. His very success
tempts him to develop a love of power and mischief for their own sake.
The fun of deception goes on for its own sake. He stabs his arm as drunkards do in sport, he deceives Cornwall, and then gets dangerous. He
plays with fire in playing off Goneril and Regan against each other without knowing why, and he orders the execution of Lear and Cordelia for
no good reason. The natural son behaves unnaturally and ends up as an
outlaw whose hand is against every man.

Gloucester begins by wanting to be an average man, looked up to,
conventional, a courtier. He is betrayed into unconventionality by his
excessive readiness to believe one son without sufficient proof, and by
his over-ready condemnation of Edgar. He is actually moved towards
catastrophe by acting again as an individual, not as a conventional figure,
when he tries to rescue Lear. He becomes an exceptional outcast: blind,
hunted, a father who becomes a child, and he dies not conventionally,
but out of a genuine individual joy.

Albany wants a quiet life, he has none of the authority by nature that
Lear has, or that, in a different way, Cornwall has. He is forced to change
to an authoritative role by the horror at what he's seen. Cornwall doesn't
change, he is what he wants to be, and he is killed by violence, a tough
who believes only in force. Edgar wants to go on by being a secure, legal
son. He is compelled not to be, but to be an unnatural son and outlaw.
He feigns to be a man nobody wants, a guilt-haunted madman, and starts
to play the role of a natural after the props of normal existence are taken
away from him. His character is thereby changed, he begins to understand what he says, and by the end of the play, he's developed into something. Kent wants to be what he is and remains, a loyal and devoted
servant. Oswald has no nature of his own, only the instinct of self-preservation. He can take on a protective coloring and can shift—he is the real
opposite of Kent.

The Fool is in a way the most interesting of the characters. One can't
really say he has a nature or a passion. He is a talent, his vocation for a
fool, nothing else. The talent? To use humor as a protection against
tragic feeling. He and Edgar are related to Hamlet and Thersites. He
stands for naked facts and therefore expresses himself not in good poetry, but in doggerel, a protective humor. Unlike Iago's honesty, which
reflects other people, the Fool's is perfectly independent. He tells simple

truths, which he divorces from feeling by making everything smaller. In Greek tragedy the hero is a fated victim and the function of the chorus is to express reverence, awe, pity, and acceptance of tragic pathos. In a Shakespearean tragedy, where characters are not victims of fate but of their own passion, the function of the chorus is to make you protest, not accept, and it is deliberately antipoetic. In comedy the clown protests against convention, and is nonconforming. The fool protests against the violence of individual manias by stating the larger general case.

Precisely because we're dealing with nature in states of being rather than in developed characters, disguises become important. Edgar, an unloved son, disguises himself as an unloving madman in order to go on loving. He becomes sophisticated, loves with knowledge, and takes upon himself the knowledge of evil. Both he and Lear see human equality, Lear seeing all humanity as weak, Edgar as bad. As Poor Tom, Edgar describes himself to Lear:

> A servingman, proud in heart and mind; that curl'd my hair, wore gloves in my cap; serv'd the lust of my mistress' heart and did the act of darkness with her; swore as many oaths as I spake words, and broke them in the sweet face of heaven; one that slept in the contriving of lust, and wak'd to do it. Wine lov'd I deeply, dice dearly; and in woman out-paramour'd the Turk. False of heart, light of ear, bloody of hand; hog in sloth, fox in stealth, wolf in greediness, dog in madness, lion in prey.
>
> (III.iv.87–97)

Edgar's speech could describe Edmund at first, but Edgar begins to see how it could be himself. He disguises himself as a peasant and it is as a peasant that he slays Oswald. Kent disguises his outer trappings to make his internal constancy acceptable to Lear.

The failure to recognize others in *King Lear* comes about either through madness or through willful passion. Gloucester and Lear fail to see their children rightly, Albany and Goneril miscalculate each other, Cornwall doesn't realize that servants exist, Oswald doesn't notice the peasant Edgar. Edgar pathetically misinterprets the cause of his father's blinding: "The dark and vicious place where thee he got," he tells Edmund, "Cost him his eyes" (V.iii.172–73). Immediately, it was his good deeds that cost Gloucester his eyes. Mistakes of madness make memory and judgment confused. Lear makes Gloucester into a philosopher, he calls a stool his daughter in the trial scene, he misconstrues Gloucester in their meeting in the fourth act.

Now the storm, what Shakespeare does *not* call nature in *King Lear*. The question of *Lear's* actability rests on how the storm is to be represented. Compare the storm in *Lear* to previous treatments of weather in the plays. The first obvious place to look is the battle of Bosworth Field in *Richard III*. It is a gloomy day at Bosworth and Richard takes it as an omen. In *A Midsummer Night's Dream* Titania says the weather has been thoroughly disturbed since her row with Oberon, and nature changes as a result of the debate between them. In contrast, in *Julius Caesar,* though Casca is fearful of the storm as an omen of the disorder in the state, Cassius denies omens and presents himself open-breasted to the storm. At the beginning of Act II of *Othello,* Montano asks about the weather at sea and is told by a Gentleman of the "molestation . . . / On the enchafed flood" (II.i.16–17). There are two kinds of storms. Either what happens is an omen, which is curiously allied to the notion that the world of nature is a macrocosm that mirrors the microcosm of human life. Or, as in *Othello,* the storm is the intervention of fate doing man's work for him, and so scattering the Turkish fleet.

You can see why you normally shouldn't have realistic scenery. There is no point in doubling, words will do it. But let's look just at the storm in *Lear.* Gloucester stands before his castle after Lear has left, and Cornwall tells him to come in: "Shut up your doors, my lord; 'tis a wild night. / . . . Come out o' th' storm" (II.iv.311–12). The Gentleman describes to Kent how Lear,

> Contending with the fretful elements;
> Bids the wind blow the earth into the sea,
> Or swell the curled waters 'bove the main,
> That things might change or cease; tears his white hair,
> Which the impetuous blasts, with eyeless rage,
> Catch in their fury and make nothing of;
> Strives in this little world of man to outscorn
> The to-and-fro-conflicting wind and rain.

(III.i.4–11)

Lear himself shouts at the storm: "Blow, winds, and crack your cheeks! rage! blow!" and calls for it to "Crack Nature's moulds, all germains spill at once, / That make ingrateful man!" (III.ii.1, 8–9). He also calls upon the "great gods, / That keep this dreadful pudder o'er our heads" to "Find out their enemies now" (III.ii.49–51). Not long afterwards he feels sympathy for the "Poor naked wretches, whereso'er you are, / That bide the pelting of this pitiless storm," and exclaims:

O, I have ta'en
Too little care of this! Take physic, pomp;
Expose thyself to feel what wretches feel,
That thou mayst shake the superflux to them
And show the heavens more just.

(III.iv.28–29, 32–36)

And he looks at the naked Edgar and says:

Why, thou wert better in thy grave than to answer with thy uncover'd body this extremity of the skies. Is man no more than this? Consider him well. Thou ow'st the worm no silk, the beast no hide, the sheep no wool, the cat no perfume. Ha! Here's three on's are sophisticated! Thou art the thing itself; unaccommodated man is no more but such a poor, bare, forked animal as thou art. Off, off, you lendings. Come, unbutton here.

[*Tears at his clothes.*]
(III.iv.105–14)

Lear's language remains the same after the storm is over. In *King Lear* the storm is *not* the macrocosm of inner passion, though Lear would like it to be. The storm is without passion, and pays no attention to who is just and who is sinful. The storm goes its way, but Lear remains the same. Lear taking off his clothes presents a contrast between the human animal and civilization. We need both the storm and green fields as contrasts to Lear's feelings, and there is a contrast between human passions and a weak body: we must see that. Lear goes mad and sees amiss: the audience must see what is really there. Also, Gloucester's attempted suicide: what is described is not there. A realism is required that the stage cannot give. *King Lear* is the one play of Shakespeare that, in the storm scene, really requires the movies. Most movies of Shakespeare make you want to say, it's very nice, but why must people say anything? You want to *see* everything. If I agree with those who don't want to see *King Lear* on stage, it isn't because I don't think it's dramatic, but that, as it *contrasts* itself with the speakers, it should be presented as real. Also, the battle in *King Lear* frees one from the idea that battles are won by the good instead of the strong. This is a profoundly unsuperstitious play. I do not agree that it is a nihilistic or pessimistic one. Certain states of being—reconciliation, forgiveness, devotion—are states of blessedness, and they exist while other people—conventionally successful people—are in states of misery and chaos.

The opposition of tempests and music in Shakespeare's plays is a theme discussed by Wilson Knight. Act I scene i begins with a sennet and pomp, Act I scene iii has a hunting horn for Lear's amusement, and the last scene has trumpets heralding Edgar for this tournament with Edmund. The Fool's plain and simple songs assert the will against the storm. The big moment is in the fourth act when the Doctor calls for music as Lear revives, music that is a rich, full, sophisticated victory over the storm. Finally, with the funeral march, there is sophisticated official music.

King Lear, like *Hamlet*, is peculiarly modern because in both, nature is no longer a home. The sensuous visual world is realized in Aristotle as a universe of things in which man is only one more thing. Augustine's new insight was that man was despairing as just one more thing. The next seven centuries depicted man and nature in the familiar Augustinian Christian tradition. Copernicus set the walls of the house crumbling with a new realization of man's limitations. Pascal's thought is opposed to the early enthusiasm of scientific figures like Bruno and Kepler. There is no new house for man. Infinity must enter the image. In the nineteenth century, man's last home is music.

Antony and Cleopatra

[2 April 1947]

Antony and Cleopatra reminds one technically of the kind of plays that lie a long way back in Shakespeare's career—the English chronicle plays. It looks back as well to *Julius Caesar,* another play of Roman history, in which the characters of Antony and Octavius are first introduced, to *Troilus and Cressida,* which also represents both public and private life, and to *Romeo and Juliet,* the only other tragedy that centers on the relationship of a boy and girl, here a man and a woman. With very great daring, Shakespeare revives the multiple scenes of the chronicle plays and makes the fullest possible use of the Elizabethan stage's resources. The action moves seamlessly from Alexandria to Rome to Messina to Rome to Alexandria to Messina to Syria to Rome to Alexandria to Athens to Rome to Actium to Alexandria. There is really no place where an interval is anything but arbitrary except from Act II scene ii to Act II scene iii, the interval of Caesar's war with Pompey. You feel the lack of an Elizabethan stage in modern productions of *Antony and Cleopatra* more than in any other Shakespearean play.

It won't do as a movie at all. The play is exclusively about human history and the effects of human will. There is no background showing farmers ploughing fields, there are no conflicts between human beings and nature, no storms. The play is concerned with the desire for world power. Movies overemphasize particular localities and their uniqueness. In a movie scene of Ventidius in Syria (III.i), for example, you would see too much particular Syrian scenery. But what is important is the contrast with the immediately preceding scene on Pompey's galley. A movie again would emphasize the particular furnishings on the galley, but it doesn't matter if it's a galley or a house. What matters is the view it presents of the lords of the world in undress in contrast to the scene of Ventidius and his troops guarding the frontier. Space is the prize, and not any particular corner of space, but the whole space of civilization.

The enemy in the play is the passage of time, in its sense both of aging and death and of the fluctuating of spirit and public opinion. There are two important acts of will in the play: Cleopatra's decision to flee at Actium and Antony's decision to follow her. The depiction of the battle itself, the movement of ships, is immaterial. The play shows an enormous advance in the treatment of history. Shakespeare has passed the stage of *histoire moralisée*—there are no symmetrical set pieces like those of a son slaying a father and a father slaying a son in *Henry VI*. There are instead impressionistic scenes that are confined to what is absolutely necessary. Take the brief scene on a Roman street between Lepidus, Maecenas, and Agrippa (II.iv): it swiftly shows Lepidus's feebleness, the slight contempt Maecenas and Agrippa have for him—the moment done, the scene is over. In the two quick scenes before the battle of Actium (IV.x–xi) Shakespeare allows the sparest of speeches to portray the indecision of Antony and the resolution of Octavius. Speeches are cut to the bone at these points, to be kept for where they are needed. A lot of history is included, some of which may *seem* irrelevant, but is not so, while other events, the war with Pompey, for example, take place off-stage or are compressed.

Julius Caesar, in comparison with *Antony and Cleopatra*, is a local play focused on the city of Rome, not the whole empire, not the world. Its subject is a single political conspiracy that draws in a person like Brutus, who is not politically gifted. It can be done successfully in modern dress, whereas *Antony and Cleopatra* cannot. *Antony and Cleopatra* deals with the unique politics of the establishment of a world empire and has a unity that develops from the particular events and persons it depicts—not the abstract pointing up of morals that forms the unity of the chronicle plays.

The representation of politics in *Antony and Cleopatra* is also different from that of *Troilus and Cressida*. Both plays represent big council scenes among heads of state. The first Grecian council scene in *Troilus and Cressida* (I.iii) presents a series of tremendous lectures by Agamemnon, Nestor and others about nature, fortune, and political authority. Everyone talks to the air or to the audience in a series of soliloquies, and the scene goes on for 392 lines. What's accomplished? Not much. There is no development of character and the result of all the talk is the decision simply to make Ajax, not Achilles, take Hector's challenge. The meeting in *Antony and Cleopatra* of Octavius, Lepidus, and Antony after Antony first returns to Rome (II.ii) is a real political conference between political figures who dislike each other but want to come to agreement. They stick to the point and poetic speeches are held in check. There is no real poetry until Enobarbus's speech describing Cleopatra's first meeting with Antony: "The barge she sat in, like a burnish'd throne . . ." (II.ii.196ff.). But the richness of the poetry is kept relevant to the political situation: will Antony leave Cleopatra or won't he? Enobarbus is telling Maecenas and Agrippa something they have to know. His rich description conveys the strength of Antony and Cleopatra's affection, as he sees it. *Antony and Cleopatra* generally contains perhaps more first-rate poetry than any other play in the canon, but not a line of it is detachable from the context either of the scene in which it occurs or of the play as a whole.

Troilus's private and public lives exist in two different compartments. His love story is parallel to the Trojan War, and history makes Cressida go away, but any other accident would have worked quite as well. In *Henry IV*, the relation between Hal and Falstaff dramatizes the gulf between the political and the a-political. Falstaff would have been the same person if he had never met Prince Hal. In *Antony and Cleopatra*, on the other hand, public and private life are entirely interwoven, and the conflict in the play is between two kinds of public life. Antony could not have a relation with Cleopatra if she were just a beautiful slave girl, nor could she with him if he were just a handsome centurion. Their worldly position is an essential part of their love. Cleopatra is Egypt and Antony is one of the rulers of the Roman empire, unlike Romeo and Juliet who are any boy and any girl separated by a family feud. Two families having a row over who borrowed the lawn mower would be interchangeable with the provincial feud in the town of Verona.

There are two themes in the play: the long tussle of wits between Antony and Octavius, and the relation between Antony and Cleopatra. Returning to *Julius Caesar*, what picture of Antony and Octavius do we get? Brutus says, "I am not gamesome. I do lack some part / Of that quick spirit that is in Antony" (I.ii.28–29). Caesar tells Antony, in describing his suspicion of Cassius, "He loves no plays / As thou dost, Antony" (I.ii.203–4). Cassius, however, in a debate with Brutus about whether to spare Antony, predicts, "We shall find of him / A shrewd contriver" (II.i.157–58). Brutus protests that "Antony is but a limb of Caesar" (II.i.165), "given / To sports, to wildness, and much company" (II.i.188–89). Trebonius, agreeing, says that Antony "will laugh at" Caesar's death "hereafter" (II.i.191). Cassius, of course, is right and Brutus wrong. After his inflammatory speech to the crowd, Antony says coolly, "Now let it work. Mischief, thou art afoot, / Take thou what course thou wilt" (III.ii.265–66). He himself takes what the moment provides without much scruple. Almost immediately afterwards, when he hears that Octavius has just arrived in Rome, he says, "Fortune is merry, / And in this mood will give us anything" (III.ii.271–72). He later quickly and ruthlessly agrees to Lepidus's proscription of the son of Antony's sister: "Look, with a spot I damn him" (IV.i.6), and he also makes clear to Octavius that Lepidus is a "slight unmeritable man" (IV.i.12) of whom they both can make use. Octavius voices no opinion, though he draws Antony out to make him say enough about Lepidus that can be serviceable to him, enough to tell Lepidus later, if Lepidus should turn out not to be a fool. At the battle of Philippi, Octavius also insists on leading the right wing, and when Antony, the older and clearly more experienced general, protests, "Why do you cross me in this exigent?" Octavius answers coldly, "I do not cross you, but I will do so" (V.i.19–20). Octavius's wing does not fight hard—not an accident, he wants to see how the wind will jump. Antony is a politician, he is ambitious, he understands the motives and weaknesses of others. Like Hal, he learns from his love of company, which is an advantage over Brutus. He can be unscrupulous and hard, as he shows in deciding who is to be proscribed, he can improvise brilliantly, as he demonstrates in his oration, and he is a good soldier. He is not good, however, at planning long-term strategy. Like many improvisers, he has a certain irresponsibility—"Let mischief work"—and he is short on patience, which is where he fails to deal successfully with Octavius, who is slow and deliberate and who prevails over Antony by his willingness to wait.

The Roman empire is shared by the triumvirate of Octavius, Antony, and Lepidus. Lepidus is the unequal member. As *Antony and Cleopatra* opens, Antony is in Egypt, Octavius in Rome. Antony's wife Fulvia and her brother have fought against each other and then united against Octavius, who has kicked them out of Italy. Syria on the frontier is lost, Fulvia dies, and Pompey revolts at sea. Pompey is formidable: "The people love me," he says, "and the sea is mine" (II.i.9). Octavius is particularly afraid that Antony and Pompey may join against him, an alliance that Pompey indeed has tried to bring about. Antony remarks to Octavius and Lepidus that

> I did not think to draw my sword 'gainst Pompey;
> For he hath laid strange courtesies and great
> Of late upon me.

> (II.ii.156–58)

Octavius calculates that with sufficient time he can deal separately with Pompey and Antony, as long as they remain apart. He is lucky. He defeats Fulvia, and Antony, moved by his own unpopularity, returns to Rome. At their meeting (II.ii), Octavius registers his complaints about Antony's failure to lend him arms and aid him, and Antony makes his excuses: I had a hangover, I forgot, etc. Antony's real reason is that he does not trust Octavius. The suggestion is then made that to create a bond between them Antony marry Miss Octavius. Antony unwisely does so, and the immediate effect is to delay Antony's joining with Pompey. Once Pompey is dealt with, the marriage doesn't matter to Octavius. If Antony treats Miss Octavius badly, Octavius gets an excuse to make trouble, and in any case he doesn't really care about his sister. Enobarbus, noting that Octavia is "of a holy, cold, and still conversation," predicts that Antony "will to his Egyptian dish again" (II.vi.132, 135–36).

In the scene immediately following, on Pompey's galley (II.vii), the characters are distinctly contrasted. Lepidus gets completely drunk and must be carted off, Antony drunkenly enjoys the party, and Octavius manages to get only a little drunk and to keep his head. As always, he knows what he is doing:

> *Eno.* There's a strong fellow, Menas.
> *[Points to the Servant who carries off Lepidus]*
> *Menas.* Why?
> *Eno.* 'A bears the third part of the world, man; see'st not?
> *Menas.* The third part, then, is drunk. Would it were all,
> That it might go on wheels!
> *Eno.* Drink thou, increase the reels.
> *Menas.* Come.
> *Pom.* This is not yet an Alexandrian feast.
> *Ant.* It ripens towards it. Strike the vessals, ho!
> Here's to Caesar!
> *Caes.*   I could well forbear't.
> It's monstrous labour when I wash my brain
> And it grows fouler.
> *Ant.*   Be a child o' th' time.
> *Caes.* Possess it; I'll make answer.
>
> (II.vii.94–106)

Shortly afterwards, with Lepidus's help, Octavius defeats Pompey, and immediately arrests Lepidus.

Octavius now turns his attention to Antony, provoking him by speaking "scantly" (III.iv.6) of him. Antony falls into the trap, and, against Enobarbus's clear counsel (III.vii.42–43), he insists upon fighting at sea. Octavius, for his part, deliberately refrains from fighting on land:

> Strike not by land; keep whole: provoke not battle
> Till we have done at sea. Do not exceed

> The prescript of this scroll. Our fortune lies
> Upon this jump.
>
> (III.viii.3–6)

Octavius knows that the Egyptian sailors will not be faithful. The slow, patient man undoes the brilliant improviser. Octavius may not be a terribly good general, but he is an extremely good politician.

The love story of *Antony and Cleopatra.* In *Romeo and Juliet* the love between Romeo and Juliet is the first affair for both of them. They discover sexual love, each other's existence, and their own, they discover that there are more things in the world than being the child of one's parents. But *Antony and Cleopatra* presents what is certainly Cleopatra's last affair, and perhaps Antony's. She has to make up very carefully indeed, and he is putting on weight—he wears corsets. They have behind them a lifetime of experience, and their worldly success makes them as unfree as children, public life taking the place of parents. Romeo and Juliet want to escape from the family into a world that contains only two people. It could be a cottage, it could be anywhere. Antony and Cleopatra want to escape from the future, from death and old age. You cannot imagine Antony and Cleopatra retiring to a cottage. They need the fullest possible publicity and the maximum assistance from good cooking, good clothes, good drink. In the comedies like *As You Like It,* the conflict is not between being a child and growing up, or remaining young and dying, it is the conflict between the wish for freedom from responsibility and the wish to marry.

Though we cannot tell how happy their marriage would have been, there is absolute trust between Romeo and Juliet, and I am convinced that Benedick and Beatrice, however much they may battle, will make an ideal couple. Antony and Cleopatra don't trust each other a yard. They know exactly what will happen in the course of their affair, and they therefore need reassurance that they have feelings left. Indeed, publicity is especially important to Cleopatra to prove that she can still inspire feelings in others, which is why she behaves so badly.

Shakespeare employs three kinds of rhetoric of love in his plays. The balcony scene in *Romeo and Juliet,* when Juliet calls Romeo back, is composed of pure Petrarchan rhetoric, right out of the book. The two are bound to use such rhetoric because they have very little experience of life and can't compare sets of emotions—they have to go to the book. In comedies like *As You Like It,* as we have seen, the rhetoric is quite different. Rosalind, in the disguise of Ganymede, instructs Orlando that "The poor world is almost six thousand years old, and in all this time there was not any man died in his own person, videlicet, in a love cause. . . . Men have died from time to time, and worms have eaten them, but not for love" (IV.i.95–98, 106–8). She tells him, also, that she, like Rosalind, "will weep for nothing, like Diana in the fountain, and I will do that when you are dispos'd to be merry; I will laugh like a hyen, and that when thou art inclin'd to sleep" (IV.i.154–57). The moment Orlando leaves, however, she confides to Celia,

> O coz, coz, coz, my pretty little coz, that thou didst know how many fathom deep I am in love! But it cannot be sounded. My affection hath an unknown bottom, like the Bay of Portugal.
>
> *Cel.* Or rather, bottomless, that as fast as you pour affection in, it runs out.
>
> *Ros.* No, that same wicked bastard of Venus that was begot of thought, conceiv'd of spleen, and born of madness, that blind rascally boy that abuses every one's eyes because his own are out—let him be judge how deep I am in love.
>
> (IV.i.209–21)

These are passages of anti-Petrarchan rhetoric, Petrarchan rhetoric being looked upon as a convention. Romeo and Juliet's Petrarchan rhetoric cannot distinguish between the feeling of love and its object. Rosalind and Celia are suspicious of those in love with love—flirting—rather than with people.

Antony and Cleopatra's rhetoric is hyperbolic and differs from that of both earlier plays. In the opening scene Antony and Cleopatra declare that a love that has bounds is not love:

> *Cleo.* If it be love indeed, tell me how much.
> *Ant.* There's beggary in the love that can be reckon'd.
> *Cleo.* I'll set a bourn how far to be belov'd.
> *Ant.* Then must thou needs find out new heaven, new earth.
>
> (I.i.14–17)

Cleopatra taunts Antony, saying that "shrill-tongu'd Fulvia" will scold him for remaining in Egypt, and Antony replies:

> Let Rome in Tiber melt and the wide arch
> Of the rang'd empire fall! Here is my space.
> Kingdoms are clay; our dungy earth alike
> Feeds beast as man. The nobleness of life

Is to do thus [*embracing*]; when such a mutual pair
And such a twain can do't, in which I bind,
On pain of punishment, the world to weet
We stand up peerless. . . .
Let's not confound the time with conference harsh.
There's not a minute of our lives should stretch
Without some pleasure now.

(I.i.33–40, 45–47)

When later Antony returns victorious from a fight on land, he cries to Cleopatra,

O thou day o' th' world,
Chain mine arm'd neck! Leap thou, attire and all,
Through proof of harness to my heart, and there
Ride on the pants triumphing!

She answers him in the same key:

Lord of lords!
O infinite virtue, com'st thou smiling from
The world's great snare uncaught?

(IV.viii.13–18)

These expressions of love are poetic, but very un-Petrarchan, entirely conscious of their exaggeration. The words are used to create feelings about which Antony and Cleopatra are in doubt, and the rhetoric is meant to prove their self-importance. When they quarrel, they express real hate, inspired by the terror of eventual betrayal:

I found you as a morsel cold upon
Dead Caesar's trencher. Nay, you were a fragment
Of Gneius Pompey's, besides what hotter hours,
Unregist'red in vulgar fame, you have
Luxuriously pick'd out: for I am sure,
Though you can guess what temperance should be,
You know not what it is.

(III.xiii.116–22)

When Romeo and Juliet express their love, they are saying, "How wonderful to feel like this." Benedick and Beatrice talk as they do about love to test each other. Antony and Cleopatra are saying, "I want to live forever." Their poetry, like fine cooking, is a technique to keep up the excitement of living.

At the moment Antony dies, Cleopatra cries out, in marvelous verse,

> The crown o' th' earth doth melt. My lord!
> O wither'd is the garland of the war,
> The soldier's pole is fall'n! Young boys and girls
> Are level now with men. The odds is gone,
> And there is nothing left remarkable
> Beneath the visiting moon.
>
> (IV.xv.63–68)

The extraordinary thing about the speech is that it comes after Cleopatra has sold Antony out and is planning to come to terms with Octavius. She eventually kills herself not for Antony but because Dolabella gives away Octavius's intention to humiliate her. She feels good in triumphing over Octavius, but her suicide is also pathetic and terrifying. Octavius, in any event, doesn't really care. It is unimportant to him whether she lives or dies. Compare the pretended deaths of Cleopatra and Juliet. Antony would have killed himself anyway. The report of Cleopatra's death only hurries it up and provides the occasion for their greatest speeches.

Cleopatra sees in Antony a great hero, slightly faded and domitable. She's excited about Antony most when he leaves for Rome. She's slightly contemptuous of him when he's obedient. She says, when she thinks of going fishing in the Nile,

> My bended hook shall pierce
> Their slimy jaws: and as I draw them up,
> I'll think them every one an Antony,
> And say, "Ah, ha! y'are caught!"

She says also, when reminded of how she once fooled Antony while they were fishing,

> That time? O times!
> I laugh'd him out of patience; and that night
> I laugh'd him into patience; and next morn
> Ere the ninth hour I drunk him to his bed,
> Then put my tires and mantles on him, whilst
> I wore his sword Philippan.
>
> (II.v.12–15, 18–23)

Cleopatra is driven to see how far she can go. The older she gets, the more she loves power, and she has the power to destroy a man who has something to lose. Antony basically wants a child's freedom to play, but he can't be a child, or even a private citizen. He is no longer innocent. The physical attraction between them is real, but both are getting on, and their lust is less a physical need than a way of forgetting time and death. For that reason, they require the support of refinements and sophistication. But their relationship is therefore selfish and destructive, and it doesn't work.

A curious opposition is made in the play between the baser elements: earth and water. There are numerous references to the Nile. Antony calls Cleopatra the "serpent of old Nile" (I.v.24), she fishes in the river, and she first presents herself to Antony on a barge on the water. Pompey says, "the sea is mine" (II.i.9), and Octavius, by beating him, acquires the sea. Enobarbus and a lone soldier try to persuade Antony not to fight at sea (III.vii.42–49,62–67). Cleopatra asks Antony's forgiveness for her flight at Actium by saying,

> O my lord, my lord,
> Forgive my fearful sails! I little thought
> You would have followed.

Antony continues the image by answering,

> Egypt, thou knew'st too well
> My heart was to thy rudder tied by th' strings
> And thou shouldst tow me after.
>
> (III.xi.54–58)

Antony's only victory over Octavius is by land, and the decisive turn of his fortunes is signaled in the beautiful scene in which common soldiers hear supernatural music, "under the earth," announcing that "the god Hercules, whom Antony lov'd, / Now leaves him" (IV.iii.12,15–16). Water is throughout associated with misfortune for Antony, with instability and fickleness, with the kind of lymphatic temperament that we see in Octavius's patience. Cleopatra can say that Antony's "legs bestrid the ocean" and that

> His delights
> Were dolphin like: they show'd his back above
> The element they liv'd in.
>
> (V.ii.82, 88–90)

But Antony is nonetheless destroyed by water. He goes to it, but he cannot control it.

The nature of the tragic flaw in *Antony and Cleopatra*. Critics have complained that the play is not strictly tragic, because Antony and Cleopatra are passive. What happens is not due to their will, they are caught: there is pathos, not tragedy. I don't think this complaint is quite true. It is true that the tragic flaw in *Antony and Cleopatra* is not of the ordinary specific kind, but this makes for the tremendous power of the play. We see malice and ambition in Richard III, ignorance in Romeo and Juliet, melancholia in Hamlet, ambition in Macbeth, paternalism and the demand for love in Lear, pride in Coriolanus, the desire to be loved in Timon, and jealousy in Othello. These are pure states of being that have a certain amount of police court cases or psychiatric clinics in them, but we are not likely to imitate them. We may feel as they do on occasion, but these people are really rather silly. We wouldn't murder a guest at a party, nor are we likely to run out of the house in the middle of a storm. We think people are crazy to behave like that. We read about such behavior in the papers. Antony and Cleopatra's flaw, however, is general and common to all of us all of the time: *worldliness*—the love of pleasure, success, art, ourselves, and conversely, the fear of boredom, failure, being ridiculous, being on the wrong side, dying. If Antony and Cleopatra have a more tragic fate than we do, that is because they are far more successful than we are, not because they are essentially different. "Now is the time when all the lights wax dim," as Herrick writes in "To Anthea." We all reach a time when the god Hercules leaves us. Every day we can get an obsession about people we don't like but for various reasons can't leave. We all know about intrigues in offices, museums, literary life. Finally, we all grow old and die. The tragedy is not that it happens, but that we do not accept it.

Antony and Cleopatra therefore must present a plenum of experience. An historian might complain of the irrelevance of the love story, a classical playwright of the irrelevance of the historical detail, and a theatrical producer of the multitude of tiny scenes. But Shakespeare needs this comprehensiveness to show the temptation of the world, the real world in all its kingdoms, all its glories. The panoramic inclusiveness is essential to the play. Pascal's remark in *Pensées* that had "Cleopatra's nose . . . been shorter, the whole aspect of the world would have been altered" is an historical falsehood, as Shakespeare's detailed depiction of the political conflict in the play shows. Loyalty and treachery, prudence and rashness: all human traits are portrayed somewhere by the multiplicity of characters in the play. But the one thing you will not find in *Antony and Cleopatra* is innocence. The characters in the play may get angry, but they won't be shocked or surprised. Even the clown is sophisticated.

Why is the weather so good in *Antony and Cleopatra?* In other plays nature reflects vices or hostility, but it is important in *Antony and Cleopatra* that the world be made to seem infinitely desirable and precious. The whole world of the play is bathed in brilliant light. In the last plays the physical tempests stand for suffering through which people are redeemed. The tragedy in *Antony and Cleopatra* is the refusal of suffering. As Kafka remarks, "You can hold back from the suffering of the world, you have free permission to do so, and it is in accordance with your nature, but perhaps this very holding back is the one suffering you could have avoided." The splendor of the poetry expresses the splendor of the world in this play, and the word "world" is constantly repeated. "Com'st thou smiling from / The world's great snare uncaught?" (IV.viii.17–18), Cleopatra asks. But Antony is caught. What Caesar calls Cleopatra's "strong toil of grace" (V.ii.351) is the world itself and in one way or another it catches us all. The moral of the play is quite simple, the same as that of Chaucer's *Troilus and Criseyde*, when Troilus looks down ironically upon the world from the eighth sphere. Shakespeare presents it without faking—there are no sour grapes, no claims that the world is not really glorious, but tawdry. You can't suggest that the world is destructive without showing it in all its seductiveness.

If we had to burn all of Shakespeare's plays but one—luckily we don't—I'd choose *Antony and Cleopatra*.

Coriolanus

[9 April 1947]

There is a certain oddity about *Coriolanus*. It is a favorite with most critics, it is rather ignored by the public, at least in English-speaking lands, and it is at the same time one of the most popular of Shakespeare's plays in France. Mr. Henry Norman Hudson, for example, one of the most dreary of critics, says the play shows Shakespeare at the maturity of his powers. Middleton Murry considers *Coriolanus* "a much finer Shakespearian drama than *King Lear*." T. S. Eliot writes that "*Coriolanus* may not be as 'interesting' as *Hamlet*, but it is, with *Antony and Cleopatra*, Shakespeare's most assured artistic success." William Hazlitt regards *Coriolanus* as a great political play, and says that anyone who studies it "may save himself the trouble of reading Burke's Reflections, or Paine's Rights of Man, or the Debates in both Houses of Parliament since the French Revolution or our own."

The play is more suited to the stage than most of Shakespeare's other mature tragedies. The parts of Hamlet and Iago are largely unactable, and *King Lear* does not benefit from a stage performance. This leaves, among the mature tragedies, *Macbeth* and *Julius Caesar*, and *Julius Caesar* does not have a concentration of interest upon a single hero. *Coriolanus* does focus upon one hero, it is well-constructed, and it keeps within the bounds of what actors can do. There are certain sacrifices. The characters are not as exciting and interesting as Hamlet or Iago are. The poetry is more restrained and has less fireworks. Except for Virgilia, who is more or less mute, there is no really sympathetic character in the play. But the play does not deserve to be neglected. The language is extremely felicitous, if restrained. Though there are lines that are untranslatable, if we listen to some of its verse, we can see how it's easier to translate into French than most of Shakespeare's verse and why the French would be drawn to it. Coriolanus's cry when he embraces Virgilia is one example: "O, a kiss / Long as my exile, sweet as my revenge!" (V.iii.44–45). The fine couplet with which Volumnia describes Coriolanus's power in battle is another:

> Death, that dark spirit, in's nervy arm doth lie,
> Which, being advanc'd, declines, and then men die.
>
> (II.i.177–78)

The rhetorical style of the play is more advanced than *Julius Caesar*'s and more translatable than *Antony and Cleopatra*'s.

Coriolanus is a very public play. Even private life in the play is public. There is more noise, more official and public music, and less private music in *Coriolanus* than in any other play of Shakespeare's. In the first Act alone the noises include: "a company of mutinous *Citizens*" as the play opens (I.i.), "*Shouts within*" in the same scene, "*Drum* and *Colours*," "*Drum afar off*," "*They sound a parley*," "*Alarum far off*," and sounds of fighting a few scenes later (I.iv), "*Alarum continues still afar off*," and "a *Trumpet*" (I.v), "*They all shout and wave their swords*" (I.vi), "*Alarum, as in battle*" (I.viii) and successively in the following scene, "*Flourish. Alarum. A retreat is sounded*," "*A long flourish*" as "*They all cry*, 'Marcius, Marcius'" and "*Flourish. Trumpets sound and drums*" (I.ix). The final scene of the Act is introduced with another "*flourish*," of "*Cornets*" (I.x). Throughout the play we hear flourishes and sennets, the sounds of armies and warfare, of noises "within," of shouts, of riots. In addition to these sounds of battles and parleys, "*Music plays*" during the feast at Aufidius's house (IV.v), ceremonial music that would be customary for such an occasion. "*A dead march*" is "*sounded*" at the very end of the play (V.vi), which we find also at the ends of *Hamlet* and *Lear*. There is no music for private life in the play, no music associated with Volumnia, for example, and the characters in *Coriolanus* don't know one note from another. The music in the play is the music of public occasions, it is not appreciated as art.

It is a misconception that the theme of *Coriolanus* is class warfare between plebians and aristocrats in which Shakespeare takes the aristocrats' part. The play might very easily have been mainly about that, since such class warfare is to be found in North's translation of Plutarch's "Life of Coriolanus," Shakespeare's source for the play. In North's Plutarch, there is class struggle in both Antium and Rome, and Coriolanus wants to combine with Aufidius in part to save the aristocrats. North's Plutarch states that in his march upon Rome, Coriolanus's

> chiefest purpose was, to increase still the malice and dissention betweene the nobilitie, and the communaltie: and to drawe that on, he was very carefull to keepe the noble mens landes and goods safe from harme and burning, but spoyled all the whole countrie besides, and would suffer no man to take or hurte any thing of the noble mens.

But Shakespeare makes no mention of these tactics and also makes it clear that Coriolanus has no special regard for the patricians. Near the end of the play, Cominius tells Menenius and the two tribunes, Sicinius and Brutus, that in beseeching Coriolanus not to burn Rome,

> I offered to awaken his regard
> For 's private friends. His answer to me was,
> He could not stay to pick them in a pile
> Of noisome musty chaff. He said 'twas folly,
> For one poor grain or two, to leave unburnt
> And still to nose th' offence.
>
> (V.i.23–28)

The main contrast in the play is not of aristocrats and plebians, but of the one and the many, of Coriolanus and the crowd. In between are the few—among the tribunes, Brutus and Sicinius, and among the patricians, Menenius and Cominius. The play deals, in passing, with ideas of society and community. I have already discussed these terms in the lecture on *Julius Caesar*. A society is temporary according to its function, which may change, or to its individuals as they grow unfit and have to be replaced. A society is threatened by an individual who through his superior gifts demands an excessive function, one greater than is consistent with that of the society as a whole. A society is dangerous when it persists in continuing after it is no longer necessary—an army in peacetime, for example. In a family, which is a society as well as a community, a mother like Volumnia is dangerous when she persists in treating her son as a small boy after he has grown up.

A community, which is defined by its common desires, is threatened by an exclusiveness of race or class, which denies admission to people with the same desires. It is also threatened by including people who don't share those desires: by a crowd, because its members are incapable of saying "I" and have no fixed desires, only fluctuating ones, and by an individual—person or society—who cannot say "we" and demands a special place. Communities are established by a common love, or negatively and more easily, by fear. Note how Audifius's servants rail at peace:

1. Serv. Let me have war, say I. It exceeds peace as far as day does night. It's sprightly, waking, audible, and full of vent. Peace is a very apoplexy, lethargy; mull'd, deaf, sleepy, insensible; a getter of more bastard children than war's a destroyer of men.

2. Serv. 'Tis so; and as war in some sort may be said to be a ravisher, so it cannot be denied but peace is a great maker of cuckolds.

1. Serv. Ay, and it makes men hate one another,

3. Serv. Reason; because they then less need one another. The wars for my money! I hope to see Romans as cheap as Volscians.

(IV.v.236–49)

There is certainly tension between the plebians and the patricians in *Coriolanus*. One of the citizens states the plebians' case against the patricians fairly and directly:

Care for us? True indeed! They ne'er car'd for us yet: suffer us to famish, and their storehouses cramm'd with grain; make edicts for usury, to support usurers; repeal daily any wholesome act established against the rich, and provide more piercing statutes daily to chain up and restrain the poor. If the wars eat us not up, they will; and there's all the love they bear us.

(I.i.81–89)

What is the case put by Coriolanus against the people? They refuse to participate in wars for the state, and in their "general ignorance" they demand the privilege of rule before they have learned to rule themselves, wanting to "lick / The sweet which is their poison" (III.i.146, 156–57). As Shakespeare shows, they're a crowd associated by appetite and passion, *not*, mind you, by desire. In the war you see them running away and refusing to follow Coriolanus. He enters the city of Corioles alone. They loot, act constantly out of both fear and greed, and are easily moved by oratory. They rejoice, *"wave their swords"* and *"cast up their caps"* at Coriolanus's triumph (I.vi), but their opinion of him is easily changed by the tribunes, who move them to go to the Capitol to "repent in their election" of him to consul (II.iii.263). "To th' Capitol, come," Sicinius says to Brutus,

> We will be there before the stream o' th' people;
> And this shall seem, as partly 'tis, their own,
> Which we have goaded onward.

(II.iii.268–71)

The same mutability of opinion is cleverly shown on a small scale in Antium, in the scene in which Aufidius's servants revise their view of Coriolanus. When they do not know who he is, they treat him as a beggar. After they learn his name and Aufidius has embraced him, they claim they sensed his identity all along: "my mind gave me his clothes made a false report of him. . . . Nay, I knew by his face that there was something in him. He had, sir, a kind of face, methought—I cannot tell how to term it."(IV.v.156–57, 161–63).

For a crowd the present moment is absolute. It lacks memory. When I was in Germany two years ago, civilians would say to me, "I was always against Hitler, I was forced, etc." This was not a lie in the ordinary sense of the word. It was not said to deceive. After what had happened, the tremendous destruction, all that remained was a sense of the moment, and they could not remember. Events had robbed them of their memory. We should not imagine such conduct is restricted to Germans. Most of us, if we are not careful, are members of the crowd. It has nothing to do with what class we belong to.

After Coriolanus returns to threaten Rome, the Roman crowd tries to renege on its earlier wish to banish him:

> *1. Cit.*   For mine own part,
> When I said banish him, I said 'twas pity.
> *2. Cit.* And so did I.
> *3. Cit.* And so did I; and, to say the truth, so did very many of us.
> That we did, we did for the best; and though we willingly consented
> to his banishment, yet it was against our will. . . .
> *1. Cit.* The gods be good to us! Come, masters, let's home. I ever
> said we were i' th' wrong when we banish'd him.
> *2. Cit.* So did we all. But come, let's home,
>
> > (IV.vi.139–45, 153–56)

Soon afterwards, a messenger reports, the crowd turns on the tribunes, capturing Brutus, haling

> him up and down; all swearing, if
> The Roman ladies bring not comfort home,
> They'll give him death by inches.
>
> > (V.iv.40–42)

In the following scene, in Antium, the Volscian crowd first greets Coriolanus with "*great shouts*," and moments later yells, "Tear him to pieces" (V.vi.48, 120). The crowd is any of us when we're not members of a society, with a definite function, or of a community, with a definite love or desire.

The tribunes have been badly used by critics. Being a politician is a dangerous trade for one's character, and there is no suggestion that democratic politicians are worse than aristocratic politicians—the question is not raised. The tribunes see their power and party threatened by Coriolanus, and they naturally take steps to combat him. Their dishing of him is not a pretty sight, but the inside of politics never is.

There is a lot of deception in politics. Volumnia and Menenius, for
their part, try to persuade Coriolanus to trick the people by seeming humble, by using the kind of strategy he uses in war. Volumnia
tells him

> that now it lies you on to speak
> To th' people, not by your own instruction,
> Nor by th' matter which your heart prompts you,
> But with such words that are but roted in
> Your tongue, though but bastards and syllables
> Of no allowance to your bosom's truth.
> Now, this no more dishonours you at all
> Than to take in a town with gentle words
> Which else would put you to your fortune and
> The hazard of much blood.
>
> (III.ii.52–61)

The patricians *can* be differentiated from the tribunes in their sense of
dignity. Menenius is a favorite of the people, partly because he doesn't
rule himself. The parts of a whole should be disciplined and restrained,
and he is governed by humour. But he shows up well when he appeals
unsuccessfully to Coriolanus to spare Rome and is mocked by Coriolanus' guards. "He that hath a will to die by himself," he says, "fears it not
from another. Let your general do his worst" (V.ii.110–12). Coriolanus
exhibits a similar patrician dignity when he takes leave of his family and
comforts them after he is exiled:

> What, what, what!
> I shall be lov'd when I am lack'd. Nay, mother
> Resume that spirit when you were wont to say,
> If you had been the wife of Hercules,
> Six of his labours you'ld have done, and sav'd
> Your husband so much sweat.
>
> (IV.i.14–19)

> Come, my sweet wife, my dearest mother, and
> My friends of noble touch. When I am forth,
> Bid me farewell, and smile. I pray you come.
> While I remain above the ground, you shall
> Hear from me still, and never of me aught
> But what is like me formerly.
>
> (IV.i.48–52)

Coriolanus is the object of much criticism in the play. In the opening scene, in a discussion between two citizens about his virtues and vices, the first citizen says of his service in war, "Though soft-conscienc'd men can be content to say it was for his country, he did it to please his mother and to be partly proud, which he is, even to the altitude of his virtue" (I.i.37–41). In a similar discussion between two officers, the second officer says of him that "to seem to affect the malice and displeasure of the people is as bad as that which he dislikes—to flatter them for their love" (II.ii.24–26). The tribune Brutus claims that Coriolanus agrees to be commanded by Cominius in battle because

> Fame, at the which he aims,
> In whom already he's well grac'd, cannot
> Better be held nor more attain'd than by
> A place below the first; for what miscarries
> Shall be the general's fault, though he perform
> To th' utmost of a man, and giddy censure
> Will then cry out of Marcius, "O, if he
> Had borne the business!"

(I.i.267–74)

Aufidius, after he has taken Coriolanus in, says that

> He bears himself more proudlier,
> Even to my person, than I thought he would
> When first I did embrace him.

(IV.vii.8–10)

Aufidius goes on to offer an analysis of the causes of Coriolanus's exile:

> Whether 'twas pride,
> Which out of daily fortune ever taints
> The happy man; whether defect of judgment,
> To fail in the disposing of those chances
> Which he was lord of; or whether nature,
> Not to be other than one thing, not moving
> From th' casque to th' cushion, but commanding peace
> Even with the same austerity and garb
> As he controll'd the war; but one of these
> (As he hath spices of them all, not all,
> For I dare so far free him) made him fear'd,
> So hated, and so banish'd.

(IV.vii.37–48)

In Rome Coriolanus is reluctant to go down and show his wounds to the people and be praised. "Your Honours' pardon," he says to Cominius and the patricians,

> I had rather have my wounds to heal again
> Than hear say how I got them. . . .
> I had rather have one scratch my head i' th' sun
> When the alarum were struck than idly sit
> To hear my nothings monster'd.
>
> (II.ii.72–74, 79–81)

He tells the citizens themselves, more derisively, "'twas never my desire yet to trouble the poor with begging" (II.iii.75–76). After his exile, however, his behavior changes a bit, and he seems to welcome adulation and exaltation. Cominius reports that "he does sit in gold" (V.i.63) in the Volscian camp, and Menenius, after his visit to him, says, "He sits in his state, as a thing made for Alexander. What he bids be done is finish'd with his bidding. He wants nothing of a god but eternity and a heaven to throne in" (V.iv.22–26).

Coriolanus illustrates the difference between classical tragedy and Shakespeare more than any other play. It looks like a classical play, a misunderstanding that may account for its popularity in France, and Coriolanus's behavior may look a little like hybris. But it's not. Coriolanus has many virtues. He can rule his body and has great physical courage, he is chaste, not greedy, and he doesn't actually crave the power over others that brings about his downfall:

> Know, good mother,
> I had rather be their servant in my way
> Than sway with them in theirs.
>
> (II.i.218–20)

His two flaws are (1) his passion to excel and (2) his passion for approval, to be approved uniquely. Why does he revolt at campaigning? Because to *ask* for approval suggests that approval is given not for the excellence of his acts but for his oratory and the display of his wounds:

> To brag unto them, "Thus I did, and thus!"
> Show them th' unaching scars which I should hide,
> As if I had receiv'd them for the hire
> Of their breath only!
>
> (II.ii.151–54)

And he hates the crowd because they are changeable and can approve of those who do not deserve approval or who do not deserve it as much as he does:

> Who deserves greatness
> Deserves your hate; and your affections are
> A sick man's appetite, who desires most that
> Which would increase his evil. He that depends
> Upon your favours swims with fins of lead
> And hews down oaks with rushes. Hang ye! Trust ye?
> With every minute you do change a mind
> And call him noble that was now your hate,
> Him vile that was your garland.
>
> (I.i.180–88)

If Coriolanus had simply wanted to excel, he wouldn't have stood for consul or spared Rome for the sake of Volumnia. If he had wanted approval only, he wouldn't have minded showing himself to the people, and he would not have joined Aufidius. Coriolanus is not reliable. His loyalty is not absolute.

Armies are societies that do not exist by themselves. For an army to function, it has to have an enemy, and there is a curious bond between the leaders and individual warriors, such as fighter pilots, on each side. They can understand and get along with each other much better than with their own civilians, and Shakespeare uses sexual imagery to describe their respect for each other. Coriolanus says to Cominius,

> O, let me clip ye
> In arms as sound as when I woo'd, in heart
> As merry as when our nuptial day was done
> And tapers burn'd to bedward!
>
> (I.vi.29–32)

Aufidius says similarly to Coriolanus, in an extended speech welcoming him to Antium,

> Know thou first,
> I lov'd the maid I married; never man
> Sigh'd truer breath. But that I see thee here,
> Thou noble thing, more dances my rapt heart
> Than when I first my wedded mistress saw
> Bestride my threshold. Why, thou Mars, I tell thee

We have a power on foot, and I had purpose
Once more to hew thy target from thy brawn
Or lose mine arm for't. Thou hast beat me out
Twelve several times, and I have nightly since
Dreamt of encounters 'twixt thyself and me—
We have been down together in my sleep,
Unbuckling helms, fisting each other's throat—
And wak'd half dead with nothing.

(IV.v.118–31)

In *Troilus and Cressida*, Achilles speaks in a similar vein of Hector:

I have a woman's longing,
An appetite that I am sick withal,
To see great Hector in his weeds of peace;
To talk with him, and to behold his visage
Even to my full view.

(III.iii.237–41)

Coriolanus would have been a great leader of the patrician class, as well as a great soldier, had he not wished to excel so much, and he could have been a brave individual standing alone, in good fortune and bad, had he not been tied to others by his desire for unqualified and unique approval. He is completely at the mercy of words that are said to him, and everyone in the play knows what they have to do to work on him. Brutus tells Sicinius,

Put him to choler straight. He hath been us'd
Ever to conquer, and to have his worth
Of contradiction. Being once chaf'd, he cannot
Be rein'd again to temperance; then he speaks
What's in his heart, and that is there which looks
With us to break his neck.

(III.iii.25–30)

Sicinius takes Brutus's advice by calling Coriolanus "a traitor to the people" (III.iii.66), and, as anticipated, Coriolanus becomes enraged at the word "traitor." At the end of the play, before an assembly of the Volscians, Aufidius also taunts Coriolanus and replays the earlier scene by calling him a "boy." Again, Coriolanus becomes instantly incensed:

Boy? False hound!
If you have writ your annals true, 'tis there,

That, like an eagle in a dovecote, I
Flutter'd your Volscians in Corioles.
Alone I did it. Boy?

(V.vi.112–16)

In two critical scenes in the play, mirror images of each other, Volumnia makes Coriolanus do what she wants. In the first, she pleads with him to speak nicely to the people, in the second, to spare Rome. In each case, she first tries to argue with him. When the arguments have no effect, she adopts the tactics of scolding him and threatening to withdraw her love, which works. In the earlier scene she tells him,

I prithee now, sweet son, as thou hast said
My praises made thee first a soldier, so,
To have my praise for this, perform a part
Thou hast not done before.

Coriolanus answers:

Away, my disposition, and possess me
Some harlot's spirit! My throat of war be turn'd,
Which quier'd with my drum, into a pipe
Small as an eunuch or the virgin voice
That babies lulls asleep! The smiles of knaves
Tent in my cheeks, and schoolboy's tears take up
The glasses of my sight!

(III.ii.107–17)

When he then protests, "I will not do't," Volumnia dissociates herself from him:

Do as thou list.
Thy valiantness was mine, thou suck'st it from me;
But owe thy pride thyself.

(III.ii.120, 128–30)

He immediately gives in:

Pray be content.
Mother, I am going to the market place.
Chide me no more. I'll mountebank their loves,
Cog their hearts from them, and come home belov'd
Of all the trades in Rome. Look, I am going.

(III.ii.130–34)

Volumnia's tactics in the later scene, in which she and his family plead with him to spare Rome, are the same. She says that he will forever stain his reputation in the annals, in which will be written, "'The man was noble, / But with his last attempt he wip'd it out. . . .'" (V.iii.145–46). When he continues to resist, she first kneels to him and then rises in anger and turns away from him in a physical gesture of rejection:

> This fellow had a Volscian to his mother;
> His wife is in Corioles, and this child
> Like him by chance. Yet give us our dispatch.
> I am hush'd until our city be afire.
> And then I'll speak a little.

(V.iii.178–82)

After this speech, as the stage direction tells us, Coriolanus, defeated once again, "*holds her by the hand, silent.*" At every point Coriolanus requires a relation where he is the only child—with the people as well as with his mother.

The character of Volumnia raises the point that any man who has achieved much in the world has had a dominating and demanding mother—a successful father is bad for him—but it is just as well that the mother die young. They must let go in time to allow their sons to set their own standards. They are apt to regard their sons as extensions of their egos. Volumnia wants power by proxy, and it is her wish, not Coriolanus's, that he become consul, a political office to which he is unsuited.

The play gives us a frightening picture of Coriolanus' little son, who would "rather see the swords and hear a drum than look upon his schoolmaster," and who is described torturing a butterfly. "I saw him run after a gilded butterfly," his aunt Valeria says,

> and when he caught it, he let it go again, and after it again, and over and over he comes, and up again; catch'd it again; or whether his fall enrag'd him or how 'twas, he did so set his teeth and tear it! O, I warrant, how he mammock'd it!

Volumnia responds, approvingly, "One on 's father's moods" (I.iii.66–72).

The real individual in this play is not Coriolanus, but Volumnia. His desire to excel and to be regarded as uniquely excellent makes him bound to the crowd as no other character in the play is, and he therefore hates them. He fears they will change their mind.

Timon of Athens

[16 April 1947]

Timon of Athens is an interim work between the great tragedies and the last batch of Shakespeare's plays, which are usually known as the romance comedies. It is rash to draw inferences from an author's works about his life. *Timon* is not a personal work, as *Hamlet* may be. The five masterpieces Shakespeare wrote in four years were succeeded by three plays—*Timon, Cymbeline,* and *Pericles*—that were only partly by him, followed by his two final plays, *The Winter's Tale* and *The Tempest.* During the period in which he wrote *Timon, Cymbeline,* and *Pericles,* Shakespeare was either ill or exhausted, and he worked on plays that he didn't finish.

The verse in *Timon* is of his late period, but the play is imperfectly constructed. The Alcibiades subplot is perfunctory—we don't know whom Alcibiades is defending. In the last scene Alcibiades changes character and style without warning, and throughout the play he has little relation to the main plot. When the senators come and plead with Timon in the cave, there is a sudden suggestion that he is a military leader. The bad senators die for no good reason. And the play is not strictly a tragedy, for Timon's death is unmotivated. He just passes away.

Timon of Athens is a psychological study of a pathological condition, showing a maniac in two phases: in the first, he gives money, and in the second, he gives curses. Timon is a pathological giver. There have been many studies of the miser, but few of the spendthrift. There was a man who was sent to Bellevue for giving away money on the Bowery at Christmas. People are divisible into those who find it easier to give and those who find it easier to take. Only those men Timon thought of as friends, those who take, have clearly motivated conduct in the play.

There are two parts to *Timon of Athens.* The first takes place in a banquet hall, with lights and music. The second takes place in wild nature, in a cave in the woods, where Timon eats roots, and finally at the verge of the sea, which has its own music. In the first phase of the action, Timon gets Ventidius out of jail for debt. He pays Ventidius's debt and vows "to support him after" (I.i.108), like the good Samaritan, who not only helped a man up, but paid an innkeeper two pence, with the promise of more, to care for him. Next, Timon arranges a match between his servant, Lucilius, and a free girl. In a gesture of contempt, her father, an old man, protests to Timon that having "from my first been inclin'd to thrift," he won't be stingy if his daughter, his only child, marries without his consent, he will give his money to a beggar (I.i.116–39). To secure the old man's consent, Timon agrees to match the girl's dowry and makes the love match possible. Timon meets the painter and poet and acts as patron to the painter. In an interesting scene, Ventidius arrives with money and offers to repay Timon. Timon refuses, saying,

> You mistake my love.
> I gave it freely ever; and there's none
> Can truly say he gives, if he receives.
> If our betters play at that game, we must not dare
> To imitate them. Faults that are rich are fair.
>
> (I.ii.9–13)

Timon feasts, he gives jewels, and people give him presents. He tells his servant that in welcoming newly arriving senators, "let them be re-ceiv'd, / Not without fair reward" (I.ii.196–97), and in the following scene, a senator notes that gifts to Timon breed still more valuable gifts in return:

> If I would sell my horse and buy twenty moe
> Better than he—why, give my horse to Timon.
> Ask nothing, give it him—it foals me straight,
> And able horses.
>
> (II.i.7–10)

During the banquet, Timon, offers a toast to his friends:

> O you gods, think I, what need we have any friends if we should ne'er have need of 'em? They were the most needless creatures liv-ing, should we ne'er have use for 'em; and would most resemble sweet instruments hung up in cases, that keep their sounds to them-selves. Why, I have often wish'd myself poorer, that I might come nearer to you. We are born to do benefits; and what better or prop-erer can we call our own than the riches of our friends? O, what a precious comfort 'tis to have so many like brothers commanding one another's fortunes.
>
> (I.ii.97–109)

"Methinks," he says in wild exaltation, "I could deal kingdoms to my friends / And ne'er be weary" (I.ii.226–27). At the end of the feast, Timon calls out "Lights, more lights!" (I.ii.234), as if afraid of the dark.

Timon has always been a person who wants to give more than he receives. Behind this behavior we see certain things that are not wholly unselfish: a desire to be in a superior position and play the mother, as well as a fear that one is in a weak position, unworthy of being loved for oneself. One must not take because one does not deserve. In sex relations, the giving of presents is a way of showing contempt and reproach. Nietzsche remarks that "In affability there is no hatred of men, but precisely on that account a great deal too much contempt of men." Timon's subsequent violent reaction shows that there was a great deal of aggression in the form of misgiving, which comes out in naked form when he can't any longer give. He wants to be related to others only as a giver, a rich man who has inherited his wealth. But as Flavius his steward says, in a sense nothing is his, he gives borrowed money. Timon is like the kleptomaniac who takes things and gives them back to the same people as presents. Lenders, like the senator who remarks on Timon's breeding gifts, begin to realize that Timon is already bankrupt, and they not unnaturally think they'd better get their money back. One basic theme of the play is that one cannot take without giving or give without taking. For better or for worse, we are all members of one society. Credit is a social and communal relation that has no objective factor, it is based on how people feel.

When he is threatened with bankruptcy, Timon approaches three friends for help. One servant goes to Lucullus, who had been expecting another gift. Lucullus says he had expected this trouble and had warned Timon: "Many a time and often I ha' din'd with him and told him on't, and come again to supper to him of purpose to have him spend less; and yet he would embrace no counsel, take no warning by my coming" (III.i.24–29). Lucullus's excuse for refusing to help may be true, but it is base. When Lucius hears Lucullus has refused Timon, he is shocked, but then refuses to give aid himself because he is afraid he won't get his money back. Strangers observe Lucius's behavior—they are not asked to help and are therefore free to profess shock at his ingratitude. Finally, Sempronius is approached. He has heard that all Timon's friends have refused him, and he, in the most base reaction, pretends to be insulted because he should have been asked first: "Who bates mine honour shall not know my coin" (III.iii.26). What is shocking is not that these friends refuse Timon, but their excuses, their lack of frankness. Timon had been trying to buy their affections, and affections cannot be bought. Either they had affection for Timon or they didn't. If they did, they should have refused Timon's gifts because he couldn't afford them. If they didn't, they shouldn't have eaten his meals, which were a test of affection.

Suddenly, Timon is without power, the power to give, which is the only relation to others that is conceivable to him, and so he severs all relations. He holds a second banquet in which he offers a prayer to the gods not to trust men:

> For these my present friends, as they are to me nothing, so in nothing bless them, and to nothing are they welcome.
>
> Uncover, dogs, and lap.
>
> [*The dishes are uncovered, and seen to be full of warm water.*]
>
> (III.vi.92–95)

We pass to the second half of the play, the depiction of Timon in a state of powerless hatred. Nothing can happen at all. Timon can make a lot of very fine speeches, but nothing can happen, except that he dies. He makes a plea for anarchy:

> Matrons, turn incontinent!
>
> Obedience fail in children! Slaves and fools,
> Pluck the grave wrinkled Senate from the bench
> And minister in their steads! To general filths
> Convert o' th' instant, green virginity!
> Do't in your parents' eyes. Bankrupts, hold fast!
> Rather than render back, out with your knives
> And cut your trusters' throats! Bound servants, steal!
> Large-handed robbers your grave masters are
> And pill by law. Maid, to thy master's bed!
> Thy mistress is o' th' brothel. Son of sixteen,
> Pluck the lin'd crutch from thy old limping sire:
> With it beat out his brains!
>
> (IV.i.3–15)

The fact that in his curse Timon has to tell matrons to be unfaithful shows that there must be some love and affection in society to make the curse meaningful. Timon giving curses is like Lear and Caliban filling the air with words. His message to all who visit: give others hell. He tells Alcibiades to kill and rape:

> Spare not the babe
>
> Whose dimpled smiles from fools exhaust their mercy.
> Think it a bastard whom the oracle

> Hath doubtfully pronounc'd thy throat shall cut,
> And mince it sans remorse.
>
> (IV.iii.118–22)

Again, his curse suggests that mercy must exist. He tells the whores who accompany Alcibiades to give diseases, and to the bandits he says, steal and be confounded. Timon's message to all: behave worse.

When Flavius, the good servant arrives, Timon believes that there is one honest man left and he calls on the gods to forgive him for his rashness, but the speech shows equal rashness in assuming that the world consists only of people he knows. He gives Flavius treasure, but advises him to shut himself off from men:

> Hate all, curse all, show charity to none,
> But let the famish'd flesh slide from the bone
> Ere thou relieve the beggar.
>
> (IV.iii.534–36)

Flavius is the worst experience for Timon, because Timon can't bear to "take" pity.

Flavius advises the senators who come to solicit Timon's help, truly, that Timon isn't interested:

> It is in vain that you would speak with Timon;
> For he is set so only to himself
> That nothing but himself which looks like man
> Is friendly with him.
>
> (V.i.119–22)

The senators invite Timon to resume his former self and come back to Athens. He refuses. Note that Timon doesn't kill himself. In his last words, he tells the senators to "say to Athens,"

> Timon hath made his everlasting mansion
> Upon the beached verge of the salt flood,
> Who once a day with his embossed froth
> The turbulent surge shall cover. Thither come,
> And let my gravestone be your oracle.
> Lips, let sour words go by and language end.
> What is amiss, plague and infection mend!
> Graves only be men's works, and death their gain.
> Sun, hide thy beams! Timon hath done his reign.
>
> (V.i.217–26)

Alcibiades says that people will weep for Timon in spite of his forbidding it and that he will be spectacularly mourned by nature, by the salt sea:

> Though thou abhorr'dst in us our human griefs,
> Scorn'dst our brine's flow and those our droplets which
> From niggard nature fall, yet rich conceit
> Taught thee to make vast Neptune weep for aye
> On thy low grave, on faults forgiven.
>
> (V.iv.75–79)

But other people must see his grave, and other people must read the epitaph saying he doesn't like them.

Timon talks a great deal to visitors. Apemantus is his shadow throughout the play. At the beginning he tests Timon's generosity. He comes to Timon's banquet and tells him, "I come to observe, I give thee warning on't" (I.ii.33), and the grace he says at the feast advises Timon to trust nobody:

> Immortal gods, I crave no pelf.
> I pray for no man but myself.
> Grant I may never prove so fond
> To trust man on his oath or bond,
> Or a harlot for her weeping,
> Or a dog that seems a-sleeping,
> Or a keeper with my freedom,
> Or my friends, if I should need 'em.
> Amen. So fall to't.
> Rich men sin, and I eat root.
>
> (I.ii.63–72)

Apemantus also mocks the "*Masque of Ladies* [as] *Amazons*":

> Hoy-day! What a sweep of vanity comes this way!
> They dance? They are mad women.
> Like madness is the glory of this life,
> As this pomp shows to a little oil and root.
> We make ourselves fools to disport ourselves,
> And spend our flatteries to drink those men
> Upon whose age we void it up again
> With poisonous spite and envy.
> Who lives that's not depraved or depraves?
>
> (I.ii.137–45)

What is the difference between Timon and Apemantus? Apemantus is a professional preacher of self-sufficiency, of the Greek idea of a god as a self-sufficient being. Timon, on the other hand, wants to be a god on whom others depend. As a professor, however, Apemantus requires an audience, he can't go into the woods as Timon later does. He's related to others by repulsion. Nietzsche remarks that "He who despises himself, nevertheless esteems himself thereby, as a despiser."

In the scene between Apemantus and Timon in the woods, both are just in their criticisms of each other. Apemantus comes in jealous. He doesn't want another professor to compete with him, and he rails at Timon for behaving as he does only because of disappointment. Apemantus sees that Timon is not interested in self-sufficiency and tells him that nature won't serve him. But he admits, "I love thee better now than e'er I did," to which Timon responds,

> *Tim.* I hate thee worse.
> *Apem.*   Why?
> *Tim.*   Thou flatter'st misery.
> *Apem.* I flatter not, but say thou art a caitiff.
> *Tim.* Why dost thou seek me out?
> *Apem.*   To vex thee.
> *Tim.* Always a villain's office or a fool's.
>
> (IV.iii.233–37)

Apemantus then says to Timon, and truly,

> If thou didst put this sour cold habit on
> To castigate thy pride, 'twere well; but thou
> Dost it enforcedly. Thou'dst courtier be again,
> Wert thou not beggar.
>
> (IV.iii.239–42)

Timon tells Apemantus that if he had been rich, he wouldn't have had to seek a position as a professor, and that he himself has

> had the world as my confectionary;
> The mouths, the tongues, the eyes, and hearts of men
> At duty, more than I could frame employment.
>
> (IV.iii.260–62)

This is what Timon thought he had gotten with his giving, but Apemantus points out to him that

The middle of humanity thou never knewest, but the extremity of both ends. When thou wast in thy gilt and thy perfume, they mock'd thee for too much curiosity; in thy rags thou know'st none, but art despis'd for the contrary.

(IV.iii.300–305)

Timon's last curse against Apemantus (IV.iii.330–49) reveals that he is disappointed that the beasts aren't self-sufficient either.

Alcibiades might have been an interesting character. Timon, unloved by the people he has helped, cuts himself off from society. Alcibiades, too, has done exceptional deeds for society as a soldier, and he demands special treatment for his friends from society in return. Society owes him something. He makes a plea to the senators for a friend who had killed a man, a friend who had fought for the state and had been brave in battle. When he is refused and banished, he doesn't cut himself off from society, but fights back. Society would be unbearable with such special treatment, but civilization is impossible without it, if extralegal entities like the state show in their behavior that civilization is incomplete. The senators judge manslaughter harshly because it does not tempt them, but they are tempted by usury. The reverse is true of Alcibiades. In a change parallel to Timon's, he wishes to turn into a tyrant god:

> I'll cheer up
> My discontented troops and lay for hearts.
> 'Tis honour with most lands to be at odds.
> Soldiers should brook as little wrongs as gods.

(III.v.114–17)

Alcibiades needs money for his rebellion, and Timon in the woods gives him the gold he has found. In the last scene, however, without warning, Alcibiades turns into a righteous judge, the senators become reasonable, and the right things are said about giving and taking. The senators invite Alcibiades into the city and offer him "decimation, and a tithed death" (V.iv.31), but dissuade him from wanton bloodshed. Alcibiades agrees and says:

> Those enemies of Timon's and mine own
> Whom you yourselves shall set out for reproof
> Fall, and no more. And, to atone your fears
> With my more noble meaning, not a man
> Shall pass his quarter or offend the stream
> Of regular justice in your city's bounds

> But shall be render'd to your public laws
> At heaviest answer.
>
> (V.iv.56–63)

The relation of giving and getting is a major theme of the play. In *How To Read a Page*, I. A. Richards talks of the ideas of giving and getting and of the union of "give" and "get"

> in the word *Agape*, standing for what it is tempting to call *the* Christian concept of love. But we should not call it that—since, from the earliest days of Christianity, this word has been the focus of a tremendous struggle to reconcile what have seemed to most people at most times to be opposite senses of GIVE and GET. The history of Christian dogma is the record of this intellectual-moral struggle. Orthodoxy has wavered between different adjustments and heresy after heresy might be described as a leaning toward one extreme or another. . . .
>
> Over against Agape as the rival concept of love is *Eros*, which is best studied in Plato's *Symposium*. Eros is that love which comes from lack. We desire or want because we are in want. He who desires something is in want of it (200). Our desires mount from bodily pleasures and beauties to the beauties of the mind, to institutions or laws, to the sciences, and at last to the all-encompassing knowledge or Idea of the Good (210–11), the final cause of the ascent. At each stage there is rebirth—a new need takes the place of the old needs. But all is need—the fulfilling of what is wanting. All desire, whatever its guise, is a striving to GET, and love, as Eros, whether it seeks pleasure or knowledge or a perfection still higher than knowledge (*Republic* V, 509), is still an effort to gain.
>
> This concept of love seemed to Plato to span all desire from its humblest stirrings to its noblest flights. When Christianity first broke with it and made an equally extreme identification of LOVE with GIVE, the opposition was recognized by men of both parties. It came to a head with St. Paul. It has often been remarked that Plato and St. Paul would have made little enough of one another. To St. Paul a new world picture had come into being with a new conception of God.
>
> To Plato, the more self-sufficient a man is the more perfect (*Republic* II, 381). And if we may let Aristotle in an early work speak for him, a perfect being would be without needs: "One who is self-sufficient can have no need of the service of others, nor of their affec-

tion, nor of social life, since he is capable of being alone. This is especially evident of God. Clearly since he is in need of nothing, God can have no need of friends, nor will he have any" (*Eudemian Ethics*, 1244b).

It is perhaps harsh to read into the last clause all that we might. Nonetheless, there is a repugnancy between this "self-absorbed object of unreciprocated love" (to use a phrase from Ross) and most Christian concepts: "For God so loved the world that he gave his only begotten Son, that whosoever believeth in him should not perish, but have everlasting life" (*John* III:16).

It is true that Eros, for Plato, did convey prophecies and such from God to man as well as man's love and desire to God. Nonetheless, Eros is a stream of GETTING and Agape is a stream of GIVINGS. As Eros, man's love to God is acquisitive, a desire to GET him for ourselves. It is the most enlightened form of self-love; the bad fail to love themselves. In it we seek our own good, and we must love him for nothing else, for no other gains than that self-fulfillment. But, as Agape, Love is all outgoing, and pure GIVING. It is not acquisitive; Charity "seeketh not her own" (*First Corinthians* XIII:5). And of this love God is the *source*; not, as with Eros, the *object*. All love is from God—overflowing in man's love for other men. It lends all value to men, who are all otherwise worthless. Our love to God is not desire for him but surrender to his love. In place of love for him we have participation in his love for other men.

Christianity teaches that "Thou shalt love thy neighbor as thyself." Who is thy neighbor? He who has need of thee. Only God is able to give in an absolute sense. One can't give without someone who needs, and one can't entirely dissociate oneself from selfishness. In the "Book of Thel," William Blake suggests two definitions of love, one the charitable generative love we find in the world of nature, the other the more selfish sexual love of human beings. He also treats the subject in "I heard an Angel singing":

> I heard an Angel singing
> When the day was springing,
> "Mercy, Pity, Peace
> Is the world's release."
>
> Thus he sung all day
> Over the new mown hay,

Till the sun went down
And haycocks looked brown.

I heard a Devil curse
Over the heath & the furze,
"Mercy could be no more,
If there was nobody poor;

"And pity no more could be,
If all were as happy as we."
At his curse the sun went down
And the heavens gave a frown.

And Miserie's increase
Is Mercy, Pity, Peace.

What are our needs? At the bottom are physical needs: hunger and thirst, which are the purest and are necessarily acquisitive. I destroy a steak and can't share it. For that very reason a meal can be a symbol of the other extreme, love as giving. Why? Eating unites us all—rich, poor, stupid, clever, male, female, black or white. If you want to know someone, the first thing you do is to ask him to dinner. Eating is purely selfish, so a shared feast becomes a symbol of generosity and love. The symbol of Agape is not the act of sex but the act of nutrition. Just because eating is the one primal act common to all living organisms irrespective of species, race, age, sex, or consciousness, the one act in which, since we demand all and give nothing, we are necessarily completely alone, therefore only this act can testify to the utter dependence of all creatures on each other, to the fact that *everyone* is our neighbor.

Somebody eating another is a symbol of aggression, and *Timon* is filled with such oral imagery. When Timon invites Apemantus to dine with him, Apemantus answers, "No, I eat not lords"(I.i.207). The other guests wish "to taste Lord Timon's bounty" (I.i.285). Apemantus remarks on "what a number of men eats Timon" (I.ii.40). Timon says to Alcibiades, "You had rather be at a breakfast of enemies than a dinner of friends," and Alcibiades answers, "So they were bleeding new, my lord, there's no meat like 'em. I could wish my best friend at such a feast" (I.ii.78–82). Later, in the woods, when Alcibiades offers him gold, Timon says, "Keep it. I cannot eat it" (IV.iii.100), and as he gnaws at a root, he says, "That the whole life of Athens were in this! / Thus would I eat it" (IV.iii.281–82). Beasts eat each other, as Timon tells Apemantus at length:

If thou wert the lion, the fox would beguile thee. If thou wert the lamb, the fox would eat thee. If thou wert the fox, the lion would suspect thee when peradventure thou wert accus'd by the ass. If thou wert the ass, thy dulness would torment thee, and still thou liv'dst but as a breakfast to the wolf. If thou wert the wolf, thy greediness would afflict thee, and oft thou shouldst hazard thy life for thy dinner. Wert thou the unicorn, pride and wrath would confound thee and make thine own self the conquest of thy fury. Wert thou a bear, thou wouldst be kill'd by the horse; wert thou a horse, thou would'st be seiz'd by the leopard; wert thou a leopard, thou wert germane to the lion, and the spots of thy kindred were jurors on thy life. All thy safety were remotion, and thy defence absence. What beast couldst thou be that were not subject to a beast? And what a beast art thou already, that seest not thy loss in transformation!

(IV.iii.330–49)

What is theft? Taking things that belong to others by right, things that by nature can't be shared. If you eat what doesn't belong to you, you steal. When the bandits come to take Timon's gold, he tells them, "Your greatest want is, you want much of meat. / Why should you want? Behold, the earth hath roots," and when they tell him they "cannot live on grass, on berries, water, / As beasts and birds and fishes," he answers, "Nor on the beasts themselves, the birds and fishes; / You must eat men" (IV.iii.419–20, 424–27). Timon then urges them to remain thieves:

> I'll example you with thievery.
> The sun's a thief, and with his great attraction
> Robs the vast sea. The moon's an arrant thief,
> And her pale fire she snatches from the sun,
> The sea's a thief, whose liquid surge resolves
> The moon into salt tears. The earth's a thief,
> That feeds and breeds by a composture stol'n
> From gen'ral excrement. Each thing's a thief.

(IV.iii.438–45)

We have to encroach on others in living. Owning something is a deprivation of others. Sex is particularly difficult. It's a hunger and also a love that wishes to give. When Timon asks Apemantus to dine with him, he answers:

Apem. No, I eat not lords.

Tim. An thou shouldst, thou'dst anger ladies.

Apem. O, they eat lords. So they come by great bellies.

(I.i.207–10)

The Fool in the play says to the usurer's servants:

> I think no usurer but has a fool to his servant. My mistress is one, and I am her fool. When men come to borrow of your masters, they approach sadly and go away merry; but they enter my mistress' house merrily and go away sadly.

(II.ii.103–8)

Giving as a physical need: Baudelaire remarks that "There are only two places where one pays for the right to spend: women and public latrines." Since love is more than simply getting, prostitution is not considered respectable. But Baudelaire sees prostitution as nonpossessive, as a symbol of Agape:

> Love is the desire for prostitution. There is, indeed, no exalted pleasure which cannot be related to prostitution. At the play, in the ballroom, each one enjoys possession of all. . . . Love may spring from a generous sentiment, the desire for prostitution, but it is soon corrupted by the desire for ownership. Love wishes to emerge from itself, to become, like the conqueror with the conquered, a part of its victim, yet to preserve, at the same time, the privileges of the conqueror. The sensual delights of one who keeps a mistress are at once those of an angel and a landlord. Charity and cruelty. Indeed, they are independent of sex, of beauty and of the animal species.

"The most prostitute of all beings is the Supreme Being, God Himself," Baudelaire writes, "since for each man he is the friend above all others; since he is the common, inexhaustible fount of Love."

We all have physical needs. We all demand food—we pray for it: "Give us this day our daily bread." If I have food to give, I give. If I haven't, I can't do anything. Love can't be priced. Parents are able to give love to their children without demanding love in return. It is never purely selfless, but it is most nearly so. Timon can't buy love—it has to be freely given. Love is unpriceable, whereas putting a price on food is easy. In between are works of art—for which it is very hard to decide on pricing and on the relation of giving and taking. The Poet in *Timon* thinks of himself as a giver: "Our poesy is as a gum, which oozes / From whence 'tis nourish'd" (I.i.21–22). He thinks that nature and experience are given to him first, and that he simply transmits them. But art does give something, and it fills some kind of need: a need for pleasure and truth. A subjective value also enters. What does my neighbor need? When one is hungry and thirsty what one feels one wants and what one should want are the same. In the arts, it's not so easy. Flattery is a problem. An artist can't demand both praise and money for his product. Timon makes a magnificent speech with conventional sentiments about the corrupting power of gold (IV.iii.24–44). But Timon has attempted to use money to coerce money in return. What he says about the corruption that gold can bring is true, but not because money itself is evil. It has a reverse side of virtues that can extend liberty. Men can have a corrupt will to break from society or to coerce others, but money can also extend Agape. If Ventidius discovered turnips, only a farmer could help him. It is difficult to price art, and impossible to price love and prestige, which involve a desire that has spiritual as well as physical grounds. Money, like science, can save lives or destroy them. Money increases relatedness, either for heaven or hell.

Some verse by Charles Williams, a poet you won't know, is relevant to *Timon of Athens*:

They laid the coins before the council.
Kay, the king's steward, wise in economics, said:
"Good; these cover the years and the miles
and talk one style's dialects to London and Omsk.
Traffic can hold now and treasure be held,
streams are bridged and mountains of ridged space
tunnelled; gold dances deftly across frontiers.
The poor have choice of purchase, the rich of rents,
and events move now in a smoother control
than the swords of lords or the orisons of nuns.
Money is the medium of exchange."

Taliessen's look darkened; his hand shook
while he touched the dragons; he said, "We had a good thought.
Sir, if you made verse, you would doubt symbols.
I am afraid of the little loosed dragons.
When the means are autonomous, they are deadly; when words
escape from verse they hurry to rape souls;
when sensation slips from intellect, expect the tyrant;
the brood of carriers levels the good they carry.

We have taught our images to be free; are ye glad?
are we glad to have brought convenient heresy to Logres?"

The Archbishop answered the lords;
his words went up though a slope of calm air:
"Might may take symbols and folly make treasure,
and greed bid God, who hides himself for man's pleasure
by occasion, hide himself essentially: this abides—
that the everlasting house the soul discovers
is always another's; we must lose our own ends;
we must always live in the habitation of our lovers,
my friend's shelter for me, mine for him.
This is the way of this world in the day of that other's;
make yourselves friends by means of the riches of iniquity,
for the wealth of the self is the health of the self exchanged.
What saith Heracleitus?—and what is the City's breath?—
dying each other's life, living each other's death.
Money is a medium of exchange."

Pericles and *Cymbeline*

[23 April 1947]

We come to the first two of the four plays that form a group making up Shakespeare's last period. During this period he also wrote bits of *Henry VIII* and *Two Noble Kinsmen.*

Somewhere or other Aldous Huxley makes the interesting suggestion of an anthology of last works, or better, late works: *Samson Agonistes* of Milton, for example, Ibsen's *When We Dead Awaken*, the last quartets of Beethoven, Verdi's *Falstaff*, the late paintings and etchings of Goya. Age doesn't enter in. Shakespeare was only 45 when he wrote *Pericles* and *Cymbeline*, Beethoven died at the age of 57. On the other hand, Verdi was 80. The works must be definitely different. The last works of Pope or Ben Jonson don't qualify—they are not a definitely different kind of thing. The difference mustn't be because of the failure of artistic power—Wordsworth, for example, wrote little of value after 1816. Other people, like Rossini and Rimbaud, just decided to stop writing—they have no late works. The difference must be a chosen difference, a choice made by the artist in light of approaching death and the end of his career.

The characteristics of such late works include, first, a certain indifference to their effect either on the general reading public or on critics. There must be no sign of a wish either for popularity or for an artistic perfection that is designed to reap critical acclaim. Late works also have a kind of obscurity that is different from that of a young artist. A young artist has an original vision that is strange and will seem strange to his audience. Secondly, he lacks the technical practice to put the vision across. He also has a wish to shock, which is a way of becoming related to his audience. There is a desire to be (a) popular and (b) *épatant.* In late works, the strangeness comes not from a given vision, but from an acquired vision. Eliot says in *Four Quartets,*

> Home is where one starts from. As we grow older
> The world becomes stranger, the pattern more complicated
> Of dead and living. Not the intense moment
> Isolated, with no before and after,
> But a lifetime burning in every moment
> And not the lifetime of one man only
> But of old stones that cannot be deciphered. . . .

> Old men ought to be explorers
> Here and there does not matter
> We must be still and still moving
> Into another intensity
> For a further union, a deeper communion. . . .

The writer of late works is sometimes shocking out of his indifference as to whether he shocks or not. It must not be a lessening of artistic power. Our difficulty must not be due to that, nor should the strangeness be due to that either. The work's strangeness must be intentional or because the author doesn't care. Nor is there a wish in late works for big, spectacular, purple effects. There *is* an enormous interest in particular kinds of artistic problems lovingly worked out for themselves, regardless of the interest of the whole work.

Some of the best things in late works come not in climaxes, but in bridge passages, in little points. Their virtues are virtues for the real connoisseur, they're not immediately apparent. Act V, scene iv of *Cymbeline*, the masque with Jupiter, for example, always shocks respectable critics, who find the writing so bad that they can't think it's by the Shakespeare who wrote the surrounding verse in the play. But the verse of one of the spirits, who comments on Jupiter's ascension, is remarkable:

> The marble pavement closes; he is enter'd
> His radiant roof. Away! and, to be blest,
> Let us with care perform his great behest.

> (V.iv.120–22)

In Act V, scene iii of *Cymbeline* there is a similarly remarkable speech of over 50 lines, often cut by directors, that describes Belarius and the royal children fighting alongside of and rallying the British troops:

> . . . These three,
> Three thousand confident, in act as many
> (For three performers are the file when all
> The rest do nothing), with this word 'Stand, stand!'
> Accommodated by the place, more charming
> With their own nobleness, which could have turn'd
> A distaff to a lance, gilded pale looks,
> Part shame, part spirit renew'd; that some, turn'd coward
> But by example (O, a sin in war,
> Damn'd in the first beginners!) gan to look
> The way that they did and to grin like lions

Upon the pikes o' th' hunters. Then began
A stop i' th' chaser, a retire: anon
A rout, confusion thick. Forthwith they fly
Chickens, the way which they stoop'd eagles; slaves,
The strides they victors made; and now our cowards,
Like fragments in hard voyages, became
The life o' th' need. Having found the back-door open
Of the unguarded hearts, heavens, how they wound!
Some slain before, some dying, some their friends
O'erborne i' th' former wave. Ten chas'd by one
Are now each one the slaughterman of twenty.
Those that would die or ere resist are grown
The mortal bugs o' th' field.

                                        (V.iii.28–51)

This is the kind of writing that is not immediately noticeable, but anyone who practices verse writing returns again and again and again to such passages, more than to spectacular things. They show real technical brilliance applied to something that is not very important in subject matter, but a writer wanting to learn his trade can find out how to write verse by studying them.

In the late works of Shakespeare, there is no real resemblance to the real world of time and place. The recognition scenes are fantastic. There are repeated shipwrecks in *Pericles* and repeated disguises in *Cymbeline*. Shakespeare is taking up an entirely primitive form—with choruses, dumb shows, and masques. One might think of a modern writer who, after mastering complex forms, takes up the Wild West. The plays show a conscious exploitation of tricks: asides, etc. Late works appeal to lowbrows and very sophisticated highbrows, but not to middlebrows, even to the aristocrat of middlebrows, Dr. Johnson. Critics do not appreciate the pleasure a writer has in consciously writing a simple form—like the masque in *Cymbeline*.

The first two acts of *Pericles* do not look like Shakespeare's in their verse, though we can't say he didn't write the Gower parts. There is very little comedy, in the sense of making one laugh. The play deals largely with suffering, except for the final conversion into joy through remembered suffering, the opposite of Francesca's "*Nessun maggior dolore*" in Dante's *Inferno*: "There is no greater pain than to recall a happy time in wretchedness." The physical sufferings, the violence, the storms are not real in these plays. Cloten's head and trunk would be horrible in *Lear*, but not here. The suffering of the characters is internal. Physical appearance is unimportant. The plays are difficult for professional actors to perform, because it's difficult to get actors and actresses to forget their audience. The parts have to be done in a completely absorbed way, forgetting the audience. The plays suffer more than any of Shakespeare's other plays if the feminine parts are taken by women. It is fatal to have the parts done by great actors and actresses. They are best done by schoolchildren with a Svengali director.

In an early essay on Dante, T. S. Eliot argues that "Shakespeare takes a character apparently controlled by a simple emotion, and analyses the character and the emotion itself. . . . Dante, on the other hand, does not analyse the emotion so much as he exhibits its relation to other emotions." That is true of Shakespeare up to the last plays, but there he turns his attention to relation, and consequently creates Märchen fairy-tale plots. Once upon a time a King and Queen and their beautiful daughter, once upon a time a charcoal burner with three sons, etc. In fairy tales, people are defined in terms of relationship. Not just Mr. Jones, Mrs. Robinson, but a son, a daughter. In Shakespeare's earlier plays, the individual is dominated and destroyed by passion, and the plot is designed to reveal his individual nature. The natures of the characters determine their relations and hence the plot, and at the end each character stands out from the others more completely than at the beginning. In the last plays, individuals are defined entirely in terms of relations. One can't talk about good and bad people, but only about good and bad relationships, and the plot creates a pattern out of these relationships. People, far from being more distinctive, are just one chord that completes the play. Compare Othello and Posthumus. Othello's jealousy is the product of the kind of man he is and of his reason for loving Desdemona, and, once released, it must rage to its end. But one can't think of Posthumus without thinking of Imogen at the same time. They are husband and wife, and jealousy is one of many strands in a plot that is designed to represent as many strands as possible. We don't have the slightest idea of what Posthumus and Imogen would be like not married.

What can happen in a relationship? People can be parted by fate, like Pericles, Thaisa and Marina, by banishment, like Posthumus and Belarius, by stealing, like Guiderius and Arviragus. People can be separated by death without the relationship ceasing. There can be misunderstanding of the relationship's nature—Imogen suspects Pisanio, and Imogen and her brothers don't understand the bond between them, at first. A relationship of positive love can turn negative: Dionyza toward Marina, for example, and Posthumus toward Imogen. And a negative relationship can become positive through repentance and forgiveness, as with Posthumus and Iachimo. As Dante explains in the *Purgatorio*, all relations imply some kind of love because love is the motive force of all human action. If it is disordered, love may be excessive, it may be defective, falling short of its duty, or it may be perverted, as in the love of harm to one's neighbor, which includes an excessive love of the self.

Relation can be tested: both time and place can serve to test relations. Real clock time is unimportant. The sea and the brothel in *Pericles*, wild Wales and the jail in *Cymbeline*, are places where people are tested and where they learn something about relation. The final purpose at the end of the play is that everyone must be related in love. For those whose relations must be altered, there are two choices. The first is death—as in the cases of Antiochus, his daughter, Cleon, Dionyza, the Queen, Cloten—which must not be felt as an event but as the removal of irreconcilable elements. Or there may be repentance, as in the cases of Lysimachus, Posthumus, Iachimo. Good relationships in the plays are balanced against bad ones.

In *Pericles* there are two bad parent-child relationships: Antiochus and his daughter, and Dionyza and hers. Antiochus and his daughter have an incestuous relationship, a perverted family relationship that prohibits the daughter from a relationship with a real husband, and both must be killed. Dionyza and Philoten's relation is one of excessive love, which causes Dionyza to be jealous of Marina for attracting love. Cleon feels guilty, but he cannot repudiate Dionyza's deed, which she calls "an enterprise of kindness / Perform'd to your sole daughter" (IV.iii.38–39).

> *Cleon.*   Thou art like the harpy,
> Which, to betray, dost, with thine angel's face,
> Seize with thine eagle's talents.
>   *Dion.* You are like one that superstitiously
> Doth swear to th' gods that winter kills the flies;
> But yet I know you'll do as I advise.
>
>   (IV.iii.46–51)

In *Cymbeline* the bad relationship of excessive love is that between the Queen and Cloten. She has spoiled Cloten and made him a selfish boor, and she hates Imogen and Posthumus for loving each other. Cymbeline's relation to Imogen is one of defective love, caused by his excessive love for the Queen. He reproaches Imogen for marrying Posthumus:

> *Cym.*   O disloyal thing
> That shouldst repair my youth, thou heap'st
> A year's age on me!
>   *Imo.*   I beseech you, sir,
> Harm not yourself with your vexation.
> I am senseless of your wrath; a touch more rare
> Subdues all pangs, all fears.
>   *Cym.*   Past grace? obedience?
>   *Imo.* Past hope, and in despair; that way, past grace.
>   *Cym.* That mightst have had the sole son of my queen!
>   *Imo.* O blessed that I might not! I chose an eagle
> And did avoid a puttock.
>
>   (I.i.131–40)

The bad relation of Cymbeline and Imogen is a contrast to the good parent-child relationship of Simonides and Thaisa, in which Simonides is willing to let his daughter go to Pericles.

Belarius's relationship with Arviragus and Guiderius is in contrast to that of the Queen and Cloten. There is no spoiling, and Belarius brings up the boys in godliness and good breeding. As he and they emerge from the cave, he teaches them to pay homage to heaven:

> A goodly day not to keep house with such
> Whose roof 's as low as ours! Stoop, boys. This gate
> Instructs you how t' adore the heavens and bows you
> To a morning's holy office.
>
>   (III.iii.1–4)

And he instructs them to bury Cloten honorably:

>   Though mean and mighty rotting
> Together have one dust, yet reverence
> (That angel of the world) doth make distinction
> Of place 'tween high and low. Our foe was princely;
> And though you took his life as being our foe,
> Yet bury him as a prince.
>
>   (IV.ii.246–51)

Shakespeare also contrasts bad and good relationships of man and wife. Cleon is dominated by his wife, and Cymbeline is dominated by the Queen. Cymbeline admits his subservience at the end of the play:

>   Mine eyes
> Were not in fault, for she was beautiful;

Mine ears, that heard her flattery; nor my heart,
That thought her like her seeming. It had been vicious
To have mistrusted her.

(V.v.62–66)

The big contrast in the play is between Cloten's feelings toward Imogen and Imogen's toward Posthumus. Cloten is conditioned by the Queen's spoiling of him. His affection for Imogen is selfish, and when it is rejected, it turns to hate. He vows to rape Imogen while wearing Posthumus's garments:

> She said upon a time (the bitterness of it I now belch from my heart) that she held the very garment of Posthumus in more respect than my noble and natural person, together with the adornment of my qualities. With that suit upon my back will I ravish her; first kill him, and in her eyes. There shall she see my valour, which will then be a torment to her contempt. He on the ground, my speech of insultment ended on his dead body, and when my lust hath dined (which, as I say, to vex her I will execute in the clothes that she so prais'd), to the court I'll knock her back, foot her home again. She hath despis'd me rejoicingly, and I'll be merry in my revenge.

(III.v.135–50)

To this is contrasted Imogen's unselfish love of Posthumus. When she and Posthumus part, she vows absolute devotion to him, and she maintains that devotion throughout. She questions Pisanio intently about how Posthumus acted at his embarkation from Milford Haven:

> What was the last
> That he spake to thee?
>   *Pis.*   It was "his queen, his queen!"
>   *Imo.* Then wav'd his handkerchief?
>   *Pis.*   And kiss'd it, madam.
>   *Imo.* Senseless linen, happier therein than I!
> And that was all?
>   *Pis.*   No madam; for so long
> As he could make me with this eye or ear
> Distinguish him from others, he did keep
> The deck, with glove or hat or handkerchief
> Still waving, as the fits and stirs of's mind
> Could best express how slow his soul sail'd on,
> How swift his ship.

> *Imo.*   Thou shouldst have made him
> As little as a crow, or less, ere left
> To after-eye him.
> *Pis.*   Madam, so I did.
> *Imo.* I would have broke mine eyestrings, crack'd them but
> To look upon him, till the diminution
> Of space had pointed him sharp as my needle;
> Nay, follow'd him till he had melted from
> The smallness of a gnat to air, and then
> Have turn'd mine eye and wept.
>
> (I.iii.4–22)

The scene is similar to, yet completely different from, Cleopatra's questioning of Alexas about Antony's departure to Rome (I.v). When Imogen first learns of Posthumus's jealousy, she protests:

> False to his bed? What is it to be false?
> To lie in watch there and to think on him?
> To weep 'twixt clock and clock? if sleep charge nature,
> To break it with a fearful dream of him
> And cry myself awake? That's false to's bed, is it?
>
> (III.iv.42–46)

In a moment of rage, she suspects that "some jay of Italy" (III.iv.51), "some Roman courtesan" (III.iv.125) has corrupted Posthumus. But in spite of all, she accepts what he has done and does not cease to love him, saying only, in the tenderest of reproaches:

> To lapse in fulness
> Is sorer than to lie for need; and falsehood
> Is worse in kings than beggars. My dear lord!
> Thou art one o' th' false ones.
>
> (III.vi.12–15)

At the end, when Posthumus strikes her, she says simply:

> Why did you throw your wedded lady from you?
> Think that you are upon a rock, and now
> Throw me again.   *[Embraces him.]*
>   (V.v.261–63)

Lovers who change in these plays include Lysimachus and, with more complexity, Posthumus. Lysimachus comes into the brothel and asks for virginities. Marina exhorts him to virtue, and he changes from a figure like Cloten to Marina's future husband. Posthumus begins in love, exchanging tokens with Imogen as he leaves her:

> And, sweetest, fairest,
> As I my poor self did exchange for you
> To your so infinite loss, so in our trifles
> I still win of you.
>
> (I.i.118–21)

But, when tested, Posthumus becomes savagely jealous:

> O that I had her here, to tear her limbmeal!
> I will go there and do't, i' th' court, before
> Her father. I'll do something—   *Exit.*
>
> (II.iv.147–49)

Posthumus here turns out to be just like Cloten, and he tries to have Imogen killed. When he believes her to be dead, however, though he still thinks she is guilty of adultery, he is repentant, and says:

> O Pisanio,
> Every good servant does not all commands!
> No bond but to do just ones.
>
> (V.i.5–7)

He continues to believe he has murdered Imogen, and he feels unable to fight against the British. Then, in prison, he thinks he ought to die:

> Must I repent,
> I cannot do it better than in gyves,
> Desir'd more than constrain'd. To satisfy,
> If of my freedom 'tis the main part, take
> No stricter render of me than my all.
> I know you are more clement than vile men,
> Who of their broken debtors take a third,
> A sixth, a tenth, letting them thrive again
> On their abatement. That's not my desire.
> For Imogen's dear life take mine; and though
> 'Tis not so dear, yet 'tis a life; you coin'd it.
> 'Tween man and man they weigh not every stamp—
> Though light, take pieces for the figure's sake;
> You rather mine, being yours: and so, great pow'rs,

> If you will take this audit, take this life
> And cancel these cold bonds.
>
> (V.iv.13–28)

At the end, when he is reunited with Imogen and she embraces him, he cries, "Hang there like fruit, my soul, / Till the tree die" (V.v.263–64).

Shakespeare also contrasts master-servant relations in the plays. In *Pericles*, perverted loyalty is shown in Thaliard's relation to Antiochus, and Leonine's to Dionyza. When Leonine reveals that he has sworn to Dionyza to kill Marina, Marina asks:

> How have I offended
> Wherein my death might yield her any profit
> Or my life imply her any danger?
>   *Leon.* My commission
> Is not to reason of the deed but do't.
>   *Mar.* You will not do't for all the world, I hope.
> You are well-favoured, and your looks foreshow
> You have a gentle heart. I saw you lately
> When you caught hurt in parting two that fought.
> Good sooth, it show'd well in you. Do so now.
>
> (IV.i.80–89)

Contrasted to Leonine and Thaliard are the good servants, Helicanus in *Pericles* and Pisanio in *Cymbeline*. When Pisanio tells Imogen what Posthumus has directed him to do, she exclaims:

>   Prithee dispatch!
> The lamb entreats the butcher. Where's thy knife?
> Thou art too slow to do thy master's bidding
> When I desire it too.

But Pisanio replies:

>   O gracious lady,
> Since I receiv'd command to do this business
> I have not slept one wink.
>   *Imo.*   Do't, and to bed then!
>   *Pis.* I'll wake mine eyeballs out first.
>   *Imo.*   Wherefore then
> Didst undertake it? Why hast thou abus'd
> So many miles with a pretence? this place?
> Mine action? and thine own? our horses' labour?

> The time inviting thee? the perturb'd court
> For my being absent? whereunto I never
> Purpose return. Why hast thou gone so far
> To be unbent when thou hast ta'en thy stand,
> Th'elected deer before thee?
>   *Pis.*   But to win time
> To lose so bad employment.

> (III.iv.98–113)

Shakespeare also explores the relation to one's neighbor in terms of one's profession. The goal of the good profession of the doctors Cerimon of Ephesus in *Pericles* and Cornelius in *Cymbeline* is to heal life. Cerimon says:

>   I held it ever
> Virtue and cunning were endowments greater
> Than nobleness and riches. Careless heirs
> May the two latter darken and expend;
> But immortality attends the former,
> Making a man a god. 'Tis known, I ever
> Have studied physic, through which secret art,
> By turning o'er authorities, I have,
> Together with my practice, made familiar
> To me and to my aid the blest infusions
> That dwell in vegetives, in metals, stones;
> And I can speak of the disturbances
> That nature works, and of her cures; which doth give me
> A more content in course of true delight
> Than to be thirsty after tottering honour,
> Or tie my treasure up in silken bags,
> To please the fool and death.

> (III.ii.26–42)

Cornelius has similar motivations in fooling the Queen in *Cymbeline*—he is committed by profession to heal. Both Cerimon and Cornelius can be contrasted with Boult and the brothel-keeper in *Pericles*, who are destined by their profession to infect people with disease. The Bawd says, "We were never so much out of creatures. We have but poor three, and they can do no more than they can do; and they with continual action are even as good as rotten" (IV.ii.6–9). And the Pander remarks that "The poor Transylvanian is dead that lay with the little baggage." "Ay, she quickly poop'd him," Boult says (IV.ii.23–25).

In *Pericles* there is a contrast between the poor, hardworking fishermen and their betters.

> *3. Fish.* Master, I marvel how the fishes live in the sea.
>
> *1. Fish.* Why, as men do aland—the great ones eat up the little ones. I can compare our rich misers to nothing so fitly as to a whale. 'A plays and tumbles, driving the poor fry before him, and at last devours them all at a mouthful. Such whales have I heard on o' th' land, who never leave gaping till they've swallowed the whole parish—church, steeple, bells, and all.
>
> *Per.* [*aside*] A pretty moral.
>
> *3. Fish.* But, master, if I had been the sexton, I would have been that day in the belfry.
>
> *2. Fish.* Why, man?
>
> *3. Fish.* Because he should have swallowed me too; and when I had been in his belly, I would have kept such a jangling of bells that he should never have left till he cast bells, steeple, church, and parish up again. But if the good King Simonides were of my mind—
>
> *Per.* [*aside*] Simonides?
>
> *3. Fish.* He would purge the land of these drones that rob the bee of her honey.
>
> *Per.* [*aside*] How from the finny subject of the sea
> These fishers tell the infirmities of men,
> And from their wat'ry empire recollect
> All that may men approve or men detect!
> Peace be at your labour, honest fishermen.
>
> (II.i.29–55)

The fisherman are good because they have to work for a living and because what they do is productive.

The exception to all of these characterizations would appear to be Iachimo. His trouble is not a defective love for his neighbor but a lack of a definite relation even to himself. Think of other villains—Iago, etc.— they directly know what they want to do, and they go about to devour others forthwith. Iachimo doesn't want to destroy, he wants to be chic. He talks so elaborately that no one can understand him. He's much more like Armado in *Love's Labour's Lost* than like anyone else. When he first attempts to seduce Imogen, he speaks to her of Posthumus with such indirectness that she has to ask, "What is the matter, trow? . . . What, dear sir, / Thus raps you? Are you well?" (I.vi.47, 50–51). Iachimo really suffers from glossolalia—a sign of no relation either with others or with himself. Even, at the end, when he is repentant, he's so elaborate and indirect in confessing that Cymbeline has to say, "I stand on fire. /Come to the matter. . . . Nay, nay, to th' purpose!" (V.v.168–69, 178). When he finally asks forgiveness, you feel he has changed, because his diction has changed. Posthumus says that he had him "down" in battle and "might/ Have made you finish," and Iachimo kneels and says:

> I am down again;
> But now my heavy conscience sinks my knee,
> As then your force did.
>
> (V.v.411–14)

Iachimo proposes the wager to Posthumus just because he has no relationship, no real identity. He is related to others by accident and through competition. He wants to win, cheats, and causes misery, but he gets no satisfaction—he is miserable and unhappy.

Everything in the plays is directed toward the final scene in which reconciliation takes place. What is past gives the reconciliation scene its power. Either a relation is changed from bad to good or, through suffering, it is valued and treasured more than it was before. Pericles' relation to Marina through suffering infects the whole world:

> *Per.*   I embrace you.
> Give me my robes. I am wild in my beholding.
> O heavens bless my girl! But hark, what music?
> Tell Helicanus, my Marina, tell him
> O'er, point by point, for yet he seems to doubt,
> How sure you are my daughter. But what music?
>   *Hel.* My lord, I hear none.
>   *Per.* None?
> The music of the spheres! List, my Marina.
>   *Lys.* It is not good to cross him. Give him way.
>   *Per.* Rarest sounds! Do ye not hear?
>   *Lys.* Music, my lord? I hear.
>
> (V.i.223–34)

In *Cymbeline*, Posthumus says to his enemy, Iachimo:

> Kneel not to me.
> The pow'r that I have on you is to spare you;
> The malice towards you to forgive you. Live,
> And deal with others better.

And Cymbeline follows with:

> Nobly doom'd!
> We'll learn our freeness of a son-in-law.
> Pardon's the word to all.

(V.v.417–22)

"Pardon's the word to all" is the note of all the late plays, the note to which everything is made to lead up. The characters are not separate individuals in their own right, you are not fond of them as you are of Beatrice and Rosalind, and they are not terrifying as they are in the trag- edies, where they are isolated in their own self-love. But like a fairy-tale story, this is the world as you want it to be, and nothing makes one more inclined to cry.

The Winter's Tale

[30 April 1947]

The Winter's Tale is a redoing of *Pericles*, in a more satisfactory way. The themes are the same: separation and reunion, death and rebirth, storm and music. In *Pericles*, good is all on one side and evil all on the other. The hero is purely pathetic, he just suffers. He is not tempted like Job to curse God and die, he is a good man. *The Winter's Tale* is more complicated, more like life, and aesthetically more satisfying. It has affinities with *Othello* and *Cymbeline* in its concern with jealousy. The subplot is like *As You Like It* in its use of pastoral convention, the meeting of the shepherds in Bohemia corresponding to the Forest of Arden.

We can start from that convention. What is the theme of *The Winter's Tale*, the interest? It's the study of the myth of the Garden of Eden. Man falls from the Garden of Eden and can only reach an earthly paradise again by a process of repentance and purgatorial suffering, as Leontes does. In the subplot there is a comic Eden, with a comic serpent, Autolycus.

We open with a dialogue that strikes a note of Paradise, of rapture in the exchange of love. Archidamus and Camillo exchange praise and humorous self-deprecation with each other and pray for the continuance of the great love of Leontes and Polixenes:

> *Cam.* They were train'd together in their childhoods; and there rooted betwixt them then such an affection which cannot choose but branch now. . . . The heavens continue their love!
>
> *Arch.* I think there is not in the world either malice or matter to alter it. (I.i.24–27, 34–37)

The main characters continue this note in the next scene, delineating an absolute equality of affection between the two kings. Hermione then succeeds in persuading Polixenes to stay on as a guest, and at that moment Eden is broken:

> Why, lo you now! I have spoke to the purpose twice.
> The one for ever earn'd a royal husband;
> Th' other for some while a friend.
>
> > [*Gives her hand to Polixenes.*]
> *Leon.*   [*aside*] Too hot, too hot!
> > (I.ii.106–8)

Before this moment, Eden even includes a play at guilt when Polixenes discusses his and Leontes' boyhood with Hermione:

> We were, fair queen,
> Two lads that thought there was no more behind
> But such a day to-morrow as to-day,
> And to be boy eternal. . . .
> We were as twinn'd lambs that did frisk i' th' sun
> And bleat the one at th' other. What we chang'd
> Was innocence for innocence; we knew not
> The doctrine of ill-doing, nor dream'd
> That any did. Had we pursu'd that life,
> And our weak spirits ne'er been higher rear'd
> With stronger blood, we should have answer'd heaven
> Boldly, "Not guilty," the imposition clear'd
> Hereditary ours.
>
> (I.ii.62–65, 67–74)

Hermione then responds, "By this we gather / You have tripp'd since":

> Grace to boot!
> Of this make no conclusion, lest you say
> Your queen and I are devils. Yet go on.
> Th' offences we have made you do, we'll answer,
> If you first sinn'd with us, and that with us
> You did continue fault, and that you slipp'd not
> With any but with us.
>
> (I.ii.75–76, 80–86)

But it is just a joke.

Compare Leontes' jealousy with two other cases of jealousy. Othello's involves a villain. Iago provokes Othello, and Othello fights his suspicions. It is very important that we see that Othello fights. First, someone works him up, and second, there is apparently evidence. Othello's sin is that once he does give way to jealousy, he doesn't trust himself to make inquiries, he puts himself entirely in Iago's hands. Othello is a very insecure person. Posthumus in *Cymbeline* also has the provocation of a villain and even better reasons for believing Imogen is guilty. He's at first unwilling to believe it and gives way on very good evidence, but to excess. "If you will swear you have not done't, you lie," he says to Iachimo:

> And I will kill thee if thou dost deny
> Thou'st made me cuckold.
>
> (II.iv.144–46)

Posthumus orders Imogen killed. When he gets her bloody handkerchief, he repents, though he still believes her to be guilty. Othello repents only when he has seen that Desdemona is innocent.

Leontes is very different. There is no cause for his jealousy, no Iago or
Iachimo, no evidence, everybody else tells him he's mistaken, and his
jealousy is absolutely instantaneous:

> Too hot, too hot!
> To mingle friendship far, is mingling bloods.
> I have tremor cordis on me; my heart dances,
> But not for joy; not joy.

(I.ii.108–11)

He becomes insane, and even his language hardly makes any sense:

> Affection! thy intention stabs the centre.
> Thou dost make possible things not so held,
> Communicat'st with dreams! How can this be?
> With what's unreal thou coactive art,
> And fellow'st nothing. Then 'tis very credent
> Thou mayst cojoin with something; and thou dost—
> And that beyond commission; and I find it,
> And that to the infection of my brains
> And hard'ning of my brows.

(I.ii.138–46)

To Camillo he says, "My wife's a hobby-horse" (I.ii.276), and when he
hears that Camillo and Polixenes have fled, he says:

> How blest am I
> In my just censure, in my true opinion!
> Alack for lesser knowledge! how accurs'd
> In being so blest! There may be in the cup
> A spider steep'd, and one may drink, depart,
> And yet partake no venom, for his knowledge
> Is not infected; but if one present
> Th' abhorr'd ingredient to his eye, make known
> How he hath drunk, he cracks his gorge, his sides,
> With violent hefts. I have drunk, and seen the spider.

(II.i.36–45)

Antigonus tries to reason with him, with no success, and when Hermione
tells him, "My life stands in the level of your dreams," he answers, "Your
actions are my dreams" (III.ii.82–83).

Shakespeare alters the original story. In the original the development of Leontes' jealousy is slow and, on hearing the oracle, Leontes repents. In Shakespeare Leontes repents only when news comes that Mamillius has died. There is no prompting of Leontes' suspicions from outside himself, only attempts to persuade him of Hermione's innocence. He undergoes an instantaneous change from faith to distrust. He is shocked back into sanity by Mamillius's death. Othello's underlying insecurity comes forth once the button has been pressed. Posthumus is a funda-mentally good man who shouldn't have made the wager. He shows ex-cessive anger, but repents quickly. With Leontes, the idea of infidelity merely crosses his mind—and he becomes jealous. The point is that in a relation of love, faith is essential and evidence is useless. You may prove a given event did or did not happen, but you can't prove that a person loves you, you can't prove that you shouldn't distrust someone. Once doubt is raised in Leontes' mind, it becomes almost an *acte gratuit.* He embraces doubt as a certainty. Leontes' flaw is a kind of hybris, though not the Greek idea of thinking, "I am a truly fortunate man, nothing can happen to me." For Leontes, it's the presumption that "I am good, I do not know evil." And suddenly he's caught by the idea of evil. Leontes has never considered the possibility of evil in himself. He doesn't just say, "That's what one does think of," but rather the idea strikes him with the force of something not considered.

In Sicilia, Leontes is his own serpent. In the Bohemian pastoral gar-den we have the comic serpent, Autolycus the thief. Why comic? "My father nam'd me Autolycus," he says,

> who being, as I am, litter'd under Mercury, was likewise a snapper-up of unconsidered trifles. With die and drab I purchas'd this capar-ison, and my revenue is the silly cheat. Gallows and knock are too powerful on the highway. Beating and hanging are terrors to me. For the life to come, I sleep out the thought of it. A prize! A prize!
> Enter *Clown.*
>
> (IV.iii.24–32)

After cheating the company of shepherds as well as the Clown, he de-clares "Ha, ha! what a fool Honesty is! And Trust, his sworn brother, a very simple gentleman!" (IV.iv.606–8), and he says later, "If I had a mind to be honest, I see Fortune would not suffer me; she drops booties in my mouth" (IV.iv.862–64). The cause of evil is the pretense, like Leontes', that there is no evil. The discovery of evil is tragic in Leontes' case be-cause the evil is in him, it is comic in the shepherds because evil is not in them, but in Autolycus. Their innocence is a temptation to him, but the proof of Arcady is that the serpent can live there without being found out. Autolycus, however, knows what he is. Leontes refuses to accept appearances and assurances. The shepherds judge by appearances: the Clown is deceived by the ragged-looking Autolycus, the shepherdesses like brightly colored ribbons, like what Autolycus says, and think that ballads are true. Though stealing could be uncomic, Autolycus remains comic because Shakespeare is careful to see that Autolycus steals from the clown and his father, who, we know, are richer than he is, so it's not serious. And, on the other side, Autolycus even in his deceptions brings pleasure, making people happy to be deceived.

Leontes is deceived, but through deception is saved. There are various deceptions in the play. Leontes is deceived in respect to Hermione's fidelity by his own self, with the evidence pointing the other way, and he's deceived in thinking Perdita dead, the evidence being his own order and Antigonus's disappearance. He is deceived in thinking Hermione is dead and that the statue is a statue by Paulina's silence and speech and by his earlier sight of Hermione seemingly dead. Polixenes is deceived by Florizel, who doesn't tell him of his love for Perdita—the lack of evidence is due to Florizel's silence. The shepherd is deceived by Florizel and Perdita about Florizel's birth—there is absence of evidence, again through silence. Florizel and Perdita are deceived about Perdita's birth, the shepherd and Clown are deceived into believing Autolycus by his clothes, and Mopsa and Dorcas are deceived about ballads and ribbons by ignorance. Florizel is deceived about Camillo's plans because of the pursuit by Polixenes. Florizel and Perdita are afraid of being parted, and Leontes has no motive to part them. Why is the shepherd silent about Perdita? Hard to say. Perhaps he's afraid of losing money. Autolycus deceives because he has to eat.

People suffer in the play, and one must consider the degree to which their suffering is innocent and the degree to which it is voluntary. Mamillius's suffering is wholly innocent, quite involuntary, and his death brings Leontes to his senses. Hermione is purely innocent. She first suffers passively, her son dies, her daughter is taken away from her, and she then endures voluntary suffering in keeping herself away for sixteen years from the husband whom she loves, which is her contribution to their reunion. Camillo voluntarily suffers exile and the hatred of Leontes, Paulina voluntarily suffers the rage of Leontes and the involuntary death of her husband. Partially guilty sufferers include Antigonus, who accepts the orders of Leontes, dreams of Hermione and believes in her guilt, and is involuntarily eaten by a bear.

Florizel and Perdita are not absolutely innocent. They have deceived their parents and stand in real risk of a tragedy occurring. Perdita sees it much more clearly than Florizel, even though there is an Edenic accent in Florizel's reassurance:

> *Flo.*   I bless the time
> When my good falcon made her flight across
> Thy father's ground.
> *Per.*   Now Jove afford you cause!
> To me the difference forges dread; your greatness
> Hath not been us'd to fear. Even now I tremble
> To think your father, by some accident,
> Should pass this way, as you did. O, the Fates!
> How would he look to see his work, so noble,
> Vilely bound up? What would he say? Or how
> Should I, in these my borrowed flaunts, behold
> The sternness of his presence?
> *Flo.*   Apprehend
> Nothing but jollity. The gods themselves,
> Humbling their deities to love, have taken
> The shapes of beasts upon them.
>
> (IV.iv.14–27)

Perdita sees the danger in her change of station. She shows the same humility in her dialogue with Camillo:

> *Cam.* I should leave grazing, were I of your flock,
> And only live by gazing.
> *Per.*   Out, alas!
> You'ld be so lean that blasts of January
> Would blow you through and through.
>
> (IV.iv.109–112)

Before Polixenes reveals himself, there is a beautiful exchange of compliments between Florizel and Perdita. "What you do," he says to Perdita,

> Still betters what is done. When you speak, sweet
> I'ld have you do it ever. When you sing,
> I'ld have you buy and sell so; so give alms;
> Pray so; and for the ord'ring your affairs,
> To sing them too. When you do dance, I wish you
> A wave o' th' sea, that you might ever do

Nothing but that; move still, still so,
And own no other function. Each your doing,
So singular in each particular,
Crowns what you are doing in the present deed,
That all your acts are queens.
  Per.   O Doricles,
Your praises are too large. But that your youth,
And the true blood which peeps so fairly through't,
Do plainly give you out an unstain'd shepherd,
With wisdom I might fear, my Doricles,
You woo'd me the false way.
  Flo.   I think you have
As little skill to fear as I have purpose
To put you to't. But come; our dance, I pray!
Your hand, my Perdita. So turtles pair,
That never mean to part.

            (IV.iv.135–55)

The storm arises when Polixenes becomes rather like Leontes and turns on them both:

  Pol. [*Discovers himself.*] Mark your divorce, young sir!
Whom son I dare not call. Thou art too base
To be acknowledg'd. Thou a sceptre's heir,
That thus affects a sheephook?—Thou, old traitor,
I am sorry that by hanging thee I can but
Shorten thy life one week.—And thou, fresh piece
Of excellent witchcraft, who of force must know
The royal fool thou cop'st with—
  Shep.   O, my heart!
  Pol. I'll have thy beauty scratch'd with briers and made
More homely than thy state.

            (IV.iv.428–37)

After Polixenes exits, Perdita says to Florizel:

      Will't it please you, sir, be gone?
I told you what would come of this. Beseech you
Of your own state take care. This dream of mine—
Being now awake, I'll queen it no inch farther,
But milk my ewes and weep.

            (IV.iv.457–61)

And the shepherd cries to Florizel that he has "undone a man of four-score three, / That thought to fill his grave in quiet" (IV.iv.464–65). They are saved by a miracle: one world cannot marry into another, but Perdita is not a shepherd's daughter.

The wholly guilty person in the play is Leontes, who has to repent. During the trial of Hermione, when he is told that Mamillius has died "with mere conceit and fear / Of the Queen's speed," Leontes cries:

> Apollo's angry, and the heavens themselves
> Do strike at my injustice.
>
> (III.ii.145–48)

But when Hermione swoons at the same moment, he can only say:

> Take her hence
> Her heart is but o'ercharg'd; she will recover.
> I have too much believ'd mine own suspicion.
> Beseech you tenderly apply to her
> Some remedies for life.
>
> (III.ii.150–54)

Leontes doesn't make a move, however, and doesn't realize what he's done. He begins to realize it when Paulina upbraids him:

> A thousand knees,
> Ten thousand years together, naked, fasting,
> Upon a barren mountain, and still winter
> In storm perpetual, could not move the gods
> To look that way thou wert!

and he responds:

> Go on, go on.
> Thou can'st not speak too much. I have deserv'd
> All tongues to talk their bitt'rest.
>
> (III.ii.211–17)

The courtiers tell her to stop, and she relents. But she tests him by saying, "What's gone and what's past help / Should be past grief" (IV.iv.223–24). He responds:

> Thou didst speak but well
> When most the truth; which I receive much better
> Than to be pitied of thee.
>
> (III.ii.233–35)

and he declares:

> Once a day I'll visit
> The chapel where they lie, and tears shed there
> Shall be my recreation. So long as nature
> Will bear up with this exercise, so long
> I daily vow to use it. Come, and lead me
> To these sorrows.

(III.ii.239–43)

During the sixteen years that pass, Paulina won't let him forget. He needs to be helped by others to remember what he's done. The rest of the court tries to make it easier for him, which isn't what he needs.

> *Cleo.* Sir, you have done enough, and have perform'd
> A saintlike sorrow. No fault could you make
> Which you have not redeem'd; indeed, paid down
> More penitence than done trespass. At the last,
> Do as the heavens have done: forget your evil;
> With them, forgive yourself.
> *Leon.*   Whilst I remember
> Her and her virtues, I cannot forget
> My blemishes in them, and so still think of
> The wrong I did myself; which was so much
> That heirless it hath made my kingdom and
> Destroy'd the sweet'st companion that e'er man
> Bred his hopes out of.
> *Paul.*   True, too true, my lord!
> If, one by one, you wedded all the world,
> Or from the all that are took something good
> To make a perfect woman, she you kill'd
> Would be unparallel'd.
> *Leon.*   I think so. Kill'd?
> She I kill'd? I did so; but thou strik'st me
> Sorely to say I did. It is as bitter
> Upon the tongue as in my thought. Now, good now,
> Say so but seldom.

(V.i.1–20)

Leontes doesn't like to be reminded, which is a proof that he needs to be. Cleomenes wants Leontes to marry, Paulina wants him not to, and he abides by Paulina's wishes. But when Leontes sees Perdita, he is drawn to her. Paulina says:

> Sir, my liege
> You eye hath too much youth in't. Not a month
> Fore your queen died, she was more worth such gazes
> Than what you look on now.

Leontes answers, "I thought of her / Even in these looks I made" (V.i.224–28). The time has come. Leontes has expiated his wrongs and is ready for reconciliation with Hermione. The technique of the reconciliation scene is different from the multiple reconciliations in *Cymbeline* and *Pericles*. The meeting of Leontes and Polixenes and Perdita is presented offstage. Shakespeare reserves full force for Leontes' reconciliation with Hermione.

Look at Act III, scene iii, the most beautiful scene in Shakespeare. Set on the desert coast of Bohemia, it is beautiful not in its actual words, but in its situation. You could tell the story and describe the scene in other words and one would know at once that it is beautiful in the way that a dream can be beautiful. We have had Leontes' storm of jealousy versus the physical beauty and peace in the description of the oracle at Delphi, and Polixenes' storm in Arcady versus the music of the shepherds. We now have the final music of reconciliation. In the middle of the desert near the scene, there is a storm and there are beasts of prey, hunters hunting bears and bears hunting hunters. We have an innocent baby, a weak and too obedient servant who has become Leontes' accomplice, the careless youth of hunters, the good poor—the shepherd and his son.

Some of it one just has to read. On stage, unfortunately, the exit of Antigonus, "*pursued by a bear*," is too funny. Note that Lear, in the storm, says:

> Thou'dst shun a bear;
> But if thy flight lay toward the raging sea,
> Thou'dst meet the bear i' th' mouth.

> (III.iv.9–11)

The shepherd is introduced, complaining, "I would there were no age between ten and three-and-twenty, or that youth would sleep out the rest; for there is nothing in the between but getting wenches with child, wronging the ancientry, stealing, fighting . . . " (III.iii.59–63). Then he sees the child. The Clown enters and tells of the shipwreck and of the death of Antigonus:

> O, the most piteous cry of the poor souls! Sometimes to see 'em, and not to see 'em! Now the ship boring the moon with her mainmast,

and anon swallowed with yeast and froth, as you'ld thrust a cork into a hogshead. And then for the land service—to see how the bear tore out his shoulder bone; how he cried to me for help and said his name was Antigonus, a nobleman! But to make an end of the ship— to see how the sea flap-dragon'd it, but first, how the poor souls roared, and the sea mock'd them; and how the poor gentleman roared, and the bear mock'd him, both roaring louder than the sea or weather.

(III.iii.91–104)

The shepherd shows his son the child: "Heavy matters, heavy matters! But look thee here, boy. Now bless thyself! thou met'st with things dying, I with things new-born" (III.iii.115–18). The scene ends with the shepherd saying, "'Tis a lucky day, boy, and we'll do good deeds on't" (III.iii.142–43). The scene has archetypal symbols of death, re-birth, beasts of prey, luck. It is one of the most extraordinary scenes in Shakespeare.

The conclusion of *The Winter's Tale* is the finest of Shakespeare's rec-onciliation scenes. Leontes, gazing at the statue, tells Paulina,

> What you can make her do,
> I am content to look on; what to speak,
> I am content to hear; for 'tis as easy
> To make her speak as move.

(V.iii.91–94)

Paulina says "It is requir'd / You do awake your faith," and then calls,

> Music! Awake her! strike!"
>
> [*Music.*]
>
> 'Tis time; descend; be stone no more; approach;
> Strike all that look upon with marvel. Come;
> I'll fill your grave up! Stir; nay, come away!
> Bequeath to death your numbness, for from him
> Dear life redeems you. You perceive she stirs:
> [*Hermione comes down from the pedestal.*]
> Start not! Her actions shall be holy as
> You hear my spell is lawful. Do not shun her
> Until you see her die again; for then
> You kill her double. Nay, present your hand.
> When she was young, you woo'd her; now, in age,
> Is she become the suitor?

Leon.   O, she's warm!
If this be magic, let it be an art
Lawful as eating.

                                        (V.iii.94–95, 98–111)

They marry Paulina off to Camillo, and in the simplest type of repentance, Leontes asks pardon of Hermione and Polixenes, and they don't
even bother to reply. Mamillius is dead, Antigonus is dead, sixteen years
have passed: all are remembered in forgiveness. Forgiveness is not in
forgetting, but in remembering.

The Tempest

[7 May 1947]

The Tempest is the last play wholly by Shakespeare, written in 1611 at or before the time he retired to Stratford. He was later brought in as a collaborator in the writing of *Henry VIII* and *The Two Noble Kinsmen.* People have very naturally and in a sense rightly considered the play Shakespeare's farewell piece. Whether or not Shakespeare was conscious of it is irrelevant. I don't believe people die until they've done their work, and when they have, they die. There are surprisingly few incomplete works in art. People, as a rule, die when they wish to. It is not a shame that Mozart, Keats, Shelley died young: they'd finished their work.

The Tempest, A Midsummer Night's Dream, and *The Merry Wives of Windsor,* which was written for a command performance, are the only plays of Shakespeare with an original plot. *The Tempest* is also his only play observing the unities of time, place, and action—which accounts for Prospero's long, expository narrative at the beginning of the play instead of action. Maybe he made a bet with Ben Jonson about whether he could do it or not.

Lastly, in *The Tempest,* Shakespeare succeeds in writing myth—he'd been trying to earlier, not altogether successfully. George MacDonald's children's books, such as *The Princess and the Goblin,* are very good examples of mythopoeic writing. C. S. Lewis remarks, in discussing MacDonald and myth, that

> the Myth does not essentially exist in *words* at all. We all agree that the story of Balder is a great myth, a thing of inexhaustible value. But of whose version—whose *words*—are we thinking when we say this?
>
> For my own part, the answer is that I am not thinking of anyone's words. . . . What really delights and nourishes me is a particular pattern of events, which would equally delight and nourish if it had reached me by some medium which involved no words at all—say by a mime, or a film. And I find this to be true of all such stories. . . . Any means of communication whatever which succeeds in lodging those events in our imagination has, as we say, "done the trick." After that you can throw the means of communication away. . . . In

poetry the words are the body and the "theme" or "content" is the soul. But in myth the imagined events are the body and something inexpressible is the soul: the words, or mime, or film, or pictorial series are not even clothes—they are not much more than a telephone. Of this I had evidence some years ago when I first heard the story of Kafka's *Castle* related in conversation and afterwards I read the book for myself. The reading added nothing. I had already received the myth, which was all that mattered.

The great myths in the Christian period are Faust, Don Quixote, Don Juan, the Wandering Jew. Among the great modern myths are Sherlock Holmes and L'il Abner, neither of which exhibits a talent for literary expression. Rider Haggard's *She* is another example of a myth in which literary distinction is largely absent. Comic strips are a good place to start in understanding the nature of myths, because their language is unimportant. There are some famous passages of poetry in *The Tempest*, including "Our revels now are ended" (IV.i.148ff) and "Ye elves of hills, brooks, standing lakes, and groves" (V.i.33ff), but they are accidental. *Antony and Cleopatra* and *King Lear* only exist in words. In *The Tempest* only the wedding masque—which is very good, and apposite—and possibly Ariel's songs are dependent on poetry. Otherwise you could put *The Tempest* in a comic strip.

Like other mythopoeic works, *The Tempest* inspired people to go on for themselves. You can't read *Don Quixote* without wanting to make up episodes that Cervantes, as it were, forgot to tell us. The same is true of Sherlock Holmes. Great writers such as Cervantes or Kafka can do this sort of thing. On the other hand, so can Conan Doyle and Rider Haggard. Browning wrote an extension of *The Tempest* in *Caliban on Setebos*, Renan did one in *Caliban*, and I've done something with it myself.

Let's begin with the comic and rather dull passage that is partly based on Montaigne, Gonzalo's imagination of the Utopia he would create if he had "plantation of this isle" and "were king on't":

> I' th' commonwealth I would by contraries
> Execute all things, for no kind of traffic
> Would I admit; no name of magistrate;
> Letters should not be known; riches, poverty,
> And use of service, none; contract, succession,
> Bourn, bound of land, tilth, vineyard, none;
> No use of metal, corn, or wine, or oil;

No occupation; all men idle, all;
And women too, but innocent and pure;
No sovereignty.
    Seb.   Yet he would be king on't.
    Ant. The latter end of his commonweath forgets the beginning.
    Gon. All things in common nature should produce
Without sweat or endeavour. Treason, felony,
Sword, pike, knife, gun, or need of any engine
Would I not have; but nature should bring forth,
Of it own kind, all foison, all abundance,
To feed my innocent people.
    Seb. No marrying 'mong his subjects?
    Ant. None, man! All idle—whores and knaves.
    Gon. I would with such perfection govern, sir,
T' excel the golden age.

(II.i.143–168)

One of the chief themes of *The Winter's Tale* is the idea of the Garden of Eden. Here we have an allied theme: the nature of the commonwealth, of the good society, which is presented by a good but stupid character whose fault is the refusal to admit evil in others that he knows to be there. In the commonwealth Gonzalo describes, there would be no money, no books, no work, no authority. This would be possible if all men were angels, which Antonio and Sebastian's reactions alone show they are not, and if nonhuman nature were perfect and obedient. Each character in the play has his daydream. The absence of evil is the daydream of all: of the good like Gonzalo, who shut their eyes to evil in others, and of the bad like Antonio and Caliban, who shut their eyes to evil in themselves.

There are various types of society represented in the play. It opens with the commonwealth of a ship, which is reminiscent of a similar scene in *Pericles* (III.i)—the parallel between ship and state is conventional. In the storm, authority belongs to those with professional skill: the Master and Boatswain take precedence over the King. The characters of the people are already revealed by their response to the situation: Alonso accepts it, Gonzalo is a little shocked, Antonio and Sebastian are angry. Gonzalo tries to cheer himself up—he tries always to look on the bright side of things. At the end of the opening scene of the play, Antonio says, "Let's all sink with th' King" (I.i.66). Gonzalo should say it—the line is misplaced.

What is society? For St. Augustine, society consists of a group of people associated in respect of things they love. Who has authority in the society of a sinking ship? How is the magic of authority maintained? All the people are threatened by death on the ship. When Gonzalo tells the Boatswain, "yet remember whom thou hast aboard," he answers, "None that I more love than myself" (I.i.20–22). Everyone is equal in the face of death, as well as of suffering. The magic of authority belongs to the person who has professional skill and courage in a crisis.

After the prologue of the ship in the storm, we listen to Prospero's narrative of the past and look back to two political states, Milan and Naples, which were at enmity with each other. We are not told why. Within Milan itself there was conflict. Prospero, "rapt in secret studies," entrusted the "manage" of his state to his brother Antonio (I.ii.77, 70). Prospero wished to improve himself, and that takes time, but government has to go on now, which poses a political problem. It is desirable for the best people to govern, but we can't wait—government must go on now.

Does Prospero tempt Antonio? Yes. Since Antonio is actually doing the work of governing, he is tempted to want the position of rightful governor. He abuses his trust and conspires with a foreign state, thereby not only breaking faith with his brother, but also committing treason to his city. Politically, the two states, Milan and Naples, soon become friends. Before, Milan had been independent, now it must pay tribute. Antonio, with the aid of Alonso, turns his brother and Miranda out. Prospero is helped by Gonzalo, who is not strong enough to break with Alonso, since he can't bear unpleasantness, but who won't countenance violence. Prospero loves self-improvement, Antonio loves personal power, Alonso loves political glory somewhat, but mostly he loves his family. He is devoted to his son Ferdinand. There is the curious story that he has been to Tunis for the marriage of his daughter, Claribel. It is suggested—and not denied—that this was an advantageous marriage of convenience, a marriage for family glory. Alonso is a fundamentally decent person who is led by his wishes for his family into deeds of which he has to be ashamed. He regards Prospero as an enemy.

The story of the island's past starts with Sycorax, who was banished from Algiers for sorcery—they would not take her life. It echoes the story of a witch who raised a storm when Charles V besieged the city in 1421. Sycorax gave birth to Caliban, the father being either the Devil or the god Setebos. Sycorax obtains Ariel either in Algiers or on the island, and confines him to a pine tree. When Prospero comes to the island, he releases him and finds Caliban. Sycorax introduces into the play a world of black magic like that of the witches in *Macbeth,* and her counterfeit city of malice and discord is presented as a parody of the city of concord and love. She saved the city of Algiers by raising a storm, but it was by accident. She can do a malicious deed, but not a good one—she can't release Ariel, for example.

Prospero is like Theseus in *A Midsummer Night's Dream,* he is like the Duke in *Measure for Measure* in his severity, and as a puppet master, he is Hamlet transformed. Prospero tried to make Caliban a conscious person, and only made him worse. He has lost his savage freedom:

> For I am all the subjects that you have,
> Which first was mine own king;

(I.ii.341–42)

and he has lost his savage innocence:

> You taught me language, and my profit on't
> Is, I know how to curse.

(I.ii.362–63)

Caliban could move from simple feeling to consciousness and from appetite to passion, but no further. He nonetheless remains essential to Prospero and Miranda.

There is a significant parallel between *The Tempest* and *The Magic Flute.* The problem posed in both works is the nature of education. Sarastro is like Prospero, the Queen of the Night like Sycorax, Monostatos like Caliban, and Tamino and Pamina like Ferdinand and Miranda. How do people react to education? You must go all the way if you start. You can be lowbrow or highbrow, you can't be middlebrow. Caliban might have been his "own king" (I.ii.342) once, but when he becomes a conscious being, he has to govern himself and he can't. Tamino, like Ferdinand, goes through tests in order to win Pamina. Papageno, who is living off the Queen of the Night, also wants things—he wants to be married. The Priest warns Tamino of his trials, and Tamino professes himself willing to undergo them. Papageno says he'll stay single if he has to submit to tests and risk death. An old woman appears and makes love to Papageno, and he eventually gives his hand to her rather than live a tough life. Though he refuses the ordeal, Papageno does get the prize when the old woman turns into Papagena. Why? He's rewarded because he's willing to pay his own kind of price—to stay single or marry an old woman. Like Monostatos, Caliban wants to have his cake and eat it. Why, through education, should he have to be obliged to exercise self-control? He wants a princess, too. Monostatos says, "*Lieber guter Mond, vergebe, / Eine Weisse nahm mich ein*": Dear good moon, forgive me, a white woman has taken my fancy. He wants to force himself on the princess and must be prevented by Sarastro. White magic, the city of love, works beneficently with Miranda, but it has to rule some by fear.

Ariel and Caliban both want freedom. Caliban wants freedom to follow his appetites, Ariel wants pure freedom from any experience. In Renan's version of *The Tempest*, Caliban goes back to Milan. He revolts and conquers, and says he's angry with Prospero for his deception, for instilling superstition in his subjects. Prospero is arrested by the Inquisition, and Caliban defends and later frees him. Prospero says that now that the people are positivists, no magic will work. But that means no government will work, because people believe only what they can touch and feel.

Hal's kingdom in *The Tempest* includes Alonso, who resembles Henry IV, a good but guilty king, Gonzalo, who is a nice Polonius, and Antonio, who is like Iago, toned down—he can govern himself, but his ego controls his conscience. It also includes the weaker Sebastian, and Adrian and Francisco, who are like Rosencrantz and Guildenstern, and take suggestion as a cat laps milk. The political reconciliation and equality of Milan and Naples is effected by both good and evil means, by Antonio and Sebastian's plotting as well as by Prospero's. Antonio suggests the death of Alonso to Sebastian, and since no immediate benefit is apparent, one suspects he has a further card up his sleeve. Antonio and Sebastian govern, but also love, their selves. Alonso loves others, especially Ferdinand, and through that love is made to suffer more.

Falstaff's kingdom is made up of Stephano, Trinculo, and Caliban. Trinculo recalls all of Shakespeare's earlier clowns, Stephano resembles Sir Toby Belch, and Caliban recollects both Bottom and Thersites. Together, they resemble the crowds in *Henry VI*, *Julius Caesar*, and *Coriolanus*. If Hal's kingdom becomes smaller, less glorious, Falstaff's becomes much uglier. Compare the filthy, mantled pool in *The Tempest* and Falstaff's being thrown into the water in *The Merry Wives of Windsor*. Stephano and Trinculo desire money and girls, Caliban wants freedom from books, work, and authority. Their magic is drink, not music, like Prospero's, and they are ruled by appetite. There are differences among them. Trinculo is good-natured, Stephano is quite brave, and both lack the passion that Caliban has, the passion of resentment. Caliban deifies those like Stephano who gives what he likes, not what he ought to like. Caliban, however, is the one who recognizes that Prospero's books—consciousness—are the danger. "Remember / First to possess his books; for without them / He's but a sot, as I am. . . . Burn but his books" (III.ii.99–101, 103). Caliban is worse, but less decadent, than the townees, Stephano and Trinculo. When Ariel plays on the tabor and pipe, the three have different reactions. Stephano is defiant. Trinculo cries, "O, forgive me my sins!" (III.ii.139). Caliban, on the other hand, is capable of hearing the music:

> Be not afeard. The isle is full of noises,
> Sounds and sweet airs that give delight and hurt not.
> Sometimes a thousand twangling instruments
> Will hum about mine ears; and sometime voices
> That, if I then had wak'd after long sleep,
> Will make me sleep again; and then, in dreaming,
> The clouds methought would open and show riches
> Ready to drop upon me, that, when I wak'd,
> I cried to dream again.
>
> (III.ii.144–52)

Caliban wishes to go back to unconsciousness. Gonzalo, on the contrary, sees Utopia in an ideal future. Both are unrelated to the present. Caliban knows what's to be done when they reach Prospero's cell. Stephano and Trinculo forget it and go for the clothes. On one side, they're not murderous people, on the other, they've no sense of direction.

Then there is the kingdom of Ferdinand and Miranda. Ferdinand is descended from Romeo and Florizel, Miranda from Juliet, Cordelia, and Marina. Both are good but untempted and inexperienced—they think that love can produce Gonzalo's Utopia here and now. In the scene in which they make vows of marriage to each other, Ferdinand says he is willing to serve Miranda and do Caliban's job of carrying logs, and Miranda offers to carry the logs herself. For both of them, love, service, and freedom are the same.

> *Mir.*   To be your fellow
> You may deny me; but I'll be your servant,
> Whether you will or no.
> *Fer.*   My mistress, dearest!
> And I thus humble ever.

> *Mir.*   My husband then?
> *Fer.* Ay, with a heart as willing
> As bondage e'er of freedom.
>
> (III.i.84–89)

Ferdinand and Miranda are far off both from the witty characters who fight for freedom in the comedies and from the great poetic tragic lovers like Romeo and Juliet, and Antony and Cleopatra. They are not allowed to say the wonderful poetic things that are so suspicious when they're said.

Before he presents the wedding masque to Ferdinand and Miranda, Prospero warns them against lust:

> Look thou be true. Do not give dalliance
> Too much the rein. The strongest oaths are straw
> To th' fire i' th' blood. Be more abstemious,
> Or else good night your vow!
>
> (IV.i.51–54)

In the masque itself, where Ceres represents earth, Iris water, Juno sky, and Venus, sinisterly, fire, there is the curious and interesting remark by Ceres to Iris, that Venus and Cupid had thought

>   to have done
> Some wanton charm upon this man and maid,
> Whose vows are, that no bed-right shall be paid
> Till Hymen's torch be lighted; but in vain.
>
> (IV.i.94–97)

Ferdinand and Miranda don't realize these difficulties and so are spared.

The Tempest ends, like the other plays in Shakespeare's last period, in reconciliation and forgiveness. But the ending in *The Tempest* is grimmer, and the sky is darker than in *The Winter's Tale, Pericles,* and *Cymbeline.* Everybody in the earlier plays asks forgiveness and gets it, but Prospero, Miranda, Ferdinand, Gonzalo, and Alonso are the only ones really in the magic circle of *The Tempest.* Alonso is forgiven because he asks to be. He is the least guilty, and he suffers most. Gonzalo, who is always good, needs to be forgiven his weakness. Neither Antonio nor Sebastian say a word to Prospero—their only words after the reconciliation are mockery at Trinculo, Stephano, and Caliban. They're spared punishment, but they can't be said to be forgiven because they don't want to be, and Prospero's forgiveness of them means only that he does not take revenge upon them. Caliban is pardoned conditionally, and he, Stephano, and Trinculo can't be said to be repentant. They realize only that they're on the wrong side, and admit they are fools, not that they are wrong. All this escapes Miranda, who says:

> O, wonder!
> How many goodly creatures are there here!
> How beauteous mankind is! O brave new world
> That has such people in't!

To which Prospero answers, "'Tis new to thee" (V.i.181–84). And the play hardly ends for Prospero on a note of great joy. He tells everyone:

> I'll bring you to your ship, and so to Naples,
> Where I have hope to see the nuptial
> Of these our dear-belov'd solemnized;
> And thence retire me to my Milan, where
> Every third thought shall be my grave.
>
> (V.i.307–11)

We come now to the inner and outer music of *The Tempest*. There are Ariel's songs:

> Come unto these yellow sands,
>   And then take hands.
> Curtsied when you have and kiss'd,
>   The wild waves whist,
> Foot it featly here and there;
> And, sweet sprites, the burthen bear.
>   Hark, hark!
>
> (I.ii.375–81)

> Full fadom five thy father lies;
>   Of his bones are coral made;
> Those are pearls that were his eyes;
>   Nothing of him that doth fade
> But doth suffer a sea change
> Into something rich and strange,
> Sea nymphs hourly ring his knell:
>
> (I.ii.376–402)

> Where the bee sucks, there suck I;
> In a cowslip's bell I lie;
> There I couch when owls do cry.

On the bat's back I do fly
After summer merrily.
Merrily, merrily shall I live now
Under the blossom that hangs on the bough.

(V.i.88–94)

There is music to put people to sleep and to waken them, "strange and solemn music" at the banquet (III.iii.18), "*Soft music*" for the wedding (IV.i.59), and "*Solemn music*," after Prospero buries his staff (V.i.57), to charm the court party. The sounds of the play also include the storm, thunder, and dogs. Some music is associated with Caliban's hate and Antonio's ambition, as well as with Ferdinand's grief for his father. There is more music in the scenes with Prospero and Miranda, Ferdinand and Miranda, and Gonzalo and Alonso than anywhere else in the play.

The nature of the magician, which is legitimately allied with that of the artist in the play, has to do with music. What does Shakespeare say about music in his plays? In the *Merchant of Venice*, Lorenzo says:

The man that hath no music in himself,
Nor is not mov'd with concord of sweet sounds,
Is fit for treasons, stratagems, and spoils.

(V.i.83–85)

In later plays, music is often used as a medicine. The Doctor in *King Lear* calls for music as Lear awakens from his madness (IV.vii.25). Cerimon in *Pericles* awakens Thaisa to the accompaniment of music (III.ii.88–91), and Paulina calls for music as Hermione's statue comes to life in *The Winter's Tale* (V.iii.98). In *Antony and Cleopatra*, sad music is played in the air and under the earth as we learn that "the god Hercules, whom Antony lov'd, / Now leaves him" (IV.iii.15–16). Balthazar's song in *Much Ado About Nothing*, "Sigh no more, ladies, sigh no more! / Men were deceivers ever" (II.iii.64–76) is a warning against the infidelity of men and the folly of women's taking them seriously. In *Measure for Measure*, when Mariana says that a song has displeased her mirth, "but pleas'd my woe," the Duke replies by stating the puritanical case against the heard music of the world:

'Tis good; though music oft hath such a charm
To make bad good, and good provoke to harm.

(IV.i.14–15)

Even the worst of characters, Caliban, is sensitive to music.

Prospero's magic depends upon his books and his robes. By himself
he is an ordinary man, not Faustian. He depends also on "bountiful Fortune" and "a most auspicious star" (I.ii.178, 182) to bring his old enemies
to the island. What does he do? He says, in his speech to the "elves of
hills" and "demi-puppets" that with their help he has

> bedimm'd
> The noontide sun, call'd forth the mutinous winds,
> And 'twixt the green sea and the azur'd vault
> Set roaring war; to the dread rattling thunder
> Have I given fire and rifted Jove's stout oak
> With his own bolt; the strong bas'd promontory
> Have I made shake and by the spurs pluck'd up
> The pine and cedar; graves at my command
> Have wak'd their sleepers, op'd, and let 'em forth
> By my so potent art.

"But this *rough* magic," he says, "I here abjure" (V.i.41–51). The first
thing we hear of Prospero doing on the island is releasing Ariel. What
magic he does between that action and the storm with which the play
begins we don't know and don't care. He raises storms to separate characters so that they may become independent. He allays the water by
music, he leads on and disarms Ferdinand, he sends all but Antonio and
Sebastian to sleep so that they can reveal their natures, he wakes
Gonzalo, he saves Alonso's life, he produces a banquet to force guilt
upon the consciousness of the members of the court, he creates a
masque just to please the lovers, he engages in fooling Stephano and
Trinculo and Caliban, and he produces the solemn music of his charms.
With the help of immediate illusions, he leads characters to disillusion
and self-knowledge, the opposite of the effects of drink and of Venus.

What can't magic do? It can give people an experience, but it cannot
dictate the use they make of that experience. Alonso is reminded of his
crime against Prospero, but he repents by himself. Ferdinand and Miranda are tested, but the quality of their love is their own. The bad are
exposed and shown that crime doesn't pay, but they can't be made to
give up their ambition. That art thus cannot transform men grieves
Prospero greatly. His anger at Caliban stems from his consciousness of
this failure, which he confesses to, aside and alone—he doesn't explain
it to Ferdinand and Miranda:

> A devil, a born devil, on whose nature
> Nurture can never stick! On whom my pains,

Humanely taken, all, all lost, quite lost!
And as with age his body uglier grows,
So his mind cankers.

(IV.i.188–92)

You can hold the mirror up to a person, but you may make him worse.

At the end Prospero himself asks forgiveness in the epilogue. Some say the epilogue is not by Shakespeare, but it is still beautiful:

> Now my charms are all o'erthrown,
> And what strength I have's mine own,
> Which is most faint. Now 'tis true
> I must be here confin'd by you,
> Or sent to Naples. Let me not,
> Since I have my dukedom got
> And pardon'd the deceiver, dwell
> In this bare island by your spell;
> But release me from my bands
> With the help of your good hands.
> Gentle breath of yours my sails
> Must fill, or else my project fails,
> Which was to please. Now I want
> Spirits to enforce, art to enchant;
> And my ending is despair
> Unless I be reliev'd by prayer,
> Which pierces so that it assaults
> Mercy itself and frees all faults.
> As you from crimes would pardon'd be,
> Let your indulgence set me free.

Rilke, at the end of his poem "The Spirit Ariel," writes of the epilogue to *The Tempest*:

> Now he terrifies me,
> this man who's once more duke.—The way he draws
> the wire into his head, and hangs himself
> beside the other puppets, and henceforth
> asks mercy of the play! . . . What epilogue
> of achieved mastery! Putting off, standing there
> with only one's own strength: "which is most faint."

Concluding Lecture

[14 May 1947]

It's a long time ago since the beginning of October. I and you are for better or worse, I hope for better, different people from what we were then.

There is very little information about Shakespeare as a person. Only the sonnets are directly personal. It is a temptation to everybody to invent their own Shakespeare. That's all right, provided that whatever they invent they base on the text. The drama from *Gorboduc* in 1561 to the closing of the theaters in 1642 is an incredibly odd phenomenon. The period of distinctly Elizabethan drama is much shorter, extending from *The Spanish Tragedy* in 1587 to *'Tis Pity She's a Whore* in 1633. The Elizabethan dramatists were all born within twenty years of each other: Peele in 1557, Greene in 1560, Chapman in 1569, Jonson in 1573, Webster in 1580, Ford in 1586, Middleton in 1570, and Shakespeare and Marlowe in 1564. Outside of Shakespeare, and of Jonson, whose works were anti-Elizabethan, I think the works of Elizabethan drama are terribly bad. Apart from *Doctor Faustus*, *Bussy D'Ambois*, and *The Changeling*, I cannot see any satisfactory plays. How completely Shakespeare dominates! And his only rival's whole approach is a direct protest against the Elizabethan era.

Why was the period of drama so short-lived, and why was one person so immeasurably better? Because of the provincial character of England: England was then a province, a hick country, compared with Italy, Spain, and France. Elizabethan drama did not develop out of the miracle plays, but the chronicle plays, and dramatists therefore had to start from scratch. That's not always a good thing. They had to build up their own conventions. As T. S. Eliot has remarked,

> The great vice of English drama from Kyd to Galsworthy has been that its aim of realism was unlimited. In one play, *Everyman*, and perhaps in that one play only, we have a drama within the limitations of art; since Kyd, since *Arden of Feversham*, since *The Yorkshire Tragedy*, there has been no form to arrest, so to speak, the flow of spirit at any particular point before it expands and ends its course in the desert of exact likeness to the reality which is perceived by the most commonplace mind. . . . In a play of Aeschylus, we do not find

that certain passages are literature and other passages drama; every style of utterance in the play bears a relation to the whole and because of this relation is dramatic in itself. The imitation of life is circumscribed, and the approaches to ordinary speech and withdrawals from ordinary speech are not without relation and effect upon each other. It is essential that a work of art should be self-consistent, that an artist should consciously or unconsciously draw a circle beyond which he does not trespass: on the one hand actual life is always the material, and on the other hand an abstraction from actual life is a necessary condition to the creation of the work of art.

Eliot says also:

What is fundamentally objectionable is that in the Elizabethan drama there has been no firm principle of what is to be postulated as a convention and what is not. The fault is not with the ghost but with the presentation of a ghost on a plane on which he is inappropriate, and with the confusion between one kind of ghost and another. The three witches in *Macbeth* are a distinguished example of correct supernaturalism amongst a race of ghosts who are too frequently equivocations. It seems to me strictly an error, although an error which is condoned by the success of each passage in itself, that Shakespeare should have introduced into the same play ghosts belonging to such different categories as the three sisters and the ghost of Banquo. The aim of the Elizabethans was to attain complete realism without surrendering any of the advantages which as artists they observed in unrealistic conventions.

That kind of freedom is to the advantage of a genius, but to the disadvantage of the simply talented man—and the distinction applies to every branch of life. Moral freedom, for example, is to the advantage of the strong, not the average, man. If the conventions of Elizabethan drama had been fixed, as in French classical drama, Shakespeare would not have done what he did, but others wouldn't have been so bad, and the period of drama wouldn't have died so quickly.

The great glory of the nineteenth century is Italian opera, which extends from Mozart's *Marriage of Figaro* in 1786 to Verdi's *Falstaff* in 1892. After that we have Puccini and the decadence of the Italian operatic tradition and its conventions that is coincident with the theory of *verismo*, of naturalism. We also have the advent of the great genius who broke previous operatic convention, Wagner—but you can't learn from great genius because it is unique. There was a long period of preparation for the golden age of Italian opera. It begins with Monteverdi and Gluck and first flowers in Mozart. It embraces not only great geniuses but all kinds of composers—including Bellini, Rossini, and Donizetti, who might not have amounted to much without the structure of conventions.

The period of Elizabethan drama has one gigantic figure, Shakespeare, and one eccentric, Jonson, and it is over in no time. The whole of Elizabethan drama has an improvised character. There was an obsession with the idea of the wicked Italian, again a provincial characteristic, and again with the exception of Shakespeare, who both understands and develops the characters of Iago and Iachimo. There developed a taste, as a consequence, for spectacular villains as in Webster, or abnormal passions as in both Webster and Ford, without an understanding of them. Dostoevsky understood abnormal passion. Elizabethans were commonplace bourgeois people with a gift for language, who read spectacular cases in the papers without understanding. Like a peep show. Very soon after Shakespeare, people applied his subtle poetry for subtle characters to unsubtle characters.

Shakespeare was born in 1564, married at eighteen, left Stratford at twenty-one, perhaps because of a charge of poaching, reached London at the age of twenty-two, and wrote *Henry VI, Part One*, at the age of twenty-seven or twenty-eight. His first poems come out when he is twenty-nine, and his sonnets are written from the ages of twenty-nine to thirty-two. At thirty-three, he's made enough money—out of the theater, not the plays, until *Henry IV*—to buy a house in Stratford. From the ages of thirty-five to thirty-seven he writes his most important comedies, from thirty-six to forty his unpleasant plays, from forty to forty-four the great tragedies, and from forty-four to forty-seven the romantic comedies. At forty-six he appears to have retired to Stratford. At forty-seven he wrote *The Tempest*. At fifty-two he dies.

Shakespeare was a comparatively late starter. He begins writing at the age of twenty-seven to twenty-eight with not terribly good work, finds himself at thirty, and then has twenty years of productive life. Not a long time, but he was incredibly productive. He wrote thirty-six plays. Contrast him with Goethe, who lives till he is eighty-three, and who was an international success at nineteen with the publication of *Werther*. Or with Dante, who dies at fifty-six, and whose whole life was a preparation for one great work. Dante was exiled at thirty-seven. Both Dante and Goethe took a prominent part in public life. Shakespeare was not a gentleman and had no kind of social importance. As Wyndham Lewis notes, Shakespeare's "representation of an agony and death, like that of Othello . . . is a show of the same nature as a public execution." Shakespeare was "in this sense," as Wyndham Lewis says,

> a public executioner, a quiet and highly respectable man, as might be expected. His *impassibility* was the professional mask of the hangman. For dramatic effect the dramatist, like the hangman, must be *impassible.* His attitude to the many kings and heroes who were done to death by him was *not* conveyed—that is the idea of this contention—by the impassible, impressive, dramatic, "unmoved" mask of the executioner. But actually the mask was incessantly convulsed with the most painful unprofessional emotions; and it was apt to be tear-stained and fixed in a bitter grimace as he left the scaffold.

Shakespeare takes himself a long time to learn the business, then pours work after work out, all of which could be better—he doesn't care much. And then he stops. In what does he get his training? He got his training in what is valuable for a genius, but not for others—the chronicle plays, which can be very heavy going indeed. For the person who has the necessary talent, however, it is the best training. You have got to start with actual historical events, and you can't eliminate a character simply because your style of writing can't deal with him. You must develop a style to suit. Events are given. The problem is, what kind of sense can I make of them when the sense is not apparent? I can't select only one significant event. I can't start with an interesting situation and create the characters to fit it—or vice versa. The study of history imposes important lessons, the most important of which is the interdependence of character and situation. The tightness of history enforces an understanding of the relation of any one thing to everything else in the world. Double plots, like the Falstaff and Hal plots, are really related. There is also in history no neat Sunday school division into good and bad, characters have mixed motives, and there can be no narrow theory of aesthetic propriety that separates the tragic from the comic. The role of fate is important, but not completely so. You can always ask, "What else might have happened if . . . ?" But the broad lines of the story are apparent. The earth is unjust, the ungodly flourish like the green bay tree, and the righteous die. At the same time there is Nemesis. History is so difficult, so complicated, that the dramatist of average talent is well advised to keep away from it and get more abstract. If such a dramatist does take an historical subject, he simplifies it into a moralized history that is neither history nor moral.

Shakespeare, like everybody else, inherits Christian psychology. You can argue for hours as to what Shakespeare believed, but his understanding of psychology is based on Christian assumptions of the kind you'd find in every man. All men are equal not in respect of their gifts but in that everyone has a will capable of choice. Man is a tempted being, living with what he does and suffers in time, the medium in which he realizes his potential character. The indeterminacy of time means that events never happen once and for all. The good may fall, the bad may repent, and suffering can be, not a simple retribution, but a triumph. The pagan conception of the mean as ideal disappears. Men must have an infinite dynamic for good or for evil. The Greek idea of the mean turns a man turn into a trimmer, like Rosencrantz and Guildenstern. *Un*-Christian assumptions include first, that character is determined by birth or environment, and second, that man can become free by knowledge, that he who knows the good will will it. Knowledge only increases the danger, as Elizabethans saw. In pure form, the quest for freedom through knowledge is rare, and it's doubtful whether it can be presented directly, but Elizabethans were fascinated by it and by its relation to the Christian concept of the *acte gratuit*. The interest in the temptation of knowledge informs Shakespeare's development of the villain from the stock and familiar Richard III to the unrecognizable figure of Iago. Other Elizabethans stayed with characters like Richard III and Aaron the Moor. The third un-Christian assumption is the understanding of God as retributive justice, where success is good and failure means wrong, and where there is no need for forgiveness or pity. In modern books, character is entirely the victim of circumstances, and there is the daydream of people as angels, transcendent in their power. Modern books are also devoted to the belief that success signifies the forward way of history and so is right.

Shakespeare's tragedies and comedies both turn on the idea of original sin and man's inveterate tendency to foster illusions, one of the worst of which is the illusion of being free of illusion, the illusion of detachment. In the comedies the characters proceed through illusion to reality. The comedies begin with Proustian illusion, but they don't stop there. They go on to marriage where illusion largely disappears and the remnants of it are accepted as a part of reality. There's plenty of suffering in the comedies, but it's different from classical and Jonsonian comedy, where people are laughing at hunchbacks and misers. In Shakespeare you suffer with the characters until you see, as they do, that they have suffered from illusion.

In the tragedies characters are sucked into illusion more and more until they become like Timon and Iago, whose illusion is of having gotten beyond illusion. The tragic flaw of the Shakespearian hero is not hybris, the classical presumption that nothing can happen to you, but pride and the anxiety of insufficiency, the determination to *become* self-sufficient. The natural reflections of a natural man to situations of difficulty can be the cynicism of Machiavelli, the Roman stoicism of Seneca, or the skepticism of Montaigne. It's impossible to prove Shakespeare's own belief or disbelief in most of these attitudes, except negatively. Maybe Shakespeare tips his hand a little in the end, since a dramatist must reflect the intellectual currents of his age. But the very unsuccessfulness of plays like *Hamlet* and *Troilus and Cressida*, dramatically, suggest that though Hamlet's skepticism and Thersites' cynicism may be reflections of current attitudes, the plays show how far the characters themselves are from being contented or happy in those feelings. Montaigne was quiet in his library, but Hamlet's skepticism is a torture of the mind, as Thersites' cynicism is a violence of the mind—there can be no identification with either state. When you see cynics, you are given all sorts of reasons for their attitudes—to show that they are not purely disinterested. Gloucester's nihilism at the beginning of *Lear* comes after we have seen him behave badly.

The basic assumptions in Shakespeare do not change very much. What does continually change is the development of his verse. He starts off his career imitatively, inheriting two possibilities. One is the style of Marlowe's choleric man of war, which we see, for example, in Talbot's speech before the gates of Bordeaux:

> English John Talbot, Captains, calls you forth,
> Servant in arms to Harry King of England;
> And thus he would: Open your city gates,
> Be humble to us, call my sovereign yours
> And do him homage as obedient subjects,
> And I'll withdraw me and my bloody power;
> But if you frown upon this proffer'd peace,
> You tempt the fury of my three attendants,
> Lean famine, quartering steel, and climbing fire,
> Who in a moment even with the earth

> Shall lay your stately and air-braving towers,
> If you forsake the offer of their love.
>
> (*1 Henry VI*, IV.ii.3–14)

On the other side is the lyrical, pathetic style, which existed outside the drama in Spenser and in the formation of Senecan rhetoric. Queen Margaret's speech to Elizabeth in *Richard III* telling of her earlier prophecy is a good example:

> I call'd thee then vain flourish of my fortune;
> I call'd thee then poor shadow, painted queen,
> The presentation of but what I was,
> The flattering index of a direful pageant,
> One heav'd a-high to be hurl'd down below,
> A mother only mock'd with two fair babes,
> A dream of what thou wast, a garish flag,
> To be the aim of every dangerous shot;
> A sign of dignity, a breath, a bubble,
> A queen in jest, only to fill the scene.
>
> (IV.iv.82–91)

Both the Marlovian and the lyrical style keep a constant pace in Shakespeare's earliest works.

Shakespeare first advances by trying to deal with characters who don't fit either style, through the development of characters as critics of convention. The tempo of the verse is not very different, but the diction and metaphor are changing, as we can see in the speech in *Love's Labour's Lost* in which Berowne compares a woman to a German clock:

> O—and I forsooth, in love? I that have been love's whip,
> A very beadle to a humorous sigh,
> A critic, nay, a night-watch constable,
> A domineering pedant o'er the boy,
> Than whom no mortal so magnificent!
> This wimpled, whining, purblind, wayward boy;
> This senior junior, giant dwarf, Dan Cupid,
> Regent of love-rhymes, lord of folded arms,
> Th' anointed sovereign of sighs and groans,
> Liege of all loiterers and malecontents,
> Dread prince of plackets, king of codpieces,
> Sole emperor and great general
> Of trotting paritors (O my little heart!)—

And I to be a corporal of his field
And wear his colours like a tumbler's hoop!
What, I? I love? I sue? I seek a wife?
A woman, that is like a German clock,
Still a-repairing, ever out of frame,
And never going aright, being a watch,
But being watch'd that it may still go right!
Nay, to be perjur'd, which is worst of all;
And, among three, to love the worst of all,
A whitely wanton, with a velvet brow,
With two pitch-balls stuck in her face for eyes;
Ay, and, by heaven, one that will do the deed
Though Argus were her eunuch and her guard!
And I to sigh for her! To watch for her!
To pray for her! Go to! it is a plague
That Cupid will impose for my neglect
Of his almighty dreadful little might.
Well, I will love, write, sigh, pray, sue, and groan.
Some men must love my lady, and some Joan.

                                        (III.i.176–207)

Such a passage shows a new freedom with the *caesura* as well as with actual imagery.

Side by side with the development of the verse is a developing use of prose that then reacts back upon the verse. In the comedies, prose is spoken by persons with a sense of humor, verse by those who are conventional. In *Hamlet*, Hamlet speaks prose to others, verse to himself. In *Troilus and Cressida*, prose is personal, verse official, in *Othello*, verse shows feeling, prose detachment. In *King Lear*, prose is used for madness. In his essays on Shakespeare's style in *Words and Poetry*, George Rylands writes:

> The first and obvious use of prose in Elizabethan drama is for low and comic characters, for servants and clowns, such as Speed and Gobbo. Shakespeare achieved his first successes in character in this realistic medium, Shallow and Quickly and Fluellen, to name only three. Gradually the more important characters caught the infection. Faulconbridge, Gloucester, Berowne, Hotspur clamoured for prose, Mercutio, the first tragic character, Shylock and Casca won it. If *Coriolanus* had been written at the time of *King John*, Menenius, like the Bastard, would have spoken verse. Further, when Shake-

speare, hampered by the limitations of the blank verse of Marlowe
and Kyd, turned to the court comedy of Lyly, he created in prose
Rosalind and Beatrice. In these he made court comedy more realistic, in Falstaff he raised low comedy to a different level. Falstaff is an
intellectual character. In him, in Hamlet, in Iago, in Edmund, and
(in lesser degrees) in Thersites and Menenius, Shakespeare used
prose for a more philosophical purpose, for reasoning, while verse
suits more emotional expression. Shakespeare with more invention
and subtlety used prose to suggest certain *traits* of character, worldliness perhaps, or cynicism, or sense of humour (like Enobarbus), or
for persons of commoner clay, not necessarily by birth, but by disposition; Sebastian, for instance, in *The Tempest,* brother to the King of
Naples. And in Act I. Sc. 2 it is to be noted that Stephano and Trinculo speak prose, while the monster, Caliban, speaks verse. Similarly
in *Othello,* Act IV. 3, the matter-of-fact Emilia, except for her last
speech, intersperses Desdemona's verse with prose.

Above all, Shakespeare found himself dramatically in prose, and his apprenticeship in that element helped him during those middle years
in which he threw over his old models and created a new form of
blank verse. It is true that as he advanced and elaborated that new
style he was able more and more to dispense with prose. But the
greatness of *Othello* and *Troilus and Cressida* and *King Lear,* and more
particularly of *Hamlet,* arises from the combination of both which
enabled him to create his characters, as it were, in another dimen-
sion. Although prose is not entirely eliminated from *Antony and
Cleopatra,* it is a *tour de force* in the use of verse. After that, Shakespeare let his obligations as a dramatist slide; he exploited his verse
style recklessly, and, where he did not feel inspired to write poetry,
filled in the gaps with prose.

The middle style of Shakespeare's verse, "packed with matter," as Rylands writes, "a style that could gallop at a touch, with freer rhythms and
higher emotional pressure," is first hinted at in a speech we've talked
about before, the King's speech on time in the second part of *Henry IV:*

> O God, that one might read the book of fate,
> And see the revolution of the times
> Make mountains level, and the continent,
> Weary of solid firmness, melt itself
> Into the sea! and other times to see

> The beachy girdle of the ocean
> Too wide for Neptune's hips; how chances mock,
> And changes fill the cup of alteration
> With divers liquors! O, if this were seen,
> The happiest youth, viewing his progress through,
> What perils past, what crosses to ensue,
> Would shut the book and sit him down and die.
>
> (III.i.45–56)

The sense stops with the *caesura* in these lines, and we have the parentheses and divisions, the broken and shortened lines—the verse giving the actors the opportunity to gesture—that we find in the great tragedies. It is a gestured verse.

The maturest form of Shakespeare's verse style can be seen in Leontes' lines after Hermione and Polixenes leave the stage at the beginning of *The Winter's Tale*:

> Inch-thick, knee-deep, o'er head and ears a fork'd one!
> Go play, boy, play. Thy mother plays, and I
> Play too; but so disgrac'd a part whose issue
> Will hiss me to my grave. Contempt and clamour
> Will be my knell.—Go play, boy, play.—There have been
> (Or I am much deceiv'd) cuckolds ere now;
> And many a man there is (even at this present,
> Now, while I speak this) holds his wife by th' arm
> That little thinks she has been sluic'd in 's absence
> And his pond fish'd by his next neighbour—by
> Sir Smile, his neighbour. Nay, there's comfort in't
> Whiles other men have gates, and those gates open'd
> (As mine) against their will. Should all despair
> That have revolted wives, the tenth of mankind
> Would hang themselves. Physic for't there's none.
> It is a bawdy planet, that will strike
> Where 'tis predominant; and 'tis pow'rful, think it,
> From east, west, north, and south. Be it concluded,
> No barricado for a belly! Know't,
> It will let in and out the enemy
> With bag and baggage. Many thousand on's
> Have the disease, and feel't not.
>
> (I.ii.186–207)

There is a complete freedom of sentence style in this speech. It is a new and remarkable lyric manner, but it had a disastrous effect on Fletcher and Webster. You have to have subtle characters for such a style.

Shakespeare initially adopts the ordinary stock of the diction and poetic properties of his time, including pastoral and rhetorical conceits. But he begins to develop his own imagery in order to represent characters whom conventional imagery didn't fit. He experiences a tremendous development of vocabulary through his use of prose. He can use austere monosyllables in *Julius Caesar*, and a Latinized style in *Troilus and Cressida*. He shows his freedom from convention by his absolute lack of snobbery toward either Latin or plain little words. He can be terribly Latinized and use dialect in the same line. He has an enormous range of vocabulary—which is not good for everyone. He's not quite unerring, but he has a fabulously good taste for words. He uses one part of speech as another, as one can in an uninflected language—a discovery made by the Elizabethans that is untranslatable into French.

Shakespeare is also remarkable in his use of metaphor. From the simple hypostasis of "art made tongue-tied by authority" in Sonnet 66, he progresses to the extraordinary, kaleidoscopic sliding from one metaphor to another in Macbeth's lines,

> If th' assassination
> Could trammel up the consequence, and catch,
> With his surcease, success; that but this blow
> Might be the be-all and the end-all here,
> But here, upon this bank and shoal of time,
> We'ld jump the life to come. But in these cases
> We still have judgment here, that we but teach
> Bloody instructions, which, being taught, return
> To plague th' inventor. This even-handed justice
> Commends th' ingredience of our poison'd chalice
> To our own lips.
>
> (I.vii.2–12)

This metaphorical license is a very dangerous practice for most writers, which is why Eliot says it is better to imitate Dante than Shakespeare.

Shakespeare also freely employs mixed metaphors, as in the speech in which Claudius tells Laertes why he has not acted openly against Hamlet:

> The other motive
> Why to a public count I might not go

Is the great love the general gender bear him,
Who, dipping all his faults in their affection,
Would, like the spring that turneth wood to stone,
Convert his gyves to graces; so that my arrows,
Too slightly timber'd for so loud a wind,
Would have reverted to my bow again,
And not where I had aim'd them.

(IV.vii.16–24)

Shakespeare also developed his own use of poetic symbols and imagery. As Wilson Knight demonstrates, in most of Shakespeare's plays there are two antithetical symbolic clusters. On the one hand tempests, rough beasts, comets, diseases, malice domestic and private vice, that is, the world of conflict and disorder, on the other hand music, flowers, birds, precious stones, and marriage, the world of reconciliation and order. Caroline Spurgeon has described the development of Shakespeare's imagery.

There is a continual process of simplification in Shakespeare's plays. What is he up to? He is holding the mirror up to nature. In the early minor sonnets he talks about his works outlasting time. But increasingly he suggests, as Theseus does in *A Midsummer Night's Dream,* that "The best in this kind are but shadows" (V.i.214), that art is rather a bore. He spends his life at it, but he doesn't think it's very important. His characters of action behave like men of action, but they talk so like Shakespeare himself, so subtly and sensitively, that if they were real, they would not be able to act, they'd be exhausted. I find Shakespeare particularly appealing in his attitude towards his work. There's something a little irritating in the determination of the very greatest artists, like Dante, Joyce, Milton, to create masterpieces and to think themselves important. To be able to devote one's life to art without forgetting that art is frivolous is a tremendous achievement of personal character. Shakespeare never takes himself too seriously. When art takes itself too seriously, it tries to do more than it can. For secular art to exist, it's highly advantageous to artists, whatever their belief, to support religion. When supernatural religion disappears, art becomes either magic that is run by authorities through force of fraud, or falsehood that becomes persecuted by science.

But in order to continue to exist in any form, art must be giving pleasure.

APPENDIX I

Auden's Saturday Discussion Classes

Shortly after Auden began his Wednesday evening lectures on Shakespeare at the New School for Social Research, he announced that he would hold discussion classes on Saturdays at 2:00 p.m. for students taking the course for credit. In the fall term, these classes appear to have covered a variety of activities, including student readings from the plays, exercises, brief discussions of various Shakespearean topics, and a final examination, which is printed in Appendix II. In the spring term, Auden turned his attention to the language of *Hamlet* and *The Tempest*, making comments on various words or phrases that he also usually underlined and annotated in his copy of Kittredge's edition of Shakespeare. Most of these philological comments can be traced to the *Oxford English Dictionary* and the *Variorum* editions of the two plays. Auden asked Ansen for his copy of the Variorum *Tempest* the week before beginning the play.

Ansen took very sporadic notes for the classes in the fall term and more detailed but still sketchy notes on the discussions of *Hamlet* and *The Tempest*. I have transcribed most of the notes verbatim, without attempting to reconstruct them, slightly reordering some for the sake of clarity and omitting a few that were too cryptic to construe. Bracketed words or sentences indicate my additions.

[19 October 1946]

Papers and work of students. A comparison with some other convention: Greek, Racine, Scribe, Ibsen. Looking for people interested in acting—getting up set speeches. In Act IV scene iii of *Love's Labour's Lost*, for example—Berowne's speech, etc., to be dressed for presentation. For stage designer, discuss principles and history of stage designing of one particular play. For people who write poems and plays, take a comedy, e.g., *Love's Labour's Lost*, or tragedy, etc., and turn it into an opera libretto. Involves problems of operatic form: tenor, soprano, mezzo soprano, contralto, mezzo contralto, baritone, bass—trio, duet, quartet, etc. *Hamlet* is not amenable to a libretto. Treatment of sources would be of interest to a historian. I don't think much of comparing Machiavelli with a shopkeeper—nothing direct, more promising than good. Literary criticism—comparison with another author. I'd advise against doing pastiche—when Shakespeare's bad, he parodies himself. His style is not specialized enough for pastiche. Antony as executive, Cleopatra as aging matron. Much better to modernize the motivations and make a new play.

Don't try to separate out sounds from a word's meaning.

Don't assume that Shakespeare's blank verse became increasingly more complex. There was a relaxation in Shakespeare's final period— he sailed into an extraordinary mildness. [Cf. "Herman Melville," *CP*, p. 251.]

[26 October 1946]

Bertram [in *All's Well That Ends Well*] is a horrid man.
Emphasize line ends.

The scene of Margaret triumphing over Elizabeth and the Duchess in *Richard III* (IV.iv) should be played evenly.

Sonnet 94, 2d quatrain—"rightly": legally, morally; "grace": physical form, theological, social form. Ambivalence of feeling, likes and likes not: (1) have power to hurt and aren't going to, (2) do harm, but *involuntarily*. The "stewards" are officially inferior, but have potentialities for superiority through humility as undercurrent. "Base": immoral and lower in chain of being; "meet": fortune, or corrupted by surroundings. Arrogance arouses envy in weeds as well as bringing destruction on person.

[2 November 1946]

Antony and Cleopatra, quotation for Election Day:

> It hath been taught us from the primal state
> That he which is was wish'd until he were;
> And the ebb'd man, ne'er loved till ne'er worth love,
> Comes dear'd by being lack'd. This common body,
> Like to a vagabond flag upon the stream,
> Goes to and back, lackeying the varying tide,
> To rot itself with motion.

(I.iv.41–47)

I.iv.44 "This common body": public opinion, public opinion judging reputation.
I.iv.45 "flag": flower, water-lily.

Zeugma : two unequally yoked things—he came home in tears and a bath chair. Chiasmus: "Blubb'ring and weeping, weeping and blubbering," *Romeo and Juliet* (III.iii.87). Aposiopesis: "A man, young lady! lady, such a man / As all the world—why, he's a man of wax," *Romeo and Juliet* (I.iii.75–76). Hendiadys, oxymoron, caesura.

Caricature is an exaggeration of a salient feature. It is designed to ridicule or to make memorable: for example, by means of abstractions, as in Tolstoy's description—in *What Is Art* [Chapter 13]—of Seigfried, described as opening his mouth, singing and going away, with no reference to Wagner's music.

Satire and comedy. Satire depicts people you're supposed not to be. A lyric puts into words sensed feelings, satire again completes, gives awareness of, sensed feeling. Satire must assume a norm. Satire involves contradiction between a legitimate universe and an abnormal specimen and may involve suffering. The cartoonist and writer James Thurber is both ironic and comic. In Thurber's *War Between Men and Women*, there are two cartoons, one showing the general headquarters of the men, the other of the women. Both have a map of the USA in the background, but in the map in the women's headquarters, Florida is cut off.

[16 November 1946]

Two possibilities in the analysis of Leontes' speech in *The Winter's Tale*, beginning "Affection! thy intention stabs the centre" (I.ii.138–46): *their* affection is undermining the bases of reality and making him mad, or *his own* passion makes him mad—jealousy—his belief in what does not exist. Jealousy can invent. Archery, assassination. Passion can do what it intends or passion can tear away, kill the reasonable order of life. Leontes believes something which is in actual fact impossible.

We filled in: "Tir'd with all these, for restful death I cry," Sonnet 66. [Auden frequently devised exercises that required students to fill in missing words or verses.]

[7 December 1946]

Next Saturday: *Antony and Cleopatra*, II.vii, and *Merchant of Venice*, III.ii.

WHA gave us a horribly difficult exercise: he took fragments of individual lines of Claudius's attempt to repent in *Hamlet*, jumbled them up, and asked us to put them in proper order.

[21 December 1946]

We read Jonson's "Vision of Delight" (WHA borrowing my copy). Scansion of "Come away, come away, death" from *Twelfth Night* (II.iv.52–67), and filling in of two missing stanzas from Campion's "Rose-cheekt *Laura*, come."

[11 January 1947]

35 spot passages: identify what play, who speaks, who is spoken to, and on what occasion. Backward and forward looking things. [This was the final examination for the fall term and is printed in Appendix II.]

Music done on second balconies above stage. Plays done in the afternoon—as it got darker you could have night scenes. Use of cyclorama.

It is very dreary to have Shakespeare out of doors. You can't hear. You need a claustrophobic feeling. Attic drama: ritual and destined, slight enclosure of amphitheater as stadium, and characters on cothurnuses hem in the hero. In Elizabethan drama the hero always has choice, and you need the claustrophobia aspect of temptation.

Ballet is nothing like modern dance.

The last century's settings for Shakespeare's plays were not necessarily worse than ours. A great work of art can be staged with a number of sets and different stage designs. There is too much culture in contemporary interpretations and cheap recreations of the Elizabethan stage. Very dreary.

[15 February 1947 ?]
[*Hamlet*]

Hamlet's positive relations turn negative, except with Horatio, who, interestingly enough, is a failure. Hamlet's mistake is to believe that relationship as such is the root of evil.

I.ii.164 "what make you from Wittenberg, Horatio?": translation of German *Was machen sie.*

I.ii.182 "dearest foe": "dear" originally strong.

I.ii.204 "distill'd" : be chilled, [OED: be melted].

I.ii.205 "act": *actus, actum*—passive meaning.

I.iii.2 "convoy is assistant": the boat's ready.

I.iii.6 "toy": origin not known, used by Skelton and Tindale, appears once in Robert de Brunne.

I.iii.9 "suppliance": pronounced either súppliance or suppliánce.

I.iii.15 "soil": *solium*, earth; *souiller*, wet.

I.iii.15 "cautel": deceit, *cautela*, precaution—*cavere*. The virtue of a drug.

I.iii.69 "censure": *censūra*.

I.iii.107 "sterling": comes from penny introduced by Normans, from *steorling*—some pennies had a star on them.

I.iii.109 "Running": [proverbial]: "That he may run that readeth it." From "rune": construe.

I.iii.117 a foot short, to mark a pause.

I.iv, v How to stage I.iv and v together. First part on the regular stage, characters going off right, then on the inner stage, with a trap door for the ghost to go out. Hamlet is relieved to find he has an identity after the murder of his father. His levity is a defense.

I.iv.2 "eager air": *acer*.

I.iv.27 "complexion": mixture of humours.

I.iv.36 "the dram of e'il": eisel, vinegar.

I.iv.37 "dout": either *dubitare* or do out.

I.iv.38 "scandal": from Greek *scandalon*, trap, stumbling-block.

I.iv.43 "questionable": something that can be questioned.

I.iv.47 "canoniz'd": buried. Cannon: *canela*, reed; canon: Greek *canōn*, rule.

Hamlet is not mad, as Ophelia is—Hamlet can look after himself.

I.iv.77 "fadoms": [outstretched arms,] embrace. Imagination changes meaning.

I.v.30 "meditation": contemplative life.

Hamlet is not really in love with Ophelia. His letter to her is terribly conventional. He wouldn't have written that way. In the grave scene, he objects to Laertes' rhetoric.

I.v.37 "process": *procès*—verbal.

I.v.71 "tetter": [eruption of the skin].

I.v.83 "luxury": lust.

I.v.124 "arrant": same as errant.

I.v.150 "truepenny": technical term from mining—sign that there's metal in the earth.

Hamlet moves around the stage to prove to others that the ghost is really there. His frivolousness is a defense against fear.

I.v.163 "pioner": *pedonem*—foot soldier, fortification forces, engineers.

Underground undermining, a pioneer undermines [old] ideas. Pawn, peon—peonage.

In criticism don't arouse emotion, but describe emotions that are there, a complaint one can make against Swinburne, who did, however, make known a lot of Elizabethan plays.

Fairy story idea in *Lear*. For all their suffering, Shakespeare's characters don't see the mistakes they make. Lear should really apologize to Goneril as much as to Cordelia, he should apologize for having demanded love. You may not be able to help it, but you should be ashamed. That's the basic mistake. He never really sees it. In criticism take other people's feelings for granted, concentrate on illuminating.

W. P. Ker—author of *The Dark Ages—Form and Style in Poetry*, George Saintsbury, *A History of English Prosody*, Thomas Campion, *Observations on the Art of English Poetry*, C. S. Lewis on alliterative verse. [C. S. Lewis, "The Alliterative Metre," *Lysistrata*, vol. II (1935), reprinted in *Rehabilitations and Other Essays* (London: Oxford University Press, 1939). At the beginning of the essay, Lewis remarks that "Mr. Auden" has revived some of the stylistic features of alliterative verse.]

[8 March 1947]
[*Hamlet*]

Nobody picked up my watch.—or perhaps somebody has. Perhaps they mean to return it.

II.ii.319 "apprehension": apprehension and intuition. Angels apprehend immediately.
II.ii.316–22 Quarto punctuation divides "how infinite."
I.ii.329 "coted": cut off, intercept a hare—technical term from coursing greyhounds.
II.ii.338 "tickle o' th' sere": from sere, trigger of a gun—light on the trigger, quick to laugh.
II.ii.354–60 Child players of the Middle Temple were competing with adult companies.
II.ii.346 "inhibition": loss of opportunity.
II.ii.355 "little eyases": unfledged eaglets.
II.ii.355–56 "cry out on the top of question": connected with the rack. Bacon's "science putting nature to the rack."
II.ii.356 "tyrannically": a tyrant on stage is the one who makes noise, so clapping is thunderous.
II.ii.359–60 "many wearing rapiers are afraid of goose-quills and dare

scarce come hither": controversy of pamphlets keeps courtiers from common stages for fear of being unfashionable.

II.ii..372–73 "the poet and the player went to cuffs in the question": have to be either battles or controversies [on] topic of children players.

II.ii.387 "Gentlemen, you are welcome to Elsinore": there is agreement that Hamlet speaks this line to Rosencrantz and Guildenstern.

II.ii.394 "aunt-mother": a pun—aunt can mean "whore," as in Autolycus's song in *The Winter's Tale* (IV.iii.11).

II.ii.398 "handsaw": should be hernshaw.

II.ii.420–21 "law of writ": classical tragedy.

II.ii.421 "the liberty": romantic pastoral.

II.ii.426 "'One fair daughter . . .'": Hamlet's song about Jephthah comes from a real ballad—the *Chanson du Pont-Neuf.*

II.ii.462 "sallets": dirty jokes.

II.ii.479 "gules": from French *gueule.*

II.ii.526 "mobled": not "mowbled" but "mob" + "led."

II.ii.540 "milch": gentle.

The first time women appeared on stage was 6 December 1660, an actress playing Desdemona in *Othello.* [Ansen asks in his notes: "Did Davenant use women in *The Siege of Rhodes?*"]

II.ii.604 "pigeon-livered": pigeons were believed not to have gall, and gall was supposed to secrete the humor causing rage and grief.

II.ii.607 "Offal": dung.

II.ii.625 "tent": a tent is the name for a bandage on a wound—to tent means "to swab out."

II.ii.625–30 Hamlet's interests keeps getting deflected, so he speaks his resolve at the end of this scene.

III.i.48 "pious action": the irony of Polonius's comment about it is that Polonius loves to draw morals, but the King takes it seriously.

III.i.59 "sea of troubles": emendations include "siege of troubles," "assail of troubles."

III.i.61 "to say": poses a difficulty because of the grammatical inconsequence. If we were looking at a MS. we'd say the texture was imperfect.

III.i.65 "rub": a technical term from bowling, if a ball grazes against another ball and is deflected.

III.i.67 "coil": may mean either "disturbance" or the modern sense of coil. Shakespeare may have thought of both meanings, "disturbance" first. A funny image, like stepping out of a pie. "Shuffle off" is "shrug off." The emendation of "coil" to "soil" is too modern, not Elizabethan.

III.i.75 "quietus": legal term meaning "settlement."

III.i.86 "pith": from sap, center; "moment": momentum, importance. From "pith" to "currents" (III.i.86–87): a mixed metaphor. ["Pith" might be] "pitch," meaning air, and correct the problem. "Currents" simply means "courses."

III.i.151–52 "you nickname God's Creatures and make your wantoness your ignorance.": Nickname means "name added," derogatory name, reference to "make up." "God's creatures" are themselves. What is really wantonness you put forth as ignorance—prudery.

[15 March 1947]

[*Hamlet*]

When we last saw Hamlet, he was in a very tense scene with Ophelia. In the beginning of III.ii, his hysterical gaiety is a distraction from his difficulties and a contrast to them.

III.ii.15 "Termagent": noisy character in the mysteries, companion of Mahound.

III.ii.27 "very age and body": every age and body.

What is Horatio to do while Hamlet praises him? For a long time we've seen Hamlet rejecting everybody, and it's important we see there's somebody he does like (he threw over Ophelia). His relation to Horatio counteracts the tendency to believe in his madness. Horatio is the kind of person with whom he can be friends. Why does Hamlet like Horatio? Horatio likes Hamlet as someone amusing to talk to. Horatio's a little skeptical—"So have I heard and do in part believe it" (I.i.165)—phlegmatic, not easily upset, as opposed to Polonius to whom nothing's happened. Horatio has accepted suffering.

III.ii.73 "blood": desire, self-confidence.

III.ii.73 "judgment": phlegm.

III.ii.98–99 "chameleon's dish": the chameleon was supposed to feed on air. A pun on "air" and "heir." Again, he's waiting to turn airy suspicion into truth. "Heir" is fooling the king as to his interests. Hamlet hasn't seen Gertrude since before he saw the ghost.

III.ii.116–17 "metal more attractive": a magnet.

III.ii.138 "for I'll have a suit of sables": "for" should be "fore."

III.ii.146ff. You can't present the dumb show with the king and queen not looking. Do it as ballet, which is obscure as all ballets are. Pantomime must be done elaborately, music, etc., a lot of action. Or else it should be out. Possibly the dumb show and the play within the play represent two variants of the text printed together. I have a particular objection to ballets anyway. Doesn't the dumb show hold up the action? There is a contrast between the badness of the play and the actual effect of it. Which are Hamlet's "some dozen or sixteen lines" (II.ii.566–67)? I think that's been forgotten about. The speeches of the player Queen are where Hamlet's comments are most likely. Hamlet talks about the "Duke" of Vienna" and they say the "King" in the text. Granville-Barker, in his preface to *Hamlet*, thinks of the dumb show characters as so stylized as to be virtually puppets.

III.ii.263–64 "leave thy damnable faces": must be connected with Hamlet's earlier advice to the players. It goes back to III.ii.36.

III.ii.286 "forest of feathers": player's clothes.

III.ii.288 "raz'd shoes": slashed shoes.

III.ii.295 "pajock". the male peacock was supposed to break the eggs of the female peacock because he didn't want her to love them more.

III.ii.307 The Folio has Rosencrantz and Guildenstern re-entering before Hamlet's "Aha!" (line 302).

III.ii.348–49 "pickers and stealers": hands, from the catechism, "keep my hands from picking and stealing and my tongue from evil speaking."

III.ii.393ff. Hamlet talks of clouds to get rid of Polonius's boring conversation.

III.iii.22 "boist'rous": from the French *boiteux lame* or Celtic *wistas*, wild.

III.iii.57 "currents": occurrences.

If you go to confession and say I'm not sorry for my sin, but I'm sorry I'm not sorry, that will do for a Catholic.

[22 March 1947]

[*Hamlet*]

The closet scene (III.iv). Hamlet can't think it's the King behind the arras if he's just passed him. But he may have been thinking of Claudius without thinking of where he was. In the Quarto, he tells his mother about the murder. Why shouldn't he? Because she has to keep quiet. How can she keep quiet on stage without arousing Claudius's suspicion? If Hamlet's going to talk about murder, he must silence any spy, since if a spy goes away and tells Claudius, he's sunk. He's under tension. You must accept the feasibility of passing a rapier through the arras. Gertrude's a stupid woman who doesn't allow herself to suspect. She's been having an affair with Claudius while the elder Hamlet was alive. It's "incestuous" (I.v.42) for her to marry her dead husband's brother.

III.iv.50 "the doom": doomsday.

III.iv.52 "index": used to come at beginning of the book.

III.iv.54 "counterfeit presentment": Hamlet must have a miniature.

III.iv.67 "moor": originally a marsh, now can be hilly.

III.iv.98 "a vice of kings": a deformed representation.

III.iv.102 "Enter the Ghost in his nightgown": Q1. F has "Enter ghost." Ghost is unarmed, should wear everyday indoor clothes. It's impossible to tell whether Shakespeare actually believed in ghosts. The audience did believe in the power of ghosts and witches. It was a great time for the actual persecution of witches. The official view was incredulous of the night-riding function of witches. James I was an extremely intelligent man, extremely intelligent, and he believed in witches. In fact, you can prove that the Ghost wasn't a figment of Hamlet's imagination because other people saw it. It wouldn't be convenient to have Gertrude see the ghost.

III.iv.169 "either [master]": a corrupt line.

III.iv.178–79 This couplet suggests the original ending of the scene.

III.ii.181–96 The chief thing is that once Shakespeare had decided not to let Gertrude know about the murder he had to have a good reason for her to keep quiet.

IV.i If you play III.iv and IV.i continuously you have the problem of the Queen rushing out and entering again. The folio cuts Rosencrantz and Guildenstern and has the King come in, which is better.

IV.i.40 "So haply slander—": not in the original, and not necessary—it reflects the editorial mania for completing lines.

IV.i.41 "world's diameter": "diameter" because the shortest way.

IV.iii.62 "cicatrice": do you pronounce it *s*icatrice or *k*icatrice? [OED has *s*icatrice.]

IV.iii.69–70 This last couplet is obviously corrupt. Last couplets are never important.

IV.iv.53–56 "Rightly to be great . . . at the stake": the line is disapproving.

[29 March 1947]

[*Hamlet*]

Act IV scene v is really the beginning of the last Act. The Folio omits the Gentleman in the stage direction. Q gives lines 14–15 to Horatio, F gives them to the Queen. It looks funny if Ophelia comes in like a showpiece. Get her forcing her way in, and Horatio should say: "Let her come in" (line 16). "Enter Ophelia distracted" (F)—"Enter Ophelia with a lute" (Q). The use of a lute is to keep Ophelia still. Nothing can keep the scene from being awful—either very indecent or a "flowers" scene.

IV.v.2 "importunate": *Portunus* is the god of harbors, a suitable season. In + *portunus* means "not in season." "Importunate" means "out of tune with herself."

IV.v.6 "enviously": *invidia* means "looking askance at," "enviously" then means "angrily."

IV.v.25 "cockle hat": Why did pilgrims' hats have shells?—they had to take ships.

IV.v.38 "Which bewept to the grave did not go": original text, but she was describing a good funeral, not Polonius's.

IV.v.41–42 "the owl was a baker's daughter": Genius arrived at a baker and asked for dough. The baker's daughter said give half, half swelled, and the daughter, astonished, turned into an owl. The moral: give freely to the poor.

IV.v.48 "Valentine's day": the first girl you see you must have for your sweetheart. The day on which birds choose their mates.

IV.v.58 "By Gis": Jesus.

IV.v.84 "hugger-mugger": old forms, "hoker-moker," "hocker-mocker."

IV.v.95 "a murd'ring piece": *meurtrière,* French gun which could sweep an area.

IV.v.97 "Switzers": guards.

IV.v.99 "list": boundary, you make it with a strip, then becomes what's written on a strip.

IV.v.110 "counter": from hunting, when hounds go back on the trail instead of forwards.

IV.v.146 "pelican": used in bestiaries for Christ.

IV.v.152 "Let her come in": probably a corrector's stage direction.

IV.v. 153 "Enter *Ophelia.*": Nicholas Rowe put in "*fantastically drest with Straws and Flowers.*" Why should she have real flowers? and mad people don't have special dresses to be mad in. You ought to have an originally good dress not put on properly. Obviously her slip is showing. Her clothes should be related to what she wears before. It's unlikely that they would have let her run around. In Bedlam and out in open you can have straw garlands. But why a garland? She should go around giving people bobbypins, etc., for flowers. Ideally she should be very obscene. But you can't do that. She should give things that are definitely *not* flowers. Mad people will give something—not just nothing.

Flowers on the table are a very modern invention—post–industrial revolution.

IV.v.171–72 "the wheel becomes it": the refrain of a song.

IV.v.177 "pansies": *pensées.*

IV.v.178 "document": lesson.

IV.v.180 "fennel": flattery (eyes).

IV.v.180 "columbines": cuckoldry , forsaken love.

IV.v.181 "rue": one exorcised a devil by making the person possessed drink a brew of rue.

IV.v.184 "daisy": daisies were warnings to young girls.

IV.v.184 "violets: fidelity.

IV.v.214 "hatchment": coat of arms.

IV.v.215 "ostentation": has no derogatory meaning here.

IV.vii.16–24 Shows when Shakespeare doesn't come off. It illustrates Eliot's business about making a fool of yourself by imitating Shakespeare, not Dante. The metaphors don't work, they clash with each other and are too complicated.

IV.vii.63 "checking": from falconry, if hawk goes after a bird other than the one it should.

IV.vii.77 "siege": seat.

IV.vii.81 "weeds": clothes, *wæd*; garden weeds, *weod.*

IV.vii.82 "health": difficulty.

IV.vii.118 "plurisy": excess water in lungs, from the Greek *pleura*, lung.

IV.vii.123 "spendthrift sigh": every time you sighed you lost blood, like bleeding for physical relief.

IV.vii.135 "remiss": used to have more general meaning.

IV.vii.142 "mountebank": *monte* + *banc*, get upon a bench—a person who sells fake medicine etc.

IV.vii.145 "simples": simple means "herb," because it was a medicine with only one ingredient—whence "to simple": go and collect herbs.

IV.vii.161 "for the nonce": [OED: orig. in the ME phrase *for þan nanes* which was altered to *for þe nanes, nones*].

IV.vii.162 "stuck": thrust, variant of stock, for *stoccado.*

IV.vii.171 "crowflowers": fair maid of France; "daisy": virginity; "nettle": death; "long purples": rampant widows.

IV.vii.180 "incapable of": can't conceive of.

IV.vii.187 "Too much of water hast thou, poor Ophelia": made fun of in Beaumont and Fletcher [*The Scornful Lady*, II.iii]. Why wasn't Ophelia saved? The person who saw her drowning couldn't swim? A description was wanted.

IV.vii.193 "douts": [extinguishes]. What's the origin of "douse"? I must look that up. [OED says, "Appears *c* 1600: origin unknown"].

This is a long scene. Why? Impossible to make [sense of] Laertes' Danes, who vanish so quickly. Big scene to show Claudius's diplomatic skill. The sudden news of Hamlet's return. Shakespeare wants a certain ending, a duel where everybody gets killed. Primarily interested in Hamlet as character. There are a lot of *grave* defects in the play. Opportunity to show Claudius's compulsive indirectness. His planning makes the scene take a long time.

[12 April 1947]
[*Hamlet*]

Do we have somebody with an accent from the old *Sooth*, from Mississippi, to play the gravedigger? (Planes overhead.) Has the war begun? Mother! Next we're going to do *The Tempest*, not a tragedy, and written for a different kind of stage, the Blackfriars Theater. The O's in the Clown's song mark blows of the pick. From the point of view of staging, where is the grave?—in the inner stage. You can set the scene for the court in the inner stage, with the curtains drawn, while Horatio and Hamlet talk in IV.ii. Hamlet shouldn't leap into the grave—that's a Rowe direction. The convention is that the Clown has on seven waistcoats which are removed one by one.

V.i.9 *"se offendendo"*: should be *se defendendo.*
V.i.10–22 In the legal case of Sir John Hale, who drowned himself in fit of lunacy, lawyers argued that a living man had done something to a dead one, and that the dead one should not be punished for suicide.
V.i.44 "confess thyself—": "and be hanged."
V.i.59 "unyoke": your work is over.

My father had to treat people who'd cut their throat and thought better of it. They were reported to the police and bound over by magistrates.

V.i.68 "Yaughan": or John, probably a bar.
V.i.69–82 The Clown's song is derived from a poem by Thomas Lord Vaux, first printed in *Tottel's Miscellany* (1557).
V.i.75–76 "property of easiness": that which belongs to you innately.
V.i.87 "politician": plotter.
V.i.97 "chapless": jawless.

V.i.101 "loggets": played indoors on a floor strewn with ashes, throwing pieces of wood, as in bowling.

V.i.115 "fine of his fines": finished.

V.i.149 "card": card line compass or card as chart of etiquette.

V.i..177 "thirty years": Hamlet's age. How should Hamlet look? He shouldn't look too Byronic—he should have a crewcut. Very nice to have him short and tubby. Get an introspective look by muscular tension—Lawrence of Arabia. Let's not be too psychoanalytical—about his feelings about his father. He's a good fencer. Bernhardt in black tights must have been out of this world. Acutely embarrassing to have a woman do it.

V.i.214–15 "to this favour she must come": favor means "look with favor," then something which makes people look with favor.

V.i.239 "winter's flaw": gust of wind.

V.i.240 "But soft!": a hint that somebody's coming. You need that, especially where people come in without having a new scene.

V.i..240 "Enter [*Priests with*] a coffin": the stage direction is wrong, should have a very small train—one priest, etc.

V.i.245 "Couch we awhile": should mean "sit or lie down"—difficult.

V.ii.6 "bilboes": Bilbao, town in Spain where iron was made.

V.ii.12 ff.: Tension aroused by story about Rosencrantz and Guildenstern. Who'll strike first? Hamlet or Claudius?

V.ii.80 "Enter young *Osric*, a courtier": the scene with Osric had to be there to provide time to prepare the inner stage. We see Hamlet lost again, playing a game with Osric, just as he did with the players. It's getting very late in the play now, people have their trains to catch.

V.ii.117 ff. meant to sound like double talk—poor Osric is scratching his head.

V.ii.203–18 The Lord business is cut in the Folio.

V.ii.270 How are the foils given? Laertes must pick from the table. The King's speech, "Set me the stoups of wine . . . ." (V.ii.278ff.), gives Laertes a chance to anoint his sword. The King must pick up the good foils and give them to Osric, then Laertes says his is too heavy.

V.ii.297 Trumpets sound—then the King puts the pearl in the cup. Noise at beginning in the Folio direction.

V.ii.313 Hamlet must be struck with the unbated point before he's ready, then he's *deliberately* determined to change swords and forces it, not conscious [of the poison].

V.ii.317 "woodcock": used as a decoy.

V.ii.359 Folio has *"Enter Osric"* as Fortinbras' drums sound.

V.ii.375 "cries on havoc": if people unsportingly kill too many birds, you "cry on havoc."

Next time *The Tempest.* They (the New School people) told me Saturday (Holy Saturday) wasn't a holiday. I told them it might not be for them, but it certainly was for me.

[19 April 1947]

Justification of rebellion. In *Richard III* rebellion is absolutely justified. Middle way: Richard II is weak, and Henry VI is weak, but those who depose them are guilty of excess.

[*The Tempest*]

Shakespeare's last plays were written for indoor theater. Sometime before 1610 Shakespeare's company moved to the Blackfriars Theater. [Auden drew a diagram of the theater, 48 feet wide, an apron 66 feet deep, and a stage and storage area 20 feet deep.] The theater included a balcony and a trap in the ceiling through which spirits could descend. What differences in effect are likely in moving from outdoors to indoors? People talk less loudly. In Shakespeare and Beaumont and Fletcher, instead of an iambic base the verse becomes much looser, doesn't have to drive. There are extra syllables, the pace slows down, and the verse is more elaborate and complicated in structure. Loud speeches won't do. Pageants will look better—processions of a few people indoors with lights work better. Music is more effective, because it's better heard. There are fewer alarums and excursions. More use of asides—whispers, like Iachimo's, are audible. Masque machinery can be introduced—gods can descend from heaven. In small villages people often get very excited when they don't see. You can't hear out of doors. They went on playing in the Globe in the summer until the Commonwealth. It was a good thing that Shakespeare had to write for an open-air theater, because his own taste would have inclined him towards more intimate and delicate verse.

I.i.18 "roarers": roaring boys, as at an American Legion convention.

I.i.32 "he hath no drowning mark upon him": a man doomed to be hanged can't die at any other time.

I.i.37 "Bring her to try": turn the ship close to the wind, lash the tiller to the lea side.

I.i.52–53 "Set her two courses!": two mainsails.

I.i.59 "merely": from application to wine, undiluted.

I.i.60 "wide-chopp'd": a wide-chopped person was supposed to be weak and stupid.

I.i.61 "the washing of ten tides": When pirates executed someone, the place was at low tide, and the bodies were left for three tides.

I.i.68 "long": might be "ling."

I.ii Would be completely impossible outdoors, nothing but a long narration of the past, terrifically difficult to make interesting—the art of the sentences, ablative absolutes, parentheses. The business about "you're not listening" is to give Miranda a chance to talk and to give the audience a rest.

I.ii.2 "allay": originally, set hounds on a scent.

I.ii.13 "fraughting": freight.

I.ii.15 "No harm.": originally given to Miranda.

I.ii.28 shows grammatical difficulty.

I.ii.30 "perdition": loss of.

I.ii.35 "bootless": *bota*, shoe; boot from *beoten*, pray.

I.ii.64 "teen": grief , Old English *téon*.

I.ii.71 "signories": states run by signor.

I.ii.81 "trash": leash for a dog.

I.ii.105 "prerogative": the early Roman republic would draw lots for the first tribe to vote.

I.ii.123 "in lieu o'": in consideration of.

I.ii.138 "impertinent": not to the purpose.

I.ii.148 "hoist": lower.

I.ii.195 "article": literally, a joint; article of death: at the moment of death.

I.ii.229 "Bermoothes": pronounced "Bermoothies."

I.ii.239 "What is the time o' th' day?": *The Tempest* is the only play of Shakespeare with unity of time.

I.ii.267 "They would not take her life.": Shakespeare must have read a story about a witch who saved Algiers from Charles V in 1541 by raising a storm.

I.ii.269 "hither brought with child": the child of a devil wouldn't be a reason for sparing her life.

I.ii.323 "A south-west": a hot, moist wind bringing plague.

I.ii.326 "urchins": hedgehogs.

I.ii.351ff. The Folio gives this speech to Miranda.

I.ii.373 "Setebos": god of Patagonian giants.

Unions and producers, who want sex, forbid Ariel to be played by a boy, who is what you should have. Sexless.

I.ii.437–38 "The Duke of Milan / And his brave son being twain": either oversight or left over from an earlier stage.

[26 April 1947]
[*The Tempest*]

I.ii.396–404 "Full fadom five": What other play does it remind you of? Clarence's dream from *Richard III*—they drowned him in a butt of wine.

I.ii.469 "My foot my tutor?": foot is Miranda.

II.i.11 "visitor": person of the parish who had to give comfort to sick people.

II.i.42 "temperance": an affected word for temperature.

II.i.55 "an eye of green": a shade of green.

II.i.76 "widow Dido's time": there was a popular ballad about "widow Dido"—"O widow Dido, aye widow Dido."

II.i.113ff. "Sir, he may live. . . .": the speech should be given to Gonzalo—it is more appropriate to him than to the negative Francisco.

II.i.140 "chirurgeonly": pronounced *sirurjonly*.

II.i.147ff. What is the point of Gonzalo's speech about the commonwealth? The whole play is about the good society. Gonzalo is a romantic. His speech is Utopian, accompanied by proof, in Antonio and Sebastian, that government is necessary. There is finally reconciliation, in the best society possible, in which suffering is necessary. Ferdinand, in the preceding scene, has to suffer.

II.i.163 "foison": abundance, Latin *fugionem*.

II.i.185 "a-batfowling": at night people went with lights and beat bushes to start birds or as a technique to get into houses at night and steal.

I.ii.235–36 "(For he's a spirit of persuasion, only / Professes to persuade)": He just wears a mask of cheerfulness without believing in it himself.

I.ii.242–43 "Ambition cannot pierce a wink beyond, / But doubts discovery there.": Ambition not only can't see beyond the hope of king-

ship, like a wall, but doubts that there's anything to see beyond kingship—like emperorship.

II.i.266 "A chóugh óf as deep chát."

II.i.298 "That you, his friend, are in": Folio text.

II.i.308 "Why are you drawn?": Staunton emends to give this line to
Alonso, and "Wherefore this ghastly looking?" to Gonzalo.

In reading, does anything strike you as odd about Antonio and Sebastian's conspiracy? How are they to get off the island? They must
suppose that other vessels of the fleet may turn back and look for them.

In the next scene, II.ii, another kind of commonwealth. Stephano's
characterization is a kind of little dig at anarchists and revolutions from
below.

II.ii.28 "poor-John": salted hake.

II.ii.35 "they will lay out ten to see a dead Indian.": in 1577 Martin Fro-
bisher brought back an Indian who died in Bath [Bristol] and whose
dead body was displayed in London. Next Indians 1611.

II.ii.61 "salvages": *silvanus—sauvage*, forest people, heathen people who
live on the heath, outside civilization.

II.ii.176 "scamels": kind of clam? kind of sea birds? Clam is more likely.
"Scamel" is a Norfolk sea bird that does not frequent the rocks, or a
diminutive of "scam," a kind of limpet—more likely than seabirds,
which are usually inedible.

III.i.1 "labour": a subject in this line.

III.i.15 "Most busiest when I do it": "Most busie lest I do it" in the Folio.

[3 May 1947]

[*The Tempest*]

III.i.46 "put it to the foil": *afoler*, put it to defeat.

III.i.91 "A thousand thousand!":—"farewells."

III.i.93 (as they) "Who are surpris'd withal."

III ii 5–6 "The folly of this island.": the line is a toast.

III.ii.19–20 "he's no standard": he's too tight, can't stand up.

III.ii.47 "Enter *Ariel*, invisible.": regular costume, light silk. Inigo Jones
in Jonson's masque, *The Fortunate Isles* (1624), attires Jophiel, "an Airy
spirit," in "light silks of various colours, with wings of the same, a bright
yellow hair, a chaplet of flowers, blue silk stockings, and pumps and
gloves, with a silver fan in his hand." [Quoted in *A New Variorum Edition*

of Shakespeare, ed. Horace Howard Furnivall, vol. 9, *The Tempest* (Philadelphia: J.B. Lippincott, 1897), 354.]

[*The Tempest*] won't do for movies, unity of place.

III.ii.71 "pied ninny": fool, sot.

III.ii.71 "patch": Italian *pazzo*, jester, fool.

III.ii.79 "stockfish": dried and salted cod, very rough.

III.ii.88 "murrain": cattle, plague.

III.ii.126 "troll": hand round from one to the other.

III.ii.161–62 Folio gives "Wilt come?" to Trinculo, and "I'll follow
Stephano" to Caliban.

III.iii.3 "forthrights and meanders": straight and crooked

III.iii.5 "attach'd with weariness": [seized by].

III.iii.21 "living drollery": a drollery was usually a puppet show.

III.iii.48 "Each putter-out of five for one": voyages were financed by
shares, in which one put down a pound, hoping to get five.

III.iii.52 *"like a harpy"*: harpies in *Argonautica*.

III.iii.52 "quaint device": how would you represent "a quaint device"?

III.iii.73 "The powers, delaying (not forgetting), have": run-on line,
something you find a lot in the last plays, beginning with *Coriolanus*.
You must make a pause, but not too much.

IV.i.3 "third of mine own life": [Miranda].

IV.i.16 "sanctimonious," and IV.i.37 "rabble": troops, are not pejorative.

IV.i.41 "vanity of mine art": illusion, conjuring trick.

IV.i.57 "coróllarý": surplus.

IV.i.63 "stover": stoves is coarse grass.

IV.i.64 "pioned": dug out? peonies?, "twilled": lattice work of flowers?
No one really knows.

IV.i.67 "dismissed": turned down.

IV.i.75 "Enter *Ceres*": daughter of Saturn and Rhea.

IV.i.81 "bosky acres": fields divided by hedgerows.

IV.i.130 "crisp": lightly wrinkled by wind, rapidly flowing stream.

IV.i.187 "stale": *stel*, standing, old; *estale*, decoy used in hawking; *stalla*,
urine.

IV.i.193 "on the line": probably not line, clothesline, but lime tree.

IV.i.197–98 "play'd the Jack with us": Jack o' lantern, will o' the wisp.

IV.i.226 "a frippery": an old clothes shop.

IV.i.222, 226 "O King Stephano": "King Stephen was a worthy peer,"
sung by Iago in *Othello* (II.iii), the drinking scene.

IV.i.237 "under the line": the Equator—south of the Equator you lose your hair.

IV.i.249 "barnacles": barnacle goose, wild goose, supposed to be born out of barnacles.

The masque in IV.i is very good, very much in this kind of style.

[10 May 1947]
[*The Tempest*]

V.i.2–3 "time / Goes upright with his carriage.": Father time is usually bent on stick, here's he's upright.

V.i.23–24 "sharply / Passions": there should be a comma after "sharply"—"passions" is a verb meaning "suffers."

V.i.29 "drift": a passageway for cattle, extended.

V.i.33ff. "Ye elves . . .": from Golding's translation of Ovid's *Metamorphoses*, Medea talking.

V.i.67 "ignorant": is transitive.

V.i.89 "cowslip's bell" : a cowslip doesn't have a bell.

V.i.118 "Thy dukedom I resign": as overlord.

V.i.124 "subtleties": kind of dessert.

V.i.129 "No": Prospero's "No" should be "Now"—he shouldn't answer Sebastian's aside.

V.i.172 "you play me false": you can't cheat at chess.

V.i.238 "On a trice": originally a single pull; German *treisen*, hoist; Spanish *tris*, shattering of glass.

V.i.244 "conduct": conductor.

V.i.271 "without": outside.

V.i.298 "luggage": lugg, lugge, ear, or forelock of hair.

V.i.314 "auspicious": *avis* + *spex*.

APPENDIX II

Fall Term Final Examination

Auden gave the following mimeographed final examination in his Saturday afternoon class for the students taking the course for credit in the fall term. Part B of the examination, which Ansen wrote in by hand with the comment "unexpected," was dictated by Auden in class.

In transcribing the excerpts from Kittredge, Auden or his typist omitted two sentences and slightly miscopied some punctuation, wording, and lineation. I have left the errors uncorrected. Auden's most notable changes are "All" for "At" in item 8, "spirit" for "sport" in item 15, "earth-braving" for "air-braving" in item 19, and "Wealth" for "breath" and "fit" for "fill" in item 22. Auden prints item 14 as verse instead of Kittredge's prose, and in item 24, after "mother," he omits the sentences, "Nay, that cannot be so neither. Yes, it is so, it is so." The identifications of the excerpts, in brackets, are the editor's.

Auden told Ansen afterward that he had sent a copy of the examination to his friend Theodore Spencer, a Shakespearean, and that "Spencer missed the second one."

Ansen describes seeing the final examination for the spring term in an entry in his "Journal" dated 3 May 1947. In addition to identifications of lines and passages in the spring exam, Auden also asked the students to provide meanings of individual words in *Hamlet* and *The Tempest* and to punctuate Hamlet's speech, "What a piece of work is man!" (II.ii.316–22).

[18 January 1947?]

New School For Social Research
66 West 12th St., NYC

Course #160—Shakespeare
W. H. Auden
Fall Term 1946

FINAL EXAMINATION

[A.]

Who says to Whom, When, Where?

(1)   How sour sweet music is
         When time is broke and no proportion kept!
         So is it in the music of men's lives.
         And here I have the daintiness of ear
         To check time broke in a disordered string;

                                   [*Richard II*, V.v.42–46]

(2)   Mark how one string, sweet husband to another,
         Strikes each in each by mutual ordering;
         Resembling sire and child and happy mother,
         Who, all in one, one pleasing note do sing.

                                   [Sonnet 8, ll. 9–12]

(3)   Let music sound while he doth make his choice:
         Then, if he lose, he makes a swan-like end,
         Fading in music.

                                   [*The Merchant of Venice*, III.ii.43–45]

(4)   I have a reasonable good ear in music.
         Let's have the tongs and the bones.

                                   [*A Midsummer Night's Dream*, IV.i.30–31]

(5)   Is it not strange that sheep's guts should hale souls out of
         men's bodies? Well, a horn for my money, when all's done.

                                   [*Much Ado About Nothing*, II.iii.61–63]

(6)   I have no brother, I am like no brother . . . .
         I am myself alone.

                                   [*3 Henry VI*, V.vi.80, 83]

(7)   By how much better than my word I am
         By so much shall I falsify men's hopes.

                                   [*1 Henry IV*, I.ii.234–35]

(8)   No, I am that I am; and they that level
         All my abuses reckon up their own.

                                   [Sonnet 121, ll. 9–10]

(9)   In the meantime let me be that I am, and seek not to alter me.
                                   [*Much Ado About Nothing*, I.iii.38–39]

(10)   Counterfeit? I lie; I am no counterfeit. To die is to be a
         counterfeit; for he is but the counterfeit of a man who hath
         not the life of a man.

                                        [*1 Henry IV*, V.iv.115–18]

(11)   The shadow of your sorrow hath destroyed
         The shadow of your face.

                                        [*Richard II*, IV.i.292–93]

(12)   What is your substance, whereof are you made,
         That millions of strange shadows on you tend?

                                        [Sonnet 53, ll. 1–2]

(13)   For since the substance of your perfect self
         Is else devoted, I am but a shadow,
         And to your shadow will I make true love.

                                        [*The Two Gentlemen of Verona*, IV.ii.124–26]

(14)   The best in this kind are but shadows; and the worst
         Are no worse, if imagination amend them.

                                        [*A Midsummer Night's Dream*, V.i.214–16]

(15)   That spirit best pleases that doth least know how;
         Where zeal strives to content, and the contents
         Dies in the zeal of that which it presents.

                                        [*Love's Labour's Lost*, V.ii.517–19]

(16)   There shall be in England seven halfpenny loaves sold for a
         penny; the three-hooped pot shall have ten hoops, and I will
         make it felony to drink small beer.

                                        [*2 Henry VI*, IV.ii.70–74]

(17)   Let us take any man's horses; the laws of England are at my
         commandment. Blessed are they that have been my friends,
         and woe to my Lord Chief Justice.

                                        [*2 Henry IV*, V.iii.140–44]

(18)   Here's a "Stay"
         That shakes the rotten carcase of old Death
         Out of his rags! Here's a large mouth indeed,
         That spits forth death, and mountains, rocks and seas;
         Talks as familiarly of roaring lions
         As maids of thirteen do of puppy dogs.

                                        [*King John*, II.i.455–60]

(19)   You tempt the fury of my three attendants,
         Lean famine, quartering steel, and climbing fire,
         Who in a moment even with the earth
         Shall lay your stately and earth-braving towers,
         If you forsake the offer of their love.
                                    [*1 Henry VI*, IV.ii.10–14]

(20)   O, he is as tedious
         As a tired horse, a railing wife;
         Worse than a smoky house—I had rather live
         With cheese and garlic in a windmill far
         Than feed on cates and have him talk to me
         In any summer house in Christendom.
                                    [*1 Henry IV*, III.i.159–64]

(21)   What; I? I love? I sue? I seek a wife?
         A woman, that is like a German clock,
         Still a-repairing, ever out of frame,
         And never going aright, being a watch,
         But being watched that it may still go right.
                                    [*Love's Labour's Lost*, III.i.191–95]

(22)   I called thee then poor shadow, painted queen,
         The presentation of but what I was,
         The flattering index of a direful pageant,
         One heaved ahigh to be hurled down below,
         A mother only mocked with two fair babes,
         A dream of what thou wast, a garish flag,
         To be the aim of every dangerous shot;
         A sign of dignity, a Wealth, a bubble,
         A queen in jest, only to fit the scene.
                                    [*Richard III*, IV.iv.82–91]

(23)   Grief fills the room up of my absent child:
         Lies in his bed, walks up and down with me,
         Puts on his pretty looks, repeats his words,
         Remembers me of all his gracious parts,
         Stuffs out his vacant garments with his form.
         Then have I reason to be fond of grief?
                                    [*King John*, III.iv.93–98]

(24)   This shoe is my father. No, this left shoe is my father. No, no
        this left shoe is my mother. It hath the worser sole.
                            [*The Two Gentlemen of Verona*, II.iii.17–20]

(25)   The passado he respects not, the duello he regards not. His
        disgrace is to be called boy, but his glory is to subdue men.
                                   [*Love's Labour's Lost*, I.ii.184–87]

(26)   Tis not so deep as a well, nor so wide as a church door; but tis
        enough, t'will serve. Ask for me tomorrow, and you shall find
        me a grave man. I am peppered, I warrant, for this world. A
        plague o' both your houses!
                                      [*Romeo and Juliet*, III.i.99–103]

(27)   For there was never yet philosopher
        That could endure the toothache patiently,
        However they have writ the style of gods
        And made a push at chance and sufferance.
                                 [*Much Ado About Nothing*, V.i.35–38]

(28)   O, who can hold a fire in his hand
        By thinking on the frosty Caucasus?
        Or cloy the hungry edge of appetite
        By bare imagination of a feast
                                        [*Richard II*, I.iii.294–97]

(29)   All things that are
        Are with more spirit chased than enjoyed.
        How like a younker or a prodigal
        The scarfed bark puts from her native bay,
        Hugged and embraced by the strumpet wind!
        How like the Prodigal doth she return.
                               [*The Merchant of Venice*, II.vi.12–17]

(30)   If he be not in love with some woman, there's no believing
        old signs. 'A brushes his hat o' mornings. What should that
        bode?
                                [*Much Ado About Nothing*, III.ii.40–42]

(31)   I remember, when I was in love I broke my sword upon a
        stone and bid him take that for coming a-night to Jane Smile.
                                          [*As You Like It*, II.iv.44–46]

(32)   There is a tide in the affairs of men
            Which, taken at the flood, leads on to fortune;
            Omitted, all the voyage of their life
            Is bound in shallows and in miseries.

                                    [*Julius Caesar*, IV.iii.218–21]

(33)   There is a history in all men's lives,
            Figuring the nature of the times deceased;
            The which observed, a man may prophesy,
            With a near aim, of the main chance of things
            As yet not come in life.

                                    [*2 Henry IV*, III.i.80–84]

(34)   Though I speak it to you, I think the king is but a man, as I
            am: the violet smells to him as it doth to me; the element
            shows to him as it does to me; all his senses have but human
            conditions.

                                    [*Henry V*, IV.i.105–9]

(35)   Belike then my appetite was not princely got; for, by my troth,
            I do now remember the poor creature small beer. But indeed
            these humble considerations make me out of love with my
            greatness.

                                    [*2 Henry IV*, II.ii.12–16]

[B.]

Write 20 lines from memory from the material covered in this half of the
course.

(Please mark every page of your paper clearly with your name. Also indicate the type of credit for which you are registered.

Please print your name, the course number and the instructor's name
on the first page of your examination also.)

APPENDIX III

Auden's Markings in Kittredge

Listed below are references to passages, words, and phrases indicated by various markings in Auden's copy of *The Complete Works of Shakespeare*, edited by George Lyman Kittredge (Boston: Ginn and Company, 1936), which he used for his lectures and discussions and which is now at the library of Texas Tech University in Lubbock, Texas.

Auden usually indicated a passage that interested him with a continuous or broken vertical line in the margin, sometimes with slash marks at the beginning and end of the passage of text, and occasionally with underlining. It is often very difficult to be sure where the vertical lines begin and end, however, and many of the passages listed are approximate. Sometimes passage references are partially repeated, because Auden marked lines or passages within passages. Kittredge's edition also prints two columns of text on each page. I have normally considered vertical lines between the two columns on a page to refer to the inner column (the column of the text nearest the spine of the book), but as evidence from both Ansen's notes and the Kittredge text itself shows, this is not always the case, and I have very occasionally had to make an educated guess at which of two possible passages Auden intended. Auden also underlined or drew lines to individual words and phrases that he annotated in the texts of *Hamlet* and *The Tempest*, the two plays he discussed in philological detail in his Saturday afternoon meetings. The annotations themselves are often illegible, and I have not attempted to transcribe them directly from the Kittredge text, but they are for the most part recorded in Ansen's notes of the Saturday meetings (see Appendix I). The listings of annotated and/or underlined words and phrases in this appendix are prefixed by an asterisk. Finally, though the markings of passages are predominantly in pencil, there are some, most often indicated in the Kittredge text by slash marks, where Auden used blue ink. The markings in ink were probably made at a different date than the others, and the references in this appendix to the passages they designate are followed by the word "[ink]."

In addition to the markings in the plays and sonnets listed below, Auden also marked off *The Rape of Lucrece*, lines 876–96 [ink], and 939–59 [ink]; and *The Two Noble Kinsmen*, III.i, 1–11 [ink], V.i.1–8 [ink], V.i.77–136, and V.i.77–173 [ink].

Henry VI, Part One

IV.ii: 3–14

Henry VI, Part Two

III.ii: 403–7
IV.viii: 19
V.i: 140, 213–14
V.ii: 71

Henry VI, Part Three

I.i: 16–17
I.ii: 22–34
II.i: 10, 20, 26–32, 48, 160–62
II.iii: 46
II.vi: 106–7
III.ii: 8–9, 124–95
IV.i: 19–22, 83, 124–26
IV.vii: 10–12, 58, 62
V.i: 105
V.v: 41–42, 49–51, 83–86
V.vi: 11–12, 57–58, 61–62, 68–69,
    80–83, 83

Richard III

I.i: 15–16, 26–31, 114–15, 117–20,
    157–59
I.ii: 72, 105–6, 109–11, 132, 156,
    176–80, 186–91, 227–36, 252–63
I.iii: 113–15, 126, 134–36, 142, 186–
    87, 233–34
I.iv: 120–48, 214–15, 228–30
II.i: 30–39, 60–64, 71–72, 91–94
II.ii: 22–26, 103, 107–10
II.iii: 36–37, 41–43
III.i: 9–11, 44–52, 81–83, 116–17,
    123–25, 129–31, 146–47, 193, 198
III.ii: 62–63, 103–4
III.iv: 24–25, 51–53
III.v: 8–11, 41–46
III.vi: 10–12

III.vii: 16, 92–97, 116, 156–60, 224–
    26, 235–36
IV.i: 81–87
IV.ii: 18–20, 28–30, 63–65, 100
IV.iv: 39–45, 150–52, 216–21, 288,
    376, 397–401, 420, 431, 459–61,
    507–8
V.iii: 19–21, 50–51, 183–204, 217–
    20, 279–88, 310–12, 348–49
V.v: 19–26

The Comedy of Errors

I.i: 140–49
II.ii: 128 [ink]
V.i: 332–34, 376, 417–21

The Two Gentlemen of Verona

I.i: 87–96
II.i: 60–62, 69–86, 176–82
II.ii: 23–28
III.i: 261–67
IV.ii: 54–72 [ink], 123–32
IV.iii: 18–21, 42–43
IV.iv: 1–42 [ink], 30–37, 109–11,
    200–210
V.iv: 26, 43–46, 74–83, 108–9

Love's Labour's Lost

I.i: 1–7 [ink], 88–92, 108–9, 143–45,
    153, 172–75, 233–36
*I.i: 8 "are"; 10 "the world's desires"
I.ii: 14–16, 34–36, 41–43, 48–51, 67–
    69, 104–11, 120–24, 155–61, 181–
    87
II.i: 15–19, 36–38, 48–51, 92–94,
    100, 104–6, 211–12, 216, 254–56
III.i: 27–30, 176–207 [ink], 191–95
IV.i: 30–35, 39–40, 144–47
IV.ii: 101–2, 124–27, 169–73
*IV.ii: 172 "game"; 173 "recreation"
IV.iii: 60–73, 72–73, 74–76, 217–19,

239–40, 274–75, 303–4, 323–30, 333–39, 350–53, 357–65
V.i: 18–21, 30–32, 39–40
V.ii: 70–72, 139–44, 323–33, 404–21, 516–22, 584–89, 632, 634, 716, 731–34, 756–60, 771–79, 803–16, 836–39, 845, 860–72

Romeo and Juliet

I.i: 21–24, 32–38, 101–3, 183–86, 205, 234–35
I.ii: 13–19, 39–42, 64–66
I.iii: 40–44, 67–68, 87–96
I.iv: 26, 37–38, 92–113
I.v: 25–29, 48–49, 54–55, 112, 142–46
II: Chorus: 9–12
II.i: 9–10, 20–22
II.ii: 42–47, 53–57, 117–20, 184–86
II.iii: 15–30, 51–56, 81–83
II.iv: 23–25, 29–32, 92–97
II.vi: 9–20
III.i: 69–76 [ink], 93–95, 102–8, 118–20, 124–25, 139–41, 187–88, 202
III.ii: 45–50, 73–85, 122–27
III.iii: 1–3, 20–23, 33–42, 71–73, 105–10, 119–21, 142–47, 166–72
III.iv: 13–14, 19–23
III.v: 46–54, 148–51, 165–69, 218–25
IV.i: 77–88
IV.ii: 30–32, 42–45
IV.v: 52–61, 86–90
V.i: 5–6, 50–54, 72–86
V.iii: 37–39, 63–70, 87, 105–11, 156–67, 210–12, 223–30, 307–10

A Midsummer Night's Dream

II.i: 88–117, 111–17
II.ii: 104–5, 115–16
III.i: 81–82, 104–8, 118, 146–50, 199–201, 205–6

III.ii: 27–29, 90–93, 115, 345–46, 382–87, 461–62
IV.i: 30–33, 39–42, 45–48, 66, 139–42, 192–95, 219–23
IV.ii: 13–14
V.i: 9–27, 59–60, 81–84, 91–105, 203–5, 214–21, 362–75, 414–25

The Taming of the Shrew

[No markings.]

King John

I.i: 174–75
II.i: 30–32, 94–98, 159–63, 183–94, 249–52, 288–93, 455–67, 510–20, 561–98
III.i: 113–34, 147–58, 262–99, 323–25
III.ii: 1–4
III.iii: 29–67
III.iv: 44–60, 90–93, 145–59
IV.ii: 103, 174–77
IV.iii: 125–34
V.ii: 103–8, 151–62
V.vii: 28–41

Richard II

I.i: 20–21, 109–10, 196
I.iii: 56–58, 97–99, 148–53, 213–15, 271–74
I.iv: 59–63
II.i: 17–23, 81–83, 222–23, 257–58
II.ii: 30–40, 64–71, 128–31
II.iii: 168–71
II.iv: 12–15, 19–22
III.ii: 6–13, 54–61, 76–90, 126–30, 172–77, 188–93, 207–13
III.iii: 70–71, 136–37, 160–75
III.iv: 75–77
IV.i: 142–44, 172–76, 192–93, 201–6, 243–44, 279–88, 292–98, 315–18

V.i: 38–50, 59–68
V.ii: 44–49
V.iii: 5–22, 111–120
V.v: 1–5, 49–50, 102–3
V.vi: 11–12, 28–29, 38–42

The Merchant of Venice

I.i: 1, 53–56, 66–67, 77–79, 138–43, 154–60, 169–72
I.ii: 1–7, 30–31,
I.iii: 36–40, 88–98, 101–3, 133–38, 159–60
*I.iii: 12 "good"; 17 "sufficient"; 42 "publican"; 119 "stranger"; 136 "enemy"; 139 "friends"; 163 "others"
II.i: 20–22
II.ii: 158–61, 170–79, 194–98
II.iii: 10–15, 17–19
*II.iii: 17 "child"; 18 "blood"
II.iv: 32
II.v: 3–4, 13, 33–39, 48
II.vi: 12–13
*II.vi: 57 "constant"
II.vii: 9–10, 18–20, 65–69
II.viii: 20–24
II.ix: 19–21, 30–32, 51–52, 66–69, 80–81
III.i: 38–39, 46–49, 61–64, 71–74, 84–86, 87–101, 113–14, 123–24
III.ii: 43–72, 73–74, 103–5, 166–70, 183–84, 211–16, 286–90, 293–94, 320–22
*III.ii: 295 "honour"
III.iii: 6, 20–24, 27–31
III.iv: 66–76
III.v: 23–28, 48–51, 66–69
IV.i: 38–39, 42–46, 66–67, 89–93, 117–18, 197–203, 259, 275–79, 309–12, 368–69, 380–87, 450–54
V.i: 1–12, 54–65, 69–88, 82–88, 107–10, 151–54, 166–69, 199–206

Sonnets

Auden marked the following sonnets with a check or cross: 8, 21, 24, 29, 31, 46, 47, 57, 61, 62, 66, 72, 75, 87, 90, 94, 109, 116, 121, 129, 141, 146 [ink], 148, 151.

Auden marked lines or underlined words in the following sonnets:
1: *10 "gaudy"
4: 10–12
9: 8–12
12: 1–6 [ink]; *7 "summer's green," "up in sheaves"; 8–14
14: 9
15: 6–12 [ink]; 9–12; *6 "Cheered" [ink], "check'd" [ink]; *10: "you" [ink], "sight" [ink]; *11: "de . . . ," "Decay" [ink]
18: 1–8 [ink]
20: 11–12
21: 1–14
22: 5–6
33: 1–10 [ink]
35: 5–11 [pencil and ink]
39: 9–14
40: 1–14
42: 5–14
44: 8–9
48: 7–12
54: 9–11
64: 13–14
66: *2 "beggar"; *3 "jollity"; *4 "forsworn"; *5 "honour"; *6 "virtue"; *7 "disgrac'd"; *8 "sway," "disabled"; *9 "art"; *10 "skill"; *11 "simple"; *12 "captive good"
93: 1–14
107: 1–10
116: 1–2 [ink]
118: 5–12
121: 9–11 [ink]
127: 1–2

129: 5 [ink]

137: 9–12

138: 13–14 [dated "1599" in ink]
    144: [dated "1599" in ink]

Auden anthologized the following sonnets in his edition of *Poets of the English Language,* 5 vols. (New York: Viking, 1950): 8, 18, 19, 29, 30, 31, 55, 57, 61, 62, 66, 73, 75, 87, 90, 94, 96, 121, 129, 138, 141, 144, 146, 147, 151.

Henry IV, Part One

A large number of markings and underlinings in *Henry IV, Parts One and Two* relate to time, and Auden occasionally wrote the word "time" in the margin.

I.i: 1, 2, 17–18, 28

I.ii: 2–4, 6–10, 28–30, 33–38, 61–63, 65–70, 82–83, 107–10, 114–17, 126–29, 131–33, 160–61, 173–78, 219–41, 221–27, 224–25, 228–30

I.iii: 14–19, 59–63, 127–30, 180, 197–200, 206–10, 253–55, 277 [ink], 288, 301–2

II.i: 1–2, 47, 73–76, 86–91

II.ii: 16–20, 28–29, 69–71, 115–18

II.iii: 13, 34–38, 63–65, 80–82, 94–97

II.iv: 6–12, 19–22, 104–07, 114–17, 122–25, 132–34, 300–301, 346–48, 354–57, 365–66, 408–9, 436–37, 463–65, 518–19, 531–32, 540–43, 552–53, 595–97

III.i: 18–20, 27–29, 96–105, 133–35, 137–40, 177–85, 236–39, 266–69

III.ii: 43–54, 46–47, 93–96

III.iii: 5–6, 10–14, 27–30, 102–3, 102 [s.d.], 155–57, 168–71, 173–75, 188–90, 203–4, 213–15, 228–29

*III.iii: 229 "tavern"

IV.i: 16–18, 28–29

*IV.i: 134 "Die all, die merrily."

IV.ii: 17–19, 25–38, 71–74

V.i: 5–9, 24–25, 44–46 [ink], 80–82, 127–28, 141–43

V.ii: 6–7, 14–15, 50–51, 82

V.iii: 62–64

V.iv: 27–28, 35–38, 59–60, 81–82, 90–92, 116–20, 167–70

V.v: 11–13

Henry IV, Part Two

I.i: 9, 153–60, 187, 200–205, 210–11

I.ii: 11–14, 86–90, 126–28, 131–36, 163–66, 210–14, 239–40, 245–47, 264–66, 278–79

I.iii: 41–50, 58–62, 85–98, 110

II.i: 100–102, 119–24, 159–62, 202–5

II.ii: 2–4, 7–8, 16–17, 31–32, 44–45, 51–54, 58–59, 71–74, 115–17, 149–51, 154–57, 174–75, 193–96

*II.ii: 116 "my dog"

II.iii: 10–11, 28–32, 68

II.iv: 41–51, 71–73, 105–8, 197, 236–41, 249–53, 257–59, 266–72, 294–96, 369–70, 391, 396–97, 412–14

*II.iv: 197 "sweetheart"

III.i: 38–40, 45–56, 72–85, 92–94

III.ii: 228–29, 276–90, 325–26, 339–42, 355–56, 358

IV.i: 54–58, 72, 74, 104, 108, 207–14

IV.ii: 26–30, 33, 51, 79–80, 110–11, 121–23

IV.iii: 20–25 [ink], 20–22, 24–25, 71–76, 95–97, 107–11, 120–24, 127–28

IV.iv: 70–75, 102, 105–10, 126–30

IV.v: 24–35, 41–46, 64–67, 107–8, 119, 134–36, 170–75, 184–87, 214–16

*IV.v: 31 "breath"

88–92, 105–7, 120–21, 130–32, 136–37, 145–47, 158, 188, 190–95, 196, 206–7, 227, 260–62, 278–80, 284–88, 296 [ink]

V.i: 7–12, 16–20, 27–29, 34–35, 45–47, 57–58, 61–63, 73–78, 89–91, 100–12, 123–25

V.iii: 33–35, 44–46, 67–69, 89–90, 93–95

V.iv: 3–6

V.v: 4–5, 24–25, 39–40, 50–51, 54, 56–57, 61–63, 67, 69–75

As You Like It

I.i: 6–10, 19–22, 49–51, 70–73, 120–25

*I.i: 151 "natural"

I.ii: 28, 30–31, 34–36, 43–45, 51–53, 110–12, 209–10, 240–41, 252–53, 265–66, 277, 295–96

I.iii: 11–12, 127, 130

II.i: 1–17

II.iii: 56–58, 63–65, 67–68

II.iv: 53–56, 68 [ink]

*II.iv: 95 "could waste"

II.v: 26–29, 40–43, 52–59

II.vi: 6–8

II.vii: 1–2, 24–28, 44–51, 59–61, 66–69, 120–27, 136–39, 142–43

*II.vii: 93 "civility"; 96 "inland"; 97 "nurture"; 200 "fortunes"

III.i: 15

III.ii: 19–23, 27–34, 40–45, 77–81, 88–90, 119–22, 172–80, 184–88, 295–96, 313–15, 326–29, 391–95, 422–27, 441–42

III.iii: 40–41, 59–62, 84–86, 98–100, 108–10

III.iv: 48–49

III.v: 23, 51–56, 66–68, 94–97

IV.i: 8–18, 26–29, 30–32, 94–98, 106–8, 209–21

IV.iii: 73–75

V.iii: 3–6

V.iv: 17–18

Twelfth Night

I.i: 14–15, 19–20, 30–31, 41

I.ii: 6, 47–50, 57–60

I.iii: 2–5, 10–12, 30–32, 40–44, 97–99, 119–21, 133–34, 146–47

I.v: 45–46, 81–82, 97–99, 165–71, 198, 211–14, 231–36, 246–53, 296, 317, 328–29

II.ii: 27–29, 34–36

II.iii: 6–8, 11–13, 30–31, 36–39, 96–99, 156–57, 196

II.iv: 3–4, 17–18, 34–36, 75–81, 101–4, 120–21

*II.iv: 19 "image"

II.v: 12–14, 58–59, 66–67, 72–73, 85, 89, 156–59, 174

*II.v: 179 "for every reason"

III.i: 5–7, 36–40, 67–75, 151–56, 170–73

III.ii: 32–34

III.iv: 2–4, 91–92, 136–38, 385–86, 388–91, 401–3

IV.ii: 21–23, 46–49, 59–60, 99–101

IV.iii: 11–16, 26–28

V.i: 45–51, 83–87, 152–53, 267–70, 279–82, 368–70, 386

Hamlet

Auden annotated many of the words and phrases he underlined or marked in the text of *Hamlet* and discussed them in his Saturday afternoon sessions. See Appendix I.

I.i: 20–22, 115–16, 136–37, 158–61

*I.i: 13 "rivals"; 19 "A piece of him"; 42 "Thou art a scholar"; 46 "usurp'st"; 63
"sledded"; 68 "gross and scope"; 72 "toils"; 83 "emulate"; 90 "moiety"; 94
"carriage"; 96 "unimproved"; 100 "stomach"; 107 "romage"; 118 "Disasters in
the sun"; 121 "fierce"; 123 "omen"; 125 "climature"; 127 "cross it"; 140 "parti-
san"; 154 "extravagant and erring"; 156 "probation"; 163 "takes"

I.ii: 47–49, 67, 84–86, 156–59, 178 [ink], 181–82, 232–33 [ink], 255–56 [ink]

*I.ii: 10 "defeated joy"; 11 "an auspicious, and a dropping eye"; 21 "Colleagued";
23 "Importing"; 33 "subject"; 38 "dilated"; 56 "pardon"; 64 "cousin"; 65 "kin,"
"kind"; 92 "obsequious"; 95 "incorrect"; 109 "immediate"; 114 "retrograde";
126 "cannon"; 127 "rouse"; 132 "canon"; 141 "beteem"; 147 "shoes"; 150 "discourse"; 154 "most unrighteous"; 159 "break my heart"; 163 "I'll change that
name with you"; 164 "what make you"; 182 "dearest"; 192 "admiration"; 198
"vast"; 204 "distill'd"; 205 "act of fear"; 248 "tenable"

I.iii: 1–4, 13–18, 45–51 [ink], 115–17, 119–20

*I.iii: 6 "toy"; 9 "suppliance"; 12 "bulk"; 15 "cautel"; 16 "virtue"; 32 "unmast'red";
59 "character"; 61 "familiar"; 63 "hoops"; 64 "dull"; 69 "censure, but"; 81
"season"; 103 "tenders"; 107 "sterling"; 120 "fire"

I.iv: 23–28 [ink], 90 [ink]

*I.iv: 2 "eager"; 17 "east and west"; 20 "Soil our addition"; 27 "complexion"; 36
"e'il"; 37 "dout"; 43 "questionable"; 77 "fadoms"

I.v: 51–57 [ink], 88 [ink], 91 [s.d.], 98–104 [ink], 114–16, 123–24, 145, 160–61,
181, 189–90 [ink]

*I.v: 11 "to fast"; 30 "meditation"; 37 "process"; 77 "Unhous'led , disappointed,
unanel'd"; 83 "luxury"; 150 "truepenny"; 163 "pioner"

II.i: 118–19

*II.i: 29 "scandal"; 34 "unreclaimed"; 38 "fetch"; 65 "windlasses," "assays of bias";
71 "in yourself"; 73 "let him ply his music"; 80 "down-gyved"; 95 "his bulk";
102 "ecstasy"; 112 "quoted"

II.ii: 54–57 [ink], 185–86, 204–6, 221 [ink], 248–50 [ink], 255–65, 317–23, 346–
47, 371–73, 463–67 [ink], 575, 584–86 [ink], 628–33 [ink]

*II.ii: 6 "Sith"; 27 "have of us"; 30 "bent"; 56 "main"; 124 "machine"; 170
"board"; 174 "fishmonger"; 182 "god-kissing"; 231 "indifferent"; 269 "beggars"; 270–71 "beggars' shadows"; 301 "have an eye of"; 329 "coted"; 338
"tickle o' th' sere"; 356 "tyrannically"; 362 "escoted"; 371 "tarre"; 394 "aunt-
mother"; 398 "handsaw"; 421 "writ and liberty"; 447 "chopine"; 450 "French";
615 "scullion"; 625 "tent"

III.i: 126–35 [ink]

*III.i: 59 "sea"; 65 "rub"

III.ii: 137–38, 144–45, 146 [s.d. for dumbshow], 247–51, 258–60

*III.ii: 15 "Termagant," "Herod"; 27 "very age and body"; 27–28 "form and pres-
sure"; 74 "blood," "judgment"; 98–99 "chameleon's dish"; 116–17 "metal

more attractive"; 138 "for"; 147 "miching malhecho"; 247–48 "Tropically"; 249 "duke's"; 254 "Lucianus"; 295 "pajock"; 348–49 "pickers and stealers"; 358 "'while the grass grows'"; 417 "seals"

III.iii: 22–23 [ink]; 71–73 [ink]; 80–81 [ink]; 97–98 [ink]

*III.iii: 22 "boist'rous"; 57 "currents"

III.iv: 64–71, 76–77, 106–11 [ink], 131–35, 178–81, 205–9

*III.iv: 46 "contraction"; 50 "the doom"; 52 "index"; 101 [s.d.] "his nightgown"; 121 "excrements"; 169 "either [master]"

IV.i: 12–13 [ink], 41–42

IV.ii: 1–3, 29–33

IV.iii: 70

IV.iv: 53–56 [ink]; 60–62 [ink]

*IV.iv: 6 "his eye"; 33 "dull" [ink]

IV.v: 37–39, 152

*IV.v: 2 "importunate"; 42 "was a baker's daughter"; 95 "a murd'ring piece"; 110 "counter"; 171–72 "the wheel becomes it!"; 177 "pansies"; 178 "document"; 180 "fennel," "columbines"; 184 "daisy," "violets"; 214 "hatchment"

IV.vii: 9–24 [ink], 16–24, 111–19 [ink]

*IV.vii: 63 "checking"; 77 "siege"; 82 "health"; 94 "brooch"; 123 "spendthrift sigh"; 135 "remiss"; 160 "for the nonce"; 162 "venom'd stuck"; 171 "crow-flowers, nettles, daisies"; 180 "incapable of"; 193 "douts"

V.i: 267–72 [ink], 318

*V.i: 4 "straight"; 9 "*se offendendo*"; 44 "confess thyself—"; 59 "unyoke"; 68 "Yaughan"; 75–76 "property of easiness"; 87 "politician"; 101 "loggets"; 107 "quiddits"; 108 "quillets"; 115 "fine of his fines"; 117 "fine dirt"; 149 "card"; 177 "thirty years"; 214 "favour"; 239 "winter's flaw"; 155 "crants"; 271 "ingenious"; 299 "esill"; 310 "couplets"

V.ii: 75–78, 117–20, 270–73, 330–31 [ink], 357–60 [ink], 400–1 [ink], 409–11 [ink]

*V.ii: 6 "mutinies in the bilboes"; 9 "pall"; 33 "statists"; 36 "yeoman's"; 42 "comma"; 43 "as's"; 63 "stand me now upon"; 120 "yet"; 122 "infusion"; 124 "umbrage"; 156 "impon'd"; 163 "margent"; 195 "comply"; 226 "gaingiving"; 242 "exception"; 268 "off indeed"; 283 "union"; 286 "kettle"; 317 "woodcock"; 369 "solicited"; 375 "cries on havoc"

Troilus and Cressida

Prologue: 29–31

*Prologue: 18 "corresponsive and fulfilling"; 26 "vaunts and first-lings"

I.i: 1–5, 22–26, 55–60, 92–94, 114–15

I.ii: 6, 20–22, 29–31, 49–52, 82–85, 97, 137–39, 178–80, 227–29, 266–68, 283–89, 292–95, 307, 312–21

I.iii: 21–23, 146, 335, 390–92, 391

All's Well That Ends Well

Measure for Measure

414–16, 442–47, 450–53, 458–59, 479–81, 487–90, 498–99, 509–10, 528–30, 538–40

Othello

I.i: 42–44, 55–60, 65, 80–81, 88–89, 98–100, 108–14, 134–38, 143–44, 148–50, 155–58, 165, 172–74, 176

*I.i: 49 "honest"

I.ii: 18–19, 22–28, 51, 69–71, 95–99, 98–99

*I.ii: 23 "as proud"; 26 "unhoused free condition"

I.iii: 48–49, 55–58, 94–98, 128–35, 161–63, 167–69, 193–98, 202–3, 218–19, 225–29, 240–41, 263–65, 284–85, 285, 293–94, 315–16, 322–24, 339–41, 345–47, 352–66, 389–96, 401–6, 409–10

*I.iii: 406 "honest"

II.i: 11–12, 61–65, 99–100, 123–24, 130–31, 149–61, 166–67, 175–77, 202–4, 218–21, 227–39, 256–65, 279–81, 295–305, 316, 321

II.iii: 6, 18–25, 35–44, 52–53, 64–65, 143–45, 242–48, 262–63, 268–72, 280–84, 329–31, 333–38, 345–48, 356–59, 368, 378–79

*II.iii: 146 "honest"

III.i: 51–53

*III.i: 43 "more kind and honest"

III.iii: 22–28, 58–61, 70–74, 90–92, 103–5, 116–17, 124–28, 137–39, 147–49, 159–60, 166–67, 197–208, 213, 229–30, 248–50, 258–60, 263–68, 278–79, 292–95, 298–99, 322–29, 335–37, 340–43, 345–57, 379–82, 427–28, 433, 479

*III.iii: 357 "occupation's"

III.iv.: 30–31, 69–72, 86–88, 93–95, 143–45, 159–62, 179–80, 185–90, 186, 196–200

IV.i: 9–10, 16–18, 31–34, 32, 34, 41–44, 56–59, 63–65 [ink], 66, 74, 96–104, 110–25, 143–44, 159–61, 185–89, 197–201, 206–10, 255–58, 286–92

IV.ii: 12–13, 20, 57–62, 134, 141–48, 165–66, 180–82, 187–93, 219–24

IV.iii: 34–40, 65, 76–79, 99–104

V.i: 8–10, 18–21, 27, 61, 103

V.ii: 76–77, 123–25, 176–77, 264–65, 293–95, 303–4, 338–56, 367–69

Macbeth

I.i: 10–11

I.ii: 1, 67

I.iii: 23–26, 79–80, 106–7, 118–20, 124–29, 134–42

I.iv: 11–14, 48–50

I.v: 19–21, 41–45, 72–74

I.vi: 6–8,

I.vii: 5–8, 21–28, 39–41, 59–61

II.i: 7–9, 54–56

II.ii: 15–16, 30–40

II.iii: 60–66, 97–101, 112–14, 123–26, 135–38

II.iv: 11–16, 24–27

III.i: 3–6, 54–57, 68–69, 91, 108–14

III.ii 4–7, 36, 45–51, 55

III.iii: 6–8

III.iv: 50–51, 80–83, 94–99, 99, 115–16, 122, 136–38

IV.i: 50–56, 83–86, 103–6, 139–49

IV.ii: 6–9, 33, 74–77

IV.iii: 12–14, 28–31, 114–15, 156–59, 168–73

V.i: 41–45

V.ii: 22–25

V.iii: 4–5, 50–56

V.v: 13–15, 43–45, 50–52

V.vii: 1–2, 28–29

V.viii: 1–2, 20–22, 43–46, 50–53, 70–73

King Lear

I.v: 50 [s.d.]
III.ii: 10–14 [ink]
III.iv: 51–58 [ink], 105–14
IV.vi: 225–28
V.iii: 196–99

Antony and Cleopatra

I.i: 33–40, 45–47, 53–54
*I.i: 20 "perchance"; 21 "scarce-bearded Caesar"; 32 "When . . . Fulvia scolds"; 35 "Kingdoms are clay"; 45 "not confound the time"; 47 "Without some pleasure now"
I.ii: 100–103, 119–21, 126–32, 150–52, 192–96, 194
I.iii: 28, 35, 42, 92–93
I.iv: 2–3, 32–33, 43, 65–71
I.v: 21–25, 73–75
II.i: 8–11
*II.i: 9 "the sea is mine"; 27 "Lethe'd"
II.ii: 42–43, 63, 81–83, 125–26, 149–53, 156–58, 165–66, 183–84
II.iii: 38–40
*II.iii: 1 "The world . . . office"
II.v: 2–3, 13–15, 21–23, 75–76, 83–84, 107–8
II.vi: 9, 24–26, 49–51, 77–79, 89–98
*II.vi: 131 "holy, cold"
II.vii: 95–105
III.ii: 3–6, 31–33, 44–45, 57–59
III.iii: 26, 50–51
III.iv: 22–23, 30–32
III.v: 20–21
III.vi: 46–50
III.vii: 11–13, 26–28, 41–45
III.viii: 1–6
III.x: 5–8, 19–20
III.xi: 1–4, 56–61, 69–74
III.xii: 7–10, 34–36

III.xiii: 60–61, 73–78, 89–96, 115–20, 151–55, 162–67, 179–85, 192–94
IV.i: 4–6
IV.ii: 9–10, 13–15, 33–37, 41–45
*IV.ii: 5 "sea and land"
IV.iii: 12
IV.iv: 6–7, 12–14, 37–38
IV.vi: 5–7, 28–31
IV.viii: 14–22, 35–39
IV.x: 1–2, 3
IV.xii: 3–5, 20–27, 48–49
IV.xiii: 6–10
IV.xiv: 50–54, 101–4, 106–13
IV.xv: 9–12, 21–23, 41–45, 63–68
V.i: 14–19, 37–40, 64–66
V.ii: 78–81, 85–92, 94, 99, 109–10, 146–48, 191–92, 224–26, 240–41, 248–49, 256–59, 276–79, 292, 320–22, 349–51, 364–66

Coriolanus

I.i: 10–11, 22–25, 30–47, 79–80, 88–90, 163–65, 173–74, 180–85, 202–4, 218–25, 229–30, 234–36, 240–41, 261–74
I.ii: 34–36
I.iii: 16–22, 35–37, 42–47, 64–71
I.iv: 28–29, 46–48, 62–63
I.v: 1–3, 20–21
I.vi: 29–36, 70–72
I.viii: 1–4, 11–15
I.ix: 2–9, 83–85, 89–90
I.x: 6–7, 17–19
II.i: 18–21, 56–58, 77–89, 130–38, 167–70, 174–78, 191–96, 218–20, 247–52
II.ii: 7–10, 24–26, 66–69, 77–78, 114–18, 142–45, 151–54
II.iii: 40–43, 47–51, 77–87, 124–28, 175–77, 211–12, 227–30, 243–45, 260–62, 268–71
III.i: 9–11, 19–20, 38–41, 43–45, 57–58, 66–68, 80–82, 93–97, 116–18,

Timon of Athens

Pericles

Cymbeline

II.iv: 24–26, 47–49, 118–28, 143–46
II.v: 2–5, 14–30
III.i: 73–75, 79–84
III.ii: 72–84
III.iii: 21–35, 65–68
III.iv: 42–46, 73–75, 104–13, 123–25
III.v: 10–19, 137–50
III.vi: 8–14, 37–40, 83–87
IV.i: 1–7
IV.ii: 22–30, 51–60, 82–85, 191–94, 230–33, 244–51, 287–90, 306–314
IV.iv: 35–54
V.i: 12–14, 30–33
V.ii: 1–10, 14–18
V.iii: 10–13, 28–51
V.iv: 1–29 [ink], 3–7, 16–29, 45–47, 101–3, 120–22, 134–37, 149–51, 168–73, 206–15
V.v: 31–33, 40–42, 62–66, 121–22, 126–28, 153–66, 192–200, 228–31, 258–64, 270–72, 321–27, 363–65, 392–99, 417–22, 474–85

The Winter's Tale

I.i: 31–48, 34–37
I.ii: 15–16, 42–44, 49–53, 62–75, 80–
87, 105–8, 129–31, 138–46, 156–58, 183–85, 186–207 [ink], 193–96, 217–20, 281–84, 292–96, 299–300, 351–57, 368–70, 426–31
II.i: 102–5, 127–28, 150–52, 188–89
II.iii: 1–2, 14–20, 35–37, 83–86, 120–23, 143–46
III.ii: 34–38, 80–85 [ink], 83, 141–42, 150–54, 180–85, 211–15, 221–24, 233–36, 239–44
III.iii: 4–6, 10–13, 46, 56–58, 61–63, 93–97, 101–4, 115–19, 134–36, 142–43
IV.ii: 22–26, 30–32, 60–62
IV.iii: 29–32, 79–83, 96–99, 112–14, 134–35
IV.iv: 3–10, 22–24, 62–66, 82–85, 89–100, 147–50, 187–90, 263–70, 286–87, 369–73, 416–21, 429–31, 459–61, 493–96, 576–90, 688–98, 732–34, 744–46, 772–74, 830–34, 862–66
V.i: 2–12, 44–46, 119–20, 135, 172–74, 225–28
V.ii: 46–61, 140–49, 164–65, 175–81
V.iii: 44–46, 49–56, 91–97, 98–135 [ink], 98–99, 109–11, 130–35, 147–50, 154–55

The Tempest

Auden annotated many of the words and phrases he underlined or marked in *The Tempest* and discussed them in his Saturday afternoon classes. See Appendix I.

I.i: 59–63
*I.i: 4 "yarely"; 9 "burst thy wind"; 18 "roarers"; 24–25 "peace of the present"; 37 "Bring her to try"; 51 "unstanched"; 52–53 "Set her two courses"; 60 "wide-chopp'd rascal"
I.ii: 28–30, 239–40, 250–51, 297–99, 351–62, 408–11, 426–28
*I.ii: 2 "allay"; 13 "fraughting," "collected"; 15 "No harm"; 31 "Betid"; 35 "bootless"; 64 "teen"; 71 "signories"; 81 "trash"; 100 "unto . . . of it"; 105 "prerogative"; 112 "dry"; 120 "condition"; 123 "lieu," "premises"; 138 "impertinent"; 146 "butt"; 148 "hoist"; 165 "steaded"; 169 "Now I arise"; 193 "quality"; 195

"article"; 207 "coil"; 209 "fever of the mad"; 218 "sustaining"; 250 "bate"; 266–67 "For one . . . her life"; 323 "A south-west blow on ye"; 364 "red plague"; 373 "Setebos"; 437–38 "the Duke . . . being twain"; 468 "fearful"

II.i: 114–16, 306–9

*II.i: 11 "The visitor"; 55 "eye of green"; 134 "Then we . . . comfort them"; 163 "foison"; 185 "a-batfowling"; 235–36 "(For he's a spirit . . . to persuade)"; 243 "But doubts . . . there"; 299 [s.d.] *"Gonzalo's ear"*

*II.ii: 28 "poor John"; 61 "salvages"

*III.i: 1–2 "their labour . . . sets off"; 15 "Most busiest when I do it"; 32 "visitation shows"; 46 "the foil"; 91 "A thousand thousand!"; 93 "withal"

III.ii: 160–62

*III.ii: 5–6 "The folly of this island"; 10 "eyes . . . head"; 19–20 "he's no standard"; 36 "natural"; 57 [s.d.]; 71 "pied ninny's," "patch"; 79 "stockfish"; 88 "murrain"; 99 "wesand"; 126 "troll"

III.iii: 3 "forthrights and meanders"; 5 "attach'd"; 21 "A living drollery"; 48 "putter-out of five for one"; 64 "still-closing"

IV.i: 51–59 [pencil and ink], 54–56, 110–17, 139–42 [pencil and ink], 154–57

*IV.i: 37 "rabble"; 41 "vanity of mine art"; 57 "corollary"; 63 "stover"; 81 "bosky"; 127 "Or else . . . marr'd"; 128 "wand'ring"; 156 "rack"; 187 "stale"; 193 "line"; 198 "Jack"; 222 "O King Stephano!"; 231 "luggage"; 249 "barnacles . . . apes"

V.i: 118–19

*V.i: 3 "carriage"; 10 "line grove"; 24 "Passion as"; 29 "drift"; 63 "show"; 67 "ignorant"; 89 "bell"; 124 "subtleties"; 129 "No."; 132 "rankest"; 155 "devour"; 156 "their words"; 157 "natural breath"; 172 "you play me false"; 227 "events"; 238 "On a trice"; 240 "diligence"; 244 "Was ever conduct of"; 271 "without"; 298 "luggage"; 314 "auspicious"

TEXTUAL NOTES

ABBREVIATIONS OF AUDEN'S WORKS

ACW   *A Certain World: A Commonplace Book* (New York: Viking, 1970).

CP   *Collected Poems*, ed. Edward Mendelson, 2nd edn. (New York: Random House, 1991).

DH   *The Dyer's Hand* (New York: Random House, 1962).

EF   *The Enchafèd Flood* (New York: Random House, 1950).

FA   *Forewords and Afterwords*, selected by Edward Mendelson (New York: Random House, 1973).

PD   *The Prolific and the Devourer* (Hopewell, NJ: Ecco Press, 1981).

SO   "Squares and Oblongs," in *Poets at Work* (New York: Harcourt Brace, 1948), pp. 163–81.

INTRODUCTION

Page

ix *"Times* reported": "Books—Authors," *The New York Times*, 27 September 1946, 21.

ix "The first lecture": There are no student notes on this lecture. According to the brief "Memories of the first lecture" that Alan Ansen recorded in his notebook—he did not take notes at the lecture itself—Auden told the class, "The poet is not like Orpheus, who is the type of Goebbels, but a mirror. The archetype, not of the poet as such, but of the poet who loses his soul for poetry, is Narcissus, who falls in love with his reflection not because it is beautiful, but because it is himself." Auden pointed out that "in a later version of the myth, Narcissus is a hydrocephalic idiot looking into a mirror saying, 'Ain't nature grand?' and in a still more sophisticated version, he is neither beautiful nor ugly, but as completely average as a Thurber husband, who instead of declaring 'I love you' to the image, asks over and over, 'Haven't we met before?'" (Cf. Auden's discussion of the artist and Orpheus and Narcissus in *SO*, 180.) Ansen records that Auden warned the class: "We are interested in art, otherwise we wouldn't be here, but be careful not to go to excess." Auden also contrasted the classical "tragic hero who is unfortunate" with the "Christian tragic hero who is tempted," a subject to which he often returned in the subsequent lectures and in his published prose, and he urged the class, "in reading Shakespeare," to "try to group characters temperamentally similar together."

ix Bernadine Kielty, "Authors Between Books," *Book-of-the-Month Club News* (December, 1946): 29. Kielty added that "always clear and concise," Auden announced at the opening lecture that those who couldn't hear him should please not raise their hands, "'because I am also near-sighted.'" In a letter to Theodore Spencer dated 21 October 1946, Auden complained, "The Shakespeare course makes me despair. I have 500 students and so can do nothing but boom away."

ix "Robert Solotaire . . . has written": Personal letter to this editor, 21 November 1998, and "Letter to the Editor," dated 18 November 1998, *Journal News,* New Rochelle, N.Y.

x "record of Auden's conversation": Alan Ansen, *The Table Talk of W. H. Auden,* ed. Nicholas Jenkins (Princeton: Ontario Review Press, 1990).

x "a series of 'Conversations on Cornelia Street' ": These conversations were published posthumously in Howard Griffin, *Conversations with Auden,* ed. Donald Allen (San Francisco: Grey Fox Press, 1981).

xi "a book by Hunter Guthrie": *Introduction au problème de l'histoire de la philosophie: la métaphysique de l'individualité à priori de la pensée* (Paris: Librairie Felix Alcan, 1937).

xi George Lyman Kittredge, ed., *The Complete Works of Shakespeare* (Boston: Ginn and Company, 1936).

xii "level of interest Auden took in different plays": Auden expressed a number of his preferences and dislikes among the plays directly in a conversation with Alan Ansen at the time of the lectures. In an entry dated 23 April 1947 in his "Journal," a typescript manuscript in the Berg collection, Ansen records Auden saying, "If I had to do an anthology [of Shakespeare] I'd have ten plays. My choice would be both snobbish *and* representative: *The Tempest, The Winter's Tale, Love's Labour's Lost, Henry IV, Parts One and Two, Much Ado About Nothing, Measure for Measure, Hamlet, Lear, Antony and Cleopatra.*" When Ansen protested that both *Hamlet* and *Lear* were "outsize tragedies" and that Auden didn't have "any representative of the other form," Auden replied, "All right, then, *Othello* and *Lear.*" Auden also said, "Do you really want *Twelfth Night?* I think it's a horrid play. Of the ripe plays, *Measure for Measure* is the least unpleasant. I really think Beatrice and Benedick are the best people in the comedies. Even compared with Rosalind. And Orlando is such a stick. I'd leave *Coriolanus* to the French. I can't follow Eliot in his exalted opinion of the play. I think Coriolanus is the most boring of Shakespeare's heroes. Macbeth is pretty dull too, he'd come second. I'm extremely fond of *The Winter's Tale.*"

xii "Clive James has remarked": "Farewelling Auden," *At the Pillars of Hercules* (London: Faber and Faber, 1979), 37, 23.

xiv "his reading of Freud": See Katherine Bucknell, Introduction to "Phantasy and Reality in Poetry" (1971), in *Auden Studies 3,* eds. Katherine Bucknell and Nicholas Jenkins (Oxford: Clarendon Press, 1995), 139–76.

xiv "elegy to Freud": "In Memory of Sigmund Freud," *CP,* 275, 274.

xiv " 'Whoso generalises, is lost' ": *PD,* 22. See also "Shorts" (1940), *CP,* 299.

xiv "a review of Ernest Jones's biography of Freud": "The Greatness of Freud," review of Ernest Jones, *The Life and Work of Sigmund Freud,* vol. 1, in *Listener,* L, 8 October 1953, 593.

xiv "article on *The Merchant of Venice*": "Two Sides to a Thorny Problem," *The New York Times,* 1 March 1953, Section 2.

xv "austere and often parched": Auden himself took issue with Eliot's doctrinaire approach to Shakespeare in a conversation with Alan Ansen. In the entry dated 23 April 1947 in his "Journal," Ansen records Auden saying, "And for all Eliot's talk about not trying to read belief from works he does it himself with Shakespeare, using "Ripeness is all," Edgar's line in *King Lear,* to show his thesis that the center of Shakespeare's philosophy is Stoicism. If one's going to do that sort of thing at all, you've got to take the whole work and see what happens to characters expressing given opinions."

xv "he later modified his view of the fall of Rome": See G. W. Bowersock, Introduction to "The Fall of Rome (1966)," in *Auden Studies 3*, 111–19. In his lecture on *Julius Caesar*, Auden relied heavily on Charles Norris Cochrane, *Christianity and Classical Culture* (Oxford: Clarendon Press, 1940), which he reviewed in *The New Republic*, lll, no.1556 (25 September 1944), and on Kierkegaard's *The Present Age* and *The Sickness Unto Death*, from both of which he quotes at length.

xvi "like Northrop Frye's": See Northrop Frye, *Fools of Time* (Toronto: University of Toronto Press, 1967), 70–74.

xvi "as Herrick writes": Robert Herrick, "To Anthea," in *The Poetical Works of Robert Herrick*, ed. F. W. Moorman (Oxford: Clarendon Press, 1910).

xvii "de Rougemont's antiromantic study": Denis de Rougemont, *Love in the Western World* (New York: Harcourt Brace, 1940).

xvii "Kierkegaard's commendation": Søren Kierkegaard, "The Aesthetic Validity of Marriage," in *Either/Or*, trans. David F. Swenson, Lillian Marvin Swenson, and Walter Lowrie, 2 vols. (Princeton: Princeton University Press, 1944), vol. 2, trans. Walter Lowrie.

xvii "Under the heading of 'Love, Romantic' ": *ACW*, 229, 230.

xviii "Northrop Frye remarks": Northrop Frye, *A Natural Perspective* (New York: Columbia University Press, 1965), 50.

xviii "isolating tendencies of his dispassionate, and prodigal, intellect": Auden wrote to Stephen Spender in 1940, using Jungian terms, "As you know my dominant faculties are intellect and intuition, my weak ones feeling and sensation. This means I have to approach life via the former; I must have knowledge and a great deal of it before I can feel anything." See John Fuller, *W.H. Auden: A Commentary* (Princeton: Princeton University Press, 1998), 371.

xviii " 'wild, extraordinary and demonic imagination' ": Oliver Sacks's phrase, in "Dear Mr. A . . . ," in *Auden: A Tribute*, ed. Stephen Spender (London: Weidenfeld and Nicolson, 1975), 191.

xix "His brother John commented on it": John Auden, "A Brother's Viewpoint," *Auden, A Tribute*, 29.

xix "episode of the pear tree in the *Confessions*": *The Confessions of St. Augustine*, trans. E. B. Pusey (London: J. M. Dent, 1932), 25–26.

xix "The drunk is unlovely . . . happens in it.": *DH*, 197.

xx "As a biological organism . . . Spirit innocent.": *DH*, 130.

xx "he quotes Goethe": Johann Wolfgang Goethe, *Torquato Tasso*, Act I scene ii.

xx "a book on Shakespeare's prose and verse": George H. W. Rylands, *Words and Poetry* (London: Hogarth Press, 1928).

xx "relied upon most directly": Auden was a friend of Theodore Spencer, and he makes occasional reference in the lectures to other Shakespeareans, including Harley Granville-Barker, G. Wilson Knight, Caroline Spurgeon, and Mark Van Doren, whose book on Shakespeare he had reviewed, but except for a stray comment or two, he was not significantly indebted to their works.

xxiii "suggestion of Aldous Huxley": Foreword to *The Complete Etchings of Goya* (New York: Crown, 1943), 7.

LECTURES

HENRY VI, PARTS ONE, TWO, AND THREE

This lecture has been reconstructed from notes by Alan Ansen. At the start of the lecture, Auden announced that an extra hour of classes would be held on Saturdays at 2:30 P.M. Ansen took no notes on the course's opening lecture, which occurred on 2 October 1946.

Page

3 "Yes . . . the interest itself": Slightly misquoted from a passage criticizing Arnold Bennett, in Henry James, "The New Novel." Auden had quoted the sentence in a review in 1933 of Violet Clifton, *The Book of Talbot*, and he drew upon it in the first line of one of his early poems, "O Love, the interest itself in thoughtless Heaven" (1932). See Edward Mendelson, *Early Auden* (New York: Viking, 1981), 163–64, and Fuller, *Auden: A Commentary*, 147.

3 "In *The Mirror for Magistrates*": Ed. L. B. Campbell (Cambridge: Cambridge University Press, 1938), 145. Ansen notes that Auden mentioned four particular editions: 1555, 1559, 1563, and 1587.

4 "force and fraud": *Forza* and *Froda* are the two modes of sin, ultimately derived from Aristotle, in the ethical scheme of the *Inferno* in Dante's *The Divine Comedy*.

4 "John Fortescue": Auden is probably referring to Fortescue's *The Law of Nature*, translated from the Latin by Chichester Fortescue, in *The Works of Sir John Fortescue*, 2 vols. (London: Chiswick Press, 1869), 1:185–372.

7 "He combines the lion and the fox": Machiavelli personified "force" and "fraud" in the figures of the lion and the fox. *The Lion and the Fox* is the title of a book by Wyndham Lewis (London: Grant Richards, 1927) from which Auden quotes in his concluding lecture.

8 "Jack Cade's rebellion": Ansen records that "Auden quotes with pleasure Cade's communist and anti-lawyer remarks."

12 "D. H. Lawrence says": "When I read Shakespeare," *Pansies* (London: Martin Secker, 1930), quoted in *DH*, 176–77.

RICHARD III

This lecture has been reconstructed from notes by Ansen and Howard Griffin.

Page

13 "an example in Marlowe": Christopher Marlowe, *The Jew of Malta*, Act II, in *Christopher Marlowe: Plays* (London: J.M. Dent, 1909), 185.

14 "Adolf Hitler's speech to his General Staff on 23 August 1939": Hitler told his staff on 22 August 1939 that he would find a reason for the invasion of Poland, and that it didn't matter whether the reason sounded convincing or not: "After all, the victor will not be asked whether he talked the truth or not. We have to proceed brutally. The stronger is always right." An excerpt from this speech is quoted in Robert H. Jackson's opening statement at the Nuremberg trials, 21 November 1945, which is reprinted in his book, *The Case Against the Nazi War*

Criminals (New York: Knopf, 1946), 57–58. The date that Jackson, as well as subsequent records, cite for the speech is 22 August 1939, but Jackson also records a similar address by Hitler on the invasion of Poland to his General Staff on 23 *May* 1939 (p. 57). Auden may have conflated May 23rd with August 22nd, and he may also have remembered August 23rd because it was the date of the notorious Non-Aggression Pact between Germany and the Soviet Union.

15 Henrik Ibsen, *Peer Gynt: A Dramatic Poem*, trans. R. Farquharson Sharp (New York: Everyman, 1922), Act II, scene 6. Auden also discussed the Troll King's distinction between men and trolls, with different emphases, in "Criticism for a Mass Society" in *The Intent of the Critic*, ed. Donald A. Stauffer (Princeton: Princeton University Press, 1941), 130–31; "Vocation and Society," in *Auden Studies 3*, 18 and note; *EF*, 88–90; and *DH*, 439–40. Auden writes in *EF*, 88–89, "To be enough to oneself means to have no conscious ego standing over against the self, to be unable to say no to oneself, or to distinguish fantasy from reality, not to be able to lie, to have no name and answer to Hi or any loud cry."

15 Hunter Guthrie, *Introduction au problème de l'histoire de la philosophie*, 54–66. Guthrie provides the basis for Auden's distinctions between the movements of the essential self and the existential self, but Auden elaborates them differently. Auden makes similar distinctions between essence and existence in *EF*, 120–22, in terms of the self and the ego. Neither Auden's discussion nor Guthrie's is particularly indebted to philosophies of existentialism at the time. Auden specifically contradicts the notion that existence precedes essence.

17 "existential drive of Don Giovanni": Auden wrote frequently of Don Giovanni's impersonal list and of its contrast to Tristan's suicidal devotion. See, e.g., *DH*, 119–23 and *FA*, 23–24.

17 "difference between anti-Negroes and anti-Semites": In his lecture on *The Merchant of Venice*, Auden said, "What is the source of anti-Semitism? The Jew represents seriousness to the Gentile, which we resent, because we wish to be frivolous and do not want to be reminded that something serious exists. By their existence—and this is as it should be—Jews remind us of this seriousness, which is why we desire their annihilation." In a column that he wrote under the pseudonym "Didymus" for *Commonweal* 37 (4 December 1942), Auden said, "Modern anti-Semitism . . . is one symptom of a Christendom which has taken offense at faith, but finding that nothing means social breakdown, is determined to replace it by a pagan political religion. The Jew is persecuted because he cannot deceive himself. His witness is this—either faith or nothing. Whereas a corrupt Christendom wants to say: 'Faith is too difficult; nothing is despair; we must have no God but Caesar. There might be no harm, though, in Caesar being a cleric.'" Reprinted in *Auden as Didymus*, ed. John Deedy (Mount Vernon, NY: Paul P. Appel, 1993), 44. What Auden meant by saying the Negro is a threat to the essential self of an anti-Negro is less clear. He may have been thinking of the anti-Negro's need to subjugate Negroes as a test of his essential strength; he may also have been thinking that the suppression of the Negro enables the white racist to believe he can achieve the ideal of his own human possibilities. In that sense, the Negro may be to the racist, what Auden believed Caliban to be to Prospero, a manichean image of the flesh. See *DH*, 130.

18 "how could . . . looking as he does?": Added from Griffin's notes.

19 "Richard really wants . . . like other people.": Added from Griffin's notes.

19 "Charles Addams cartoon of a little man . . . engaged in a life-and-death struggle with a large octopus": *New Yorker* cartoon, reprinted in Charles Addams,
Drawn and Quartered (New York: Random House, 1942), as described by Auden
in *EF*, 32–33. Auden may have presented an incorrect description of the cartoon
in the lecture. Ansen's notes record Auden saying, "man takes octopus out of
manhole." Griffin, in a handwritten note, records him saying, "hauling a huge
octopus out of a manhole." Griffin's typescript account, however, has Auden
saying the man is "struggling with a large octopus, coming out of a manhole."

21 "Carmen reading the cards": Georges Bizet, *Carmen*, Act III, "Trio des Cartes."
Griffin records that Auden also mentioned the omens in August Strindberg's
Inferno (1897).

THE COMEDY OF ERRORS AND *THE TWO GENTLEMEN OF VERONA*

This lecture has been reconstructed from notes by Ansen and Griffin.

Page

23 "We'll begin with the nature of the comic . . . right particulars.": The first three
paragraphs of the lecture are amplified from *DH*, 371–75, 379–81.

23 "Goliath," "prostitute": These two examples are derived from Søren Kierkegaard, *Concluding Unscientific Postscript*, eds. David F. Swenson and Walter Lowrie
(Princeton: Princeton University Press, 1941), 459–60, note. Auden prints the
story of the innkeeper and the prostitute as an epigraph to "Notes on the
Comic," *DH*, 371.

23 "New Yorker cartoon": By George Price. The cartoon is reprinted in *The New
Yorker Album 1942* (New York: Random House, 1942).

23 Sydney Smith: Hesketh Pearson, *The Smith of Smiths, Being the Life, Wit and
Humour of Sydney Smith* (New York and London: Harper and Brothers, 1934),
268, said the impromptu remark occurred in "an alley close to St. Paul's
Cathedral."

24 "Many years ago . . . With reasons for your choice.'": From *DH*, 32.

24 "effect of Greek tragedy": See *DH*, 172–76, and also, *FA*, 18–22.

25 "'Either she's dead'": Groucho Marx, as Dr. Hugo Hackenbush, in *A Day at the
Races* (1937).

25 "Icelandic saga . . . son.": Auden's reference to killing the son may be an error.
There is a little saga called Hrafnkel's Saga in which the chieftain Hrafnkel
swears such an oath to his friend, the god Feyr, and through demonic or supernatural power of some sort the horse tricks a wonderful young man into riding
him. It is this young man Hrafnkel kills. See *Hrafnkels saga Freysgoðda* (Cambridge: Harvard University Press, 1932).

25 "Jepthah's daughter": Judges 11.30–31, 34–35. Ansen's notes read "Jethro's
daughter," who was the wife of Moses, almost certainly a mishearing of
"Jepthah."

26 "Hard cases": Auden often cites the phrase, "hard cases make bad law." See,
e.g., *PD*, 22: "The artist's maxim: 'Whoso generalises, is lost.' The politician's
maxim: 'Hard cases make bad law.'" See also "Shorts" (1940), *CP*, 299.

26 "There is a difference . . . knowledge of others.": Auden writes fully about this distinction, in somewhat different terms, in *DH*, 171–73.

27 "use of servants": Auden discusses the servant-master relationship at length in *DH*, 107–45. I have made occasional use of Auden's discussion to amplify Ansen's notes on this subject.

28 "Kierkegaard discusses the imperative": In "Thou *Shalt* Love," "Thou Shalt Love Thy *Neighbor*," and *Thou* Shalt Love Thy Neighbor," in Søren Kierkegaard, *Works of Love*, trans. David F. Swenson and Lillian Marvin Swenson (Princeton: Princeton University Press, 1946), 15–74.

29 "From the personal point of view . . . mammals do.": From *DH*, p. 375.

30 "Kierkegaard discusses the implications": In "Remembering the Dead," in *Works of Love*, 286–88.

32 "It is nonsense . . . the Germans, for example.": Charles Williams makes this observation in *The Forgiveness of Sins* (London: Geoffrey Bles, The Centenary Press, 1942), 109–10.

32 "Many promising reconciliations . . . to be forgiven.": A slight rephrasing of Charles Williams, *The Forgiveness of Sins*, 113. Auden's discussion of forgiveness in this lecture is generally influenced by Williams, "Forgiveness in Shakespeare," in *The Forgiveness of Sins*, 5–14.

LOVE'S LABOUR'S LOST

This lecture has been reconstructed from notes by Ansen and Griffin.

Page

33 "not *specific* satire": Auden may have been protesting against the disposition of many Shakespeare scholars to stress contemporary references in the play, e.g. Frances A. Yates, *A Study of "Love's Labour's Lost"* (Cambridge: Cambridge University Press, 1934).

34 "Plato's *Symposium*": *The Dialogues of Plato*, trans. B. Jowett, 2 vols. (New York: Random House, 1937), 1:331–32, 334–35.

35 "neo-Platonists, Ficino, Pico della Mirandola": Auden's discussion and references in this section of the lecture are drawn from Erwin Panofsky, *Studies in Iconology* (New York: Oxford University Press, 1939): active and contemplative life, pp.138–39; Ficino's cosmology, p.132; Ficino's microcosm, pp.136–37; and Pico della Mirandola, pp.144–45 and note 51. Panofsky refers to many works, but principally to Ficino's Commentary on Plato's *Symposium* and Pico's Commentary on a long poem by Girolamo Benivieni.

35 "Biblical characters of Leah and Martha . . . Rachel and Mary": Ansen notes that "Auden combined Leah and Rachel as Active—a significant slip."

37 " 'I want to write' ": Auden returned to this subject in *SO*,165–67; and *DH*, 72–76.

37 "Mozart's *The Magic Flute*": See "Vocation and Society," *Auden Studies 3*, 15–18 and notes; and Auden and Kallman's "Preface" to their translation and adaptation of *The Magic Flute*, in W. H. Auden and Chester Kallman, *Libretti*, ed. Edward Mendelson (Princeton: Princeton University Press, 1993), 129–33.

37 "traditions of courtly love": Auden's discussion of courtly love and Andreas

Capellanus is drawn from C. S. Lewis, *The Allegory of Love* (Oxford: Oxford University Press, 1938), 1–43. Lewis discusses Andreas on pp. 32–43, and Andreas's allegorical story of the three troops of ladies on p. 38.

38 "Spenser's House of Busirane": *Fairie Queene*, III.xii.25, in the version of the text cited in Lewis, *The Allegory of Love*, 341, almost certainly Auden's source.

39 "a German work": Thomasin von Zerclaere's didactic poem, *Der Wälsche Gast* (around 1215), cited in Panofsky, *Studies in Iconology*, 105.

39 "Anteros": Discussed by Panofsky, *Studies in Iconology*, 126–27.

41 "Shakespeare makes fun of the Euphuists . . . and he knew it.": From *DH*, 17.

ROMEO AND JULIET

This lecture has been reconstructed from notes by Ansen and Griffin. Auden later published an introductory "Commentary on the Poetry and Tragedy of *Romeo and Juliet*," in the Dell-Laurel edition of the play (New York: Dell, 1958). The Dell-Laurel introduction does not include a discussion of the idea of romantic love, a major theme of the lecture.

Page

44 "Dog bites man": Cf. *DH*, 173.

44 "There is a story of a comic conflict": Ansen records Auden saying that "John B. Waugh reports" the story, but Auden probably said "Evelyn Waugh." Griffin records Auden saying, without any attribution for the story, that the two women were wives of the French and Belgian ambassadors and that the neutral party was the wife of the British ambassador.

44 "Inwood": A neighborhood in upper Manhattan in New York City.

45 "the idea of romance and of falling in love": Cf. *ACW*, 228–29.

46 "Ovid is mock heroic": Auden's discussion of Ovid is drawn from C. S. Lewis, *The Allegory of Love*, 5–8.

46 Roland: The most famous of the paladins of Charlemagne and the hero of the medieval French *Chanson de Roland*.

46 "Troubadour poems": See Lewis, *Allegory of Love*, 12.

46 "Catharist heresy": The source of Auden's reference to the Catharists is Denis de Rougemont, *Love in the Western World*. Auden reviewed de Rougemont's book in *Nation*, 152; no.26 (28 June 1941): 56–58, with high praise, and draws upon de Rougemont's skeptical views of romantic love considerably in this lecture as well as elsewhere in his work.

46 Martin Buber, *I and Thou*, trans. Ronald Gregor Smith (Edinburgh: T. & T. Clark, 1937).

46 A. E. Housman, *A Shropshire Lad* (New York: Henry Holt and Company, 1924), XVIII.

47 "For the intoxicant of romantic love . . . religious mystery, of Romantic Love": From Donald Pearce's account of Auden's lectures at the University of Michigan in the fall of 1941, "Fortunate Fall: W. H. Auden at Michigan," in *W. H. Auden: The Far Interior*, ed. Alan Bold (London: Vision, and Totowa, NJ: Barnes and Noble, 1985), 138.

48 "jobs that are really vocations": The decline of vocations, a repeated theme in Auden, is discussed by Eugen Rosenstock-Huessy, an author whom Auden ad-

mired, in *The Christian Future Or The Modern Mind Outrun* (New York: Scribner's, 1946), 15–29.

49 "Tybalt . . . Mercutio": Some details in the discussion of the minor characters are borrowed from Auden's "Commentary" in the Dell-Laurel edition of the play.

50 "Kierkegaard distinguishes": In "The Aesthetic Validity of Marriage," *Either/Or*, 2:112–14.

51 "Paolo and Francesca": Dante Alighieri, *Inferno*, Canto V, *The Divine Comedy*, trans. Carlyle-Wicksteed (New York: Modern Library, 1932), Canto V, pp. 40–41.

A MIDSUMMER NIGHT'S DREAM

This lecture has been reconstructed from notes by Ansen and Griffin. In the upper margin of one of his pages of notes on this lecture, Ansen writes: "WHA's trick of beginning negative part of antithesis (which comes 1st) with 'No!' or 'No,' and positive part by 'Yes!' "

Page

53 "subplot . . . English drama itself declined.": Auden, as he told Ansen in conversation, was indebted for this observation to William Empson's discussion of "Double Plots," in *Some Versions of Pastoral* (London: Chatto & Windus, 1935), 27.

53 "stone Dr. Johnson kicked": In *Boswell's Life of Johnson*, eds. George Birkbeck Hill and L. F. Powell, 4 vols. (Oxford: Clarendon Press, 1934), 1:471.

54 Alfred North Whitehead, Lecture VII, "Nature Lifeless," in *Modes of Thought* (New York: Macmillan, 1938), 173–201. All four of Auden's subcategories of nature are indebted to Whitehead.

54 "Plato's 'noble lie' ": *The Republic*, III.414, in *Dialogues of Plato*, ed. Jowett, 1:679. Jowett's translation is "royal lie."

54 "*Credo ut intellegam*": Cf. Auden, "New Year Letter," 1.422, and *ACW*, p. 34. The phrase is Anselm's, quoted by Charles Williams, *The Descent of the Dove* (New York: Oxford University Press, 1939), 109.

55 "St. Paul": Romans 7.15.

55 Sigmund Freud, *Totem and Taboo* (1913, tr. 1918).

55 "animism . . . polytheism . . . myths": Cf. *Auden as Didymus*, 25–28.

55 " 'Nativity Ode' ": John Milton, "On the Morning of Christ's Nativity," XIX.

55 "Gods become accidents in substance.": Following Aristotle, medieval philosophers defined an accident as an entity whose essential nature it is to inhere in another subject. It is thus to be contrasted with substance. Accidents and substance are fused, however, in Scholastic explanations of the Eucharistic Presence, and it is apparently such fusion that Auden sees in polytheistic gods and myths and that he calls attention to in Dante's description of love in the *Paradiso*. Ansen's notes here read: "Gods become accidents in substance. (Dante so says on love), myths."

55 Dante, *Paradiso*, *The Divine Comedy*, trans. Carlyle-Wicksteed, Canto XXXIII, p. 599.

57 "Nature never intended . . . in the USA": Cf. *DH*, 317 note.

58 "taking the frivolous too seriously": See *DH*, 429–32.

59 "Dr. Johnson remarked": *Boswell's Life of Johnson*, 2:461.
59 "myth of Tristan and Isolde": Cf. *DH*, 119–23, and *FA*, 23–24.
60 "BMT": A subway line in New York City.
61 Virginia Woolf, *Between the Acts* (New York: Harcourt, Brace, 1941), 218–19. Auden considered the novel Woolf's "masterpiece," *FA*, 414.

THE TAMING OF THE SHREW, KING JOHN, AND RICHARD II

This lecture has been reconstructed from notes by Ansen and Griffin.

Page

63 "Groucho ... Grock.": Groucho Marx (1895–1977) of the Marx brothers. Grock (Charles Adrien Wettach, 1880–1959), a famous Swiss clown.
63 *The Great Dictator* (1940) had Charlie Chaplin's first speaking part.
65 "An earlier play, *The Troublesome Reign of King John*": At the time Auden gave this lecture, most scholars assumed *The Troublesome Reign* was earlier than *King John*, and some argued that it might have been Shakespeare's own first draft, views that were questioned some decades later.
68 "such a lyric as Peele's": George Peele, lyric from *David and Bethsabe*. Text from *Poets of the English Language*, eds. W. H. Auden and Norman Holmes Pearson, 5 vols. (New York: Viking, 1950), 2:65.
68 "writer is the husband and language the wife": Cf. *SO*, 171–72.
71 Mark Van Doren, *Shakespeare* (New York: Henry Holt, 1939), 109. There is some evidence that Auden looked through Van Doren's book while composing his lectures, but the occasional echoes are of phrasing, not thought. Auden had praised Van Doren's book in a review, "The Dyer's Hand," *Nation*, 149, no. 17 (21 October 1939, 373–74).

THE MERCHANT OF VENICE

This lecture has been reconstructed from notes by Ansen and Griffin. Auden discusses *The Merchant of Venice* in "Brothers and Others," *DH*, 218–37, and he wrote an article on the play, "Two Sides to a Thorny Problem," for *The New York Times*, 1 March 1953, section 2.

Page

75 "The only racial remark ... Christians refute it.": This statement is neither persuasive nor clear. Auden may be referring to Shylock's assertion that he takes revenge "by Christian example" (III.i.73–74) and the Duke's statement in pardoning him: "That thou shalt see the difference of our spirit / I pardon thee thy life before thou ask it" (IV.ii.368–69).
75 "Religious differences ... treated frivolously": For the connotations of Auden's use of the word "frivolous" throughout this lecture and in others, see *DH*, 429–32.
76 "The first four suitors": The first suitors, on the contrary, leave because they wish to win Portia "by some other sort than your father's imposition, depending on the caskets" (I.ii.113–15).

76 "Today there are . . . *laissez-faire* society.": Ansen's notes read, "Today there are no personal obligations in a *laissez-faire* society, which comes round to status in totalitarian states."

76 E. M. Forster, "I Believe," in *I Believe*, ed. Clifton Fadiman (New York: Simon and Schuster, 1939), 81.

76 "aesthetic awareness": Auden's sense of the word "aesthetic" depends, in part, on Kierkegaard. See, e.g., "Equilibrium Between the Aesthetical and the Ethical in the Composition of Personality," *Either/Or*, 2:133–278; and *FA*, 172–74.

77 "At a lunch party . . .": After this sentence in his notes, Ansen inserts, with a caret, "Adrian and Francisco." This may be Ansen's interpolation, though his notes also suggest that Auden may have thrown it out to him as a hint during the lecture. In Part II of "The Sea and the Mirror," Adrian and Francisco say: "Good little sunbeams must learn to fly, / But it's madly ungay when the goldfish die," *CP*, 415. Ansen was writing a paper on "The Sea and the Mirror" at the time of this lecture. See also Fuller, *Auden: A Commentary*, 361.

77 "the noise, and the *people*": Auden also recounts this story in *ACW*, 383.

79 "back to Aristotle": *Politics* I. iv.

79 Dante, *Inferno*, Canto XI, *The Divine Comedy*, trans. Carlyle-Wicksteed, p. 68. In *DH*, 231, Auden quotes the same passage from the *Inferno*, and says about the collocation of Sodom and Cahors, which was known for its usurers, that it can "hardly be an accident that Shylock the usurer has as his antagonist a man whose emotional life, though his conduct may be chaste, is concentrated upon a member of his own sex."

82 "law *of* or a law *for* . . . at present ignorant": From Auden's review of Kierkegaard, *FA*, 177.

82 "Utilitarian theory . . . are identical.": Ansen's notes read, "Utilitarian theory doesn't consider the choice of means, put as caprice, but argues that utility and right are identical."

82 "Kant and Fichte ask": See, e.g., Immanuel Kant, "On a Supposed Right to Tell Lies from Benevolent Motives."

83 "A 'Profile' ": Richard Rovere, "Profiles: 89 Centre Street: II, The Weepers," *The New Yorker*, 30 November 1946, 48–49.

84 "But life is not a game . . . hang himself.": From *SO*, 169.

84 "The Greeks . . . sticky end.": From *SO*, 170.

84 "A society constructed to be . . . cellars.": Details from *SO*, 178, and *DH*, 85.

84 "The only serious . . . their neighbor.": From *SO*, 168–69, and cf. *DH*, 431–32.

85 "behave well out of a sense of social superiority": After this sentence in his notes, Ansen writes, "can't be friends?" The context of the phrase is unclear.

85 "What is the source of anti-Semitism?": See *Auden as Didymus*, 42–44, and lecture and notes on *Richard III*. Auden also discusses Jewish seriousness, "the Jewish passion for truth," in "The Greeks and Us," reprinted in *FA*, 14.

SONNETS

In addition to Ansen's holograph notes and Griffin's typed notes on this lecture, there is a typescript of the lecture in the Berg Collection of the New York Public Library that Ansen made from his holograph notes. Ansen's typescript, which is unsigned and undated, is the basis of this text of the lecture, with some small changes in phrasing derived from Ansen's original holograph notes and a few minor bits and pieces from Griffin. Auden published an essay on the *Sonnets* in *Listener*, 2 and 9 July 1964, which was reprinted as an introduction to the Signet Classic edition of *The Sonnets* (New York: New American Library, 1964), xvii–xxxviii, and also reprinted in *FA*, 88–108. This lecture differs materially from the published essay, though there are also significant parallels between the two. In the lecture, for example, as opposed to the essay, Auden argues that the relationship between Shakespeare and the young man depicted in the *Sonnets* suggests sexual infidelity, "which wouldn't make sense if there hadn't been a prior sex relationship."

At the start of the lecture, Auden said, "I have two announcements to make, and I'm very sorry to be forced to make the first one. A good many of you have been handing in papers for me to read. Now I don't say they aren't very good, but unfortunately this is not a creative writing class, and I really have other obligations to fulfill. So, I'm afraid I'll have to ask you not to hand in any more writing. The Saturday class will not be held this week—I have to go to Washington." Ansen notes, "I am aware of one of the particular facts leading to this decision. The previous Wednesday as I was trailing along after Auden down 12th Street a would-be poet had leapt from the dark covert of an empty building and cornered him about some MSS. he had given Auden. At bay, the Master promised him an audience at four the following Monday in the Waldorf Cafeteria." Later, Auden told Ansen, and Griffin, that "he didn't know what to say, as the man's poetry was exceedingly bad."

Page

86 William Wordsworth, "Scorn not the Sonnet," in *The Poetical Works of William Wordsworth*, ed. Ernest de Selincourt, 4 vols. (Oxford: Clarendon Press, 1940–47), vol. 3.

86 Robert Browning, "House," *in The Poetical Works of Robert Browning* (London: Oxford University Press, [1940]).

88 "difference between essence and existence": See Hunter Guthrie, *Introduction au problème de l'histoire de la philosophie* and the lecture and notes on *Richard III*.

88 "My feelings, desires . . . pretending to be him.": From *FA*, 171.

90 "Dr. Johnson refuted": See *Boswell's Life of Johnson*, 1:471.

91 "what would be a good poem to illustrate that?": Ansen notes that while Auden was "leafing through his Kittredge," someone in the audience called out, "Sonnet 66," and Auden said, "Yes, that's very good, but perhaps Sonnet 65 will do."

93 "we can never tell if he's proud": Auden often makes this observation; see, e.g., *DH*, 95, and *FA*, 21, 171–72.

95 "the sonnet about the rival poet": There are several sonnets alluding to a rival poet, but Auden is possibly thinking of Sonnet 80.

95 "aren't any pure accidents in love": Ansen records that at this point, "Auden's eyes glaze slightly, Auden increasingly [looks hard at the] audience."

96 "though he may destroy others": Ansen records that Auden delivered this phrase "sotto voce."

96 "Yeats writes": *The Collected Poems of W. B. Yeats* (New York: Macmillan, 1933), 315–16.

97 Friedrich Hölderlin, *Gesammelte Werke*, ed. Wilhelm Böhm 5 vols. (Jena: Eugen Diederich, 1924) 2:38; translation mine. Auden may have referred to the German and English texts of "Sokrates und Alkibiades" in *Some Poems of Friedrich Hölderlin*, trans. Frederic Prokosch (Norfolk, Conn.: New Directions, [1943]), though he would have been likely to have translated the poem himself in class. For Auden's other references to the poem, see Fuller, *Auden: A Commentary*, 208, 221, 358.

98 "speech of Palamon" Ansen notes that Auden read the speech in a "determined, slightly angry voice." He notes also that Auden's "readings from Yeats, Hölderlin, and *The Two Noble Kinsmen* were conducted in [a] far less placid style" than his readings from the sonnets.

HENRY IV, PARTS ONE AND TWO, AND HENRY V

This lecture has been reconstructed from notes by Ansen and Griffin. There is an account of Auden's lecture on *Henry IV* and *Henry V* at the University of Michigan in the fall of 1941, by Donald Pearce, "Fortunate Fall," in *W. H. Auden: The Far Interior*, ed. Bold, 144–48. Auden later wrote an extended analysis of the plays in "The Prince's Dog," *DH*, 182–208. The lecture presents the main outlines of the later essay, though Auden's praise of Falstaff is somewhat more qualified in the lecture. Ansen records the following conversation with Auden immediately after the lecture: "Do you really think Shakespeare would have approved of your interpretation? WHA: I don't care whether he would or not. It's in the text, and that's what counts. As a matter of fact, I think that probably Shakespeare's young man was only a would-be Prince Hal—a failure really, and Shakespeare wrote the plays with a double idea: he showed the young man how horrible that kind of character could be, and showed him what a real success was. And it is Falstaff who is really remembered."

Page

101 "different kinds of time": In his copy of Kittredge's edition, Auden marked passages concerned with time in these plays profusely, sometimes also numbering them and writing "Time" next to them. He did not make such systematic annotations for any other play.

110 "Hal and Falstaff are eternal antitypes": Cf. "Under Which Lyre ... *Phi Beta Kappa Poem, Harvard, 1946*," in which Auden wrote,

> Related by antithesis,
> A compromise between us is
>   Impossible;
> Respect perhaps but friendship never:
> Falstaff the fool confronts forever
>   The prig Prince Hal.

111 "eat humble pie . . . and swallow their pride": Cf. Stephano's lyric in Part II of "The Sea and the Mirror":

> Embrace me, belly, like a bride;
> Dear daughter, for the weight you drew
> From humble pie and swallowed pride,
> Believe the boast in which you grew:
> Where mind meets matter, both should woo. . . .

111 "The Greeks thought of . . . borne it all by himself.": From *DH*, 196.

111 "Greenwich Village": The neighborhood in lower Manhattan in New York City in which the New School was located and in which Auden himself lived.

112 "Tammany Hall": The Democratic party political machine in New York City.

MUCH ADO ABOUT NOTHING

This lecture has been reconstructed from notes by Ansen and Griffin.

Page

113 "Bandello, Ariosto, and a Greek romance": Matteo Bandello, *Novelle* (1554); Ludovico Ariosto, *Orlando Furioso* (1532), Cantos IV–VI; and *Chæreas and Callirhoë* (late fourth or early fifth century).

113 "Where and how songs are placed in Shakespeare": To amplify Ansen's notes in this section of the lecture, I have used a number of details from Auden's discussion of songs in "Music in Shakespeare": *DH*, 515 ("Who is Silvia"), 521 ("O mistress mine"), 514 ("Take, O, take those lips away"), and 516–18 ("Sigh no more, ladies").

115 "personal fidelity versus arranged marriage": See lecture and notes on *Love's Labour's Lost.*

121 "post-Freudian-analytic rhetoric": This phrase is in Griffin's notes, not Ansen's.

122 "more a British than an American attitude": This phrase is in Griffin's notes, not Ansen's.

122 Jean-Nicholas-Arthur Rimbaud, "Génie," in *Prose Poems from the ILLUMINATIONS*, trans. Louise Varèse (New York: New Directions, 1946). Ansen's notes state: "Arthur Rimbaud, *Le Génie* (read)—applied by WHA (implicitly) to Christ."

THE MERRY WIVES OF WINDSOR

This brief "lecture" is reconstructed from Alan Ansen's notes only. Ansen records that Auden proceeded to play 18 sides of a recording of Verdi's *Falstaff* during the hour, giving very brief plot summaries for each side. Ansen notes that early on "One young student started to get very nasty and complained that WHA should have been talking." After the lecture, Auden spoke to Ansen of his annoyance over the interruption, saying, "Why do they behave like that? I'll make him act a play and then tell him it's awfully boring. There are people who will listen to you gurgle water for the hour, just so long as you're doing something."

JULIUS CAESAR

This lecture has been reconstructed from notes by Ansen and Griffin.

Page

125 "In the later Roman plays, history is superficial . . . essential in *Julius Caesar.*": Auden contradicts this view when he takes up these later plays. See lectures on *Coriolanus* and *Antony and Cleopatra.*

126 "There are three types of groups of people": For a full discussion of the ideas of society, community and the crowd, see *DH*, 63–65. Auden returns to the subject in his lecture on *Coriolanus.*

127 "A cello player . . . community of music lovers.": From *EF*, 31.

127 Kierkegaard, *The Present Age*, trans. Alexander Dru and Walter Lowrie (London: Oxford University Press, 1940), 39–45. Auden also quotes from this passage in *EF*, 28.

130 "'Disingenuous compliances,' Dr. Johnson called it": Auden probably had Johnson's essay on marriage in mind, *Rambler* 45 (21 August 1750), in which Johnson speaks of couples who, through "studied compliance" disguise their real temper and desires until they are married. Ansen's notes say, "Johnson's indiscriminate compliances," Griffin says "disingenuous compliances." Griffin, in this case, seems right. Auden used the term "disingenuous compliances" in the same way in *PD*, pp. 15–16: "No one who is dependent upon the good-will of others (and even headmasters are dependent upon the good-will of the parents, just as a dictator has to cajole the masses) can avoid becoming a politician, and that involves not only many disingenuous compliances but a good deal of downright lying." See also *EF*, 70.

130 "As Hegel wrote": Auden was likely to have been quoting from memory— Georg Friedrich Hegel's reference to "the owl of Minerva" was well known. The T. M. Knox translation of Hegel's *The Philosophy of Right* (Oxford: Clarendon Press, 1942) reads: "One word more about giving instruction as to what the world ought to be. Philosophy in any case always comes on the scene too late to give it. . . . The owl of Minerva spreads its wings only with the falling of dusk" (12–13).

130 "The Greek's ethical cosmology . . . didn't work.": Amplified from Auden's review of Cochrane, *Christianity and Classical Culture* in *The New Republic*, 25 September 1944, reprinted as "Augustus to Augustine," in *FA*, 34–35. In later years Auden came to rely less on Cochrane's tendentious view of classical idealism. See "The Fall of Rome" (1966) in *Auden Studies 3*, 120–37, and G. W. Bowersock, *Auden Studies 3*, 111–19.

130 "archaistic or futuristic": Auden derived these terms from Arnold Toynbee, *A Study of History*, vol. 6 (London: Oxford University Press, 1939), 49–132. Auden cites Toynbee explicitly at the end of the lecture.

132 "General Patton": George S. Patton was a famous American World War II general, known for his ungovernable temper as well as his military fortitude.

134 "he has to run on someone else's sword": Someone else, his servant Strato, holds the sword Brutus runs on, but it is his own sword. Both Ansen and Griffin

report "someone else's sword," though Griffin mistakenly says it is Cassius who runs on the sword.

134 "Toynbee writes": *Study of History*, 6:140.

134 "in A. E. Housman's poetry": *A Shropshire Lad*, XXXII and XXXI, respectively.

135 Epictetus, Book III.xiii.7–13, *The Discourses as Reported by Arrian*, 2 vols. (London: William Heinemann, 1935), 2:91. In the midst of his notes on this section of the lecture, Ansen writes, "Bevin, *Stoic and Epicurean*." Perhaps Auden was referring to R. D. Hicks, *Stoic and Epicurean* (Oxford: Clarendon Press, 1910). He may have also been thinking of Edwyn Bevan, *Stoics and Sceptics* (Oxford: Clarendon Press, 1913), though Bevan discusses Zeno, not Epictetus.

136 Kierkegaard, *The Sickness Unto Death*, trans. Walter Lowrie (Princeton: Princeton University Press, 1941), 71–73. Ansen inserted a reference to these page numbers in his notes.

137 T.S. Eliot, "Coriolan," *Collected Poems 1909–1935* (London: Faber & Faber, 1936), 137–39. It is difficult to know how much of the poem Auden read in the lecture. Ansen's notes say simply, "Poem of T. S. Eliot *Coriolanus* [sic] 'Cry what shall I cry.' " "Cry what shall I cry" is the first line of the second section of the poem, "Difficulties of a Statesman."

AS YOU LIKE IT

This lecture has been reconstructed from notes by Ansen and Griffin. Ansen's notebook pages for this lecture are very badly smudged and often nearly illegible. I have indicated one reading of his notes that seems especially problematic below. Ansen records (obscurely) that Auden announced at the start of the lecture, "*Life* magazine is going to do some photographs for a piece on education in the Village—so nobody must yawn. Inquired for a drink afterwards. Un-Elizabethan institution primal test: please nobody yawn, they promise to be out soon. People who haven't handed in papers have been marked incomplete—an alarmingly great number of them. Read the plays a little more carefully than I have reason to think you do. There is no point in my getting up here and talking about the plays if you don't." *Life* magazine did not follow through on the project.

Page

138 Erwin Panofsky, *Studies in Iconology* 40–42.

138 Hesiod, *Works and Days*, in *The Homeric Hymns and Homerica*, trans. Hugh G. Evelyn-White (London: William Heinemann, 1924), 11, 15–17.

139 "Aidôs and Nemesis": *Aidôs*, as a quality, is that feeling of reverence or shame that restrains men from wrong; *Nemesis* is the feeling of righteous indignation aroused especially by the sight of the wicked in undeserved prosperity.

139 " '*Ils sont dans le vrai*' ": The phrase is quoted in Auden's "New Year Letter," ll. 540–41, "Well, FLAUBERT didn't say / Of *artists: 'Ils sont dans le vrai.'* " In a note to the poem in *The Double Man* (New York: Random House, 1941), 103, Auden wrote, "He said it of peasants." The source in Flaubert is unidentified.

140 "Spengler's premise": Oswald Spengler, author of *The Decline of the West* (1918–22).

141 "The Sea God's Address to Bran," in *Selections from Ancient Irish Poetry*, trans. Kuno Meyer (London: Constable, 1913), 7–8.

142 Luis de Góngora, *Las Soledades* (1613).

143 Lao-tse, sixth century B.C., Chinese philosopher and reputed author of *Tâo Teh King*, which put forth the doctrine of simple, spontaneous, childlike, unselfish action, in the individual and in government, as the foundation of general happiness.

143 "animal in contrast with man": Just before this phrase in Ansen's notebook is a nearly illegible phrase that may read "one form back, ahistorically."

143 Walt Whitman, *Leaves of Grass* (Philadelphia: David McKay, [1891]), "Song of Myself," ll. 684–91.

143 "If men were as much men": From D. H. Lawrence, "Lizard," *Pansies*. Auden also used these lines as the epigraph to "D. H. Lawrence," *DH*, 277.

143 "Alice in Wonderland": Griffin's notes add, "Alice and Jabberwocky."

143 John Gay, *The Beggar's Opera* (1728).

144 Mickey Spillane, Raymond Chandler: American detective story writers.

144 "vicarage or college": Cf. *DH*, 146–58.

144 William Wordsworth, *The Prelude* (1805–6), ed. Ernest de Selincourt (Oxford: Clarendon Press, 1926), Bk. VII, lines 695–704. Auden cites part of this passage in *EF*, 28.

144 "Sydney Smith's comment": Cited with slightly different wording in Hesketh Pearson, *The Smith of Smiths*, p. 92. Auden cites Smith's comment in his introduction to *Selected Writings of Sydney Smith*, reprinted in *FA*, 156.

144 "in Pascal's words": Blaise Pascal, *Pascal's Pensées*, [trans. William Trotter], intro. T. S. Eliot (London: J. M. Dent, 1932), fragment 260, p. 76: "To deny, to believe, and to doubt well, are to a man what the race is to a horse." Auden cites this sentence, in French, in a note to "New Year Letter," l. 962, "Our faith well balanced by our doubt." See *The Double Man*, 120. He also cites the sentence, in English, but with the order changed: "to believe, to doubt, and to deny well," in *ACW*, 34.

145 "There is no distinction, rightly none . . . affects matter.": Ansen's notes read: "No distinction (rightly none) between nature and art—psychosomatic constitution—nature, use of it partly on grace."

149 "the truest poetry is the most feigning'": Auden later used Touchstone's line as the title of one of his poems, *CP*, 619–21. See also Fuller, *Auden: Commentary*, 452–53.

150 "Goethe writes": Johann Wolfgang Goethe, *Torquato Tasso*, Act I scene ii.

151 "Civilization . . . diverse.": Cf. "The Sea and the Desert," *EF*, 3–39.

151 "Alice dances so": Lewis Carroll, *Through the Looking-Glass* (New York: Random House, 1946), 53–54. Empson quotes and discusses this passage in *Some Versions of Pastoral*, 261.

TWELFTH NIGHT

This lecture has been reconstructed from notes by Griffin, Helen Lowenstein, and Bea Bodenstein. Ansen missed this lecture. For the passages in *Twelfth Night* Auden marked in his Kittredge text, see Appendix III. See also his discussions of the play in *DH*, 375–76, 520–22. In an entry in his "Journal" dated 10 May 1947, Ansen records Auden saying to him in conversation, "*Twelfth Night* is really a very nasty play. Everybody reads it in school and says, 'How lovely,' because it has no sex in it. If it were frankly an unpleasant play it would be all right. But he started out to write a pleasant play like *As You Like It*, and he was trapped by his own convention. Oh yes, it's well written, all right. But I don't like it."

Page

152 "The comic convention in which . . . around the 'fun.' ": From *DH*, 520.

153 "more intimate audience than at the Globe": The first recorded performance of *Twelfth Night*, on 2 February 1602, was for an audience of law students at the Middle Temple.

154 "The Duke, who up till . . . make a good husband.": From *DH*, 521.

155 "These lines are charming . . . old drunks.": Amplified from *DH*, 521–22.

155 A. E. Housman, *A Shropshire Lad*, XXXIII. Lowenstein's notes read: "A similar thought in a poem by Housman." She does not specify the poem; and neither Griffin nor Bodenstein mentions Housman. Lowenstein also records that Auden mentioned "Dante's sestinas (some)" in connection with "O mistress mine," but what he meant is not clear.

157 "Shakespeare has so placed . . . Viola has to endure.": From *DH*, 522.

158 "in contrast to classical tragedy": For Auden's extended comparisons of Shakespearean and classical tragedy, see *DH*, 172–76, and *FA*, 18–22.

HAMLET

This lecture has been reconstructed from notes by Griffin, Lowenstein, and Bodenstein. Ansen missed this lecture. For Auden's discussions of *Hamlet* in his Saturday classes, see Appendix I, and for the passages from *Hamlet* he marked off in his Kittredge text, see Appendix III.

Page

159 "If a work is quite perfect . . . left open for a tragedian.": The material in this opening paragraph appears only in Griffin's notes, not Bodenstein's or Lowenstein's. Auden may have said it in conversation with Griffin sometime later.

159 "T. S. Eliot has called": In "Hamlet," *Selected Essays* (London: Faber and Faber, 1934), 143. Much of this lecture is under the spell of Eliot's essay.

160 "George H. W. Rylands's book": *Words and Poetry*, 119–44. Auden's preceding comments on Shakespeare's style are largely derived from Rylands.

161 "This business of being a mirror": Auden explores this subject at length in "The Sea and the Mirror."

161 Saxo Grammaticus, *Historia Danica* (ca. 1200; first printed in 1514); Belleforest, *Histoires Tragiques* (1576).

162 "Hamlet's disgust . . . mother": Cf. Eliot, *Selected Essays*, 145–46.

163 "last speech . . . vanity": The apparent vanity of Shakespeare's heroes at their death is a fixture of Senecan tragedy that Eliot criticizes in "Shakespeare and the Stoicism of Seneca," *Selected Essays*, 126–40.

164 "Hamlet lacks faith in God . . . play at possibilities.": From *DH*, 451–52. See also *EF*, 113, where Auden writes, "Shakespeare . . . had a new vision of the

nature of revenge, and transformed the old Hamlet into the first hero of the romantic type. I.e., Shakespeare's Hamlet is made a hero by the situation in which he finds himself of having a mother who has committed adultery with his uncle, who has murdered his father. Before this happened he was no hero, just an ordinary pleasant young man. The result is that, instead of just avenging his father and getting it over with, he secretly cherishes the situation and cannot bear to end it, for who will he be then?"

164 "Hamlet should be played by an actor brought in off the street": In 1941, while Auden was teaching Shakespeare at the University of Michigan, he said to Charles H. Miller, "When a director seeks an actor to play the role of Hamlet, he may as well go out on the street and take the first person who comes along. Because the role doesn't require an actor. One has only to recite Hamlet's speeches, which are instructions and arguments to himself on how to act the roles he decides to play." See Miller, *Auden: An American Friendship* (New York: Charles Scribner's Sons, 1983), 61.

164 Kierkegaard, *Either/Or*, 1:234, 239.

TROILUS AND CRESSIDA

This lecture has been reconstructed from notes by Ansen, Griffin, Lowenstein, and Bodenstein.

Page

166 Ronald Firbank (1886–1926). Auden wrote a review of Firbank for the *New York Times*, 20 November 1949, and an essay on his work for *The Listener*, 8 June 1961.

170 "In the foreground . . . sea and earth.": From *FA*, 17.

170 "at the end of the Iliad": Homer, *Iliad*, Bk. 24, trans. Andrew Lang, Walter Leaf, Ernest Myers, *The Complete Works of Homer* (New York: Modern Library, 1935), 456.

170 *The Battle of Maldon*, ll. 312–13.

172 "biblical story of David and Jonathan": 1 Samuel.20.

172 "Steig cartoons": William Steig was a regular and extremely sardonic cartoonist for *The New Yorker.*

173 "Nestor . . . Patroclus . . . queen": a conflation of Bodenstein's and Ansen's notes. Bodenstein's notes say, "Nestor must be an old, tiny, dribbling 52nd Street Queen," Ansen's say, "Patroclus must be 52nd Street Queen." Cf. "September 1, 1939": "I sit in one of the dives / On Fifty-Second Street," and see Fuller, *Auden: A Commentary*, 290–91.

173 "the Second Mrs. Tanqueray": In Arthur Wing Pinero, *The Second Mrs. Tanqueray* (1893).

173 "like Mildred": In W. Somerset Maugham, *Of Human Bondage* (1915).

173 "Dares": Dares of Phrygia, reputed author of a lost pre-Homeric account of the Trojan War. A supposed Latin prose translation survives, *Daretis Phrygii de Excidio Trojae Historia* (5th century?), and was widely used by medieval authors.

173 Giovanni Boccaccio, *Il Filostrato* (ca. 1338).

173 Robert Henryson, *Testament of Cresseid* (1593).

173 "C. S. Lewis sees": *The Allegory of Love*, 183–89.

176 John Wilmot, Earl of Rochester, "The Maim'd Debauchee," *Collected Works of John Wilmot Earl of Rochester*, ed. John Hayward (London: Nonesuch Press, 1926).

177 "'the smale bestes . . . .'": Geoffrey Chaucer, *Troilus and Criseyde*, III. 1781.

178 Robert Graves, "The Cool Web," *Poems (1914–26)* (London: William Heinemann, 1928).

179 Martin Buber, *I and Thou* (1937), Part One.

179 G. K. Chesterton, "The Sword of Surprise," *The Collected Poems of G. K. Chesterton* (London: Cecil Palmer, 1927), 55.

ALL'S WELL THAT ENDS WELL

This lecture has been reconstructed from notes by Griffin and Lowenstein. Ansen missed this lecture. For Auden's markings of passages in the play in his Kittredge text, see Appendix III.

MEASURE FOR MEASURE

This lecture has been reconstructed from notes by Ansen, Griffin, Lowenstein, and Bodenstein.

Page

185 Cicero, *De Re Publica* I. xxv.

185 "Augustine": In *The City of God* (II. xxi) Augustine recapitulates Cicero's definition of the earthly city, as men united by a common sense of right, *iuris consensu*, and contrasts it with the idea of the heavenly city, men united in respect to the things they love, *rerum quas diligit* (XIX. xxiv). Auden's discussion of Augustine's conception of the two societies is indebted to Charles Norris Cochrane, *Christianity and Classical Culture*, 488 ff.

185 "vanity of the secular hope for creative politics": Cf. Cochrane, 510, "the pretensions of creative politics."

185 Karl Marx, *Capital* (New York: Modern Library [1936?]), 268, 284–89, 510–11. Ansen's notes read: "Whether hypocrisy or as Marx claims a moral advance." The word "or" is probably misplaced, since Marx stresses the manifest hypocrisy of justifications of child labor in *Capital.*

190 "Hard cases make bad law.": See note to lecture on *Comedy of Errors* and *Two Gentlemen of Verona.*

192 "The difference between the superego and conscience": See *ACW*, 87–88.

192 "to make her fond of melancholy music": See lecture on *Much Ado About Nothing* and *DH*, 514.

192 "aesthetic authority, ethical authority and religious authority": Auden draws these categories from Kierkegaard. See *Either/Or*, 2:131–278; Auden's preface to his anthology of Kierkegaard, *FA*, 172–77; and *EF*, 93–98.

193 "Religious authority is shown through forgiveness": See lecture on *The Comedy of Errors* and *The Two Gentlemen of Verona*. Both discussions are influenced by Charles Williams, "Forgiveness in Shakespeare," *The Forgiveness of Sins*, 5–14.

194 "Many promising reconciliations . . . to be forgiven.": A slight rephrasing of Charles Williams, *The Forgiveness of Sins*, 113.

OTHELLO

This lecture has been reconstructed from notes by Ansen, Griffin, Lowenstein, and Bodenstein. There is an account of Auden's lecture on *Othello* at the University of Michigan in the fall of 1941, by Donald Pearce, "Fortunate Fall," in *W. H. Auden: The Far Interior*, ed. Bold, 139–43. Auden later published an extended essay on the play, "The Joker in the Pack," in *DH*, 246–72. I have used the text of the essay to elaborate a few points in Ansen's notes that needed clarification. The concepts of Iago as a practical joker and a scientist do not appear in the lecture, and the discussions of the *acte gratuit* and Iago as an inverted saint do not appear in the essay; otherwise, the arguments of the lecture and the essay are similar.

Page

195 "The particular kind of tragedy . . . participant as well as a spectator.": Auden compares Shakespearean and Greek tragedy in *DH*, 172–76, and *FA*, 18–22. See also "The Christian Tragic Hero," *The New York Times*, 16 December 1945, section 7, pp. 1, 21.

196 "In the original story": By Giovanni Battista Giraldi (surnamed Cinthio), *Hecatommithi* (1565).

197 "the idea of the *acte gratuit*": Cf. *FA*, 36–37; *SO*, 167–68; and *DH*, 430–31.

197 "episode of the pear tree": *The Confessions of St. Augustine*, 25–26.

198 "St. Augustine was the first real psychologist . . . through an act of pure choice.": From *SO*, 167.

198 "it depends upon your view of psychology.": In *SO*, 167, Auden seemed to conclude that the *acte gratuit* was essentially "primary": "The psychoanalyst can doubtless explain St. Augustine's robbing of the pear-tree in terms of natural desire as, say, a symbolic copy of some forbidden sexual act, but this explanation, however true, misses the point which is the drive behind the symbolic transformation in consequence of which what in its original form was felt as a given desire now seems to the actor a matter of free and arbitrary choice."

198 "At the same time man . . . to make free with necessities.": Largely from *SO*, 167–68.

198 Charles Williams, *He Came Down From Heaven* (London: Heinemann, 1938), 16–19; Williams reprinted his discussion of the Fall in *The Forgiveness of Sins*, 19–21, which is likely to have been Auden's source.

200 "Leopold and Loeb": In the late spring of 1924, two well-to-do University of Chicago students, Nathan Leopold and Richard Loeb, kidnapped and murdered a fourteen-year-old neighbor, Robert Franks. They said they had done it for the exhilaration of planning and executing "the perfect crime."

200 "We are able to see what other characters are like. . . .": Ansen's notes at this point read: "Other characters emerge through interactions with Iago as more conscious."

205 "Othello learns nothing . . . and is damned.": Auden's judgment reflects T. S. Eliot's celebrated comment, "What Othello seems to me to be doing in making this last speech is *cheering himself up*." *Selected Essays*, 130.

205 "the villain as an inverted saint . . . govern or trouble most living.": Amplified from Donald Pearce, "Fortunate Fall," in *W. H. Auden: The Far Interior*, ed.

Bold, 143. Ansen's notes record simply, "With Iago's knowledge, he should be a saint."

206 Fyodor Dostoevsky, *Notes from Underground*, in *The Short Novels of Dostoevsky* (New York: Dial Press: 1945), 148–50. Auden also quotes from this passage in "The Greeks and Us," reprinted in *FA*, 37, and in *EF*, 57.

MACBETH

This lecture has been reconstructed from notes by Ansen, Griffin, and Lowenstein. Auden's "The Guilty Vicarage," *DH*, 146–58, rehearses some of the issues treated in this lecture, and I have used the essay to clarify several points. Griffin, *Conversations with Auden*, 16–18, appears to be a rehearsal of his notes on Auden's lecture on the play.

Page

208 "There are three classes of crime . . . abolishes the party it injures.": Amplified from *DH*, 149.

209 "As to the murderer's end . . . I disapprove of capital punishment": From *DH*, 152.

213 "Henry IV's speech": Ansen records: "WHA said Warwick."

218 "The Hecate scene . . . another author.": Editors usually attribute this scene (III.v) to Thomas Middleton. Two stage directions in the First Folio call for songs that are preserved in Middleton's play *The Witch*.

218 "why does he act in this completely crazy way?": Ansen records that Auden said to him immediately after the lecture: "But don't you think really that the business about Macduff and his family is unsatisfactory? The first thing a man did in feudal times when he was planning to cast off his allegiance was to see to it that his wife and children were out of the way."

KING LEAR

This lecture has been reconstructed from notes by Ansen, Griffin, Bodenstein, and Lowenstein. Auden discusses *King Lear* in "Balaam and His Ass," *DH*, 124–28. Auden announced at the start of the lecture: "Papers have to be in by May 7th. The last lecture is on the 14th. I will be leaving afterwards, out of the reach of mail or phone. Anything later than the 7th will not be accepted."

Page

220 "to the kind of states of being . . . that Blake wished to represent in his prophetic books.": Charles Williams makes this point in *The Forgiveness of Sins*, 92.

220 "The quality common . . . big ensemble.": From *DH*, 470.

224 "Pascal asks": *Pensées*, fragments 72, 347; pp.16–18, 97.

226 Ludwig von Beethoven, *Fidelio*, Act II. Near the end of *Fidelio*, Florestan says to Leonora, with whom he has just been reunited, "*Was hast du meinetwegen erluldet*"—"What have you suffered for my sake?" Leonora answers, "*Nichts, mein Florestan! Meine Seele war mit dir.*"—"Nothing, my Florestan! My soul was with you. . . ." : Both Ansen's and Bodenstein's notes read: "Nichts, nichts, mein Florestan."

230 G. Wilson Knight, *The Shakespearian Tempest* (Oxford: Oxford University Press, 1932).

230 "nature no longer a home.": After this phrase, Ansen's notes read: "Rosenstock? or Cochrane? 'Dilthey says of Aristotle that he becomes 3rd person.'" Dilthey refers to the German philosopher, Wilhelm Dilthey; Eugen Rosenstock-Huessy was the author of *Out of Revolution, Autobiography of Western Man* (New York: Morrow, 1938); and Charles Norris Cochrane was the author of *Christianity and Classical Culture*, Auden's review of which is reprinted in *FA*, 33–39.

ANTONY AND CLEOPATRA

This lecture has been reconstructed from notes by Ansen, Griffin, and Lowenstein. See Howard Griffin, *Conversations with Auden*, 35–59, for Griffin's account of a conversation with Auden on the play, a substantial portion of which appears to have been derived from Griffin's notes on the lecture.

Page

240 "the beautiful scene . . . supernatural music": Cf. *DH*, 509.

241 "police court cases or psychiatric clinics": Cf. *DH*, 176.

241 "as Herrick writes": Robert Herrick, "To Anthea," in *The Poetical Works of Robert Herrick*, ed. F. W. Moorman (Oxford: Clarendon Press, 1910). The opening lines of the poem are:

> Now is the time, when all the lights wax dim;
> And thou (Anthea) must withdraw from him
> Who was thy servant.

241 Pascal, *Pensées*, fragment 162, p. 48. See also fragment 163, p. 48: "*Vanity.* —The cause and effects of love: Cleopatra."

242 "The whole world of the play is bathed in brilliant light": Cf. Mark Van Doren, *Shakespeare*, 268, "Light plays on everything with undiscouraged luxury."

242 Franz Kafka, *Reflections on Sin, Suffering, Hope, and the True Way*, No. 103, cited in *The Viking Book of Aphorisms*, ed. W. H. Auden and Louis Kronenberger (New York: Viking, 1962), 90. For a discussion of the text of these *Betrachtungen*, see Franz Kafka, *Dearest Father Stories and Other Writings*, trans. Ernst Kaiser and Eithne Wilkins (New York: Schocken Books, 1954), 398–99, notes 2 and 3.

242 "I'd choose *Antony and Cleopatra*.": Auden printed the whole of *Antony and Cleopatra* in his selections from Shakespeare in *Poets of the English Language*, his anthology of English poetry.

CORIOLANUS

This lecture has been reconstructed from notes by Ansen, Griffin, Lowenstein, and Bodenstein.

Page

243 Henry Norman Hudson, ed., *Shakespeare's Tragedy of Coriolanus* (Boston: Ginn and Company, 1909), 12–13. Auden could have come upon Hudson's commentary, as well as Hazlitt's, below, in a number of early twentieth-century editions

of Shakespeare's collected or individual works that reprinted excerpts from earlier criticism.

243 John Middleton Murry, *Shakespeare* (London: Jonathan Cape, 1936), 350.

243 T. S. Eliot, *Selected Essays*, 144.

243 William Hazlitt, *A View of the English Stage*, in *Complete Works*, ed. P. P. Howe, 21 vols. (London: J. M. Dent, 1930–34), 5:347.

243 "The parts of Hamlet and Iago . . . stage performance": See the lectures on *Hamlet, Othello,* and *King Lear.*

244 "In North's Plutarch": "The Life of Caius Martius Coriolanus," *Lives of Noble Grecians and Romanes Translated by Thomas North,* 8 vols. (Stratford-Upon-Avon: Shakespeare Head Press, 1929), 1:414–15.

245 "I have already discussed . . . in the lecture on *Julius Caesar.*": See also *DH,* 63–65.

245 "A society is threatened by an individual . . . society as a whole.": Griffin's notes record that Auden read anonymous verses on "The Choir Boy" to illustrate this point:

> And when he sang in choruses
>   His voice o'ertopped the rest,
> Which is very inartistic,
>   But the public like that best.

These verses are quoted in *ACW,* 73.

247 "When I was in Germany two years ago": Auden worked in Germany for the U.S. Strategic Bombing Service, with the equivalent rank of Major, for part of the spring and summer of 1945.

TIMON OF ATHENS

This lecture has been reconstructed from notes by Ansen, Griffin, and Lowenstein.

Page

255 Bellevue: A psychiatric hospital in Manhattan.

255 Bowery: At the time, an area of derelict people in lower Manhattan.

255 "good Samaritan": Luke 10. 33–35.

257 "'In affability'": Friedrich Nietzsche, Chap. 4, "Apothegms and Interludes," No. 93, *Beyond Good and Evil,* in *The Philosophy of Nietzsche* (New York: Modern Library, 1940).

261 "'He who despises'": Nietzsche, Chap. 4, Apothegm No. 78, *Beyond Good and Evil.* Quoted in *DH,* 95, with a slight variation.

263 I. A. Richards, "Love," *How to Read a Page, A Course in Efficient Reading With an Introduction to a Hundred Great Words* (New York: Norton, 1942), 153–55. Auden discusses Eros and Agape in a review of Denis de Rougemont, *Love in the Western World* in *The Nation,* 152, no.26 (28 June 1941): 756–58; and in his introduction to Anne Freemantle, ed., *The Protestant Mystics* (Boston: Little, Brown, 1964), reprinted in *FA,* 63–70.

264 William Blake, "I heard an Angel singing," *Blake's Poems and Prophecies,* ed. Max Plowman (London: J. M. Dent, 1927).

265 "The symbol of Agape . . . *everyone* is our neighbor.": From Auden's review of
de Rougemont in *The Nation*, 757. Auden also discusses eating in *PD*, 43, and
ACW, 134.

267 "Baudelaire remarks": Charles Baudelaire, *Intimate Journals*, trans. Christopher Isherwood, intro. T. S. Eliot (London: The Blackamore Press; New York:
Random House, 1930), 45, 29–30, 79, respectively. Auden wrote an introduction to a later edition of *Intimate Journals* (Hollywood: Marcel Rodd, 1977),
which includes slightly different translations of parts of the text.

268 Charles Williams, *Taliessin Through Logres* (London: Oxford University Press,
1938), 44–45. Quoted in *ACW*, 265–66.

PERICLES AND *CYMBELINE*

This lecture has been reconstructed from notes by Ansen, Griffin, and Lowenstein.

Page

270 Aldous Huxley, foreword to *The Complete Etchings of Goya*, 7.

270 T. S. Eliot, *Four Quartets* (New York: Harcourt, Brace, 1943) "East Coker," V.

272 "aristocrat of middlebrows, Dr. Johnson.": Johnson wrote of *Cymbeline*, for example: "To remark the folly of the fiction, the absurdity of the conduct, the
confusion of the names and manners of different times, and the impossibility of
the events in any system of life, were to waste criticism upon unresisting imbecil-
ity, upon faults too evident for detection, and too gross for aggravation." See
Johnson on Shakespeare, ed. Walter Raleigh (London: Oxford University Press,
1946), 183.

272 Dante, *Inferno*, Canto V.

273 T. S. Eliot, *The Sacred Wood*, 3rd ed. (London: Methuen, 1932), 168.

274 "As Dante explains": *Purgatorio*, Canto XVII.

THE WINTER'S TALE

This lecture has been reconstructed from notes by Ansen, Griffin, and Lowenstein.

Page

287 "the original story": Robert Greene, *Pandosto. The Triumph of Time* (1588), a
prose romance reprinted as *Dorastus and Fawnia* (1607).

THE TEMPEST

This lecture has been reconstructed from notes by Ansen, Griffin, and Lowenstein.
For an account of Auden's lecture on *The Tempest* at the University of Michigan in
the fall of 1941, see Donald Pearce, "Fortunate Fall," in *W. H. Auden: The Far Interior*, ed. Bold, 148–53. Auden adapted the play in his long poem, "The Sea and the
Mirror" (1941–43), published in *For the Time Being* (New York: Random House,
1944), and he discusses it in "Balaam and His Ass," *DH*, 128–34. See also Appendix I. In an entry in his "Journal" dated 30 April 1947, Ansen records Auden saying
in conversation that there have been so many adaptations and continuations of *The*

Tempest both because "Shakespeare really left it a mess" and because, like all myths, it "has value independent of the way it is written about." "You don't have to have any poetry, the myth itself is enough, you can go on with it yourself once you've got the point." Auden added, "No, I don't think 'Our revels now are ended' is such a purple patch or the one passage one would want to take as the high point of Shakespeare's art. It's all right, but *Antony and Cleopatra* is much better poetry. It has to be—they've nothing else to live on. . . . Yes, the words are absolutely vital for the masque. But afterwards, when he hears of Caliban making mischief, you could tell the story any which way and it would be just as effective. What he's saying is simply, 'I want to die.' He's very tired and doesn't want to be bothered. No, Alonso doesn't want to die—not in the earlier part of the play, anyway. Oh no, Prospero doesn't want to die rebelliously, but he will be quite glad when he can go."

Page

296 C. S. Lewis, ed., *George MacDonald: An Anthology* (London: Geoffrey Bles, 1946), xxvi–xxvii.

297 "Like other mythopoeic works . . . forgot to tell us.": Slightly amplified from *DH*, 407–8. See also *FA*, 268.

297 "I've done something with it myself": Auden is referring to his adaptation of the play in "The Sea and the Mirror."

297 "based on Montaigne": Michel de Montaigne, "Of the Cannibals," *Essays*, trans. John Florio, Vol. 1, Chap. 30.

298 "good but stupid character": In his 1941 lecture on *The Tempest* at the University of Michigan, Auden appears to have been somewhat more sympathetic to Gonzalo. See Pearce, in "Fortunate Fall," 151–52.

300 "Prospero . . . only made him worse.": Auden took a similar view of Prospero and his relation to Caliban in his lecture on the play at the University of Michigan in 1941, but was considerably less sympathetic in "The Sea and the Mirror" and in "Balaam and His Ass," *DH*, 128–34. He does indicate in the New School lecture that *The Tempest* is darker than the other plays of the final period, and that Prospero himself does not end on a note of joy, but there is less suggestion of the beliefs that subsume "The Sea and the Mirror" and that he expresses explicitly in *DH*, 130–31, that Prospero is cold and self-righteous, that Caliban represents a condition of all human beings, and that *The Tempest* is "a manichean work."

300 "He has lost his savage freedom . . . 'know how to curse.' ": From *DH*, 130.

300 "*The Tempest* and *The Magic Flute*": Auden discusses parallels between the two works in *DH*, 134–35.

301 "Monostatos says": Mozart, *Die Zauberflöte*, Act II.

301 "Renans's version": Ernest Renan, "Caliban," in *Drame Philosophique* (Paris: Michel Levy Frères, 1888), 1–103.

301 "the people are positivists": It is Ariel who announces that "Le peuple est positiviste," *Drame Philosophique*, 78.

305 "What does Shakespeare say about music": Some details in this section of the lecture are borrowed from "Music in Shakespeare," *DH*, 500–527.

307 Rainer Maria Rilke, "The Spirit of Ariel (After reading Shakespeare's *Tempest*)," in *Later Poems*, trans. J. B. Leishman (London: Hogarth Press, 1938), 57–58.

CONCLUDING LECTURE

This lecture has been reconstructed from notes by Ansen and Lowenstein.

Pages

308 "The drama from *Gorboduc*... Marlowe in 1564.": Some of Auden's dates vary by a year or two from those commonly accepted at the time of his lectures and afterwards; the widest discrepancies from currently accepted dates are those of *The Spanish Tragedy* (1589) and the birth of Middleton (c. 1580).

308 "As T. S. Eliot has remarked": In *Selected Essays*, 111, 115–16.

309 "The great glory... *verismo*": See *DH*, 475–82.

310 "publication of *Werther*": Johann Wolfgang Goethe, *The Sorrows of Young Werther* (1774).

311 Wyndham Lewis, *The Lion and the Fox*, 144–45.

311 "He got his training ... the chronicle plays": Cf. *DH*, 173–74.

312 "Christian psychology": Cf. *DH*, 174–76.

312 "infinite dynamic for good or for evil": Ansen notes that "Auden said [sic] 'for good or for virtue.'"

313 "cynicism ... stoicism ... skepticism": Ansen's notes indicate that Auden added "Petrarchanism" to this list. Auden may have been referring to the idolatrous illusions of Petrarchanism, but the reference is not clear.

313 "What does change continually is the development of his verse.": Auden discusses Shakespeare's verse and prose in similar terms, though without the examples, in his lecture on *Troilus and Cressida*.

315 "George Rylands writes": In *Words and Poetry*, 164–65.

316 "packed with matter ... emotional pressure": Rylands, *Words and Poetry*, 150.

318 "why Eliot says": T. S. Eliot, *Selected Essays*, 252.

319 "developed his own use of poetic symbols": Ansen's notes read: "Development of his own use of poetic symbols—Dover Wilson, Caroline Spurgeon: imagery Tempest-Music." The reference to Dover Wilson is not clear.

319 "As Wilson Knight demonstrates ... reconciliation and order": From *EF*, 12. The reference is to Knight's *The Shakespearian Tempest*.

319 Caroline F. E. Spurgeon, *Shakespeare's Imagery and What It Tells Us* (New York: Macmillan; Cambridge: Cambridge University Press, 1935).

319 "that art is frivolous": See *SO*, 170–71, 173–74, and *DH*, 429–32.

319 "When art takes itself too seriously ... more than it can.": This issue is one of the principal concerns of "The Sea and the Mirror," which Auden completed a few years before these lectures.

INDEX